# Analyzing Form, Function, and Financing of the U.S. Health Care System

# Analyzing Form, Function, and Financing of the U.S. Health Care System

Paula Stamps Duston, PhD

**CRC Press**
Taylor & Francis Group
Boca Raton  London  New York

CRC Press is an imprint of the
Taylor & Francis Group, an **informa** business
A PRODUCTIVITY PRESS BOOK

CRC Press
Taylor & Francis Group
6000 Broken Sound Parkway NW, Suite 300
Boca Raton, FL 33487-2742

First issued in paperback 2021

© 2016 by Taylor & Francis Group, LLC
CRC Press is an imprint of Taylor & Francis Group, an Informa business

No claim to original U.S. Government works

Version Date: 20151030

ISBN 13: 978-1-03-209812-8 (pbk)
ISBN 13: 978-1-4822-3653-8 (hbk)

Publisher's Note
The publisher has gone to great lengths to ensure the quality of this reprint but points out that some imperfections in the original copies may be apparent.

**Visit the Taylor & Francis Web site at
http://www.taylorandfrancis.com**

**and the CRC Press Web site at
http://www.crcpress.com**

To

Dr. William A. Darity, who gave me a chance,

and to

All the students at the University of Massachusetts,

who kept asking questions.

# Contents

## SECTION III  POLITICAL AND ECONOMIC VALUES AND HEALTH CARE FINANCING

# Acknowledgments

Every book has its genesis in multiple personal and professional experiences and has contributions from many people, and this is no exception. This volume is the result of my attempts to explain to both students and the many health care professionals I have worked with over my career WHY we have the health care system we do. This explanation has required an integration of the fields of medical care organization, public health, policy, ethics, and politics.

The many students I have had in class have all contributed directly to this book, and my thanks to them are expressed in the dedication. Two particular groups of students worked directly with me in writing this book. Both were in formal classes that revolved around their independent work. The first group of students helped by preparing background papers on many of the topics in this book, including finding and updating references. They also suggested several topics they thought should be included. The second group of students spent a semester working as my staff. They read and commented on drafts of chapters, did both fact and reference checking and helped me in the process of cutting down on some excess material. They also found all those words faculty like to use and called my attention to them. Thanks to them, the word obviously is not in this book. Several were especially involved in creating figures and providing suggestions about including graphics. Each of these students is acknowledged in the relevant chapters so their work can be recognized. Less easy to acknowledge is the perspective they helped me develop. This book is different because of their influence.

Several colleagues at the University of Massachusetts were especially supportive, and their specific contributions are noted in the relevant chapters. I especially thank Dan Gerber, who has been continually supportive of my desire to include students in this venture. Both Gloria DiFulvio and Megan

Griffin made it possible for me realize this by assisting in the practical arrangements necessary, including some manipulations in the formal course schedule of the department.

I very much appreciate my daughter Jessi, for her excellent work on many of the figures in this book. She was calm and always available on my time schedule. (Jessi, your travel debt is now forgiven.) My son Christopher and his wife Jen gave me several small, but incredibly important, technical tips that saved me precious time over the course of writing this book. Who knew what a mouse could do? On a different note, I must acknowledge that my writing was always accompanied by Van Cliburn playing the music of Liszt, Beeethoven, Schumann, and Rachmaninoff, among others. I may never be able to listen to this music again.

Finally, my greatest thanks go to my husband, Dr. Thomas Duston. He contributed directly to several chapters as my highest level but unpaid research assistant. His ability to find relevant and helpful sources was impressive. He also prevented me from using his field of economics for my own purposes. He was patient with my mental distraction as the deadline neared, and always understood my need to work on this project.

# Author

 **Dr. Paula Stamps Duston** earned her PhD from the School of Public Health at the University of Oklahoma. She has spent most of her career at the University of Massachusetts/Amherst, with several years at Dartmouth College where she held joint appointments in the Departments of Sociology and Family and Community Medicine. She is best known for her research in developing validated scales to measure the level of satisfaction of direct care providers, including both nurses and physicians. Her nurse satisfaction instrument, the Index of Work Satisfaction (IWS), is the most widely used in the field and is recommended by the American Nursing Association and The Joint Commission (JCAHCO) for use as a quality indicator. The IWS is also widely used internationally, currently in over 25 countries.

This book is the result of her many years of teaching about the U.S. health care delivery system. Both the content and organization of this text have been influenced by undergraduate and graduate students, as well as the many health care professionals with whom she has worked.

She is currently teaching in the Commonwealth Honors College at the University of Massachusetts. She also serves as the graduate program director for public health in the university's School of Public Health and Health Sciences.

# Introduction

This book tells the story of the U.S. health care system by using a narrative approach identifying function rather than the more common data-driven focus on structure. This does not mean there are no numbers here and no attention to structure: there is both. Shifting the major focus to function changes the primary question from *how* the health care system operates to *why*. This shift in emphasis came after years of trying to explain the U.S. health care system to students and many different health care professionals. After a detailed explanation of how, the major question remaining is always, "But why do we do things this way?" Answering this question requires thinking about the U.S. health care system in a different way.

This includes integrating ideas from fields that are generally separated, such as the fields of public health, medical care organization, and health policy. This gives a more comprehensive view of the U.S. health care system, as well as an explicit discussion of philosophical and political values. The people who are usually interested in books such as this are students who want some kind of career in the health field. The multidisciplinary approach utilized in this book is also the most appropriate way to prepare for a health-related career. By focusing on telling the story of the American health care system, this book is accessible to those who do not want to work in this sector of the economy, but who need to understand it to utilize it better. This approach helps those already employed in the health care field. Since the training is so specialized, many do not understand anything other than their own small piece of the puzzle.

The U.S. health care system is an amazingly complicated puzzle: deconstructing it in order to describe and then analyze it is like the proverbial onion. Each topic reveals additional layers, but each layer is related to several others, so it is difficult to know where to begin. Almost no topic can be described without requiring knowledge of another. In the case of this book, there are three programs frequently referred to before they are fully explained. Two are long-standing programs that are part of our casual conversation about the health care field, but which few people actually understand. The Medicare program is a completely federally funded social insurance program that provides health care access to people over the age of 65, as well as disabled people of all ages. The Medicaid program is a joint federal–state entitlement program that provides access to people who are defined as poor, with an additional emphasis on women and children, as well as frail elders. These two programs are described in Chapters 18 and 19, but their impact is felt throughout the health care system, so there are many earlier references.

A similar situation occurs with the 2010 Patient Protection and Affordable Care Act, known colloquially as Obamacare, although this book will use the term Affordable Care Act (ACA). This Act has significantly influenced the entire health care system, and there are many references to it before it is fully explained in Chapter 17.

There are several topics included in this book that are not usually found in books about the U.S. health care system, even though their influence is very important. These are described in the summary of each section below. Three different fields are used in this book: medical care organization, public health, and health policy. Also included in this analysis are two philosophical frameworks. The first is based on the traditional economic values of free enterprise, where those with more money get more and better goods and service. Applying this allocation model to the health field produces some difficult situations, especially when we are faced with people in need of health care that they cannot afford. A different allocation model is based on medical need, without reference to ability to pay. This creates a different financing system: one that is funded by all through general taxes, and accessed when needed. The term social justice is used for this to emphasize the additional public health principle of believing that access to health care is a human right.

The tension between these two perspectives is an overarching theme of this book, as is the cost of our health care system. Cost and the desire to control expenditures are a primary driver for much of health policy, so it must be included as a major theme. However, this book is unusual in including two additional levels of analysis. The first is organizational structure, so there is much attention to whether medical care is being provided in a nonprofit or for-profit organization. This is important because of the second level of analysis, which covers the philosophical and political values that guide our health care system. Any discussion of the American health care system without understanding these values is incomplete and misleading. This perspective is woven through every chapter in this book.

There is no perfect health care delivery system. The overall goal of this book is to present policy decisions we have made about our health care system, and analyze some of their consequences in order to better understand the choices we have. To facilitate this analysis, this book is arranged in four major parts, each of which is described here.

## Section I: Introduction: Setting the Context

The first set of chapters is mostly "about" the health care system. The first two chapters are conceptual, with the first (Definitions of Health and Illness) describing several theoretical models that are the foundation for the structure of the U.S. health care system. The second chapter (Public Health: Defining Determinants of Health) focuses on the perspective of the public health field, and reminds us that many health problems are actually social problems that cannot be solved by the health care system. Conceptual frameworks are probably more important to academics than anybody else, but the intent of these two chapters is to translate these models into an understanding of why the health care system is structured in the way it is.

Of course, this is in the context of our social and cultural traditions, which is why Chapter 4 (Role of Culture in the Organization of Health Care Delivery Systems) is devoted to the impact of culture on both beliefs about health and illness and on the structure of the health care system. This includes a description of healing activities that are placed outside the formal health care system and labeled alternative, even though these practices are used by a great many people.

Chapter 5 (Political and Philosophical Values that Influence the U.S. Health Care System) describes several specific examples of the political dimension by identifying some explicit limits that are part of our health care system. These examples include a group of people—noncitizens—and a group of services—women's reproductive services. The cultural, political, and philosophical values discussed in this chapter are incredibly important, because they quite literally define our health care system in its form, function, and financing.

Chapter 3 (Health Status Indicators) is included in this beginning part of the book for a slightly different reason. This chapter explains some very important analytical tools that are used repeatedly throughout this book to describe and assess our health care delivery system. Health status indicators are ubiquitous in the health and medical field, but are seldom explicitly explained.

## Section II: Functional Description of the U.S. Health and Medical Care System

Section II is a description of the form—or organization—of the U.S. health care delivery system. The first chapter (Do We Have a System? A Functional Analysis) in this section provides a comprehensive overview of the entire health care delivery system, including identifying all levels of care, those defined as public health and/or preventive health care and those that are medical. The rest of this section—and of the book—then focuses more narrowly on the medical care system. Even with this more narrow focus, this is challenging information to present because of its complexity. The goal of this section is to provide necessary background information on the various sectors in the medical care system so the important policy issues can be identified. Chapter 7 (People Who Make the Medical Care System Go: The Workforce) focuses on the health care workforce, with the most detail on two important clinical providers: physicians and nurses. Both medical degrees are described, and the increasing use of mid-level providers is likewise described. Also included are many clinical professionals usually left unmentioned, such as podiatrists, pharmacists, paramedics, and several different types of allied health professionals known as therapeutic science practitioners. This chapter concludes with a policy discussion about how many—and what type—health care providers we need.

The next two chapters describe two important sites of care: hospitals (Chapter 8) and ambulatory care settings (Chapter 9). In both cases, these chapters integrate important structural and organizational information with a discussion of relevant policy issues, especially the role of the for-profit sector.

The last chapter (Other Components of the Medical Care System, Chapter 10) in this section describes several other parts of the health care system that are usually left out of books like this, with a particular focus on the mental health system. Also described here are long-term care and dental and vision care services.

# Section III: Political and Economic Values and Health Care Financing

The focus of Section III is financing, beginning with a description of the economic and political values that determine how we finance our system (Health Economics 101: Do Health Care Goods/Services Follow Standard Economic Rules?). Chapter 12 (From Economics to Health Policy and Regulation) links this economic framework to several specific examples of health policies related to paying for medical care services. This chapter also includes a more general description of the role of policy and regulation in the health care field.

Two chapters—Chapters 13 (Health Care Financing: Health Insurance) and 14 (Health Insurance: Two Conceptual Models)—describe health insurance, from the perspective of both the consumer and the provider. Included in these two chapters is a detailed explanation of the concept of primary care and managed care, a discussion that is continued from Chapter 9 (Ambulatory Care: Functions, Structures, and Services), where it began. Chapter 15 (The Payment Function: Money Moving through the System) integrates all the financing information by describing how money moves through the system, sometimes also known as the payment function.

Section III concludes with a discussion and analysis of cost and cost control efforts. Although the overall topic of this section is financing, the administrative complexity—and inefficiency—of the health care system is revealed through these six chapters.

# Section IV: Health Care Reform in the United States: Targeted Programs and Consequences

The title of the final section of this book is purposeful, because a common myth is that once health care systems are designed, they are static. In fact, they are in a constant state of change or reform, and this is as true in the United States as it is in other countries. Chapter 17 (Health Care Reform: Past as Prologue to Present) summarizes several attempts at reforming the U.S. medical care system, with special attention to Medicare and Medicaid. The ACA stands on the shoulders of these two early efforts, and continues in their tradition of creating a targeted program for a group of people without employment-related health insurance. Many describe our health care system as fragmented, implying an accidental occurrence. Chapter 17 demonstrates that the belief in targeted, independent programs is a purposeful, intentional design of the U.S. health care system, one that the ACA continues.

Chapter 18 (Taking Care of the Elderly: Medicare) and Chapter 19 (Taking Care of the Poor: Medicaid) describe the Medicare and Medicaid programs, respectively. In both cases, the actual program is described in some detail. Each chapter then also discusses several important issues related to the health care program and the group it takes care of. In both cases, the larger social problems are identified.

Chapter 20 (Taking Care of Almost Everybody Else) describes eight other targeted programs. Some are very specific, such as the Program of All-Inclusive Care for the Elderly, which is designed for the poor, frail elderly. Some are for groups already targeted, such as children. Two are for groups not usually covered by other programs: Native Americans and U.S. military and veterans. Each of these groups has specific needs, and most books do not include these.

Chapter 21 (A Persistent Problem: Racial and Ethnic Disparities in Health Outcomes) describes a very persistent problem in the U.S. health care system, which may very well be related to the targeted program structure. This chapter describes the wealth of research identifying racially based health disparities, with an additional focus on how this research is conducted.

The book concludes with a summary of a different method of organizing a nation's health care system. This is termed universal, because all people are eligible, without any further specifications. Chapter 22 (Alternative Models for Health Care Systems: International Perspectives) describes the health systems of seven countries and compares these systems to our own. There is an impressive range of methods of organizing health and medical care services in these countries. The book ends as it begins, by making explicit the cultural and political influences on the U.S. health care system.

# INTRODUCTION: SETTING THE CONTEXT

**I**

The five chapters in the first section of this book provide an understanding of the rich and complex context of the U.S. health care system. Chapter 1 (Definitions of Health and Illness) describes several conceptual models, with an emphasis on defining health, illness, and disease—terms that significantly impact the structure and organization of the U.S. health care system. This chapter also explores how patients decide to utilize this system. Chapter 1 concludes with the distinction between a health care system and a medical care system.

Chapter 2 (Public Health: Defining Determinants of Health) expands this framework by exploring the concept of health as a positive state, rather than a state in which illness is absent. Focusing on health or wellness rather than illness has many ramifications, including a switch in emphasis from individualistic healing to population-based efforts to promote and/or maintain the health of groups of people. This highlights the difference in perspective between two major professional groups: medical care providers, who mostly focus on individual determinants of health, and public health professionals, who tend to emphasize social determinants of health.

Chapter 3 (Health Status Indicators) explains a set of basic tools that are utilized when analyzing a health care system: health status indicators. This chapter provides basic information and several examples of the more commonly used indicators. These will be used throughout this book.

Chapter 4 (Role of Culture in the Organization of Health Care Delivery Systems) is a reminder that a health care system exists within a cultural framework, and the U.S. system is no exception. It is partly this cultural context that determines the difference between socially and legally legitimate medical care services and those that are described as alternative healing practices.

The final chapter (Political and Philosophical Values That Influence the U.S. Health Care System) in this section describes the philosophical and political values that are the foundation of the U.S. health care system. Not only do these values set an overall context, they also limit the types of services as well as the population to which certain health services can be provided.

It may seem that this section is too much *about* the U.S. health care system instead of a true description. However, these five chapters include essential information necessary for answering the question, "But why do we have this kind of health care system?"

# Chapter 1

# Definitions of Health and Illness

This first chapter presents several conceptual models that are necessary to understand the foundation of the U.S. health care system. The first framework is known as the Biomedical Model, and it developed at the same time as scientific understanding of pathogenic organisms, which is why it is also called the germ theory. This conceptual framework defines the U.S. health care system in terms of services offered as well as how these are financed. Several modifications have been made to the Biomedical Model, primarily to enlarge its focus because of the changing pattern of disease in the United States. These modifications enlarge the narrow focus of the Biomedical Model to explain chronic illness. Other conceptual models are organized around the idea of health or wellness instead of just illness. These modifications support the inclusion of services that promote health as well as those dedicated to resolving sickness.

People must have access to whatever services are offered, but identifying the beginning of this process is not always easy. Another conceptual model is used to describe how people decide to seek professional help for symptoms they are experiencing. This is called Becker's Health Belief Model, and it is used widely in many ways in the health care field.

Language is a very important part of these conceptual models, so this chapter distinguishes between several terms we use too casually in common speech—including health, illness, and disease. Language is linked to process, including the method by which some health services are labeled alternative health care practices, as will be discussed in Chapter 4.

This chapter also introduces the differences between two fields that are concerned with the U.S. health care delivery system: medicine and the field of public health. Although there are some very clear differences in emphasis, there are also many common goals of these two professions.

## Health and Illness: Language Issues

The most traditional definition of health is from the World Health Organization (WHO): "Health is a state of complete physical, mental and social well-being and not merely the absence of disease or infirmity" (WHO, 1948). This is more of a mission statement than a definition, and like most such broad guiding principles, it provides a valuable vision, but not many specifics. A more pragmatic definition of health relates to functional status in terms of being able to successfully carry out defined social roles. The simplest expression of this is: if we can do our jobs, then we are not sick. One of the major theoretical contributions of the WHO definition is to state clearly that health is more than the absence of illness. This is important because it is far easier to define and discuss illness or disease than to describe health. There is more language—and resources—dedicated to explaining and treating disease and illness than ensuring various levels of good health.

Illness and disease are not interchangeable terms. Illness is defined as personal perceptions of physical symptoms. The importance and description of these symptoms is determined partly by family patterns that are, in turn, highly impacted by cultural expectations, which will be the topic of Chapter 4. In many situations, it is enough to state we are ill and thus excused from work or personal responsibilities. However, in other cases, a formal definition of a disease must be made by a legally recognized clinical health care provider, such as a physician. This formal definition is created by the health provider utilizing a recognized diagnosis, based not only on description of symptoms (illness narrative), but also on evidence from a variety of tests and other clinical signs (May, 1993). It is only when the physician authenticates individual perceptions that one is truly excused from normal role expectations and pronounced sick. Everything in the medical care system is based on this act of diagnosis, including the financing of services. A person may also be defined as having a disease—being sick—without feeling ill, as in the case of hypertension, which may be first discovered in a routine medical encounter. Conversely, and more commonly, a person may feel ill, but cannot be given a specific diagnosis. It is this situation that provides frustration for both physicians and patients.

Two general categories of describing diseases are important to define. Acute conditions are those that are severe enough to require the services of a physician, but which are limited in time and are treatable, as well as being diagnosable (Timmrock, 1994). Examples of acute conditions include common ones seen in primary care practices such as upper respiratory infections, gastrointestinal symptoms, and headaches. Acute conditions are also those that require hospital-based interventions, including surgeries. In contrast, a chronic disease is one that is diagnosable but not episodic, and usually long term. Chronic diseases are treatable, but generally not cured by treatment, so we often term them as being managed, not cured (Timmrock, 1994). Common examples include many cardiovascular problems ranging from hypertension to strokes, but also include diseases for which there are more technological interventions such as many types of cancer.

Medical care services are based on the framework for characterizing illness, the Biomedical Model, or germ theory. This model presents illness being diagnosed by finding one specific causative agent and then treated by developing strategies for an intervention specific for that agent. All bacterial infections fall into this fairly simple understanding, in which symptoms are caused by one pathogenic organism that can be isolated and identified. A person may then be cured by a specific treatment—usually an antibiotic specifically designed to kill a particular bacterium. This is a very successful model as long as most of the illnesses involve acute, bacterial ones. This model also works well for those acute conditions that require more technological interventions, such as surgery. The cause of the symptoms is identified and a remedy of surgery cures the symptoms, thus restoring the person to health. However, this Biomedical Model does not work so well for those who feel ill but for whom there is no specific diagnosis. This model also does not explain illnesses that can be diagnosed, but not actually treated, as in the case of chronic illnesses. Additionally, over time, it became clear that not everyone who was exposed to the pathogens necessarily got the disease. These three observations led to a more ecological model that could be used to more successfully explain the range of illness episodes seen by clinicians.

## Modification of the Biomedical Model: Epidemiological Model

In this model, disease is viewed as being caused by an imbalance between agent, host, and environmental factors (Oleckno, 2008). Agent factors include biological, chemical, and/or physical properties that cause disease or injury, ranging from pathogenic bacteria to toxic chemicals or a car accident. Host factors include intrinsic characteristics of the host, which are identified as risk factors, influencing the susceptibility to a causative agent. Environmental factors are a whole range of extrinsic characteristics that impact this balance.

This model significantly enlarges the scope of the germ theory by including the idea that some people are more or less likely to become ill. The application of this more ecological model helps to identify a variety of possible interventions, which may be targeted to the person, the agent, or the environment. All three of these factors—the agent causing the illness, the host, and the environment—help research efforts better understand why some people seem to get ill more than others, especially with respect to chronic disease. Of all the factors, the one that receives the most attention in the clinical setting is the impact of stress on an individual's susceptibility to illness episodes.

## Stress as Cause of Illness

The original idea of the impact of stress on health came from Selye, an early biologist who coined the term fight or flight, which refers to the immediate and sudden flow of adrenaline as a result of something startling or surprising to us. As research continued, the perspective switched from the immediate impact of these chemicals to consideration of the impact of exposure over a long time. Now, there is a plethora of biochemical and molecular evidence to support what was previously merely anecdotal, observational, and often controversial evidence. This has occurred because of identifying actual chemicals circulating in the bloodstream as a result of exposure to perceived stressful situations. It is now well accepted that exposure to chronic stress is related to the production of increased levels of cortisol, as well as increased levels of C-reactive protein, a marker of systemic inflammation. Both of these have significant impacts on the body, including a lowered immune system response and increased vulnerability to both acute and chronic diseases, including diabetes, hypertension, and cardiovascular diseases. Research in this area includes the impact of stress on increased susceptibility to all sorts of illness episodes, ranging from acute to chronic illnesses (Hankin, 2006), the impact of bullying on children (Copeland et al., 2014), and the impact of long-term unemployment (Wanberg, 2012). Some of the most provocative areas of research are explored in Chapter 21, which describes some of the racial differences in health status as being increasingly attributed to the chronic stress of minorities experiencing discrimination over the course of their lifetimes.

One of the advantages of this expansion of the Biomedical Model is a shift from the narrow focus on a specific causative agent to a broader consideration of various risk factors that might make a person more vulnerable to diseases and/or illness episodes, both acute and chronic. This is more realistic in terms of diagnosing and treating diseases, especially chronic ones.

However, these models still focus on the experience of illness rather than the level of health. There are some models that emphasize health, not illness, all of which are drawn from the field of public health rather than medicine and which are inspired by the vision of the WHO definition. These models generally support the importance of focusing on promotion of health and prevention of illness, and require that language reinforce this perspective. Although these models are primarily based in the field of public health, they also provide a way to emphasize the importance of the primary care part of the medical care system (Adashi et al., 2010).

## Models of Health Not Illness

Several models describe an illness–wellness continuum (Figure 1.1) to express the idea that health or wellness is more than the absence of illness. Where traditional illness-centric models of health care focus on bringing a

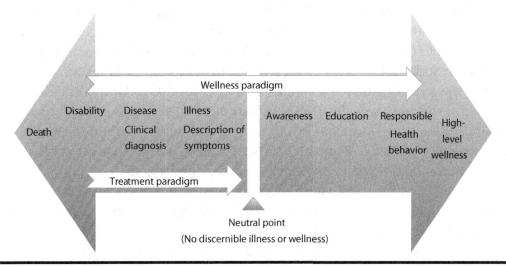

**Figure 1.1   Illness/wellness continuum. (Adapted from Travis, J.W. and Ryan, R.S., *Wellness Workbook: How to Achieve Enduring Health and Vitality*, 3rd edition, Ten Speed Press, Berkeley, CA, 2004.)**

patient's health from illness to neutral, this continuum promotes attaining a higher level of wellness than simply a neutral point. This model is a bridge between the germ theory perspective and the paradigm of wellness, which emphasizes self-responsibility and self-motivated movement toward improving health (Travis and Ryan, 2004). One of the major strengths of this framework is the focus on health as a positive, specific status, rather than just not being sick. This model also identifies a full range of services that people need, as opposed to only those needed by sick patients, an idea that will be further described in Chapter 6. Although the language used is of health, it is important to note that the emphasis on services is still within the medical care orientation, including emphasizing the individual's personal responsibility in complying with all medical recommendations.

There are a number of weaknesses associated with this framework, the primary one being the two-dimensional representation of the illness–wellness continuum, which oversimplifies the concepts of both illness and wellness. For example, a physically disabled person may not view themselves as physically ill. Also, with its heavy focus on individual responsibility, the model does not sufficiently address ecological, environmental, or social determinants of health, all of which clearly impact the ability of the person to exercise responsible health behavior. Chapter 2 addresses this topic.

The umbrella term "holistic health" is used for a set of models that focus on health as opposed to illness, and includes a more comprehensive perspective by including social determinants of health. There are a number of holistic models of health, all of which include multiple factors that contribute to level of health. These multiple factors include the ideas of agent, host, and environment contained in the epidemiologic models, but enlarge environment to include factors such as lifestyle, human biology, and resources available in the health care system (VanLeeuwen et al., 1999). One of the original models of this idea was developed by Blum (1974) and included five "background" influences—population, culture, mental health, natural resources, and ecological balance. Figure 1.2 shows VanLeeuwen's expansion of these factors in a model representing these complex interactions.

The value of health-oriented models is they enlarge the concept of which services should be included in a health care delivery system, as opposed to a medical care system. Barriers to implementing these concepts have been long identified (VanLeeuwen et al., 1999; Adashi et al., 2010). The value of a holistic model of health is that it provides guidance in converting the vision of the WHO to actual services offered by an organized system whose goal is to produce health. As shown in Figure 1.2, helping people achieve a high

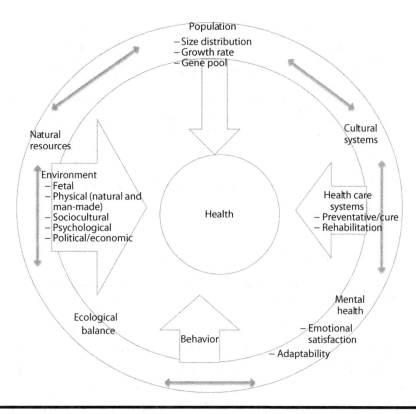

**Figure 1.2  Holistic health model. (Adapted from VanLeeuwen, J.A. et al., *Ecosystem Health*, 5, 205, 1999.)**

level of wellness involves consideration of many factors besides those simple ones contained in the germ theory. This Holistic Health Model incorporates important concepts from both the fields of public health and medicine.

The ideas expressed in the illness-oriented models and the health-oriented models come together in the concept of preventive health, a field which is claimed by both medicine and public health. For example, preventing the original episode of disease by screening healthy people (mammograms, hypertension screenings) or administering vaccinations to prevent the occurrence of specific diseases are both examples of primary prevention, and occur in physician's offices as well as public health settings. Secondary and tertiary prevention are used to describe the activities used to prevent more or worse episodes of illness and are almost always used in conjunction with medical treatment. Figure 1.3 shows these levels of prevention for three examples: smoking behavior, risk of heart disease, and musculoskeletal pain.

In the public health field, prevention and promotion activities are usually based on educating people to make better lifestyle choices, such as not

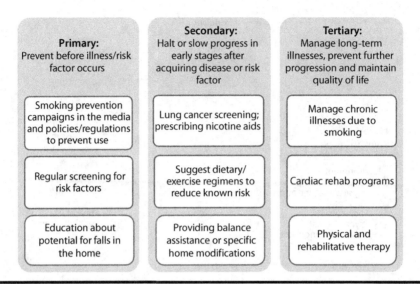

**Figure 1.3   Tiers of prevention.**

smoking, not using drugs, and not texting and driving. The failure of these educational activities to produce responsible health behavior leads to the many well-known regulations and laws aimed at requiring such behavior. As described in Chapter 5, this regulatory focus influences the public perception of the field of public health.

Understanding the language used and the conceptual basis of the health care delivery system is essential to gaining a better understanding of how the system is meant to operate, and also of the services that should be offered to the patient. These will be described in Chapter 6 as the various levels of care involved in the health care system. A critical aspect of how the system is meant to operate is to identify how people decide to seek care for a health problem.

## From Language to Behavior: Access

Access includes a whole range of factors that express the likelihood that a person will actually utilize a needed health or medical service. These are usually described in four groups of factors: availability, affordability, accommodation, and acceptability (Barton, 2007).

*Availability* begins with geographic location but also includes both numbers and type of providers available. This includes individual providers such as physicians and other clinicians, as well as institutional providers such as hospitals and clinics. *Accommodation* includes the idea of time, such as the hours the providers are available for delivering services. It also includes factors such as physical access, as in accordance with the Americans with Disabilities Act. More technological aspects such as telemedicine or whether the provider is available through e-mail are part of this component. *Affordability* describes financial access, but not only prices of services. This important construct includes the relationship between the clinical provider and the health insurance company in negotiating coverage and costs. This very important aspect is described in Chapter 15. *Acceptability* includes whether the attitudes of the patient and the providers are suitable for each other. When this fit is good, the person has better access to the services they need. When the fit is bad, there are barriers to access that may prevent utilization. Being able to have adequate access to health and medical care services directly impacts a person's health. It also significantly impacts costs and expenditures in the health care delivery system.

One of the most important steps is to identify the beginning of this process, which is the individual's decision to seek care. One very important conceptual model that explains this process is Becker's Health Belief Model, which has now been specified for several different types of health services, including acute care, mental health care, chronic care, and preventive health behavior. This model has been specified for various groups of people, such as children versus adults, as well as for exploring differences in health behavior related to cultural factors. Because of the ubiquity and importance of this model, the general form of it will be briefly described here.

## Health Belief Model Helps Explain Utilization

The original goal of the research project that led to this important model was to understand why people were so reluctant to participate in health promotion activities. The researcher who refined this model is Marshall Becker, who conducted numerous research projects, all aimed at identifying and quantifying the impact of each of these components that contribute to the decision to seek some sort of care (Becker, 1974; Champion and Skinner, 2008).

A modified version of Becker's Health Belief Model in its most general form is shown in Figure 1.4. The more susceptible a person feels and the more severe the risk, the higher the perceived threat to health, which is then

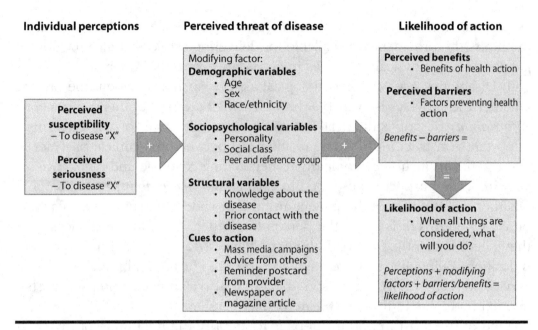

**Figure 1.4 Becker's Health Belief Model (modified general form).**

more likely to result in some health-related action. This may involve a visit to the doctor or participation in screening. These views are strongly influenced by several factors, all of which act to modify the perceptions of the individual. Some of these relate to demographic characteristics or sociopsychological variables, as shown in Figure 1.4. A third group of modifying factors are structural variables, which include knowledge about and/or experience with a certain illness or health condition. A final category of factors that influence the perceived threat or risk is a set of variables called cues to action. These may be intentional, such as the reminder cards mailed by health providers, or a public service notice on a TV station. Sometimes cues to action are unintentional, such as learning about an illness in a family member or close friend, or even seeing an illness portrayed in a movie.

The perception of threat, as influenced by these factors, is linked to the likelihood of a person taking action, but the likelihood of action is also based on a personal risk/benefit analysis that accompanies any health-related behavior. This is balancing the potential benefits of health behavior against the barriers. The predicted likelihood of taking action is a result of this personal risk/benefit analysis, which includes all of the factors shown in the Health Belief Model. If the benefit does not seem strong or immediate enough; or if the barrier (affordability; pain involved) is too strong, a person is less likely to take action.

The Health Belief Model has been used extensively for a variety of purposes ranging from designing an educational program explaining why patients do not take all their prescribed medication, to identifying factors that may lead to intravenous drug use. This model has been used to predict any action that involves either use of medical care services or participation in any type of health promotion activities.

Even though this model focuses on the individual level, it also incorporates social, cultural, and environmental factors that impact that individual decision. As will be shown in Chapters 2 and 3, the social and cultural factors that impact a person's decisions are critical to the decision to utilize any type of health or medical service.

## Health Care System or Medical Care System?

The focus of this chapter is on the conceptual basis for the U.S. health care delivery system, with an additional focus on the language used to describe the most important concepts underlying this system. This is not an idle exercise in semantics. The very definition of the types of health and/or medical care services offered people is based on these concepts. Despite the known limitations, the Biomedical Model forms the primary conceptual basis of the conventional or legally sanctioned medical care system. Services that cannot be justified by this Biomedical Model are usually not paid for by a health insurance policy, although they may be well utilized by consumers. These services are called "alternative," complementary, or sometimes "integrative," depending on the perspective, and will be described in Chapter 4.

A second theme of this chapter is to explore the differences between two very different perspectives: the medical field and the field of public health. It is not true that the medical field is only interested in disease and the public health field is only interested in community-oriented health practices. Both groups are interested in improving the health of the people with whom they interact. However, the medical field is more oriented to treating individuals who have already gained access to them—that is, people who have defined themselves as being ill and are seeking a diagnosis and treatment. This perspective is clearly more illness oriented and is firmly anchored in the scientific explanations supported by the Biomedical Model. It is also much more individually oriented, and as such is consistent with Figure 1.1, even though this does also show health-oriented services.

The focus of the public health field is not primarily on an individual, but rather a group of people and most frequently not a group that needs specific services. Although many medical interventions can be classified as preventive, a major focus of the public health field is community-based preventive activities, all designed to promote or improve health. This perspective leads to consideration of larger social and environmental factors that impact the health of a group, as shown in Figure 1.2. This perspective also leads to an important shift in language, which is to talk about determinants of health rather than risk factors for disease. Chapter 2 describes this shift to determinants of health.

Health or wellness is not easy to define, and although there are challenges in defining illness, it is far easier to think about health in terms of illness and disease. This is not only true conceptually, it is true at a practical level. When people are healthy, their health status is not something they think about. When people are sick or ill, regaining their health status is a priority. It is partly because of this that there is some tension between the medical and public health approaches, even though their ultimate goal is the same thing. Far more resources are devoted to what can be termed the medical care system, which is those services available to diagnose and treat, than to the public health system, which includes all services that promote and preserve health. This resource allocation issue will be discussed more thoroughly in Chapter 6, but it is appropriate to note here that the three top causes of premature death in the United States arise from personal health behavior. Although cancer, cardiovascular disease, and accidents are treated in the medical care system, prevention occurs primarily in the public health sector.

The ethical basis of the field of public health is to allocate resources so that the greatest number of people are helped: greatest good for the greatest number. The ethical basis of the medical field is to devote as many resources as necessary to provide an effective treatment to one person. In an ideal world, the physician does not want to think about resources that might be better used elsewhere. Physicians are trained in this patient-intensive Biomedical Model, and patients want this model when they are the sick person. When group-level health outcomes are analyzed, however, public health professionals feel that increased resources would not only improve health status indicators (discussed in Chapter 3), but would also decrease costs of the medical care system.

It should be obvious from this short discussion that our health care delivery system is based on the theory and concept of the WHO's vision of health; at the functional level, however, the U.S. health care system is actually based on treating illness episodes, and therefore is more accurately termed a medical care system.

# Acknowledgments

The following people made significant contributions to the content of this chapter, including gathering material and references, as well as writing and analysis: Irene Eberbach, Michael Goulart, Sam Taylor, and Pratiksha Yalakkishettar. Jillisia James and Sydney Leone made substantive comments and revisions, and Jillisia constructed the original versions of Figures 1.1 and 1.2. Pratiksha suggested the idea for Figure 1.3. Josh Smith suggested the modification of Becker's Health Belief Model (Figure 1.4) for teaching purposes. I appreciate the work of Jessi Duston, who finalized all the figures in this chapter.

# Chapter 2

## Public Health: Defining Determinants of Health

Although the goal of the health care system is to produce health, the functioning of the health care system is more focused on diagnosis and treatment of illness, consistent with the Biomedical Model. The major focus of the field of public health is identifying how to improve or promote health, usually in terms of a community rather than an individual. The reason for this emphasis is the public health belief that environmental and socioeconomic circumstances significantly impact a person's health. According to the public health perspective, health cannot be achieved only through an individual effort, even when wellness services are included, as noted in Chapter 1. This chapter describes the public health contribution of identifying the importance of social and environmental factors by describing determinants of health, and ends with a description of a major federal effort to apply this framework: The Healthy People Project.

## What Are Determinants of Health?

The simplest definition of determinant of health is any factor that contributes to a person's health, although this understates the complexities. Historically, both the fields of medicine and public health concentrated on improving people's health, with medicine gradually evolving to devoting more time to restoring health than to improving health, especially as the scientific basis of contagious illness became more well developed. Overall health status was improving before the discovery of specific causes of illness, primarily because of improvement in public health efforts, including general sanitation, food, and housing; as well as isolation and quarantine to control epidemics. One of the earliest examples of the importance of social factors on health status was in 1850, when Virchow noted that a typhoid outbreak was worse because of a widespread famine. He was the first to use the term determinants when he observed education, freedom, and welfare were three factors that could prevent future typhoid outbreaks (Maio, 2010).

However, Virchow was still focused on determinants of illness, because he was trying to prevent a more extensive outbreak of an illness. As public health professionals studied health determinants more carefully, it became obvious that many factors improve health and contribute to health status. Gradually, a consensus developed that determinants of health could be described by examining biological factors, such as genes, individual health behaviors, social and physical characteristics of the environment, and the availability of health services. Although there was broad agreement with these five general categories, there was no agreement on the specific definition of each category. There was also little agreement on the relative importance of each category. Today, determinants of health are described as being either primarily individual or primarily social, depending on how strongly one holds the public health model.

## Individual Determinants of Health

Individual determinants of health are viewed as factors that originate within an individual, but which cannot be modified or changed. Within the field of public health, there is a consensus that only three variables completely fit into this definition. These include genetic history, age, and gender. Medical technology is rapidly developing techniques to modify the genetic code, but these are not yet widespread enough to modify their inclusion as an individual determinant (Wang and Watts, 2007). Demographic variables have a fairly obvious impact, especially on a population basis. For example, there are more episodes of illness in an older population than in a younger one, and several illnesses such as various cancers are much more common in older people. Women seem to have more chronic disease conditions than men (Case and Paxton, 2005), although they also live longer than men (Arias et al., 2003).

Many studies have tried to estimate the relative importance of these three factors, with the overall conclusion being that these individual determinants

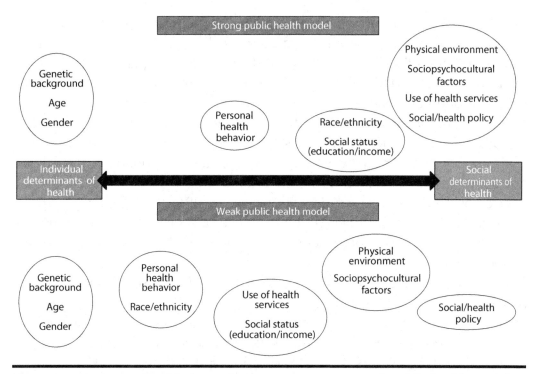

**Figure 2.1   Impact of health determinants: strong versus weak public health model.**

only contribute about 10% to a person's overall health status (Shi and Singh, 2014).

Figure 2.1 demonstrates there is some variation in this public health perspective, ranging from a weak identification with this perspective to a strong affiliation. From both a strong and a weaker public health perspective, these three categories of variables—genes, age, and gender—are viewed as being individual determinants of health. From the strongest public health framework, these are the only three factors that can be considered individualistic.

## Social Determinants of Health

Social determinants of health mean that economic and social conditions strongly influence the health of both individuals and communities. This includes the circumstances in which people are born, grow up, live, work, and age, as well as the systems put in place to deal with illness (WHO, 2008).

As shown in Figure 2.1, there is broad agreement that three categories are very clearly social determinants of health: physical environment, sociopsychocultural factors, and social and health policy.

The physical environment includes not only safe drinking water, clean air, and safe houses, but also food safety, as well as control of toxic chemicals, including radiation and other hazards. Healthy workplaces and safe roads are also included here, as are habitat alterations, such as the increase in urbanization and decrease in green and outdoor spaces. This set of variables has long been a mainstay of the public health efforts to improve health of both individuals and communities. The current definition of the physical environment has recently been expanded to include the notion of the impact of climate change on health (Frumkin et al., 2008).

Sociopsychocultural factors is a very large set of factors encompassing a range of variables. These include the presence of social support networks, individual psychological perceptions, and cultural beliefs and traditions. Chapter 4 expands on these.

Increasing attention has been paid to the role of both social and health policy and their impact on health. Many examples will be noted throughout this book, ranging from minimum wage regulations to the passage of the Affordable Care Act (ACA). Both health and social policy impact the full range of our daily lives as we travel on roads, spend time at work, and eat out in restaurants (Robert and Booke, 2011). More frustrating is the difficulty of translating knowledge about health determinants into policies that could prevent many deaths from preventable causes (Beaglehole et al., 2004).

As can be seen in Figure 2.1, there is less agreement in how to characterize three other sets of variables: race/ethnicity, personal health behavior, and utilization of medical services. All three of these were originally thought to be closer to individual determinants of health, but most in the field of public health now consider these to be strongly impacted by social, political, and cultural factors. Each will be briefly discussed here.

How to consider the impact of race and ethnicity on health has experienced the most dramatic shift in perspective. Much of the early research was framed around identifying the biological basis of the racial differences that exist in health status. Today, the presence of health disparities is viewed as a product of institutional racism, not biology. The exceptions are a small set of specific diseases for which we can identify the genetic markers, including sickle cell anemia or diseases such as Tay–Sachs, in which clear genetic markers have been identified in a group of people from a defined geographic area. For those with strong connections to the public health field, the racial and ethnic health differences in health status are considered to be very highly impacted by social and cultural factors and are considered to be an important part of the social determinants of health. Chapter 21 provides a summary of this research.

Personal health behavior is another example of a group of variables that used to be thought of as having a very large component of individual responsibility, although people with strong views of the public health perspective never included this as a completely individual determinant. One of the best examples of the complexities involved in personal health behavior is smoking. Although some characterize this as an individual lifestyle choice, this can only be understood when smoking is viewed in the larger social and cultural context that begins with the $1.5 billion in taxpayer-provided federal financial subsidies provided to tobacco farmers in 2012 (USDA, 2014). Tobacco advertising, although limited, is still very prevalent; and prices of tobacco products, although increasing, are still well within the ability of people to purchase. The impact of just this one health behavior is profound. Fifteen percent of all preventable deaths are a direct result of smoking (Sultz and Young, 2014b). There are 21 different diseases that are specifically caused by smoking and many others for which smoking is a significant contributor. Mortality among smokers is two to three times higher than among nonsmokers (Carter et al., 2015). For those with a strong public health orientation, this is not a choice made freely by one individual.

Use of appropriate health care services is a third variable that is viewed by a strong public health model as a social determinant of health. Those with a weaker affiliation to a public health perspective recognize that factors such as financial barriers may limit accessibility, but have always viewed seeking help for health problems as mainly an extension of the individual level of responsibility portrayed in Figure 1.1. Research using the framework of accessibility described in Chapter 1 has helped expand the understanding of the impact of health policy on personal health behavior. This does not remove the importance of emphasizing increased personal responsibility, but it does acknowledge how difficult it is to encourage better health-related decisions in a culture in which a variety of poor health habits are not only tolerated, but often either financially subsidized or even encouraged. Additionally, the financial subsidies of the medical care system frequently make the most expensive part of the medical care system—an emergency room—more accessible to patients without insurance than a primary care physician's office, so responsible health-seeking behavior is further eroded (Newman and Anderson, 2005).

A collection of variables are contained in the category of social status, which includes both education and income. It has long been known that poverty is linked to poor health indicators, including higher death rates as well as higher rates of disease (Nandi et al., 2014; Shi and Singh, 2014).

However, more recent research indicates that high levels of income inequality impacts everybody in a region, not just the individuals who are poor. The greater the economic gap between the rich and the poor in a defined area, the worse the health status of that population as a whole (Wilkinson and Marmot, 2003; Starfield, 2004; Marmot et al., 2008). Countries more committed to income equalization policies through various social policies are more successful in improving various health status measures of a whole population, including death rates (Navarro and Shi, 2001; Wilkinson and Marmot, 2003; Starfield, 2004).

## Why Do Health Determinants Matter?

The focus of this chapter is the perspective of the public health field, which believes that all determinants of health, even those involving high levels of personal decision making, must be interpreted in the context of the social and cultural network that impacts those decisions. Figure 2.2 shows a summary of the relative impact of each of these determinants of health. Although it may be important to identify specific areas of personal responsibility; social, economic, and cultural factors are crucial influences on health behavior. Together, these two categories are responsible for 60–80% of our health status.

It is also important to be aware of the interconnections between these categories. Two examples of this effort relate to obesity and smoking. Increasingly, the presence of what are called food deserts are related to poor health outcomes, including higher obesity rates as well as higher rates of diabetes (Gordon et al., 2011). Food deserts involve areas in which an affordable supply of nutritious foods, especially fresh fruits and vegetables, is simply not available. These areas are almost always located in low-income neighborhoods, which reinforces Marmot's observations of the overall importance of income and socioeconomic status in whole communities, not just individuals (Marmot et al., 2008).

Research on smoking habits reinforces this notion of the overall importance of socioeconomic status. Adults who live below the poverty line are 27.9% of current smokers, as opposed to 17.0% of those whose incomes are higher; and those in lower income areas seem to be less accepting of smoking cessation programs (Pampel et al., 2010).

Two final observations are warranted. There is a political dimension to this topic, which will be mentioned here and developed more fully in

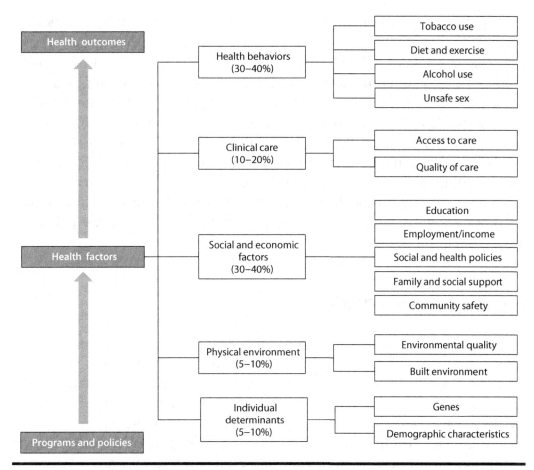

**Figure 2.2   Relative impacts of determinants of health. (Adapted from University of Wisconsin Population Health Institute, 2010. Available from: http://www.countryhealth rankings.org.)**

Section III. The importance of individual responsibility is not only a central aspect of the Biomedical Model as described in Chapter 1, it is also the basis of a politically conservative position. The understanding that a person's health is very significantly impacted by his or her social and cultural surroundings is one of the components of a more liberal political position. In focusing so strongly on the importance of social determinants of health and by gradually enlarging their conceptual importance, the public health field is taking a more liberal political approach to improving the health status of people.

The second observation is about language. Much of the distinction between the various categories of determinants of health seems like semantics. However, being clear about all the factors that impact health status is very important to allocating resources for programs and for health services.

Many policies are regulatory, most of which are developed after educational efforts fail.

Within the field of public health, it has long been recognized that interventions at the community level have a much better chance of improving the social determinants of health, which in turn provide support for those personal lifestyle decisions that are necessary to improve health status at an individual level. The Healthy People Initiative is an example of an effort to improve health status through an integrated model of both individual and social determinants of health while using a community-based intervention. This is a significant policy effort aimed at improving the health of the entire U.S. population, using interventions from both the medical and the public health fields.

## Healthy People Initiative

The Healthy People Initiative began in 1990 with a goal of significantly improving the overall health status of Americans by the end of the century. The Department of Health and Human Services (DHHS) identified 319 main objectives grouped into 22 priority areas (Lurie, 1999). Consistent with the perspective of the field of public health, the areas of interest were all concerned with health promotion, health protection, and prevention. The final priority area focused on the necessary data and surveillance efforts to keep track of progress. The National Center for Health Statistics (NCHS) was in charge of gathering data to measure the progress on each of the goals (CDC/NCHS, 2009).

This was a huge project with idealistic goals, so it is not surprising that by the end of the 10-year mark only 21% of the objectives completely met the targets set for 2000. Another 41% showed some progress; 16% showed mixed results, and only about 2% showed no change from the baseline data (NCHS, 2001). Some of the more important successes included reducing deaths from coronary heart disease, cancer, and gun violence. The incidence of AIDS and syphilis were reduced, and participation in screening examinations such as mammography increased.

The revised objectives for Healthy People 2010 were organized around two major goals. The first was to increase quality and years of healthy life and the second was to reduce health disparities. The 2010 initiative refocused its efforts to identify a specific group of health behaviors that lead to increased risk of experiencing poor health, which would then translate into lower health status indicators. As will be more fully described in Chapter 3, health indicators are quantifiable characteristics of a population that can be used to predict the health status of that population. Health indicators can also be used to identify areas in which interventions need to be designed. Healthy People 2010 identified 10 health indicators to track progress toward improving Americans' health. As can be seen in the following list, each of these health indicators have a strong connection to a person's health status (ODPHP, 2010).

Twenty-first century leading health indicators (CDC/NHCHS, 2009)

- Physical activity
- Overweight and obesity
- Tobacco use
- Substance abuse
- Responsible sexual behavior
- Mental health
- Injury and violence
- Environmental quality
- Immunization
- Access to health care

The mid-decade evaluation of the Healthy People 2010 project showed substantial improvements in many of the targeted health behaviors. Of the 28 specific focus areas, about half showed substantial improvement. Some of the most notable improvements were in access to health services, improvement in air quality, and occupational health and safety. Several specific preventive health behaviors were targeted, with significant improvements in immunizations and also in control of infectious diseases. Moreover, the homicide rate decreased enough to exceed the established target (Koh, 2014). In December 2010, the DHHS launched Healthy People 2020, which emphasizes monitoring health-enhancing social and environmental factors. Prevention activities are also more fully integrated into the 2020 project. One of the most important goals is to eliminate racially based health disparities by the year 2020 (Koh, 2014).

The Healthy People Project stresses the importance of setting and measuring population-based health objectives. The scope of the objectives provides an important message that improving health involves not only curing diseases, but also promoting health through social policies as well as more targeted health policies. This initiative is based on a strong public health orientation, because it assumes that individual personal health choices that are at the basis of many of the major health problems are strongly influenced by social, cultural, and economic factors. The challenge is including health services that build on this conceptual understanding. As just one example of this, the ACA requires all health insurance policies to cover screening for sexually transmitted diseases with no copayments on the part of patients (Fielding et al., 2012). This is based on data collected by Healthy People 2010 that determined that almost 25% of young women between the ages of 14 and 19 have at least one sexually transmitted disease. Removing the financial barrier to this preventive service is essential to improving access, as will be explained in Chapter 11.

This example speaks to the issue of resource allocation in the health field. Almost 95% of the total amount of money on health care in the United States goes to the medical care sector, an area that seems to impact about 10–20% of our health status. Only about 5% of health care dollars are spent on activities that promote health, hopefully decreasing the need for more costly medical care services (see Figure 6.2). This is an old argument between the fields of medicine and public health, with public health proponents noting that some of the biggest improvements in health status have been the result of overall public health measures—including improved sanitation and isolation/quarantine for infectious diseases—rather than medical measures.

This continued debate is largely attributable to the difference in perspective, as noted in Chapter 1. For those in public health, the focus of improving health is a group. For those in the medical field, the perspective is one sick person. Despite this very real difference, it is not true these two perspectives are mutually exclusive, as will be shown in Chapter 6.

A final contribution of the Healthy People project lies in the effort to quantify various aspects of our health behavior. We now have data on nearly everything related to health behavior, ranging from actual utilization of medical services to number of people in each age group who continue to smoke. The ultimate goal is to relate these health behaviors to outcomes, which is primarily done by measuring what are called health status indicators. As these important measures will come up repeatedly throughout this book, they will be described in Chapter 3.

# Acknowledgments

Thanks go to all of the students enrolled with me in PH 494CI for the Spring 2014 semester at the University of Massachusetts. Their comments and suggestions about the structure and content of this chapter were very helpful. The following people made significant contributions, including gathering materials and references, as well as writing and analysis: Irene Eberbach, Michael Goulart, Evan Hill, Tiphanie Jones, Sarah Schlosstein, Sam Taylor, Kylie Wojcicki, and Pratiksha Yalakkishetter. Annie Beach, Bianca Doone, and Nicolas Dundas significantly improved this chapter with their very helpful comments and suggested revisions. Bianca constructed the figures and Irene constructed the table.

# Chapter 3

# Health Status Indicators

The field of public health has developed a set of numbers to describe and summarize the health of a population. These quantitative estimates are similar to those used by physicians to summarize our individual health status, such as weight, blood pressure, cholesterol levels, and temperature. This chapter will describe the most commonly used population-based health status measures, including death (mortality) rates, sickness (morbidity) rates, and life expectancy rates. A rate includes a denominator that defines the context of the number. Simply reporting the total number of people who died in one year does not provide nearly as much useful information as specifying the number of deaths for a certain defined group of people, which may be 1000, 10,000, or 100,000, depending on the measure that is being utilized.

Health status indicators are used in a wide variety of ways. They are used to track trends in diseases, such as increased influenza cases, or a widening outbreak of food poisoning. They are used to track the success in treating or preventing specific diseases such as cancer, by comparing death rates over several years. They are used to identify where additional resources may be needed. They are also widely used to assess the effectiveness of a nation's health care system and to make international comparisons, as will be discussed in Chapter 22. Health status indicators are referred to throughout this book, so it is appropriate to give a general understanding of them here.

## Measuring Death: Mortality Rates

Mortality rates represent the proportion of people in a population who die over a specified length of time, usually one year. Crude death rates are the broadest measure and include all deaths from all causes in one year in a defined population. Many death rates are age-adjusted to control for different age distributions in communities. Others are age-specific, which is a rough measure of the risk of dying in a certain age group, or cause-specific, which is an expression of risk of dying from a specific cause, such as heart disease or a specific cancer.

Figure 3.1 shows an example of age-adjusted mortality rates for each of the top five causes of death for three different years. In this case, the rate is expressed as the number of people dying per 100,000. Comparing rates over time allow for decisions about resources needed, for both screening and treatment.

### Infant Mortality Rate

The one death rate that is most commonly used for international comparisons is an age-specific rate: the infant mortality rate (IMR). This is defined as the number of infants who die before 1 year of age. It is expressed as a ratio, with number of deaths in the numerator and number of 1000 live births in the denominator.

Figure 3.2 shows a very common way of using the IMR, which is to compare the IMR across different countries. As can be seen from this figure, nations with higher IMRs tend to be poorer, less well developed, and also tend to have fewer resources devoted to their national health care system. The differences between the countries with very high IMRs and those with very low IMRs is very dramatic.

The IMR is viewed as a good overall estimate of a country's health care system, so data are routinely collected by most countries around the world. Both the World Health Organization (WHO) and the Organization for Economic Cooperation and Development (OECD) collect data and monitor IMRs around the world. Major causes of infant mortality worldwide include infection, dehydration due to a diarrhea-related illness, premature births, birth defects that lead to death, sudden infant death syndrome, and complications with the mother during pregnancy (CDC, 2012b; OECD, 2013).

A very puzzling aspect of the IMR is the poor showing of the United States, as can be seen in Figure 3.2. Despite the resources available in the

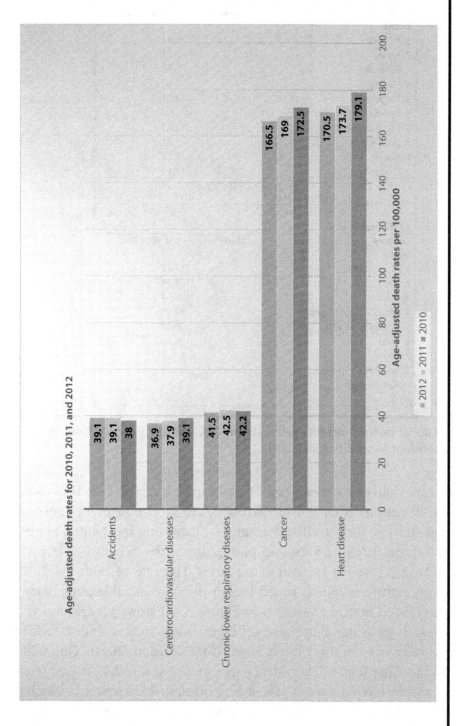

**Figure 3.1  Top five causes of death in the United States. (From Centers for Disease Control, *National Vital Statistics Report,* 61, 4, 2015.)**

| 10 Lowest | |
| --- | --- |
| Country births | Mortality rate per 1000 live |
| 1. Monaco | 1.81 |
| 2. Japan | 2.13 |
| 3. Bermuda | 2.48 |
| 4. Norway | 2.48 |
| 5. Singapore | 2.53 |
| 6. Sweden | 2.60 |
| 7. Czech Republic | 2.63 |
| 8. Hong Kong | 2.73 |
| 9. Macau | 3.13 |
| 10. Iceland | 3.15 |
| **United States** | **6.17** |
| 10 Highest | |
| Country births | Mortality rate per 1000 live |
| 1. Afghanistan | 117.23 |
| 2. Mali | 104.34 |
| 3. Somalia | 100.14 |
| 4. Cental African Republic | 92.86 |
| 5. Guinea-Bissau | 90.92 |
| 6. Chad | 90.30 |
| 7. Niger | 86.27 |
| 8. Angola | 79.99 |
| 9. Burkina Faso | 76.80 |
| 10. Nigeria | 74.09 |

**Figure 3.2   Global infant mortality rates. (From CIA World Factbook, Country Comparisons: Infant Mortality Rates, 2013.)**

U.S. health care delivery system, the overall ranking of the U.S. IMR is 50th among all nations (CIA World Factbook, 2013). The primary cause of infant deaths in most industrialized countries, including the United States, is low birth weight (under 5.5 lb) and premature births, which is a baby born at less than 37 weeks (Martin et al., 2015). The rate of both low birth weight and premature babies is much higher in some racial groups than others in the United States, as shown in Figure 3.3. Figure 3.3 and much of other research indicates that these differences are attributable to lack of access to primary care in the United States (MacDorman, 2011). This will be described in Chapter 21. The IMR is an especially sensitive measure of a group of people having access to a strong primary care system, which explains why some countries with fewer economic resources have lower IMRs than the United States.

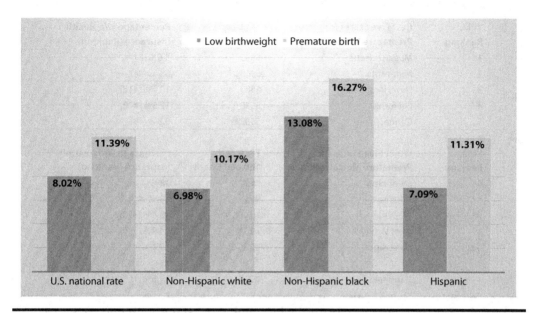

**Figure 3.3   Percent of low birth weight and premature births in the United States by race (2013). (From Births: Final Data for 2013,** *National Vital Statistics Report,* **64, 1, 2015.)**

## Premature Death Rate

Another sort of age-related mortality rate involves premature deaths, which are those that occur before the age of 75. This measure is also expressed as years of potential life lost (YPLL). For example, if a 20-year-old were to die there would be 55 YPLL, but if a 70-year-old were to die there would be 5 YPLL. The premature death rate is especially important to public health researchers because the assumption is that premature deaths are preventable through lifestyle modifications. The most important causes of premature deaths are cancer (especially lung cancer), accidental injury, heart disease, and suicide (United Health Foundation, 2013a).

Using premature deaths as a health status indicator allows public health researchers to track the success of various intervention programs. The premature death rate is also viewed as a good indicator of access to medical care, especially primary care services. For example, in the United States, those who are insured are less likely to die before the age of 75 (Bailey, 2012). Another way to look at this is presented in Figure 3.4. In general, the states with the fewest uninsured also have the lowest rate of premature deaths.

The rate of premature deaths in the United States has fallen over the past 20 years. In 1990, the YPLL before age 75 was 8716 per 100,000 people

| YPLL Ranking | Best Five States for Premature Mortality Rates | YPLL per 100,000 Deaths | Percentage w/o Health Insurance (Ranking) |
|---|---|---|---|
| 1 | Massachusetts | 5345 | 3.8% (#1) |
| 2 | Minnesota | 5358 | 8.1% (#4) |
| 3 | New Hampshire | 5580 | 10.7% (#12) |
| 4 | California | 5590 | 17.5% (#43) |
| 5 | Connecticut | 5603 | 9.3% (#8) |

| YPLL Ranking | Worst Five States for Premature Mortality Rates | YPLL per 100,000 Deaths | Percentage w/o Health Insurance (Ranking) |
|---|---|---|---|
| 46 | Oklahoma | 9654 | 18% (#44) |
| 47 | Arkansas | 9656 | 19.5% (#47) |
| 48 | Alabama | 10,008 | 13.4% (#25) |
| 49 | West Virginia | 10,159 | 14.2% (#30) |
| 50 | Mississippi | 10,354 | 17.1% (#40) |
| | National | 6976 | 14.6% |

**Figure 3.4 Rate of premature deaths by best and worst states with percentage of citizens without health insurance, 2014. (From United Health Foundation, America's Health Ranking, 2013.)**

as a national average. Comparatively, in 2013 the YPLL before age 75 was 6976 per 100,000 people (United Health Foundation, 2013a). This decline is explained not only by improved medical treatment, but also by improved prevention based on understanding the social determinants of health. One of the best examples of this is the focus of the public health field on the national antismoking campaign. Between educational campaigns, laws and regulations, and improved medical treatment, 8 million lives have been extended over the past 50 years. This is about one-third of all premature deaths that occurred between 1964 and 2012 (Meza and Pletcher, 2014).

This health status indicator is also widely used for international comparisons. In 2011, the United States ranked 29th for women and 27th for men in premature death rates out of the 31 OECD countries that had data available (OECD, 2011a). As with the IMR, this is largely explained by overall lack of access to health care services, especially to primary care services.

## Cause-Specific Mortality Rates

It is very common to use various disease-specific death rates, either to focus on the need for more resources or perhaps to highlight particular progress over time, as in Figure 3.5, which demonstrates more progress in reducing the death rate from heart diseases than from cancer.

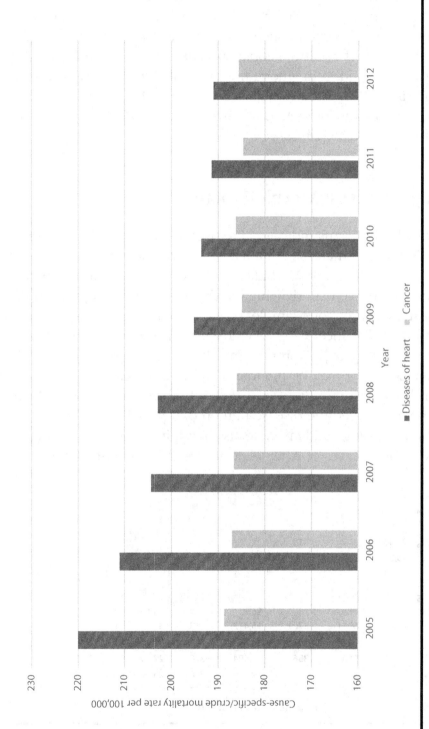

**Figure 3.5   Cause-specific/crude mortality rates for the United States from 2005 to 2012. (From CDC/NCHS, *National Vital Statistics Report, Mortality,* 2013.)**

Cause-specific death rates can also be used to track progress in larger social problems, such as gun violence, considered a health status indicator by the public health field. Reduction in gun violence was included as one of the objectives of Healthy People 2010, as described in Chapter 2. In 2010, homicide dropped from among the top 15 leading causes of death for the first time since 1965. The age-adjusted death rate for homicide (5.3 per 100,000 standard population) fell to its lowest since 1962, decreasing 3.6% from 2009 to 2010 (NCHS, 2012).

## Measuring Diseases: Morbidity Rates

Another set of health status indicators are used to assess the level of disease in a population, rather than the deaths that occur. Morbidity encompasses disease, injury, and disability. Morbidity is also expressed as a rate, which is the number of people experiencing the disease over the population that is at risk for the disease. For example, breast cancer rates are expressed as the number of breast cancer cases diagnosed over the population of women within a specific age group. Morbidity may be newly diagnosed cases, known as incidence, or may be the total number of cases at a certain point in time, which is prevalence (Oleckno, 2002). Both of them are very helpful in tracking what is called the disease burden of a population.

An example of using incidence rates is shown in Figure 3.6. Although the total number of new cases of AIDS is declining, the decrease is not even

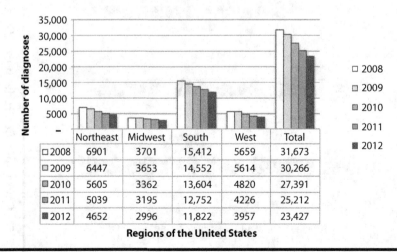

| | Northeast | Midwest | South | West | Total |
|---|---|---|---|---|---|
| □ 2008 | 6901 | 3701 | 15,412 | 5659 | 31,673 |
| □ 2009 | 6447 | 3653 | 14,552 | 5614 | 30,266 |
| ▨ 2010 | 5605 | 3362 | 13,604 | 4820 | 27,391 |
| ▨ 2011 | 5039 | 3195 | 12,752 | 4226 | 25,212 |
| ■ 2012 | 4652 | 2996 | 11,822 | 3957 | 23,427 |

**Regions of the United States**

**Figure 3.6    AIDS diagnosis by region: 2008–2012. (From CDC 2012 HIV Surveillance Report.)**

over the entire country. There are regional differences that highlight the need for additional resources in some parts of the country.

Morbidity data are also used in routine surveillance to identify unusual and/ or emerging diseases, including regional or national episodes of food poisoning. For example, between March 1, 2013 and December 26, 2013, there were 430 individuals diagnosed with a strain of *Salmonella heidelberg* in 23 states and Puerto Rico (CDC, 2014a). The majority of the infected patients were from California. An epidemiological analysis of the pattern of cases revealed that chicken products at three facilities in California caused the outbreak (CDC, 2014a). The infected poultry was recalled and the outbreak ended.

Monitoring the incidence of influenza is another way to understand surveillance. Predicting epidemics helps identify the need for increased resources, especially in hospitals, and helps control the death rate for a seasonal disease such as influenza.

## Life Expectancy Rates

Life expectancy is a statistical term used to predict the probable number of years a person will live. It is most frequently calculated at birth, but is also determined at age 65, as shown in Figure 3.7. This health status indicator is viewed as a more comprehensive measure of a health care system's performance, and is also impacted by all the social determinants of health that were discussed in Chapter 2. It is also significantly impacted by one of the individual determinants of health, noticeably gender, as can be seen from

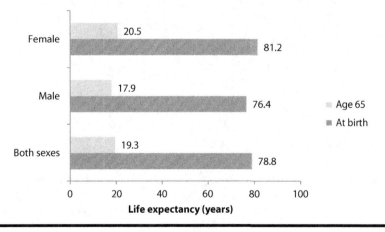

**Figure 3.7** **U.S. life expectancy by sex and age: 2013. (From Kochanek, K.D. et al., Mortality in the United States, 2013. CDC/NCHS Date Brief. # 178; Dec. 2014.)**

Figure 3.7. On average, women live almost 5 years longer at birth than males and about $2\frac{1}{2}$ years longer at age 65.

A common way of using the life expectancy rate is to compare international rates, as shown in Figure 3.8. Not surprisingly, the five countries with the best life expectancy are more industrialized and have more resources overall than the countries with the lowest life expectancy. As with the IMR, the U.S. ranking is a little puzzling, as we are only 16th in overall life expectancy (World Bank, 2011). Public health researchers attribute at least some of this to cultural values that limit the role of government both in the health system, and in social policy. Countries with longer life expectancies have a much lower percentage of uninsured and lower levels of poverty. These countries also have far less gun violence. The Institute of Medicine (IOM) recently estimated that homicide and suicide account for 25% of premature deaths, which contributes to the lower life expectancy in the United States (Woolf et al., 2013). Despite the progress through the Healthy People

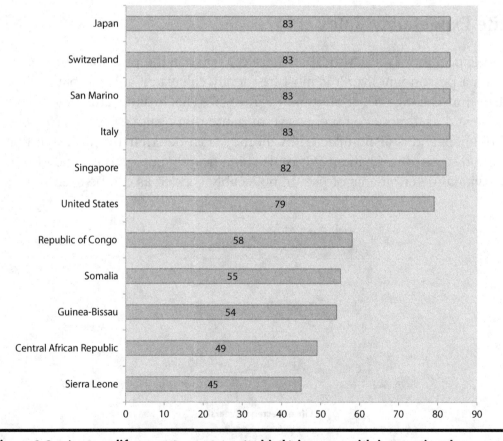

**Figure 3.8   Average life expectancy rates (at birth) in years with international comparisons, 2012. (From The World Bank, Life Expectancy at Birth, 2012.)**

Imitative, in the United States, firearms are the second leading cause of death due to injury, after car accidents (CDC, 2014b).

Life expectancy rates provide data that exemplify global variations and act as a strong statistical tool in identifying areas in which more resources are needed. Life expectancy rates reflect not only access to medical care services but also access to public health services, as well as the various social determinants of health described in Chapter 2. Life expectancy rates also provide a more positive way to characterize the impact of a health care system on a population.

# Other Measures of Health Indicators

With the exception of life expectancy rates, all of the morbidity and mortality measures focus on disease, not health. There are other health status indicators that focus on measuring health as opposed to sickness. Although these are occasionally used to make international comparisons, these health indicators are mostly used for research purposes. Two examples will be described here: one that is used to describe an individual's health status and one that summarizes the health of a group.

## Individual Functional Health Status Measures

This set of health status indicators arises from the fact that the most practical definition of health relates to function, as noted in Chapter 1. These measures are primarily used to assess disabilities and the level of assistance needed among elderly people. There are two scales that are most commonly used. The first is the Activities of Daily Living scale, which measures six basic variables: eating, bathing, dressing, using the toilet, maintaining continence, and transferring from bed to chair (Katz and Akpom, 1979). The second scale is the Instrumental Activities of Daily Living scale, which assesses 10 variables that are necessary for living independently in a community setting, including activities such as driving a car, using mass transportation, shopping, preparing meals, going up and down stairs, and walking a half-mile without help (Ostir et al., 1999).

## Community Health Status Indicators

A newer approach is to characterize the health of a whole community. The most commonly used is a technique developed by the World Health

Organization called Health Impact Assessments (HIAs). This is an explicit technique to develop health programs and policies based on social determinants of health, including the availability of health and medical care services (Joffe and Mindell, 2002; O'Mullane, 2013). Although developed for international use, HIA studies have also been done in the United States. One example analyzed the decisions low-income families make in using cheaper methods of heating homes, such as kerosene or space heaters and identified the health impact on their children, especially with increased medical visits for respiratory problems (Dannenberg et al., 2008).

The Institute for Health Metrics and Evaluation has created measurements to quantify global health problems based on functional health, and calculated on a community or national basis instead of for one individual. This approach uses the concept of premature death and disability days to estimate the total years of life lost on a national basis. One interesting result was that in 2010, road accidents resulted in a global loss of 75 million years of healthy life, which was more than years of life lost from any other cause (Smith, 2014). The purpose of this research is to emphasize the importance of a comprehensive approach to estimating the health of a nation.

## What to Do with This Information?

Chapters 2 and 3 have a similar theme, which is to quantify health, either individually or as a group. The medical field uses a set of numbers to describe an individual's health, and the field of public health uses a set of numbers to quantify the health status of a whole group. Both are very useful, and neither is a complete description. In both cases, it can be fairly asked why we depend on these estimates. The answer is that the phenomenon of health is very complicated and impossible to describe without using some sort of proxy measure. The use of a numerical estimate allows us to identify risk factors, to summarize health trends, to identify the need for resources, and to do comparisons.

These comparisons are often not very favorable to the United States, as has been seen throughout this chapter. This is difficult to understand, because the United States spends so much more money on its health care system than any other country. The most common health status indicator used internationally is the IMR. Some criticize this indicator as assessing the health of only a small portion of a population. However, the IMR has a very high correlation to life expectancy, including when life expectancy is adjusted for disabilities (Allotey and Redipath, 2003). Although the IMR is a very sensitive measure of the impact of a strong and accessible primary care system, life expectancy also captures the more technological aspects of a medical system.

Many researchers have demonstrated that the presence of a well-funded primary care system has a very significant impact on all of the health status indicators (Tarlov, 1999; Starfield, 2004). The United States is better characterized as a medically sophisticated system with known unequal access for some segments of our population, which we address with programs specifically designed to provide care for the underserved segments. Although the United States does perform better in life expectancy measures than in infant mortality measures, we are still far from being among the top 10 countries. Whether this is related to the greater racial and geographic diversity of our population or to the structure of our health care system will be part of the discussion throughout this book, culminating in Chapter 22. Cultural beliefs and expectations and the U.S. political culture must be examined first in order to complete the picture of the larger context for the U.S. health care delivery system.

## Acknowledgments

The following people made significant contributions to the content of this chapter, including gathering material and references, as well as writing and analysis: Rachel Brown, Susannah Gleason, Maria Kardaras, and Samantha Calabrese. Emily Assarian, Christopher Lukasik, and Derek Luthi made substantive comments and revisions that greatly improved the quality of this chapter. Emily created Figures 3.1 through 3.3 and 3.5, Derek created Figures 3.7 and 3.8, and Chris created Figures 3.4 and 3.6.

# Chapter 4

## Role of Culture in the Organization of Health Care Delivery Systems

This chapter focuses on the role of culture on the structure and type of health care delivery system. This is the last conceptual piece of the puzzle that explains the relationship between the views of health and illness, the type of organized health care system, and the health care services available. All healing practices are based on a complex network of cultural beliefs about what causes illness and what types of practices are used to restore health. Each culture has a whole range of healing practices, as well as people identified as "healers." Inevitably, some of these become more legitimate than others, with the less legitimate healing practices usually termed alternative medicine. Alternative medical practices are frequently culturally based, but not always. This chapter begins with a description of the impact of culture on health beliefs and the organization of the health care delivery system. It then describes the process of differentiating alternative from legitimate healing practices in the United States. The chapter describes some of the most common of the culturally based healing practices, as well as several of the nonculturally based practices, all of which are labeled as alternative to the U.S. traditional biomedically based medical care system. The chapter concludes with some observations about alternative healing practices and how they fit into the U.S. health care system.

## Role of Culture in Defining Health and Illness

There are two large categories of beliefs about what causes illness: personalistic and naturalistic (Helman, 2007). Personalistic beliefs identify the cause of illness as primarily resulting from offending a supernatural deity or an ancestor, usually by behavior that is contrary to social norms. Naturalistic beliefs focus on the balance between an individual and his/her natural or social environment, with illness being the result of some sort of imbalance. There can be an overlap between these two theories, and healing practices frequently use techniques of both.

Naturalistic systems are more common around the world, with the humoral theory especially common in Asia, India, and Latin America. This focuses on maintaining balance by regulating one's diet by season and by being attentive to a quality (not temperature) called hot or cold. In addition to the quality of hot–cold, illness was also thought to originate from exposure to a miasma, which was a noxious emanation from water or air. This belief persisted throughout the late 1800s, including explaining diseases such as cholera and smallpox (Helman, 2007). Once pathogenic organisms were discovered, it led to a more refined version of this theory, with miasma being increasingly defined as microbes, and becoming the basis of the Biomedical Model described in Chapter 1.

The idea of health being a balance and illness being a disturbance requiring some sort of treatment to restore balance is very common across almost all health belief systems. The belief about what causes an illness episode is very important, because it strongly predicts what the person expects in terms of the type of healer, the types of healing practices offered, and often where the healing takes place. In the United States, which is a naturalistic system with a belief in the Biomedical Model, healing almost always takes place in an individual setting. Balance is restored by eliminating the specific organism causing the imbalance.

There are two important caveats in discussing the impact of culture on the structure of any health care system. The first is that the beliefs and approaches included throughout this chapter represent what are known as traditional values. These are the core, basic, and—in some cases—conservative values. These core values can and do vary with technological discoveries. For example, once miasma was more technologically defined as pathogenic organisms, healers in the United States were trained in the Biomedical Model. Even though the limitations of the Biomedical Model are recognized, as discussed in Chapters 1 and 2, the germ theory is still our traditional belief, or what is often called our ethnomedical model.

A second caveat is the importance of avoiding oversimplification when explaining cultural practices in health beliefs and their impact on health care systems. Cultures are full of diverse groups, so it is important to not make too many generalizations. For example, although the humoral system of healing is widespread in several Asian and Latin American countries, the expression of it is very different on these two continents (Helman, 2007; Galanti, 2008). The use of personalistic beliefs is also very common in many Asian cultures, including in those with humoral-based healing practices, resulting in a mixture of practices that is sometimes difficult to distinguish. More important than distinguishing between the various categories is recognizing beliefs as the basis for all therapeutic services offered to patients, for the training of health care healers or providers, and also for how health practices are financed.

## Impact of Culture on Organized Health Care Systems

Within every culture, there is not just one health or medical care system, but rather three: the popular, the folk, and the professional (Helman, 2007). Although only the professional system is usually considered as the health care system, the folk and popular sectors are important to understand, as they are utilized by many people and are an important part of the overall context of the formal system.

The first system is the most informal, and is usually termed the *popular sector* (Helman, 2007). It is a lay, nonprofessional sector, and involves a strong reliance on family members and friends, as well as self-treatment. The importance of this sector cannot be underestimated, because individual perceptions of symptoms are the beginning of the whole health behavior process, as summarized in Figure 1.4 (Chapter 1).

Also included in the popular sector are self-help groups, including Alcoholics Anonymous (AA), Narcotics Anonymous, Overeaters Anonymous, and Weight Watchers, just to mention a few. These well-recognized groups are usually led by a person with some special knowledge based on personal success rather than any professional training. Since the founding of the first one (AA in 1936), there are now more than 500,000 individual self-help groups in the United States. Nearly 20% of the U.S. population participates in at least one of these groups annually (Helman, 2007).

The *folk sector* is partly defined by not being formally recognized as a part of the legitimate, professional medical care system, although these health practitioners often have their own licensing and certification process. The definition of the folk sector depends primarily on culture, with the legal system (also culturally defined) used to enforce the distinction. For example, in many Asian countries, acupuncture is viewed as part of the professional system, whereas in the United States, it is considered part of the folk system. The folk sector is often described by terms such as quackery, charlatans, or folk healers. More formally, the terms alternative or complementary medicine are used, as will be described later in this chapter.

Folk healers are of two general types, depending on the belief system about what causes illness. In the more personalistic belief systems, the healers are sacred and may also involve organized religion. In the naturalistic systems, the healers are more secular, and use practices that are relevant to their view of the cause of the imbalance underlying the person's reported symptoms. Some of the types of folk or alternative healing practices used in the United States include acupuncture, faith healers, herbologists, reiki masters, and chiropractors. Some of the most frequently utilized ones will be described later.

Professionalization occurs in the folk sector of a health care system just as it does in the socially legitimate medical care sector. Many alternative healers have their own professional associations, and some have professional certification from their own schools and/or apprentice training organizations. Globally, folk healers provide a very valuable resource, not only for economically challenged countries, but also for the United States and other resource-rich countries. The World Health Organization's goal of having adequate primary care for people in all countries cannot be achieved without utilizing the full range of all folk healers (WHO, 2008b).

The *professional sector* is the socially and legally legitimate health or medical care system. This formalized sector is noted for its high level of organization and hierarchy, as well as its extensive education and certification requirements. It is the health care providers in the professional sector who have the legal right to treat patients and those who do similar treatments without the appropriate licensure can be punished. The Western Biomedical Model described in Chapter 1 is the basis for the professional system in the United States as well as globally. This is based on allopathic medicine, whereas the alternative healing practices described above as part of the folk system are usually based on homeopathic medical models that rely on healing practices that restore balance.

Even though this allopathic system is the basis for the medical care systems of many countries, there is variation based on cultural and political values in the expression of this system, both clinically and in terms of providing access. For example, in almost every industrialized nation, part of the medical care system is the belief that access to health care is a right, based on medical need alone. In the United States, the philosophical and political values related to access are more conflicted. As will be described in Chapter 5, there is a strong belief that access to medical care should be income based, although there are many programs that provide access to those who cannot afford it. In the multiple financing system used by the United States, medical treatments provided by the professional sector are usually covered by health insurance, whereas treatments that arise in the folk sector are usually not—unless access is controlled by a physician.

For all its knowledge, technical ability, and dominance, this Western biomedical allopathic model provides only a small proportion of all the medical care delivered globally. Part of this is because folk medical practices are well developed and well accepted in every culture. Also, the level of training and technology required by this Western Biomedical Model is not easily available to nations with few resources. Even in the United States, where this Biomedical Model is a strong part of our culture, the folk sector remains an important part of the health care delivery system, at least when judging by the number of people who use the services of one of these alternative healing practices.

## Alternative or Complementary Medical Systems and Practices

The folk sector in the United States is termed complementary alternative medicine (CAM), which is defined by the National Center for Complementary and Alternative Medicine (NCCAM) as "a group of diverse medical and health care interventions, practices, products or disciplines that are not generally considered part of conventional medicine" (NCCAM, 2011). In other words, any healing practice that the traditional Biomedical Model rejects is viewed as alternative or complementary. There is a distinction between alternative and complementary care, although both are included as CAM. Alternative medical therapies are often used in place of conventional medicine, whereas complementary medical practices are used alongside or as an adjunct to conventional medicine. The term alternative is preferred by those who believe their healing practice is a viable alternative to traditional medicine. U.S. physicians prefer to consider them as adjunct or complementary to their own healing techniques. The overall increased acceptance of at least some of these healing practices on the part of both patients and physicians is represented in the term CAM.

Views of U.S. health professionals about alternative care vary, although an increasing number accept them as complementary rather than alternative (Barnes et al., 2004). The National Institutes of Health (NIH) has encouraged medical schools to incorporate some of these healing practices into their medical school curricula, partly so the practices could be controlled more by the formal medical establishment (Helman, 2007).

CAM has a large impact on the U.S. medical system, because about 30% to 45% of the U.S. population utilizes some form of alternative medicine every year (Barnes et al., 2004; Kuehn, 2009). CAM practices are used by patients for a wide variety of reasons, including acute, self-limiting diseases, life-threatening conditions, and chronic illnesses. The most common symptom that is related to seeking alternative care is acute or chronic pain (Barnes et al., 2004; Ruggie, 2004). In the United States, these treatments are most commonly used as a complementary option as opposed to a replacement of Western medicine (Rakel and Faass, 2006). The vast majority of the money spent on alternative care is paid for by the consumer, whereas the majority of traditional medical therapy is paid for by insurance.

There are several ways of categorizing the many different types of CAM practices in the United States, but this chapter will only examine a few examples in two very broad categories. The first category includes healing practices embedded within a strong cultural system of health beliefs, which will be the topic of the next section. The second will be a group of those healing techniques that are based on a different view of causation of illness, but not necessarily embedded within a systematic cultural belief system.

## Culturally Based CAM Medical Practices

Culturally based alternative medical care practices exist within an organized system of cultural values and beliefs about health and illness, as well as expectations for the healers, and the type of healing practices used. This section will describe three important culturally based alternative health belief systems: the traditional Chinese, Indian, and Mexican health belief systems. Within their original countries, each belief system interacts with the Western biomedical medical care system. Many of these healing practices are seen by U.S. physicians as they encounter immigrant patients with strong cultural ties to one of these traditional systems (Galanti, 2008).

## Traditional Chinese Health System

The best known of the culturally based medical care systems and the most widely used in the United States is the traditional Chinese system. Beliefs about health are based on the philosophical foundation of Taoism, which believes that people are interconnected in a chain of relationships that create harmony in the universe. This harmony is an expression of the balance of two forces in the universe: *Yang*, which is a positive energy that produces light, warmth, and energy, and *Yin*, which is a negative energy that provides darkness, cold, and emptiness. The physical symptoms of disease are caused by an upset of the balance between these two opposing forces (Lam, 2001).

This is an ancient health belief system, with the first documented source describing Chinese medicine written in 300 B.C. and called the *Yellow Emperor's Book of Internal Medicine* (Lam, 2001). The healing practices used in this system include extensive herbal remedies, acupuncture, acupressure and massage, diet, and exercise regimens; and moxibustion, which is the application of heat to specific areas, commonly with stones (Hesketh and Zhu, 1997). The purpose of all the individual healing remedies is to restore balance to the body.

Traditional Chinese doctors are professionally trained in schools teaching traditional Chinese medicine (TCM). The duration of this educational program is 3 to 4 years, after which graduates are certified practitioners of TCM and become an integral part of China's professional health care system (Hesketh and Zhu, 1997).

The two best-known healing practices within this system are acupuncture and herbal therapy. The Chinese have an extensive and sophisticated herbal system that differs from other herbal systems by emphasizing health-promoting herbs as well as curative ones. Of the 7000 different herbs and combinations that are available in the traditional Chinese system, 500 are devoted to health promotion and are known as Imperial herbs. TCM practitioners mix selected herbs to specifically address the imbalance that is causing the symptoms (Lam, 2001).

TCM views the body as a network of energy involving the forces of Yin and Yang. This energy network is known as Qi (or "chi"). Qi goes through the entire body, within 14 primary meridians that correspond to 12 different organ systems (Povolny, 2008). Qi is adjusted by using the six different pulses within these meridians. There are 15 ways to characterize each pulse to identify blockages of energy causing symptoms. The acupuncturist inserts 6–12 very thin needles in various locations for up to 45 minutes, sometimes twirling the needles, other times leaving them stationary (Povolny, 2008).

In the United States, people use acupuncture for a variety of reasons, mostly related to chronic pain (including back pain), joint pain, headaches, and postoperative pain as well as systemic and generalized muscle pain from syndromes such as fibromyalgia. Acupuncture treatments can be curative, but are more likely to be viewed as part of continuing therapy (Povolny, 2008).

In the United States, state licensure is required to practice acupuncture. Acupuncturists practicing in the United States must also pass a national board examination given through the National Certification Commission for Acupuncture and Oriental Medicine (Povolny, 2008). Medical doctors, chiropractors, and clinical nurses can become certified to practice acupuncture by taking a training course shorter than the required 4 years (White, 2009).

Although widely practiced in many Asian countries, acupuncture was not practiced in the United States until the early 1970s when President Nixon normalized political relations with China, and the Internal Revenue Service allowed expenses related to acupuncture to be deducted as medical expenses (Frum, 2000).

It is estimated that more than 3 million people receive acupuncture yearly (Kuehn, 2009). It is increasingly common for a medical practice to establish acupuncture as part of its own practice, with a physician trained and certified as an acupuncturist. This makes it possible for health insurance to cover the cost of acupuncture treatments (White, 2009).

## Traditional Indian Health Care System

*Ayurveda* is another ancient healing system, this one originating in India. It is a holistic system of using natural resources in order to regain balance of the body's five basic elements and seven basic tissues. This traditional Hindu medical system views the universe as being composed of five basic elements: earth, water, fire, air, and ether. The human body has three humors; products of the body are derived from the five basic elements and are defined as three basic energies (Mukherjee and Wahile, 2005; Galanti, 2008). Poor health is caused by an imbalance between all these elements and humors, and Ayurveda medical healing practices are used to restore balance. There are eight branches of Ayurveda and 16 specialties (Mukherjee and Wahile, 2005). A practitioner of Ayurveda creates individualized prescriptions that include herbal compounds, special diets, exercise, and development of lifestyle practices. In India, the majority of the population utilizes Ayurveda, often on its own, but also frequently in conjunction with conventional Western medicine (NCCAM, 2005).

Although there are Ayurvedic medical schools in India, there are no state or federal regulations on practitioners of Ayurveda within the United States. There is a professional accreditation process, however. The National Ayurvedic Medical Association was formed in 1998 in order to "establish and maintain standards of education, ethics, professional competency, and licensing" (NAMA, 2013). They maintain a list of schools and certificate programs they have reviewed, and they group schools and programs according to intensity of requirements.

The practice of yoga, which is used to restore and maintain balance, is an integral part of Ayurvedic medicine. This practice is the best known part of Ayurvedic medicine in the United States. About 9% of the U.S. population practices some form of yoga, although it is not generally connected to the Ayurvedic health system (Peregoy et al., 2014).

## Traditional Mexican Health Care System

The traditional Mexican health belief system is based on the hot–cold theory of illness described earlier. Illness is caused by the person being exposed to something that causes that individual to become cold or hot—not in terms of temperature, but rather to a quality of being. Every food, drink, and medicine has a hot or cold quality, as do emotions and interactions with others. The practitioner uses a variety of healing practices to restore the body to a neutral balance. This belief system has more followers globally than any other system of health belief, including the Biomedical Model. There are variations across cultures as to what can be considered hot or cold, but the core beliefs are similar.

This belief system gives rise to several healing practices, including extensive dietary modifications. Two specific healing practices that are very common are *coining* and *cupping*. Both are used to restore balance to a person by drawing the illness out of a person's body. Coining involves heating an oil-covered metal object, such as a coin or a spoon. The heated metal is rubbed over the body, most frequently over the spot where symptoms are present. Illness is diagnosed if the heated coin produces welts. The welts also demonstrate that the illness is being drawn out of the body (Helman, 2007). Cupping is a similar process, involving a heated glass. This is placed on the body where the vacuum creates a red welt. As in coining, the red welt is both proof of illness and also demonstrates the beginning of healing. Cupping is extensively used in many parts of the world, including Asia, Latin America, Russia, and parts of Europe. It is likewise taught in most acupuncture colleges, because TCM also has some therapies related to moxibustion.

The clinical medical literature is full of examples of Western doctors misdiagnosing welts that result from either coining or cupping (Galanti, 2008). As will be shown in Chapter 5, the largest group of immigrants in the United States comes from a country in which the Mexican traditional health beliefs are an important folk healing system. For this reason, it is important for U.S. physicians to be aware of these healing practices.

## Nonculturally Based CAM Healing Practices

There are many alternative health practices that do not have a strong association with a cultural background. Some of these involve a trained and certified practitioner whereas others are far less regulated. Table 4.1 shows some examples of the more common of these healing practices. This section will describe the most well known and most commonly used of all the alternative medical practices, which is chiropractic medicine.

Chiropractic medicine is based on a view of illness being caused by an imbalance, but focuses on the structural and biomechanical balance of the body rather than an energy flow. Illness and/or physical pain is a result of an imbalance between the spine and overall health. The imbalance is caused by subluxation, which is a partial dislocation of the vertebrae of the spine, but also has a spiritual aspect and represents a separation from a vitalistic life force, usually expressed as the spirit of God. The misalignments of the spinal vertebrae interfere with the innate intelligence of the body's ability to heal itself. Correction of the dislocation is done by spinal manipulation (Ernst, 2011). The formal definition of chiropractic care has changed numerous times in the past decade, and in 2003, NCCAM described it as "a form of health care that focuses on the relationship between the body's structure, primarily of the spine and function" (Ernst, 2011).

**Table 4.1   Examples of Some Nonculturally Based CAM Healing Practices**

| Therapy | Description and Use | Notes on Practitioners/ Method of Access | Comments |
|---|---|---|---|
| Biofeedback | • Uses mind to control/modify bodily functions such as blood pressure; muscle tone; pulse rate; brain waves.<br>• Instruments (such as skin electrodes) are used to provide quantitative measures in order to train the person to control these functions.<br>• Used to treat anxiety; chronic pain; hypertension; headaches; and structural problems including pelvic muscle dysfunction. | • Practitioners are both certified and licensed by one of three national certifying agencies.<br>• May be used in conjunction with a physician, but frequently practiced independently. | • Practice has a strong laboratory and research basis, but most studies show mixed results.<br>• Seems to be most effective treating headaches, especially migraines. |
| Chelation therapy | • Uses chemicals to bind to heavy metals in the body so they will be excreted safely.<br>• Used to treat autism; heart disease; cancer. | • Used in a very limited fashion in a medical setting through intravenous infusion of chelating agents.<br>• When used by individuals, chelating agents are purchased and self-administered orally. | • Used as a medical treatment primarily for lead and mercury poisoning.<br>• Viewed as very dangerous by the Food and Drug Administration (FDA) and the American Medical Association (AMA), but more than 1 million people use this technique yearly. |

*(Continued)*

**Table 4.1 (Continued)   Examples of Some Nonculturally Based CAM Healing Practices**

| Therapy | Description and Use | Notes on Practitioners/ Method of Access | Comments |
|---|---|---|---|
| Dietary supplements (nonvitamin/ mineral) | • Includes many products such as antioxidants; herbal remedies; individual large dose vitamins; omega-3; large dose minerals, such as calcium.<br>• Primarily used for prevention and overall health promotion. | • Self-administered by buying over-the-counter products.<br>• No regulation by FDA, because these products are viewed as food.<br>• Nutritional Foods Association has a certification process that involves a label demonstrating safety of production: Good Manufacturing Process (GMP). Products are not required to have this label to be sold. | • Almost 20% of the U.S. population takes some kind of self-directed supplement.<br>• If daily multivitamins are included, 50% of the U.S. population takes a self-directed supplement. |
| Homeopathy | • Based on theory of vitalism: the body can heal itself when given help.<br>• Therapy is based on law of similars, so remedies are designed to produce the same symptom the person is experiencing, but in a much smaller range. | • Self-administered by buying products over the counter or from a practitioner.<br>• No professional certification for practitioners.<br>• Some states prohibit the practice of homeopathy, whereas others require a license in order to practice.<br>• Homeopathic remedies are not regulated by the FDA. | • This is an historically important healing method, as it was quite common in the United States in the 1800s and is very common globally.<br>• There are many internal studies on clinical trials, called "provings," the results of which are still used to guide the production of the remedies. |

*(Continued)*

**Table 4.1 (Continued)   Examples of Some Nonculturally Based CAM Healing Practices**

| Therapy | Description and Use | Notes on Practitioners/ Method of Access | Comments |
|---|---|---|---|
| | • Remedies are compounded by the practitioner by using the smallest active particle possible, involving many dilutions. <br> • Used for a wide variety of ailments, with more than 3000 specific remedies created. | | • Many studies have been performed but none have demonstrated any effectiveness for any of the remedies. <br> • A popular cold remedy (Zicam Cold Remedy) is marketed as being based on homeopathic theories. |
| Massage therapy | • Manipulation of superficial and deeper muscle/connective tissue to aid in healing process and to promote wellness. <br> • There are more than 80 distinct types of massage therapy. <br> • Mostly used for relief of chronic pain; relaxation; anxiety; sports injuries; and to promote wellness. | • Practitioners are professionally certified through a professional organization and licensed by states. <br> • There are many different types of schools and professional associations, depending on the type of massage therapy. <br> • There are more than 300,000 licensed massage therapists in the United States. | • This therapy is widely used, with almost 20% of the U.S. population having some sort of massage therapy every year. <br> • This therapy is studied but most studies use self reports of pain levels. <br> • Massage seems to be most effective for musculoskeletal pain, including low back pain. <br> • Personal reports indicate the usefulness in alleviating depression and anxiety. |

*(Continued)*

**Table 4.1 (Continued)   Examples of Some Nonculturally Based CAM Healing Practices**

| Therapy | Description and Use | Notes on Practitioners/ Method of Access | Comments |
|---|---|---|---|
| Naturopathy | • This alternative healing system is an outgrowth of vitalism, which recognizes the body as having a vital energy that can be harnessed to promote healing.<br>• Naturopaths encourage the body's natural healing ability by using nutritional and herbal remedies, including some homeopathic remedies as well as aromatherapy and massage therapy. | • Independent practitioners are required to obtain a Doctor of Naturopathy from one of several accredited Schools of Naturopathic Medicine.<br>• They are licensed to practice as nondrug prescribing physicians in 17 states and either not recognized or banned in all other states.<br>• The national association for Traditional Naturopaths has about 2000 practitioners as members. | • The profession does not support any studies of effectiveness, because they reject the Biomedical Model.<br>• The profession does not support vaccinations and also reject antibiotics.<br>• Some physicians have become trained in naturopathy in order to integrate it into their allopathic medical practice. |
| Reiki | • Japanese method of controlling the "Universal Life energy" to balance the body's energy. This makes it a biofield energy healing method.<br>• The energy field is modified by the palms of the hands held above the body, not generally touching the body.<br>• Used mainly for chronic pain and anxiety disorders. | • Practitioners are not certified or licensed, but there are training programs designed for a therapist to become a Reiki Master. This indicates a higher level of understanding of not only the use of the hands, but also the spiritual aspect of the body's energy field. | • Some studies have been conducted, but outcomes are mixed and mostly based on self-reports. |

Chiropractic medicine arose in the United States in the 1890s under the direction of one individual and his son: D.D. and B.J. Palmer, respectively (Keating, 2005). These two had medical practices that focused on the idea of treating illness based on biomechanics and spinal manipulation. They founded the Palmer School of Chiropractic, which grew rapidly. As will be shown in Chapter 7, this structured training predates the formalization of medical schools in the United States. Two subgroups developed within chiropractic medicine. The first subgroup consisted of practitioners called straights, because they used spinal manipulation exclusively. They also viewed the spiritual aspect of subluxation as being important. The second group was composed of mixers, so termed because they utilized other healing and diagnostic practices, including x-rays and the emerging medical knowledge and technology of the time, instead of the spiritual emphasis. As medical knowledge and technology increased, mixers gradually became more prominent, and remain so today. By 1930, chiropractic medicine was the main alternative to medical practice, as it still is (Keating, 2005; Villanueva-Russell, 2011).

Organized medicine understood the professional challenge presented by chiropractors. In 1966, the American Medical Association (AMA) labeled chiropractors as an "unscientific cult" and through the 1980s strongly discouraged their patients from using chiropractors (Cherkin, 1989). The AMA legally prosecuted chiropractors for practicing medicine without a license, but the American Chiropractic Association successfully fought these prosecutions by maintaining that chiropractic medicine was different from allopathic medicine. They argued that chiropractors "analyzed" rather than "diagnosed" and adjusted subluxations rather than treating disease (Keating, 2005). Throughout all of this controversy, chiropractic medicine continued to establish itself as an independent profession with standardized, professionally accredited schools, as well as state licensure procedures. In 1987, the AMA lost a landmark case when it was judged to have participated in "unreasonable restraint of trade and conspiracy" against chiropractic practitioners (Cooper and McKee, 2003).

Today, there are 30 professionally accredited schools that graduate almost 4000 chiropractors each year (Ernst, 2011). Most schools offer 4-year programs, and grant one of two degrees: the Doctor of Chiropractic (DC) or the Doctor of Chiropractic Medicine (DCM) (NCCAM, 2007). There are more than 50,000 actively practicing chiropractors in the United States (CCE, 2008), some of whom are in primary care, whereas others are in specialties such as chiropractic orthopedics, sports chiropractic, and also radiological chiropractic (Coulter et al., 1997). Chiropractors are licensed by states, which also control their scope of practice. Some states such as New Mexico allow chiropractors to prescribe some medications, but most states do not. Chiropractors are not allowed to do surgery nor do they admit patients to hospitals.

Patients seek the care of a chiropractor for many reasons, but especially for pain, such as back and neck pain, as well as headaches. In 2012, about 9% of the U.S. population (more than 25 million) reported using a chiropractor within the past year (Peregoy et al., 2014).

Physicians increasingly refer patients to chiropractors, especially for chronic pain, a syndrome for which traditional biomedical treatments can do little but offer drugs that have significant side effects. Most health insurance policies today cover chiropractic medicine, as long as the patient is referred by a physician, but some cover a limited number of yearly visits made without a referral. Between $2 billion and $4 billion is spent each year on chiropractic care (Peregoy et al., 2014).

As will be shown in Chapter 7, this increased utilization and acceptance is the way in which health care systems evolve and change the definitions of conventional versus alternative healing practices. The most controversial aspect of chiropractic medicine today goes back to their historical split. Some chiropractors serve as primary care providers for families, including children. Almost one-third of chiropractors do not believe there is any scientific evidence to support the idea that vaccination prevents disease, and the majority of these identify as straights (Campbell et al., 2000).

More than any of the other alternative healing practices, chiropractic medicine rejects the term complementary. They embrace the term alternative, because they view themselves as just that: a viable alternative to mainstream medicine. Their own medical profession is one that is in competition with the conventional medical system.

## What Really Works?

These very different healing practices challenge our core cultural beliefs about health and illness, and also about the way the U.S. health care system is structured and financed. The allopathic model depends on the idea that medical therapies are based on scientific principles; their impacts can be observed through collection of data and their effectiveness can be determined, thus providing evidence-based therapies. This belief in science—more accurately, Western scientific principles—is one of the most important beliefs underlying our medical system, as will be noted in Chapter 5. Therefore, it should not be surprising that we have tried to apply the principles of our Western medical scientific model to assess the effectiveness of these alternative medical practices. The NCCAM and NIH both provide funding for many studies of effectiveness. Some observations related to this effort will be made here to provide a summary of this chapter.

## From Herbs to Drugs

Every healing system involves the use of herbal remedies. In the U.S. biomedical orientation, the word drug designates pharmaceutical therapies that are standardized, studied, and regulated. The word supplement describes the many other types of health-related products available. In 1994, herbal remedies became regulated by the Food and Drug Administration, but under a different category than either a food or a drug. Under this classification, herbal remedies do not have be proven effective (as do drugs), but can be removed from the market if shown to be unsafe. This classification resulted in increased use of herbal remedies and supplements, as well as increased clinical trials to determine their effectiveness. More than 25% of Americans use some sort of specific herbal remedy, not counting vitamins or nutritional supplements. About two-thirds of adults use these herbs for a specific illness, and in accordance with the recommended use—indicating a good knowledge base about these remedies (Bardia et al., 2007).

One of the standard herbal remedies of the TCM system is artemisnin, or yellow wormwood. This has been shown to be so effective against a drug-resistant malaria parasite that it has now become the recommended treatment (WHO, 2014). This has created a supply problem, with some drug companies trying to identify the active ingredients so they can prepare a synthetic version. Others are researching ways of increasing the dosage by drying and powdering the leaves (Elfawal et al., 2012).

Identifying active ingredients in plants to synthesize them in order to convert them into drugs is very common, and provides the foundation for many of the pharmaceuticals used in the United States. Three of the most well-known examples include the widely used cardiac drug digitalis, which came from the foxglove plant and was used extensively by Native Americans; tamoxifen, used to prevent recurrence of breast cancer, originated in the bark of the yew tree; and cyclosporine, a powerful immune suppressant drug used with organ transplants, which was an accidental discovery from a fungus (Galanti, 2008). The continuation of this process is the Herbalome study, an effort begun in 2008 to catalog all the active ingredients in the herbs used in the TCM system. This has already produced the possibility for a new nonnarcotic pain relief medication (Zhang et al., 2012).

## Acupuncture

Acupuncture has been widely studied, because many people seem helped by it. Demonstrating how it works according to Western science models, however, has been challenging. Studies report a range of effectiveness, with patient reports indicating at least 28 specific diseases, symptoms, or conditions that have been helped by acupuncture, including a variety of pain symptoms, as well as depression; nausea and vomiting; and hypertension (Langevin and Yandow, 2002; Xie and Dong, 2003; Berman et al., 2010; Lee and Ernst, 2011).

## Importance of Belief

One of the most common criticisms of all alternative healing practices, including acupuncture, is that it works only because people believe in it. Belief in a treatment is the basis for placebo therapy, when a person is given an inert substance, but told it will help them. The placebo effect has long been known, with the original research demonstrating that in many cases, a nonactive ingredient such as sugar was as effective as morphine in relieving severe postoperative pain. Placebo research has expanded into several other areas including orthopedic surgery. One important placebo study examined 5 years of patients being given either a true arthroscopic surgical procedure or a sham surgery. Surprisingly, there were no significant differences between these two groups, in either reported pain or in functioning (Moseley et al., 2002).

In fact, it has been understood for a long time that belief or faith in the physician is an integral part of healing and of medicine (Balint, 1957). Recent research into the relationship of the mind and the body has popularized this (Weil, 1995). It is now recognized that the ritualistic aspect of all our healing practices, even the most technical ones, is very important (Helman, 2007). The placebo effect is clearly found in alternative therapies, but there is no evidence that these therapies have a higher placebo effect than biomedical treatments (Kaptchuk, 2002).

Not all conventional medical practices meet the standard of proof of the Western scientific model. As with alternative healing practices, much of conventional medicine is based on observations of what works for individual patients rather than scientific evidence (Helman, 2007). This is not to say that conventional therapies do not have a scientific basis, nor is it to say that the social and legal regulations supporting the conventional U.S. health care system are unnecessary. Rather, it is to acknowledge that an increasing number of health problems cannot be helped by the conventional Biomedical Model, and that some of the CAM practices may be helpful, and at a lower cost. Treatment of chronic disease accounts for more than 75% of the nation's $1.4 trillion medical costs. The most common reasons for using CAM practices are "relief from symptoms," mostly from a chronic health problem (Thorne et al., 2002; Rakel and Faass, 2006).

Although many of the health practices described in this chapter are controversial, their continued use speaks to the importance of recognizing the limitations of the traditional, conventional medical care system. After all, if everybody were helped by the biomedical system, there would most likely be less need for the existence of the many alternatives, including those listed in Table 4.1.

## Acknowledgments

The following people made significant contributions to the content of this chapter, including gathering material and references, as well as writing and analysis: Tia DiNatale, Nolis Espinal, Avery Henniger, Sarah Kelly, and Laura Norton. Jennifer Salop, Daniella Stern, and Elyssa Williams made significant contributions to this chapter through their careful review and suggested revisions, as well as finding additional references.

# Chapter 5

# Political and Philosophical Values That Influence the U.S. Health Care System

This chapter examines several important political and philosophical values that are at the very foundation of the U.S. health care delivery system. This begins with political values regarding the nature of the U.S. economy and whether health care goods and services are commodities to be bought and sold just as are other goods and services. This economic value significantly impacts the view of the appropriate role for the government in the health care system. There are different political and philosophical values among health professionals on this question, including some tensions between medical and public health professionals. Cultural beliefs in science and technology are very important in the health care system, although these beliefs are challenged by the apparent success of some of the alternative healing practices, as discussed in Chapter 4. The chapter concludes with two specific examples of how these political, philosophical, and cultural values dictate health care services that are available to people. Examining these values helps us understand the idiosyncrasies of the U.S. health care system, as well as the challenges of reforming the U.S. health care system.

## The Private Market and the Role of Government

The U.S. economy is based on a strong belief in the capitalistic model, which is frequently referred to as the free or private market. Various goods and commodities are sold to consumers based on competitive prices, with consumers responsible for making informed choices. Economists use the term allocation of resources in describing how the free market works, which is basically that people with more money have access to either more or higher quality goods. This economic value system can be described as market justice (Shi and Singh, 2014), which implies that this method of allocating health care goods and services results not only in an efficient distribution, but also a fair or equitable one. In this allocation model, each individual is primarily responsible for their own health status, as well as in purchasing health services, as discussed in Chapters 1 and 2. Because individuals are responsible, they must also be free to make choices. This leads to a mistrust of government, because that is the entity that prevents the private market from operating freely and restricts the freedom of individuals.

Not everybody in either the health field or in politics accepts that health and medical care services are fairly distributed by the free market. Some reject this allocation model because of a humanitarian concern for those who do not have enough money to buy needed health care services. This is especially strong for those who are viewed as innocent, such as children, disabled and/or sick people, and the elderly. Others have a more pragmatic view: they recognize those who do not receive health care when they first need it will most likely eventually require more expensive care, thus increasing overall costs. There are also those who reject the whole concept that health care services are a private good. Their view is that access to health care is a basic human right and is an important philosophical principle.

Viewing health care as a human right rather than a commodity to be purchased involves an alternative method by which health care services are allocated. This is called social justice and views health care services as being primarily a social good, not an economic good (Shi and Singh, 2014). Under this allocation theory, health care services should be paid for collectively, not individually, so that everybody who needs medical services can receive them as needed instead of based on income. The role of government in a social justice allocation model is to protect those who are not able to receive health care services under a free market system. This is in stark contrast to the view of government's role in a market justice system.

There are political values associated with each of these two allocation systems. In general, those who favor a market justice approach are politically conservative and those who favor the social justice approach for allocating health care services are politically liberal. Chapters 11 and 12 describe this in more detail, with some examples of health policies.

Two large and diverse groups of professionals are intricately involved in the U.S. health care system: medical care services providers and public health professionals. There are differences in philosophical values between these two broad groups of health professionals, although it is far more nuanced than the political positions noted above. Medical care providers include a wide variety of licensed and/or certified professionals, who give direct care services to individuals in response to illness symptoms and in accordance with the professionally recognized disease classifications. As noted in Chapter 1, their healing activities are based on the Biomedical Model. These professionals include not only physicians and mid-level providers, such as physician assistants and nurse practitioners, but also nurses, many types of therapists, and various technicians who provide supportive services to these caregiving professions. The range of these will be described in Chapters 6 and 7. The emphasis of this group of providers is individualistic, because they focus on sick individuals. Their view of the importance of social determinants of health varies, but is mostly on the weak end of the public health model, as shown in Figure 2.1.

The field of public health is strongly anchored in the importance of social determinants of health and community-based interventions, as a way to prevent illness, improve health, and also to save money. Public health professionals may be involved in provision of direct services, especially educational, but most public health efforts involve working with groups, not individuals. A significant focus for public health professionals is the policy and regulatory work to ensure accessibility to health and medical care services for all, especially those with no insurance coverage. Another important role of public health is to ensure patient safety throughout all parts of the health care system. These two roles mean that the public health field is often viewed as part of government, as it takes on the primary role of regulation and restriction. This can produce some tension between the fields of public health and medicine.

Under the politically liberal view of the public health profession, it is the responsibility of the government to ensure adequate access to health care services for all. Under this view, allocating health care services based on income is unfair because some are not able to purchase health care goods and services. Under the view of social justice, regulation is a way of ensuring both equal access and also patient safety. Under the view of market justice, regulation restricts the ability of the free market to find the lowest price for a good. In the United States, we have a mixed model that involves as much privatization as possible to appease our political beliefs while regulating the health care system to protect people from unsafe practices and to ensure adequate access to health care services when needed. This results in a highly regulated, but not centralized health care system, with many distinct and specific programs designed for those who do not have enough money—or health insurance—to purchase health care. Throughout this book, the term targeted programs will be used to describe them, because these programs are designed for those who do not have adequate access to health care services.

Most of these targeted programs are publicly funded through tax revenues, which completes the circle, because increased taxes are an anathema to most Americans and a symbol of too much government. One activity that is triggered by the involvement of public money is the determination of who is eligible to receive services from which program. Our fear of fraud and waste has evolved into a system where we spend more money than any other country making sure only those who are eligible receive services from specific programs. This persists despite evidence of significant cost savings in several European countries that provide publicly financed health and social services without any determination of eligibility. This will be explored more fully in Chapter 22.

## Cultural Belief in Science and Technology—Sometimes

The belief in science and technology is at the very foundation of the Biomedical Model. The basic thrust of medicine is toward evidence-based, quantifiable, and technological interventions, with concomitant training for these skills in medical schools. The result is medical care providers primarily trained to recognize and treat physical symptoms and an emphasis on physical health. As the science and technology knowledge base has increased, it is necessary to have increased professionalization of health care providers. This was seen first in physicians, as will be described in Chapter 7. Increased certification is now also occurring among the public health professions. This takes place in the overall context of the U.S. culture, which places great reliance on certification of various professionals. Increased professionalization actually results in less free market activity, because it restricts the pool of providers that consumers can select to provide health care services. And, as noted in Chapter 4, this process defines the conventional medical care system as well as the alternative care system. In the United States, this distinction also extends to the financing system, because most alternative health care services are not covered by health insurance. Ironically, the most free market activity in the U.S. health care system is actually in the alternative health care sector, not in the socially sanctioned Biomedical Model.

Despite the overall belief in science and technology and the strong cultural and legal support for the Biomedical Model and highly certified medical care providers, alternative healing practices are substantially utilized by the American public, as described in Chapter 4. Because of this use, much research is devoted to trying to understand the science involved in some of these alternative healing practices.

Another challenge to the view that science and technology are the most effective methods by which we can be made healthy is that this is not consistent with the leading causes of both death and illness in the United States, as shown in Chapter 2. Purely medical responses based on the most technological approaches are responsible for resolving only about 10–20% of the total disease burden of the United States. This further contributes to the tension between the fields of medicine and public health, as noted above.

# When Political Values Restrict Health Care Services

One of the myths of the U.S. health care system is that everybody who needs medical care gets it. The reality—detailed throughout this book—is more complicated. For example, having health insurance—termed financial access—results in having more and better health services, as well as improved health outcomes. This financial access may be provided through employment-based health insurance or through one of the several publicly funded, targeted programs. Cultural and political values also help determine which services are available and to whom. This chapter will discuss two specific examples of this: health care to noncitizens and reproductive health care services for women.

## *Health Care Services Are for Citizens*

The U.S. health care system has several legislative guidelines that require citizenship to receive health care services, although there are some exceptions.

Full discussion of this issue is beyond the scope of this book, but enough information will be included here to provide an understanding of the impact of this political issue on the health care system.

Two important observations start this discussion. The first is that this is not a recent issue. The 1965 legislation creating Medicare and Medicaid limited these programs to citizens (Teitelbaum and Wilensky, 2013). Second, this limitation is not unique to the United States, as will be shown in Chapter 22. The United States has a larger population of noncitizens, both legal and undocumented, so the discussion is more prominent in the United States. Those with a strong orientation to the social justice allocation model believe that access to health care should be based on medical need rather than citizenship.

Several different terms are used for noncitizens. The U.S. Census Bureau prefers the term foreign-born; others use the term noncitizen, whereas many use the term immigrant. Noncitizen and foreign-born include both immigrants and nonimmigrants. *Immigrants* have the intention of staying and include several different groups, as shown in Table 5.1. The total number of immigrants in the United States is generally estimated to be about 40 million people, which is 12% of the total U.S. population. An accurate estimate is difficult because of the group that receives the most political attention: the undocumented, the unauthorized (U.S. Census Bureau), or the popularized term illegal alien. The most reliable estimate for the number of undocumented people is around 11 million or 12 million (Passel, 2005; Baker and Rytina, 2013). This is about 28% of the total group of legal immigrants and is 4% of the total U.S. population.

Table 5.1 also shows a second category of noncitizens, those who are here temporarily on a specific visa. *Nonimmigrants* are counted as arrivals, which includes about 39 million people annually (Batalova, 2009). The largest category of this group comprises those entering the United States for reasons related to tourism (Monger, 2013). If they get sick while in the United States, their process of accessing health services is sometimes complicated, as will be noted later.

Two regions of the world provide about 80% of all noncitizens: 53% come from one of the Latin American or Caribbean countries and 28% come from one of the Asian countries. Immigrants (and nonimmigrants) are not equally distributed in the United States. The states with the largest absolute number of immigrants include California, New York, Texas, Florida, and New Jersey (Monger, 2013). California has the largest percentage of immigrants in comparison to their population (27%), with

**Table 5.1 Categories of Noncitizens**

| | Immigrants | | Nonimmigrants | |
|---|---|---|---|---|
| Category | Description | Category | Description | |
| Lawful Permanent Resident (LPR) | • Green card holder<br>• Allowed to reside/work in the United States permanently | Students | • Provided student visa to study in United States<br>• May be renewed as long as a person is enrolled in educational program | |
| Conditional Permanent Resident (CPR) | • Spouse/children of a citizen or an LPR<br>• Supported by the LPR<br>• Often applying for LPR | Temporary worker | • Allows employment for a fixed length of time<br>• May be skilled or unskilled | |
| Violence Against Women Act (VAWA) self-petitioner | • Allows for battered immigrant to petition for CPR or LPR status without support of abusive spouse or parent | Visitors | • Persons who want to enter United States temporarily, including for business, tourism, or family visit | |
| Special Immigrant Juvenile Status (SIJS) | • Person under age 21<br>• Juvenile court declares not in the best interest of juvenile to be returned to country of origin | | | |
| Refugee/asylee status | • Allowed to stay in United States due to fear of political reprisal if returned to country of origin | | | |
| Special immigrant | • Some religious workers<br>• Specific highly trained workers<br>• Some foreign medical graduates | | | |
| Undocumented immigrants | • People who enter United States without authorization<br>• Those who enter legally but who overstay their visa | | | |

*Source:* Data from the State Justice Institute (2014) and the U.S. Department of Homeland Security.

New York, New Jersey, and Nevada each having populations that are almost 20% immigrants (Batalova, 2009).

*How do noncitizens get health care services?* Two factors impact the access of noncitizens. The first is health insurance. About 16% of the U.S. workforce are immigrants, and noncitizens are as likely as citizens to have a full-time worker in the family, although they have lower incomes (Stephens and Artiga, 2013). Many of these employees are undocumented; with almost one-third of undocumented immigrants working in the service industry, 16% in construction, and about 17% in production, installation, or repair (Passel, 2005). These types of jobs do not usually involve health insurance. Only about half of all immigrants have health insurance, and undocumented adults are three times less likely to have health insurance than citizens (CBO, 2007). This means this group is largely uninsured.

The second factor determining access of noncitizens is state and federal legislation. Formally, either citizenship or documented permanent residence is required in order to receive health care services. Lawfully present noncitizens have several paths available to obtain health insurance. Documented immigrants may be able to obtain health insurance from their jobs, although some health insurance companies require a green card and a residency requirement ranging from 3 to 60 months. Documented immigrants who do not have employment-based insurance are not eligible for most publicly funded programs, including Medicaid, until they have been in the United States for 5 years, although individual states can modify this (NILC, 2014).

Most of the nonimmigrants shown in Table 5.1 are able to obtain health insurance. For example, international students are eligible to enroll in their university's health plan. Visitors and tourists are strongly encouraged to purchase a private, specific short-term health insurance policy to cover their health needs while in the United States. Otherwise, their access to the U.S. health care system is limited to hospital-based emergency rooms or independent for-profit clinics that accept payments from individuals (see Chapter 9).

There are several federal laws that specifically prohibit undocumented immigrants from having access to any sort of health insurance, including private health insurance but especially to any publicly funded government programs, such as Medicaid. This includes participating in Medicare, even if the undocumented person has contributed to the Social Security system enough to be eligible for it. The exception to this prohibition is emergency care, which is covered in the Emergency Medical Treatment and Active Labor Act, which specifically prohibits hospitals from asking about immigration status until the medical situation—including childbirth—has stabilized. Afterward, however, the hospital is asked to determine immigration status so it can be determined whether Medicaid will reimburse the hospital for the cost of services (Galewitz and Kaiser Health News, 2013). The Affordable Care Act (ACA) itself specifically forbids all undocumented people from buying any health insurance from any of the exchanges, as all have some sort of federal or state subsidy (NILC, 2014).

There are several specific targeted programs aimed at providing medical care services to uninsured people, and these programs do become a source of nonemergency care for undocumented people, especially migrant farm workers (NILC, 2014). For example, there are 150 federally funded clinics that provide medical care to agricultural workers, with the understanding that some of these are undocumented. These will be described in more detail in Chapter 20. In some states (Florida, Alabama, and Georgia), state legislators allowed immigration officials to set up checkpoints by these clinics in order to try to restrict access (Monga et al., 2014).

Although this is a hotly contested political topic, there is a far more practical approach within the health field. Medical providers have little interest in a person's immigration status, except as it might influence their ability to cooperate with their medical care. Medical personnel do not wish to get involved with determining immigration status of patients and are frustrated when the immigration status of one of their patients interferes with their ability to get needed medical care (Ofri, 2013). However, the cost of caring for uninsured people cannot be overlooked. Because undocumented people are provided emergency care, physicians are frequently faced with patients in the emergency room that could be less sick if they had care available to them earlier, or who might not actually need the services of an emergency room but have no other options available. Medical care delivered in an emergency room setting is far more expensive than in other care settings. Also, when primary care services are restricted, sicker people do cost the system more (Kullgren, 2003; King, 2007; Nandi et al., 2009). A main concern of hospitals is that they will not be reimbursed for the cost of caring for undocumented people (Appleby, 2013). The economic impact on hospitals of caring for uninsured people will be detailed in Chapter 8.

Public health professionals have two main arguments about why a full range of health services should be provided to everybody regardless of citizenship. The first is philosophical and involves support of the United Nations' Declaration of Human Rights. This document states that every person has the "right to a standard of living adequate for the health and well-being of himself and his family, including food, clothing, housing and medical care and necessary social services..." (Sokolec, 2009). Public health professionals view this as an important component of the social justice framework, which is the anchor of their profession. The American Public Health Association has a statement of professional ethics that supports providing services for members of all "disenfranchised communities" (Sokolec, 2009).

Second, public health professionals believe that providing all needed health services to undocumented people provides many benefits to the larger community, including improving the health status of the whole community. One example is improved control of communicable disease, especially for vaccine-preventable diseases. Many undocumented immigrants postpone treatment of acute illness as well as vaccinations because they are afraid their immigration status will be detected. This increases the risk to others in the community (Kullgren, 2003; Nandi et al., 2009). It also increases overall costs in the health care system.

This is a difficult political and philosophical issue. Nearly two-thirds of undocumented people have lived in the United States for more than 10 years (Passel and Cohn, 2012). There are about 65,000 undocumented children who graduate from U.S. high schools every year (Passel and Cohn, 2012). The Congressional Budget Office analyzed 29 different reports over the past 15 years to ascertain the economic burden of undocumented people on local and state governments. On a national level, this impact was small, but the impact is clearly greater in some states than in others (CBO, 2007). The economic impact of providing health services is felt most strongly in the hospital sector, primarily because emergency rooms are more accessible than any other site of medical care. However, the most salient point in this discussion is that this is not a political problem for health care professionals—both medical and public health—but is a practical one.

## Legislative Restrictions on Legal Medical Care Services

There are many examples of legal restrictions on medical services, ranging from certification and licensure of physicians to accreditation of hospitals, which will be described in the next group of chapters. However, one type of health services in the United States is especially susceptible to legislative restrictions. These health services fall under women's reproductive health and include abortion, but more recently also include family planning services. A full discussion of this topic is beyond the scope of this book, but it is essential to have at least a rudimentary understanding of the issues involved in women's reproductive health care services.

The most contested medical service is that of abortion. The landmark 1973 case of *Roe v. Wade* set the legal definition of abortion services, with several important modifications added during the 1990s (Teitelbaum and Wilensky, 2013). This case was an effort to create a balance between two sets of competing rights: the pregnant woman's and the unborn fetus. The decision was framed in the scientific knowledge and technology of the time, which was fetal viability. In 1973, this was determined to be reliably 28 weeks, although it was recognized at the time that a fetus might survive with intensive medical interventions as early as 24 weeks. This issue of fetal viability has become more ambiguous as technology and neonatal care has increased, although no fetus has survived earlier than 21 weeks (Nash et al., 2014). At the time of *Roe v. Wade*, public perception of abortion was split, and both federal- and state-level politicians began proposing many different policies to limit abortions in the only arena in which they could, which was for women whose abortions would be paid for with public funds.

The 1977 Hyde Amendment prohibits the use of any federal funds to provide abortions except in the cases of rape, incest, or if the life of the woman is in danger as a result of the pregnancy continuing (Guttmacher Institute, 2014; Nash et al., 2014). This means that women who receive health care through Medicaid (described in Chapter 19) are not able to receive an abortion unless only state funds are used. Over time, state legislatures have introduced a variety of policies designed to limit a woman's ability to have an abortion using state funds. These actions include limiting the number of abortion clinics allowed in the state, restricting the number and type of providers that can perform abortions, requiring counseling and/or imaging services before an abortion, and requiring parental notification for younger women.

Over the past 5–10 years, there has been enormous political activity at the state level so that today 41 states have significant restrictions on the use of state funds to pay for medically necessary abortions (Guttmacher Institute, 2014). States have used a variety of restrictions including limits on doctors performing abortions (requiring them to have hospital privileges); additional limits on fetal viability (most frequently 20 weeks); as well as banning abortion outright unless in the case of rape or incest or to save the woman's life. In 2013, more than half of all women in the United States live in one of the 27 states that have at least four different restrictions on providing abortion services (Nash et al., 2014). States are free to choose to use state funds to also provide medically necessary abortions, which are defined as those requested by a woman and supported by a physician. Only 17 states currently allow this, with 13 of them doing so because of court cases (Guttmacher Institute, 2014).

In no other area of health care services has there been more legislative activity restricting medical services than in women's reproductive health. Restrictions on the availability of this service are based on political and religious ideology and impact access to abortion only when public funds are utilized. As a result, women who have private health insurance have more access to abortion than women on Medicaid. However, the boundary between private health insurance and public funding has become much more ambiguous with the passage of the ACA, because federal subsidies are involved in health insurance purchased on the exchanges (see Chapter 17). Increasingly, states now require women with private insurance to buy separate riders for their health insurance if they want abortions to be covered (Nash et al., 2014).

The ACA has also inadvertently caused other parts of women's reproductive health services to be limited by requiring contraception to be covered as a required preventive health care service. This has caused significant controversy, and the result is 20 states passing legislation limiting contraception services, especially for low income women, but also for women purchasing health insurance policies on the new exchanges (Nash et al., 2014).

Regulations surrounding women's reproductive health services and care to noncitizens dramatically underscore the idea that the type of health care delivery system any country has is the product of its cultural and political values. It is very important to keep this framework in mind as the rest of this book explores the structure, form, and financing of the services that are available to the American public.

## Acknowledgments

The following people made significant contributions to the content of this chapter, including gathering material and references, as well as writing and analysis: Loreiny Peñaló, Sheighlyn Knightly, Jasmine Offley, and Halicia Lyttle. Alexandra Amaral-Medeiros and Diana Griggs made substantial contributions as a result of their careful comments and suggested revisions.

# FUNCTIONAL DESCRIPTION OF THE U.S. HEALTH AND MEDICAL CARE SYSTEM

This section is analogous to a demographic description of the entire health care system, including an analysis by both form and function as a system. After an initial differentiation between a health care and a medical care system, the chapters in this section, and in the remainder of the text, will focus on the medical care system. The first chapter in this section (Do We Have a System? A Functional Analysis) describes a functional way of analyzing the U.S. health care system by utilizing a form of systems analysis. Even though the health care system does not completely meet the definition of a system, this is the best way to both describe and analyze all the component parts.

Chapter 7 (People Who Make the Medical Care System Go: The Workforce) describes the people who make this system work, including clinical and nonclinical professionals, with some of the nonclinical providers being public health professionals. Within the clinical domain, there are many types of health care providers, and this chapter cannot do justice to them all. The emphasis will be on physicians and nurses, and the associated mid-level providers that arise from both of these professional roots.

The next chapter (Hospitals) focuses on one of the most prominent type of facilities in the health care system: the hospital. This includes a brief description of the history of hospitals as well as a description and classification of current hospitals in the United States. One of the important issues in the hospital sector is the increasing role of for-profit companies in buying and managing hospitals. Of course, hospitals are a very significant cost center of the medical care system, so both costs and control of costs are covered in some detail.

Chapter 9 (Ambulatory Care: Functions, Structures, and Services) focuses on ambulatory care services and the most common sites in which such care takes place. This is the most heavily utilized part of the health care system, with several innovations in delivery of services, many of which involve for-profit corporations. Primary care services are a subset of ambulatory care, and this is described in this chapter. Primary care is also a concept of how to manage all needed health care services, and this will be discussed in relation to managed care.

The final chapter in this section is best termed as "what is left over" (Other Components of the Medical Care System). The U.S. health care system is complex and large, so it is necessary to choose what to emphasize. As a result, some parts are left out and in many cases those parts are very important. This chapter seeks to provide at least a partial remedy for this by describing four especially important subsystems of the U.S. health care system: the mental health system, the long-term care system, and the dental and vision care systems.

## Chapter 6

# Do We Have a System?
# A Functional Analysis

The term system generally implies a group of departments, organizations, or agencies under a centralized administrative structure. The individual parts are thought of as operating as a network of components designed to work together in an integrated fashion to achieve some common goal. The U.S. health care system does not actually meet this definition. Even though the concept of system seems an oxymoron, it is a very valuable perspective when analyzing the U.S. health care industry. The field of systems analysis uses an analytical perspective based on function rather than form, which is very useful in describing how this fragmented system actually works.

Figure 6.1 presents a functional description in a manner consistent with systems analysis. This figure also identifies the chapters in this book that are relevant to each of these functions or sectors of the overall system, thus providing an overview of the topics in this book. As is customary in systems analysis, the actual health care delivery system is shown at the center of Figure 6.1. This book follows the convention of using health care delivery systems to include all health-related services, including those that involve the public health field. The medical care system is considered to be a subset of the larger health care system, even though it is the largest component in terms of services, resources, and influence. All chapters in this second section of the book are devoted to a description of the form or structure of the U.S. medical care system.

There are two categories of factors that impact the system's ability to function and perform its goals. The first category comprises specific *inputs*

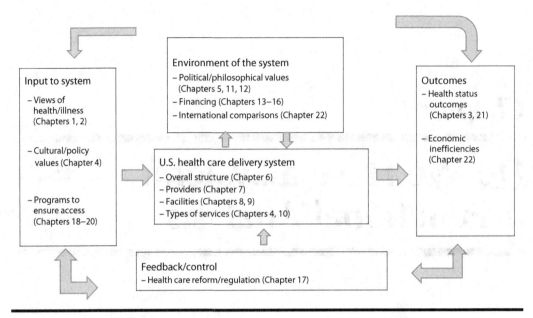

**Figure 6.1   U.S. health care system.**

to the system, which include patients, whose beliefs about health and illness influence health behavior, including how health and medical services are utilized, as described in Chapters 1, 2, and 4. These are not the only inputs, as specific health policies and programs create different abilities of accessing health services, as described in Chapter 1. Some of the most important of these are programs that described in this book as "targeted," which is to say they are designed to create financial access for a specific group of people, as in the Medicare program (described in Chapter 18). The second group of factors impacting the system is composed of the more general political and cultural values of the U.S. economic system that provide the context for the health care system, as described in Chapter 5.

Systems are dynamic and changing, not static, and sometimes general *environmental* factors become inputs to the system, especially when they become specific. For example, the general belief in a private market economic system is an environmental factor, but a specific way of paying physicians (described in Chapters 13–16) is better described as an input. Sometimes a component defined as being outside the system becomes part of the system itself. One example of this is some of the alternative care healing practices that are defined as being outside the conventional medical care system, as described in Chapter 4. The term "complementary" indicates greater acceptability of these healing practices, and an effort to include them in the medical care system.

Every system produces something. In this case, the goal is to produce health, a difficult concept to quantify, as discussed in Chapters 1 and 2. However, as this is the desired *outcome*, there are several ways to measure this, as described in Chapter 3. Making comparisons with other countries' outcomes helps better define the strengths and weaknesses of the U.S. health care system, and also highlights some of the economic inefficiencies that are present.

Every system has a *feedback/control* mechanism. This is the process by which the system is changed, and is known as health care reform efforts. These are activities mostly designed to regulate components of the system in order to improve financial access for certain defined groups of people. The Affordable Care Act of 2010 is a very good recent example, with Chapter 17 providing a summary of several other previous reform attempts.

The purpose of Figure 6.1 is to give a conceptual description of the health care delivery system and an overview of this book. Not all parts of the complex health care system are covered in this book. For example, the medical educational system may be considered both an input as well as part of the system itself. However, details about this system are beyond the scope of this book. An important environmental component of the health care delivery system that is not explicitly represented in Figure 6.1 includes stakeholders. These are a diverse group of people and organizations that have powerful influences in their advocacy and/or lobbying roles. These are discussed in Chapter 12.

## Describing the Health Care System: The Numbers

More than 10 million people are employed in some capacity in the health care delivery system, which makes it the largest sector of the U.S. economy. This includes more than 800,000 physicians, 2 million nurses, 226,000 pharmacists, and more than 700,000 administrators (Shi and Singh, 2014). There are more than 5000 hospitals and thousands of different sites for outpatient care. This system is very well utilized, with 100 million outpatient visits per year, about 136 million visits to emergency rooms, and 16 million hospital admissions (CDC, 2010). Financial access is varied, with about 60% of people accessing medical care services through a private health insurance policy, about 20% being provided access by some sort of publicly financed program, and the rest receiving what is called uncompensated care, as will be described in Chapters 13–16.

It is not easy to capture the total amount of money spent in the U.S. health care system, for two reasons. The first is the multiple and nontransparent financing systems, as described in Chapter 15. The second is that all estimates of the amount of money spent on health care services are political, and definitions used for each financial category create different conclusions. The most common indicator used to describe the financial size of the U.S. health care system is that about 17.9% of the gross domestic product (GDP) goes to this sector of the U.S. economy. This is about $2.8 trillion. One of the most frequently made political observations is the large proportion of this amount that comes from public sources. It is true that about 37% comes from tax funds at either the state or local level. However, a little more than 20% comes from businesses with about one-third coming from individuals, either by purchasing health care services or health insurance (CHCF, 2014). This means that well over one-half of all the money spent in the U.S. health care system comes from private—not public—sources. Chapter 16 provides more detail on this.

Figure 6.2 shows an estimate of how this money is allocated within the U.S. health care system. The resource allocation issues discussed in Chapters

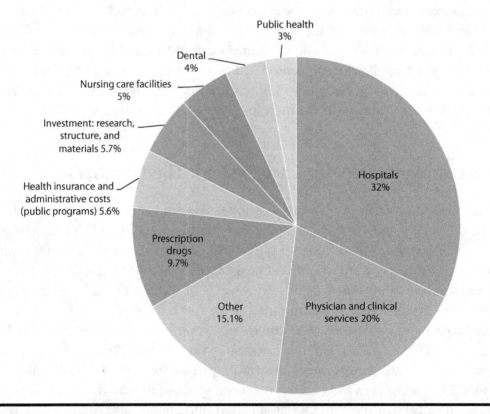

**Figure 6.2  U.S. health care spending breakdown. (Data from Centers for Medicare and Medicaid Services, *National Health Expenditures, 2014,* http://www.cms.gov; California HealthCare Almanac, *Health Care Costs 101: Slow Persists,* http://www.chcf.org; Centers for Disease Control and Prevention, *Health Care, United States 2013,* http://www.cdc.gov.)**

2 and 5 are very clear here. This is a treatment-oriented medical care system, with only about 3% spent on the health promotion and community-based prevention activities advocated by the public health field. Another political observation should also be noted. The estimate of 5.6% for administrative costs is limited to the costs of managing publicly funded health programs, specifically Medicare and Medicaid. This estimate does not include the administrative costs of the private insurance market and, as such, it is a significant underestimate of this category of expense, as will be discussed in Chapter 13.

# Functional Description: Levels of Care

A more functional analysis is to describe and categorize the full range of health services that are contained in the U.S. health care system. There are eight distinct levels of health services available, depending on the health needs of the individual. Figure 6.3 shows these eight levels in relation to differentiating between the health care system and the medical care system. The *health care delivery system* includes all eight levels of care, with three levels being primarily associated with the field of public health and the remaining five levels being properly considered part of the *medical care system*, which is a subsystem of the whole.

## *Classic Public Health Levels of Care*

Both health promotion and health protection represent classic public health approaches to health care. Both are oriented at groups of people; both are focused on modifying social determinants of health to improve overall health status.

   *Health promotion* activities promote health and wellness, primarily by educating groups of people about individual health risks or about community-based risks to health. These programs include education to facilitate better individual health behavior, but also emphasize social determinants of health that may be improved by community-based action. Educational programs to improve individual health behavior are designed for primary prevention, as discussed in Chapter 1. The Drug Abuse Resistance Education (DARE) program is an example, because it is designed for school-age children before it is likely they will have much experience with drugs. More community-based examples include establishing a recreational area

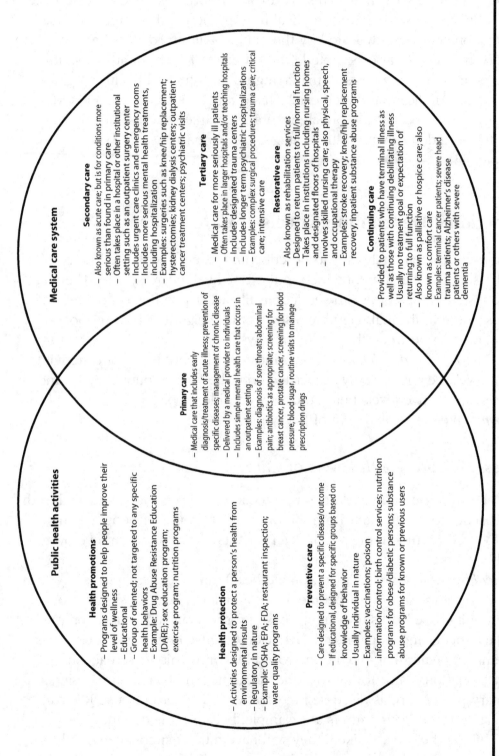

**Figure 6.3    Levels of care in the U.S. health care system.**

near a residential neighborhood or mounting political action to keep a trash incinerator from being located near a residential area.

*Health protection* is largely regulatory in nature and is extensive, involving almost every sector of the U.S. society, and significantly impacts every person's life. As noted in the discussion of political and philosophical values in Chapter 5, this level of care is controversial, because it involves laws and regulations designed to protect the health and safety of either individuals or communities. In addition to the examples noted in Figure 6.3, other examples include traffic safety laws such as speed limits, seat belt laws, and motorcycle helmet laws.

Health protection activities are decentralized, even at the federal level. This means there is no central or federal agency involved in protecting people from health risks. Instead, there are many agencies, each of which has its own sphere of responsibility. For example, federal agencies such as the Occupational Safety and Health Administration and the Environmental Protection Agency handle issues related to occupational safety and environmental safety, whereas federal agencies such as the Food and Drug Administration (FDA) are responsible for oversight of the safety of food, prescription drugs, cosmetics, and veterinary products. The scope of the FDA includes safety testing of products as well as monitoring the manufacturing processes.

Many health protection laws and regulations occur at the state level, such as restaurant inspections. The restaurant industry is literally a billion-dollar-per-year industry, which makes up 4% of the nation's GDP. Nearly one-half of all the money spent on food is spent in restaurants (NRA, 2014). There are more than 600,000 restaurants and each one must be inspected by state health departments, and in many states results of these inspections are now made public. Some of the public notification methods are by newspaper announcements whereas others are through the use of report cards that must be posted in the window of the restaurant where it can be seen by customers.

This category of public health has a very large mission, including protecting food hygiene, water purity, environmental sanitation, drug safety, as well as eliminating as much as possible all adverse effects of a wide variety of environmental hazards. This is a core function of public health and represents an important level of care that contributes greatly to improved health status.

## *Classic Medical Care Services*

There are five distinct levels of care that are clearly defined as components of the medical care system. As shown in Figure 6.3, these include secondary and tertiary care as well as restorative and continuing care. These levels of care have in common their focus on one sick individual. Access begins with a person deciding to obtain care, as described in Chapters 1 and 4. Once that process is begun, a medical professional decides which level of service is most appropriate.

*Secondary care* services are also known as acute care services, but are more specialized than routine outpatient care (this will be described later). Several examples are noted in Figure 6.3. An individual can almost never access this level of care without a referral from a primary care physician, a function that will be described later.

*Tertiary medical care* services are still more specialized, and are generally needed for progressively sicker people. This level of care is usually administered by an even more narrowly trained medical specialist practicing at a teaching or specialty hospital and is almost always as a result of a referral, often from a secondary-level physician. For example, a general surgeon is usually considered a secondary level of medical specialist, whereas a neurosurgeon is considered a tertiary care surgeon (Niles, 2011).

The level of *restorative care* services focuses on rehabilitation with the goal of returning a person to their previous level of functioning. Restorative care programs provide skilled services to help patients recover independence in terms of their ability to live independently and to perform all activities related to what is called daily functioning. The scales described in Chapter 3 for functional health status are often used to evaluate the effectiveness of the rehabilitation process.

*Continuing care* services are also known as palliative care services and include hospice services. In this level of care, emphasis shifts from rehabilitation to the comfort of the patient. The goal of this level of medical service is not treatment, but rather pain relief. This level of medical care is for those who are living with either terminal or severely debilitating chronic illness, with little hope of much functional recovery. These services may be delivered in an institutional or home care setting.

## Services Involving Both Medical and Public Health Perspectives

As can be seen in Figure 6.3, there are two levels of care that have not yet been described. These are appropriately displayed as being in between the medical care system and the classic public health system, because they have characteristics of both fields and share some activities.

*Preventive care* services are usually included under the scope of the field of public health, despite the fact that they are usually provided to individuals rather than groups of people. Preventive care services are used to prevent specific illnesses. One of the simplest examples of this level of care is vaccination. However, also included in this category are other sorts of activities meant to prevent specific individual outcomes, such as contraceptives. Some universities have a required alcohol education program for all incoming freshmen, regardless of individual drinking behavior. This is classified as health promotion, whereas alcohol education programs designed for those who have been caught violating campus drinking regulations are prevention programs. As described in Figure 1.3, prevention can be subdivided into three subcategories—primary, secondary, and tertiary—and can be provided by both public health and medical professionals.

*Primary care* is recognized as the formal beginning of the medical care system. There are three important functions of primary care, and prevention is the first one of these. Screening examinations such as pap smears, mammograms, cholesterol, blood pressure, and blood sugar are part of primary care services, as are vaccinations. Some of these services are offered under the auspices of state public health agencies, but nearly always in some sort of association with physicians, because medical follow-up may be required. The other two functions of primary care are more clearly defined as being part of the medical care system. These two functions include diagnosis and early treatment of acute illnesses and management of chronic health problems. This level of care is delivered by medical specialists trained in primary care and also by what are known as mid-level providers, both of which will be described in Chapter 7.

Primary care services are an important concept in organizing medical care service. The primary care doctor is responsible for providing basic medical care services and is also viewed as the point of entry into the rest of the medical care system. Related to the idea of a gatekeeper is the function of coordinating all other services needed by the patient. Although primary care providers are concerned about social determinants of health, their main focus is on each individual patient. The role of primary care is important in medical care (Chapter 9) and also in a form of health insurance called health maintenance organizations (Chapter 14).

## Resource Implications of Levels of Care: Issues of Balance

The tension between public health professionals and medical professionals arises when considering the relative importance of these levels of care and the resources allocated to each one. As noted in Chapter 2, public health professionals view the biggest contributors to poor health and illness episodes as being related to social determinants of health—especially poverty and social policies that contribute to continued economic inequality. Many damaging health behaviors either are a result of poverty or are made worse by low socioeconomic status. For example, the four factors that are responsible for 75% of preventable deaths discussed in Chapter 3 include injury, alcohol consumption, tobacco use, and gaps in primary prevention (CDC, 2011). All of these factors are made worse by low income level (Bodenheimer et al., 2009). The medical field has to deal with the consequences of these poor health behavior decisions, but the field of public health focuses on preventing poor decisions in the first place.

However, the level of understanding about modifying individual health behavior seems limited. The traditional trajectory of most public health initiatives is to begin with health promotion activities, especially educational campaigns. When behavior change is less than desired, the next efforts occur within the health protection level of care and are primarily regulatory in nature. A particularly good example of this is the national antismoking campaign. Smoking rates dropped from about 43% in the 1960s to about 33% in the 1980s after nationwide public education campaigns. Smoking rates today are about 25%, but this is a result of many regulatory efforts, as well as various tax policies designed to decrease use (Gruber, 2002; CDC, 2004). This one health behavior is often used as an indicator, because it alone contributes significantly to the overall disease—and cost of care—burden of the United States, as noted in Chapter 2.

As can be seen from Figure 6.2, only about 3% of the total amount of money spent on health care goes to levels of care that could prevent about 80% of the disease burden cared for by the medical care system (CDC, 2000). One of the more recent estimates indicates that a $2.9 billion investment in community-based public health programs would save $16.5 billion in medical costs and reduce preventable deaths by about 5% (Mays and Smith, 2011; APHA, 2014).

Of course, when individual patients seek care, their desire is to receive as much individualized attention as possible from the medical care system. However, there is a similar resource imbalance within the medical care field. As shown in Figure 6.2, the largest share of resources goes to hospitals, which are the most expensive segment of the health delivery system. The level of services that occur within hospitals includes secondary and tertiary care, which are usually technologically intensive and expensive medical care services. As will be discussed in Chapters 9, 14, and 22, the most cost-effective use of the medical care system is increasing resources to the primary care component of the medical care system.

Occasionally, a system-wide reform tries to create a slightly different balance. The Affordable Care Act of 2010 (described in Chapter 17) focused on increasing access to medical care services. Other parts of the legislation designated money for the Prevention and Public Health Fund and also created a National Prevention, Health Promotion, and Public Health Council (APHA, 2014). Furthermore, the legislation specified 15 different preventive services that must be provided to all adults (including contraceptives) by all health insurance companies with no copayments (APHA, 2014).

The need for balance between the resources devoted to these levels of care is more strongly felt by the public health field than either the medical field or the general public. The American cultural orientation is a healing system that is based on a technical approach to curing illness episodes without interfering too much with how we live our lives, and resource allocation within the health field reinforces this.

The rest of this book focuses on the subsystem of the medical care system, rather than the entire health care delivery system. The next chapter begins this description by examining the various types of providers that work in some aspects of the medical care system. The health care sector of the U.S. economy is very labor-intensive, and each group is professionally licensed and certified, creating a large and diverse workforce—these are the people who make the whole medical care system work.

## Acknowledgments

The following people made significant contributions to the content of this chapter, including gathering material and references as well as writing and analysis: Chandler Kaplan, Alex McGowan, and Michael Renkawitz. Ryan Barry, Rashinda Key, Daphna Raz, and Renee Williams-Sinclair provided careful review and comments that improved the content of this chapter. Ryan created Figure 6.1 and Daphna constructed Figure 6.2. Figure 6.3 had many contributors, beginning with Rebecca Kinney Baldor while she was employed as my teaching assistant. Rashinda contributed one version of this, and Jonathan Rosenblatt and Julie Minnisch created the final design.

---

# Chapter 7

# People Who Make
# the Medical Care System
# Go: The Workforce

---

The health care industry is the largest single sector in the U.S. economy, employing more than 12% of the total workforce of the United States. This sector contributes almost 18% to the overall U.S. economy. Although most think first of capital, such as physical facilities and technological equipment, the health field is very labor-intensive. There are more than 200 different occupations and professions in the health care sector. These can be divided into two distinct groups, as shown in Table 7.1.

The first general category includes those who provide direct, hands-on medical care. These are called either direct care providers or clinicians. Some of these providers practice completely independently (such as physicians, dentists, and optometrists); others practice semiautonomously such as physician assistants (PAs) and nurse practitioners (NPs); and a third group practices under the direction and legal responsibility of others, including nurses and other allied health care professionals, such as physical therapists.

All of the direct care providers are governed by professional, educational, and legal regulations. The professional method of regulation is *certification*, which is often synonymous with the granting of a degree, but frequently also requires a separate examination. Professional certification gives the provider more credibility but is not sufficient for professional practice. The legal method of regulating clinicians is through *licensure*. Clinical professionals who practice medicine without a license can be legally prosecuted. For each

**Table 7.1    Health Care Workforce**

| *Direct Care Providers* | *Indirect Care Providers* |
| --- | --- |
| Independent clinical providers | Health/hospital administrators |
| MD physicians | Health information specialists |
| DO physicians | Laboratory technicians |
| | Medical records technicians, transcriptionists |
| Mid-level clinical providers | Public health professionals |
| Physician assistants | Health policy analysts |
| Nurse practitioners | Public safety staff |
| | Receptionists/secretaries |
| Nurses | Business office staff |
| RNs | Biomedical engineering |
| Specialty RNs | Dietary food services |
| LPNs | Legal services |
| | |
| Other independent clinical providers | |
| Dentists | |
| Podiatrists | |
| Chiropractors | |
| Optometrists | |
| Psychologists | |
| | |
| Clinical providers with varying degrees of independence | |
| Pharmacists | |
| Paramedics | |
| Therapeutic science practitioners | |

of the direct care providers shown in Table 7.1, there is a separate licensure arrangement, all of which are at the state level (Sultz and Young, 2014).

The second large category shown in Table 7.1 are those whose activities make it possible for the direct care providers to do their jobs, but who do not themselves provide direct patient care services. This very large and diverse group of health professionals consists of indirect care providers or nonclinicians. A few examples of this group are shown in Table 7.1. Many of these nonclinicians are professionally certified and some are licensed. All are necessary for the provision of medical and health care services, but are seldom recognized for their contribution or considered part of the health care system.

Of necessity, this chapter must curtail its scope. The first narrowing is the exclusion of this whole category of indirect care providers. Within the category of direct care providers, this chapter focuses on those defined as being part of the traditional, biomedical care system. This leaves out the many alternative and complementary care providers described in Chapter 4, some of whom are either certified by their professional groups, or even licensed by the state. This more narrow focus does not imply these alternative care providers are not important and/or do not treat many people. As discussed in Chapter 4, this is not true. Rather, this focus allows a more complete description of those who are part of the conventional, socially recognized medical care system. Although all direct care providers are important, this chapter will present more detail on physicians, as they are legally responsible for medical care. Also, the story of physicians is in many ways the story of the development of the U.S. health care delivery system.

## Physicians: The Story of Professionalization and the Development of the Biomedical Model

The history of the development of medicine as a profession is also the story of how the Biomedical Model came to be the traditional, socially accepted framework for the U.S. health care system, with its reinforcing infrastructure of laws and regulations as well as cultural mores. This is also the process by which some healing practices came to be labeled as alternative. Because this is so important to the very foundation of the health care system, this will be briefly described here.

From the early history of colonial America until the early 1900s, medical care can best be described as a free market, highly competitive system. There were many healers, almost all of whom were part-time and had other occupations, especially blacksmiths and barbers, the latter being the earliest surgeons. Many of these healers were women. Some declared a self-defined specialty, based on success of treatment. Consumers chose freely what type of healer to consult, usually based on word of mouth or by early advertising related to treatment success, which did occur frequently.

Some healers took on apprentices and these gradually evolved into medical schools. There were hundreds of small, for-profit medical schools in the late 1800s, with no entrance examinations. Whoever could pay the tuition was admitted. Most had a yearlong academic curriculum, with 2–3 years of apprentice training (Cox and Irby, 2006). All types of healing techniques were taught. A degree called Medical Doctor (MD) was granted at the end of the apprentice period, and all graduates were referred to as doctors.

Gradually, scientific discoveries such as the germ theory described in Chapter 1 began to emerge. Scientifically based innovations were often controversial and slow to spread. Commonly, doctors would try several different therapies, including some of the newer approaches, using more often those approaches that seemed to work better. The mid to late 1800s were a vibrant time in terms of the range of healing arts being taught. Some doctors strongly identified with homeopathic healing traditions whereas others adopted the new osteopathic model, which gave rise to chiropractors, as described in Chapter 4. An increasing number began to include the new scientific discoveries, and identified themselves as allopathic doctors.

European medical schools were becoming more formalized as they emphasized the allopathic model of medicine based on the germ theory. This influenced the medical culture in the United States, and by 1850, there were four European-style schools in the United States, all located at universities. These were small schools that required entrance examinations and had a longer academic curriculum, but no standardization. The early allopathic treatments were not necessarily more successful, but the people practicing them had invested more into their education and believed this model was scientifically superior to the homeopathic or osteopathic models. By the late 1800s, two schools (Harvard and Johns Hopkins) instituted an entrance examination and a standard 4-year medical school curriculum, which culminated in an MD degree. The American Medical Association (AMA) had formed and supported the idea of restricting medical practice to those holding a degree from one of these two schools. However, these two schools and the AMA recognized that professional certification would not be enough to restrict all the other healers.

This set the stage for the watershed moment in medical education. The AMA and the Carnegie Foundation hired Abraham Flexner to survey 155 of the more organized medical schools in the United States. Of that number, about 10 had a European-style curriculum and were located at universities, although only Harvard and Johns Hopkins had a required 4-year curriculum. All the others were the individual proprietary medical schools teaching several different kinds of medical therapies and primarily using the apprentice system.

Flexner's report *Medical Education in the United States and Canada* was published in 1910 by the Carnegie Foundation (Flexner, 1910). The details of this report frame the current structure of medical education today. Flexner recommended a standardized entrance examination (today the Medical College Admissions Test [MCAT]) and a standard 4-year curriculum based on allopathic medicine, with the last year being a structured apprenticeship or internship year. He predicted the need for additional apprentice training as scientific knowledge grew, foreseeing the graduate level residency training of today. He suggested that all medical school attendees should have training in basic, generalist medicine, with more specialized training later. He also specified the importance of continuing medical education with periodic required recertification, a system used today. He rejected the for-profit medical schools, arguing that medical education should take place only within the structure of a nonprofit college or university.

Perhaps most importantly, he recommended that certification and a medical degree was not enough to treat patients. He recommended that states restrict who could treat patients by a formal and legal licensure process. This state licensure would require graduating from one of the newly sanctioned medical schools meeting the standards described by a new organization created to accredit medical schools.

It is difficult to overstate the impact of this report. It was released at a time with several important factors contributing to a moment of reform. First, the AMA created a Council for Medical Education, which in turn created the Association of American Medical Colleges. This established the principle of professional certification and created the organizations enforcing this. Second, the value of government regulations to ensure safety of the consumer was perceived as being important, especially in the food industry. As scientific knowledge increased in the medical field, consumers were viewed as being more vulnerable to unauthorized healers. Finally, as more people graduated from one of these European-style schools, they were interested in protecting their investments. It is important to note that this period of reform in medicine rested on a mistrust of the private economic market and significantly increased the presence of government in the health care system. This will be explored more fully in Chapter 11.

Not surprisingly, Flexner's report found that only 31 schools met the proposed criteria for professional certification and licensure (Mitka, 2010). Many of the small, for-profit apprentice-based medical schools immediately closed, although it took another decade for all the state and professional regulations to be implemented.

This report defined the allopathic physician as the only legally legitimate type of doctor. All other healers became alternatives to scientifically based allopathic medicine. This combination of education and regulatory reform transformed the number, type, and nature of healers available to the American public. The number of people identifying as a doctor dropped precipitously, which reduced access to health care services. Medical care from an educated, licensed doctor cost more, and did not always produce a better result, especially at the beginning of this professionalization process. The diversity of healers was also negatively impacted. The only people who could afford a formal medical school education were affluent, white males. The number of female and minority healers dropped quickly.

This reform is clearly—and rightly—recognized as an important step in protecting the health of the American people. However, it also secured the income of those licensed as a doctor by significantly limiting competition. As there now was a significant economic investment into medical education, the job of physician became a full-time profession. This reform did not eliminate all other healing arts, as noted in Chapter 4. But it did move all nonallopathic healers outside of the conventional medical care system, which had a financial impact on consumers continuing to use these services. However, health care systems are dynamic, including the delineation of what is legal and what is alternative. An excellent example of this is the survival of one of the alternative models—osteopathic medicine—and the gradual evolution of the acceptance of two different types of degrees for doctors.

## Medical Education: Two Degrees

A relative latecomer to the battle between healing systems was osteopathic medicine. This method of healing was begun by Andrew Still, who founded the American School of Osteopathy in Missouri in 1892. Osteopathy is closely related to allopathy but includes an additional theory of manipulative medicine. Osteopathic Manipulative Medicine (OMM) is based on the same theories as chiropractic medicine by restoring balance through manipulation of the bones. Dr. Still, like the Palmers who established chiropractic medicine (see Chapter 4), believed in establishing a professional alternative to the allopathic MD degree. Osteopathic medical schools developed a degree called Doctor of Osteopathy (DO). He modeled the curriculum of osteopathic medical schools after the European and later the Flexner model, with an added component of OMM. He then began a state-by-state political effort to get each state to license a physician with a DO degree as being equivalent to an MD degree. The AMA formally opposed this degree, just as it opposed chiropractors, because this biomechanical model of treating patients was in conflict with their allopathic model of medicine. The result of this opposition was the establishment of two parallel—and legal—medical systems. States licensed these two types of physicians separately, and each had their own hospitals for their own patients (Stanfield et al., 2012).

By 1990, the AMA altered its opposition and accepted the DO degree as equivalent to an MD. This occurred primarily because of public response to the increasing lack of primary care physicians. Primary care is emphasized in osteopathic medical schools, and at this time, nearly all DO graduates became primary care physicians, many of whom were willing to practice in rural, underserved areas. This increased the public support for osteopathic medical schools, hospitals, and doctors, which created substantial competition for allopathic MD physicians.

Today, there are 141 schools that offer the MD degree and 30 that offer the DO degree (Chick et al., 2010). In both cases, the curriculum is 4 years, with the second 2 years involving core clinical training, as well as some specialty training. The curriculum in osteopathic schools includes training in OMM techniques. All states now recognize these two degrees as being equivalent, and all hospitals recognize both degrees as being equivalent. Admission to both medical schools requires the MCAT, and both types of schools are very competitive. Graduates of both types of schools complete graduate residency programs. Osteopathic physicians may compete for MD residency programs or they may choose to attend osteopathic residency programs. Historically, osteopathic medical schools focused on training primary care physicians. As will be seen later, the trend for specialization, including surgical specialties, is increasing among osteopathic physicians, just as with allopathic physicians.

## Graduate Medical Education

The term graduate medical education refers to residency programs. These programs last from 3 to 7 years, depending on the specialty and differing state requirements for licensure. Residents are paid for their work, but the pay is low and the hours are extremely long, leading to state-level regulations on how many hours per week residents may work. There are nearly 7000 different residency programs, each of which is separately accredited. Graduates of osteopathic schools are eligible to compete for the same residency spots as graduates of allopathic schools, although there are some residency programs that are specifically designed for osteopathic training (Sultz and Young, 2014).

## Financing of Medical Education

Medical schools are financed from several streams of revenues, the primary one of which is student-generated tuition and fees. Each medical school is associated with an academic medical center, which includes both a hospital and an outpatient site for providing medical care to patients. Medical school faculty all have some sort of practices, and the revenues from those practices are used to support the medical school. By some estimates, they account for about one-third of revenues for medical schools (Sultz and Young, 2014). There are both state and federal subsidies to medical schools, as well as tax subsidies for nonprofit schools. Some of these subsidies are from the Medicare program, which pays for residency slots, and some are reimbursements for providing medical services to uninsured patients.

Training physicians is very expensive, because it is both technology- and labor-intensive. Academic medical centers have two distinct objectives: one is to deliver medical care, especially tertiary care services; and the other is to train new physicians. Because of these two objectives, medical care services obtained at hospitals associated with medical schools are 20–30% more expensive than similar care obtained at other types of hospitals. This is at least partly attributable to the need for medical students and residents to do more diagnostic tests and to consult with more senior physicians (Sultz and Young, 2014). As many academic medical centers receive public subsidies, they must care for a larger proportion of uninsured and usually sicker patients.

## Licensure, Board Certification, and Continuing Medical Education of Physicians

In order to practice medicine, all physicians must pass a state-administered licensing examination. Allopathic (MD) and osteopathic (DO) physicians may—and often do—take the same examination. There is also another set of licensing examinations specific for osteopathic physicians, which they may also choose to take (Stanfield et al., 2012). Although not required for practice, most physicians also become board-certified in their particular specialty, usually after several years of being in practice.

Both allopathic and osteopathic physicians are required to participate in continuing education each year in order to maintain licensure, a requirement first set by Abraham Flexner. Continuing medical education is also governed by states, and there are ranges of requirements, although most states require between 20 and 25 certified hours per year. Some states require up to 50 certified hours per year. Each specialty board has specific requirements. Continuing medical education is not without controversy, as many of the educational opportunities are offered by the pharmaceutical industry (Sultz and Young, 2014).

## How Many Physicians Are There and Where Do They Practice?

There are several interrelated policy issues regarding physician supply. The first is how many physicians there are; however, counting physicians is not a simple problem. The main interest is in physicians who are in active practices, which is not the same as graduates of medical schools or as those holding a license to practice. The complications of accurately counting the physician supply is beyond the scope of this book, other than to recognize that all numbers given in this book and elsewhere vary depending on the procedure used to develop the count (Stamps and Cruz, 1994). The most recent report of the AMA State Physician Workforce Book (AAMC 2013 Masterfile) is used in this book. This provides an estimate of 817,850 actively practicing physicians in the United States, with 92% of these holding an MD degree (AAMC, 2013).

As shown in Chapter 3, knowing the total number of actively practicing physicians is not very helpful, so rates are used, which are expressed as the number of physicians per population (usually per 1000). This allows for monitoring of the physician supply, and also for comparisons between geographic areas. Urban states have a higher physician/population ratio, as demonstrated by Massachusetts, which has the highest ratio of 3.2/1000. Mississippi, as a rural southern state, has the lowest ratio, at 1.6 physicians per 1000 people (AAMC, 2013).

Is this number of physicians enough? This is a subject of much debate. In the 1960s, the rate was 2.0/1000, which analysts thought to be insufficient. Several policies were instituted to increase the number of practicing physicians, and by 2000, there were almost 3 doctors per 1000. This caused policy discussions to evolve into questions of oversupply. As of 2012, the estimate of physician supply was 2.2/1000 (Sultz and Young, 2014). Although the total number of physicians is an important indicator, more sensitive indicators include estimates of diversity and specialty.

The physician workforce has historically been predominated by white males. Nationwide, about 70% of active physicians are males, although this is shifting with older doctors retiring and younger physicians entering the workforce. The number of female doctors is increasing at a larger rate (8%) than the number of male doctors (2%) (Young et al., 2011). The percentage of minority physicians has remained stubbornly low, at less than 3%. The lack of diversity has been long recognized, and there have been several policies developed to increase the proportion of women and minorities. Because of the long training period, policy changes impacting physician supply take more than 10 years to be realized (Sullivan, 2004).

## Specialization and Primary Care

Besides issues related to geographic distribution and diversity, one of the most important policy issues is the type of specialty physicians practice. Physicians can choose among 125 different specialties or subspecialties, which are certified by 24 different specialty boards (Young et al., 2011). These specialties are generally described as being divided into three groups: primary care specialties, medical care specialties, and surgical care specialties.

Table 7.2 gives a few selected examples of each of these categories of specialties. Primary care specialties are those that are the first point of contact for a patient, as will be discussed in Chapter 9. Primary care specialties include internal medicine, pediatrics, and family medicine. Most health insurance policies allow women to see a specialist in obstetrics–gynecology (OB/GYN) as their primary care physician. This particular specialty is a good example of overlap between specialties, depending on the individual choice of the physician. OB/GYN can be included in all three categories, because this type of physician may serve as a primary care physician, or may be consulted for more acute or specialized medical problems. Some, but not all, perform surgery. All physicians are trained in a specialty, but some specialties are more narrow than others. Primary care specialists are trained most broadly; medical specialties have more specific training and most practitioners in this category perform some sort of diagnostic procedure. Surgical specialties are characterized as those physicians who operate.

**Table 7.2   Examples of Physician Workforce by Specialty Groups**

| *Primary Care Specialties* | *Medical Specialties* | *Surgical Specialties* |
|---|---|---|
| Family practice | Cardiology | Cardiothoracic surgery |
| Internal medicine | Gastroenterology | General surgery |
| Pediatrics | Hematology | Orthopedic surgery |
| Obstetrics/gynecology | Oncology | Neurosurgery |
| | Urology | Plastic surgery |
| | Radiology | Anesthesiology |
| | Dermatology | Plastic surgery |
| | Psychiatry | Vascular surgery |
| | Neurology | |
| % MD 30% | % MD 69% | |
| % DO 65% | % DO 35% | |
| Average income: $168,000 | Average income: $350,000 | Average income: $550,000 |

These range from general surgery to increasingly narrowly defined surgeons, such as neuro- or cardiovascular surgeons.

Within each specialty, there are several subspecialties. For example, internal medicine has 18 recognized and independently certified subspecialties, each with its own residencies and certification examinations (ABMS, 2013).

As Table 7.2 shows, only about 30% of the U.S. physician workforce is in a primary care specialty, although a higher percentage of osteopathic physicians remain in primary care practices. Although the number of female practitioners is slowly increasing in medicine, they are not equally distributed among the various specialties. Women are far more likely to practice in one of the primary care specialties. For example, the specialties with the greatest percentage of females include pediatrics, child and adolescent psychiatry, OB/GYN, and geriatric medicine. In each of these, the percentage of females ranges from 34% to 50%. Women are less likely to practice within one of the surgical specialties: only 15% of general surgeons are female (Young et al., 2011).

Table 7.2 also gives some information on average income levels for each broad specialty category. Physician income is a very complex and nuanced issue that includes the highest level of debt than any other graduate or professional degree program. Almost all medical school graduates (85%)

have a significant level of debt upon completing medical school, often approaching $200,000 (Greyson et al., 2011). This contributes to choosing a higher income specialty. The incomes shown in Table 7.2 are average values, and they are gross—not net—incomes. These figures include all operating expenses of their practices, such as malpractice premiums. Physician salaries in the United States tend to be higher than those in other countries, but this is at least partly explained by more highly subsidized medical education and much lower practice costs of physicians in other countries (Rampell, 2009; Saltman, 2009).

Physicians control almost 70% of expenditures in the health care sector, so many policy initiatives are directed at reducing costs related to their role in the health system. Some policies are efforts to increase the total number of physicians in the workforce, but most are directed at specialty choice or geographic distribution, which interact with each other. This is a frustrating and complex area, because policy changes are realized many years later, as noted, and also because it is very difficult to exert exact control over physician supply. For example, although the overall number of physicians greatly increased in response to policy decisions of the 1960s, this was not even across all specialties, nor across geographic distribution. For example, the number of primary care physicians only increased by 18% between 1960 and 2000, whereas the number of more narrowly defined medical and surgical specialties increased by 118%. Physicians practicing in rural areas only increased by about 50% over this period (Shi and Singh, 2014).

Of particular interest is the link between primary care physicians and health status. International research strongly supports a positive link between a strong primary care system and health status, as will be shown in Chapter 22. Even in the United States, those states with a higher number of primary care physicians (such as Minnesota and Hawaii) have higher health status indicators than states with a lower number of primary care physicians such as Mississippi and Alabama (United Health Foundation, 2013b).

Whether the United States has too many or too few physicians remains an open question. More consensus exists around the observation that the physician supply is not evenly distributed in the United States, leaving some rural areas in great need of access to all sorts of medical care services. There is also broad agreement that the U.S. physician supply needs far more primary care physicians, especially as the Affordable Care Act (ACA) continues to be implemented. Others suggest that we should greatly increase the number of mid-level providers instead of primary care physicians. This trend is currently happening, as the latest survey by the National Center for Health

Statistics shows that 53% of primary care practices included either a PA or an NP in 2012 (Hing and Hsiao, 2014).

# Mid-Level Independent Clinicians

These clinical providers are sometimes called nonphysician practitioners, or physician extenders. They were originally meant to extend the ability of physicians while working directly under their supervision or to practice in rural, underserved areas of the United States. Over time, they have evolved into a more independent practice model. There are two main types of mid-level providers: PAs, arising from the medical model; and NPs, arising from the nursing care model. Although they share several similar practice characteristics as well as similar policy issues, they are very different in training and orientation, and so will be discussed separately here.

## PAs

The impetus for a mid-level physician provider arose in the 1960s, partly because of the perceived shortage of physicians, as described previously. Another influence was the large number of corpsmen returning from Vietnam who had significant clinical experience. Because of this, the first school for PAs at Duke University used a military orientation for training (Sultz and Young, 2014). Originally, all PAs were male, but today almost 65% of PAs are female (Cawley and Hooker, 2013).

There are 181 PA programs in the United States, with 85 more seeking accreditation (Cawley and Hooker, 2013). The programs have a very similar curriculum, which includes about a year of concentrated coursework and a year of at least 2000 hours of supervised clinical experience. As with graduates from medical schools, a degree from a PA school does not permit the person to practice. This takes certification and licensure from a state. To maintain licensure, PAs must take 100 hours of approved continuing medical education experiences every 2 years (Cawley and Hooker, 2013).

There are about 89,000 PAs in practice today, working in a wide variety of practice settings, including primary care practices, hospitals, and military health care settings. Their incomes range from $64,000 to $125,000 with a mean income of $90,000 (Cawley and Hooker, 2013). As with medicine, this profession is largely white: about 4% are black and about 4% are Hispanic or Latino (AAPA, 2011).

The original impetus behind this profession was to increase the number of resources in primary care, especially in rural underserved areas. However, the pattern within the PA profession is that of specialization, just as it is within medicine. Currently, about 40% practice in primary care, whereas 26% are in a surgical specialty; another 26% work in a more narrowly defined medical specialty such as dermatology, gastroenterology, psychiatry, or emergency medicine (Cawley and Hooker, 2013). These specializations require a year of additional graduate level training and a certification examination.

Although the original concept of PAs was that they would work directly under the supervision of a physician, this varies considerably by state. In most states, a physician and a PA file a plan that outlines the level and type of supervision. PAs in all states have a large range of medical responsibilities, including diagnosing and treating acute illness; ordering and interpreting various laboratory and other diagnostic tests; making rounds in hospitals; performing minor office-based procedures; and assisting in more complex hospital-based surgical procedures (Cawley and Hooker, 2013). All states allow PAs to prescribe drugs, but not all states allow them to prescribe controlled pain medications.

PAs carry malpractice insurance on themselves, but physicians have the ultimate legal responsibility. Medical malpractice lawsuits are less common among PAs than among physicians. Between 1991 and 2007, there was one malpractice claim paid for every 32 PAs in contrast to one claim paid for roughly every three physicians (Wright, 2012).

PAs earn less money than physicians, and they seem to be able to do about 85% of what a primary care physician does (Henry et al., 2011). This results in suggestions to replace primary care physicians with PAs. Patient acceptability of PAs is increasing, although not all patients are satisfied with a primary care visit involving a PA instead of a physician. There is some evidence that patients who consult a PA are more likely to make a repeat visit to a physician (Everett et al., 2013). Another concern relates to the ability of a PA to accurately diagnose a more complex illness and properly refer a patient to a specialist (Henry et al., 2011). Some analysts worry about further diminishing the role of primary care specialties. Already paid less, and with lower status in medical schools, they worry about even fewer people choosing one of these specialties.

## NPs

The origins of NPs also occurred in the 1960s as a result of the perceived physician shortage. Added to this was a long-standing perception of nurses not being fully appreciated for their clinical skills, but being recognized for being more patient-centered than either physicians or PAs (Hooker and McCraig, 2001). The original idea was to extend physician resources, especially in primary care practices located in rural and underserved areas.

The various degree paths in the nursing field as well as the philosophy of that field will be more fully discussed in the next section. NPs must first have a registered nurse (RN) degree, which is the basic licensure requirement in the field of nursing. Most also have a Bachelor of Science in Nursing (BSN), which is the degree that leads up to RN. NPs also usually practice for a while as an RN before seeking the extra training and credentials to become an NP. The accepted degree for an NP is a Master's Degree in Nursing (MSN), which is one of the four different types of advanced practice nurses. The training programs are typically 2 years in length, although some are shorter, certificate programs designed for more experienced nurses. There are more than 300 accredited programs, most of which are located in universities and colleges with schools of nursing (Shi and Singh, 2014). NPs are both certified and licensed. Certification is obtained by a test, usually specified for a practice population such as primary care, women's health, and pediatrics. State licensure is through the State Board of Nursing. There are about 115,000 licensed practicing NPs in the United States. The average salary for an NP varies quite a lot by practice setting, but for full-time work, the average is $95,000 (AANP, 2007). Their scope of practice is similar to PAs, including the ability to prescribe drugs. As with PAs, this varies by state.

It is expected that both of these two professions will grow, especially with the further implementation of the ACA, which emphasizes the role of primary care. For both of these mid-level providers, the issue of more independent practice is a serious one. For both, there is a concerted effort to pass state-level laws that allow for more independent practice authority, including the ability to practice without physician supervision (Fairman et al., 2011).

## The Nursing Profession

The nursing profession is the largest group in the U.S. health care field. Its history is probably also the best known, because of Florence Nightingale as the mother of nursing and of nursing schools. Less well known is the fact that her emphasis on simple measures of good hygiene was responsible for a reduction in the death rate in British hospitals in the 1850s from nearly 40% to less than 5% (Starr, 1982). Nursing schools following the Nightingale model were established in the United States starting in 1873. The emphasis was on recruiting upper-income women to improve their domestic abilities as well as to serve their communities (Stevens, 1989). World Wars I and II greatly increased the need for hospital-based nurses. Prior to this, most nurses were employed in private duty responsibilities in the homes of sick people (Stevens, 1989).

The nursing profession is characterized by numerous educational paths that are specific to each level of nursing, but not hierarchical or sequential. The lowest entry level is the certified nurse assistant (CNA). This is the only level of nursing that is not state-licensed but is professionally certified. The next level is licensed practical nurse (LPN), sometimes called the licensed vocational nurse (LVN). This is a 12-month program, often offered in a community college. LPNs generally work under the direction of either an RN or a physician.

The first level of professional nursing requires an RN degree, and there are three independent paths for this degree (Barton, 2007). The original training for the RN license occurred in diploma programs located in hospitals. There are still more than 100 such programs although today they only train about 8% of the nursing workforce (Sprately et al., 2001). The second educational path to licensure as an RN is an associate degree program, known as the AA or AS program. This is usually offered at a community college level and currently trains about 65% of RNs. The most recently developed path is the BSN, an undergraduate bachelor's degree. It is this path that is now preferred by the profession and is often required in order to gain one of the advanced practice degrees. After completing one of these three degree, a nurse must take a state licensure examination (Sultz and Young, 2014).

There are almost 3 million licensed nurses in the U.S. health care field (Kovner and Knickman, 2011). Nurses work in a wide variety of practice settings, including primary care, nursing homes, private-duty care, schools, and community clinics, but about 60% work in some sort of hospital environment (DHHS, 2003). The nursing profession is female dominated, with only about 10% men. The nurse workforce is also largely white: about 15% are minority, with about 5% being African-American (Sprately et al., 2001).

## Advanced Practice Degrees

Degrees above the RN are termed advanced practice degrees. There are four types of advance practice nurses. The first is the clinical nurse specialist (CNS), which involves a master's degree, and training in more specialized nursing practices including pain management, ordering routine tests, and doing physical assessments for hospital admissions. CNSs are often involved in hospital practices and do not have prescribing authority. The second—certified registered nurse anesthetists (CRNAs)—is more specialized; these individuals hold a master's degree and generally work under the direction of a physician, although about 20% of anesthesia delivered to patients is by a nurse anesthetist working alone (Sultz and Young, 2014). The third level of advanced practice is the NP, which was described previously. The fourth level is composed of certified nurse midwives (CNMs). These are RNs who have completed a certificate program that allows them to manage routine gynecological care as well as deliver babies, either in a home or hospital environment. In some states, physicians oppose CNMs delivering babies outside of hospitals and without direct supervision of physicians, although the nursing profession argues this is an unreasonable restriction. Each state sets its own limitations on the scope of practice for midwives (Pushfor, 2013).

## Issues in Nursing

The nursing profession is the backbone of personal and individualized care, especially in the hospital setting. However, this profession has suffered because of gender and economic issues. Hospitals are the most expensive component of the U.S. health care system. Much of the cost of a hospital is in labor costs, and nurses make up a large proportion of that workforce. Average salaries for RNs have been historically low, ranging from $38,000 to $70,000, depending on the practice setting (Kovner and Knickman, 2011). Increased specialization and unionization have increased nurse incomes.

Trends toward unionization have increased as cost-saving nurse staffing adjustments are implemented in hospitals. A fairly common approach is to have staff ratios involve more lower-level nurses, such as LPNs, and fewer RNs. State legislatures sometimes get involved in setting parameters for nurse staffing patterns. Nursing research suggests that low staffing levels in hospitals is linked to poor health outcomes, including higher mortality rates (Needleman et al., 2011). Occupational dissatisfaction among nurses often leads to high turnover, with rates as high as 50% annually. This impacts hospital costs, because it is very expensive to recruit and train a nurse. Besides the cost, the impact on patient outcomes is very negative. For both of these reasons, level of nurse satisfaction is used by hospitals as one of several required quality indicators required by the accrediting organization (Stamps, 1997).

All of these factors result in a prediction of a shortage of nurses in the next 10 years (Brewer and Kovner, 2001). Shortage of nurses in hospitals leads to the hiring of contract nurses, who work as a temporary employee to bring the staffing ratios up to what is required either professionally or legally. Although these RNs are competent and licensed, they often provide discontinuous care and also contribute to nurse dissatisfaction, because of the differences in payment for services (Barton, 2007).

## Other Independent Clinical Providers

Table 7.1 shows several different types of independently practicing direct care providers. Each of these is certified and state licensed, which means that these professionals are able to practice independently. The only one that will be briefly described here are podiatrists. Chiropractors were discussed in Chapter 4; the other independently practicing providers will be described in Chapter 10.

### Podiatrists

Podiatry is the medical specialty that most people have never heard of or assume that it is related to orthopedic surgery. Podiatrists are independently trained, with their own schools and their own degree, which is totally independent of either the MD or DO degree. Podiatrists specialize in the care of feet, including diagnosis and both medical and surgical treatment of feet and ankles. As with chiropractors and osteopaths, they have maintained an independent set of schools and degrees since the Flexner Report of 1910 (AACPM, 2013).

There are nine professionally accredited colleges of podiatric medicine in the United States (AACPM, 2013). Entrance requirements are very similar to those of medical schools, including the MCAT examination. The curriculum is standard and lasts 4 years, after which a graduate receives the Doctor of Podiatric Medicine (DPM) degree. As with physicians, practice requires a residency, which is a standard 3 years long. After completing residency training, podiatrists become licensed to practice and may choose to also become board-certified. There are several specialties available, some of which require more training. These include pediatrics (podopediatrics), sports medicine, orthopedics, and reconstructive foot and ankle surgery. All podiatrists can perform surgery, although there is separate certification for rear foot surgery (AACPM, 2013).

Podiatrists may practice in a private practice, in a managed care practice, or in a hospital setting. Each state sets their scope of practice, but all states include the right to perform foot and ankle surgeries, including amputations, nonsurgical treatment of the foot as well as the tendons that go from the ankle to the foot, and the ability to perform physical assessments and to order and interpret diagnostic tests. Patients with foot and ankle problems may consult either an orthopedic specialist with an MD or a DO, or a podiatrist, but only the podiatrist is actually specialized in treating foot and ankle problems. Podiatry is a high-paying specialty, with income ranging between $250,000 for surgical podiatrists and $170,000 for nonsurgical podiatrists. Forbes recently listed it as the 15th best-paid professions in the United States (Forbes, 2007).

# Clinical Providers with Varying Levels of Practice Independence

This final category of health care providers, often called allied health professionals, provide direct patient care, usually—but not always—under the supervision of a physician. These clinical groups are professionally certified, but are not all licensed by the state. Of the many examples of allied health professionals, only three groups will be described here: pharmacists, paramedics, and therapeutic science practitioners.

## *Pharmacists*

Pharmacists have always served as an important source of information, for both over-the-counter and prescription drugs. Today, through state-regulated practice compacts, pharmacists have a more formally structured role. Each state has a Collaborative Practice Agreement identifying the practice arrangement between physicians and pharmacists. Some pharmacists work directly with patients to do assessments, referrals, and even to order laboratory tests. All states allow pharmacists to do immunizations, although a few states restrict this to influenza injections only. Some states require a specific physician prescription, whereas others use the Collaborative Practice Agreements to identify the range of immunizations that can be given by pharmacists, once they are trained in this skill (CDC, 2013).

There are 124 Doctor of Pharmacy (Pharm.D) professionally accredited schools. This doctoral level curriculum involves 4 years of course work and also includes practical experience in a variety of medical care settings, including hospitals and retail pharmacies. Pharmacists are licensed by states and must take two separate examinations, one of which focuses on state-level laws about drugs (Stanfield et al., 2012).

Pharmacy incomes vary somewhat by region of the country. The highest range is from $117,000 to $130,000 (in Maine, California, Vermont, and Delaware), whereas the lowest range of $76,000 to $109,000 prevails in such states as Montana, Wyoming, Nevada, Oklahoma, and Pennsylvania (BLS, 2013). The proportion of women in pharmacy is increasing: in 1990, 31% of licensed pharmacists were female, but by 2007, almost half are female. Women earn about 8% less than their male counterparts (Manasse and Speedie, 2007). The pharmacy profession is largely white: only about 8% of pharmacists are African-American (ASHSP, 2008).

Many predict shortages in pharmacists, especially as the Collaborative Practice Agreements allow pharmacists more direct contact with patients. The use of both prescription and over-the-counter drugs is anticipated to continue to increase.

## Paramedics

A paramedic is a professional who provides medical services for patients in an emergency situation in the field, often as a part of a response team on an ambulance. The term paramedic is used broadly but actually refers to the third tier of training for emergency medical personnel. The first tier is an emergency medical technician (EMT) and the second tier is advanced EMT. The difference between these three levels of training is not only in education and certification, but also in delineation of specific clinical tasks. For example, an EMT can assess and/or manually reposition breathing assistance devices, but a paramedic can insert emergency airway support devices. An EMT can conduct cardiopulmonary resuscitation, including an external automatic defibrillator, whereas a paramedic can also administer cardiac support drugs as well as a manual defibrillator. An EMT can assess wounds, whereas a paramedic can do treatment of wounds, including suturing (Stanfield et al., 2012).

Paramedics are not professionally certified through a national organization, although some states have a certification process. They are not licensed by states. They are enrolled on the National Registry of Emergency Medical

Technicians, which is recognized in most, but not all, states. This profession continues to grow, but it remains diverse in educational standards, which vary depending on state requirements. A traditional curriculum involves between 700 and 1300 hours of training, including both didactic and clinical experience. Because of the lack of certification and variability in training, the professional recognition and the incomes of paramedics are lower than other allied health professionals.

Despite this, the role of paramedics is slowly moving beyond the original concept of providing only emergency medical services. Paramedics are increasingly employed in hospital settings, especially in emergency rooms. Paramedics are also often used to transport critically ill patients in helicopters, a role that used to require an RN. In a few states, ambulance companies employ paramedics to provide home-based medical care services in an effort to prevent more expensive hospital stays (McCluskey, 2014).

## Therapeutic Science Practitioners

This is a large category of allied health professionals that includes physical, occupational, and speech-language therapists. All three require graduate training from an accredited program, and all are also licensed by states.

*Physical therapists* help with physical recovery and rehabilitation from an injury or debilitating illness such as a stroke. There are 227 professionally accredited programs, which are 3 to 4 years long and involve both didactic and clinical work. The degree is the Doctor of Physical Therapy (DPT) (Stanfield et al., 2012). Physical therapists work in a variety of settings, including hospitals, nursing homes, health centers, and increasingly, in an independent practice. Most insurance policies require a referral from a physician in order to pay for the cost of a visit, but some states allow patients to see a physical therapist without a referral. As might be expected, salary range varies depending on practice setting, but the national average is about $80,000 (BLS, 2013).

*Occupational therapists* provide supportive activities for a variety of activities of daily living. They tend to be involved with a range of ages and types of patients, including autistic children, or people with specific physical or mental disabilities. The requirement for practice is at least a master's degree from one of the 322 certified occupational therapy programs (Stanfield et al., 2012). Occupational therapists work in either hospitals or in some other setting such as a school or nursing home. The average salary is similar to that of a physical therapist (BLS, 2013).

*Speech-language therapists* assess, diagnose, and treat communication and swallowing disorders in patients. They frequently work with children, but also with adults who have suffered a stroke or some sort of other brain injury. The degree requirement is a master's degree, along with a certification and/or licensure examination, depending on the state in which the therapist would like to practice. Most programs are 2 years long (Stanfield et al., 2012). Incomes for speech therapists are somewhat lower (BLS, 2013).

All three of these professions are female-dominated and all three are predicted to grow, with increased demand from the increasingly aging population.

## Policy Issues

This chapter demonstrates there are many different, highly trained professionals that comprise the workforce of the U.S. health care system. The most detail has been devoted to physicians and nurses, primarily because physicians control most of the spending decisions in the health care system and nurses are the largest single group of professionals. However, there are many other nonphysician, nonnurse health care providers. Nearly all of those who have some sort of direct care relationship with patients are highly regulated, not only by professional certification, but also by state level licensing and specific regulations that govern the scope of practice.

The process of professionalization begun by the Flexner report has resulted in this highly regulated health care system, which influences not only the type of health care providers available, but also the financing of their services. Professionalization increases patient safety but decreases the power of the private market, as will be shown in Chapter 11. This system is not static, as demonstrated by the gradual acceptance of osteopathic medicine, as well as the continued evolution of the acceptance of chiropractic medicine. Despite professional certification and state licensure, people in the United States seek medical care in many settings, some of which are not acceptable to the mainstream medical system. It is unfortunate that providing health care services is not straightforward, and cures and remedies often defy the extremely technological interventions we have developed.

An important policy issue facing the U.S. health care system is whether we have enough health care providers, what types we need more and less of, and where they practice. This is a very complicated question that has no easy answers, partly because of the dynamic nature of the workforce and patient behavior. Also complicating this decision-making process is that it is not easy to quantify the number of actively practicing health care professionals. Figure 7.1 provides guidance in how to think about the issues involved in planning the nation's health care workforce. The composition of the U.S. health care workforce is directly impacted by three separate groups of variables: demographic influences, the education system, and the structure of the health care system itself. Influencing these factors is the overall economic situation of the country and various policies and regulations set by state and federal levels of government.

*Demographic influences* include the changing nature of the U.S. population, especially with respect to an increasingly aging population. Age does not in and of itself mean that an individual person automatically needs more health care services. However, when examined as a population, older people almost always need more health care resources, and often expensive services. Demographic variables include the changing pattern of diseases, especially the increasing number of chronic diseases. Based on past and current information, it is anticipated that the number of Americans with a chronic disease will increase 42% from the current 133 million to nearly 160 million by 2023. The current total cost of treatment of chronic illness is about 75% of total health care spending (Bodenheimer et al., 2009).

The *structure of the medical care system* helps determine the way in which diseases are treated. This includes innovations in both treatment and screening technology; restructuring of medical practices to accommodate the increased size and corporatization of health care institutions; and the roles

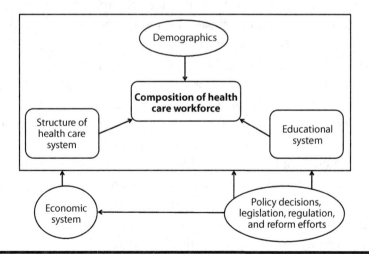

**Figure 7.1 Factors influencing workforce supply and demand. (Adapted from Dumpe, M.L. et al., *Nursing Economics*, 16, 174, 1998.)**

of the health care professionals. Most agree it is more cost-effective to have primary care physicians manage chronic diseases. However, a substantial number of patients have multiple chronic illnesses (Rhoman and Wagner, 2003). As primary care physicians become involved in the management of more complex patients, they increasingly refer patients to specialists and/or subspecialists (Colwill et al., 2008). Referring patients with multiple illnesses often results in fragmentation of care and higher spending on care of chronic illness, but not necessarily better outcomes (Ostibye et al., 2005).

This is relevant to the changing roles of primary care physicians and increasing utilization of mid-level providers. Cost is lower and outcomes seem to be at least the same, if not better (Link et al., 2014). However, there is the continuing issue of patient acceptability and the further diminution of the role of the primary care physician. Whether we have enough physicians—or any other health care professional—depends a lot on how they are used in patient care, so this discussion of who should treat chronic disease is very important.

There is a consensus that there is a need to increase the number and percentage of primary care physicians, where only about 30% of the physician workforce is employed (Bodenheimer et al., 2009). The *educational system* for health care professionals is controlled by many different factors, some of which include studies that predict future demand. Increasing capacity in any of the educational institutions is not simple. Each educational institution is accredited, and receives either direct or indirect public subsidies. This means that increasing the number of students enrolled is subject to both professional and governmental approval. In the case of physicians, for example, the National Council on Graduate Medical Education advises the Department of Health and Human Resources, which submits a recommendation to the U.S. Congress (Kovner and Knickman, 2011). Also, increasing the number of students accepted does not immediately increase the number of practitioners, as has been noted.

The larger *economic situation* in the United States is important here, because any potential health care provider must consider how much money they will spend to become trained, certified, and licensed. Then they must consider how much money they will likely earn, in comparison with other potential occupations. This chapter has given some information on average incomes, which are diverse. A very important influence noted in Figure 7.1 is *policy and legislation*, and several examples have been included here to illustrate this. Although many policy and legislative decisions are based on data, the influence of politics and philosophical values is always present.

One important policy issue noted throughout this chapter is the striking lack of diversity in the health care workforce. Although women are increasingly practicing as clinicians, progress with respect to minorities has been poor. Although African-Americans make up about 13% of the U.S. population, the percentage of physicians who are Black has been at slightly less than 3% for 50 years. Hispanic or Latinos make up about 12% of the U.S. population, but only 4% of the physician workforce. Only about 5% of nurses are African-American (Sullivan, 2004). Chapter 21 discusses some of the consequences of this lack of diversity.

The next two chapters describe two of the major settings in which many health care professional work: hospitals and ambulatory care settings.

## Acknowledgments

The following people made significant contributions to the content of this chapter, including gathering material and references, as well as writing and analysis: Molly Barlow, Rachel Brown, Samantha Calabrese, Tia DiNatale, Irene Eberbach, Susannah Gleason, Michael Goulart, Avery Henniger, Maria Kardaras, Sarah Kelly, Sheighlyn Knightly, Ariana Lymberopoulos, Alexandria McGowan, Hayley Mandeville, Jasmine Offley, Loreiny Peñaló, Joshua Prevatt, Kylie Wojcicki, and Pratiksha Yalakkishettar. Reema Chapatwala, Julie Minnisch, and Jonathan Rosenblatt improved the quality of this chapter with their suggestions and feedback. All three contributed to the redesign of Table 7.2 and Jonathan constructed Figure 7.1.

## Chapter 8

# Hospitals

Hospitals employ the largest percentage of health care workers in the entire health care system—42% in 2005. At least one-third of all money spent in the health care sector is spent on medical services delivered in a hospital setting (Shi and Singh, 2014). The actual definition of a hospital is quite simple: an institution with at least six beds, the primary function of which is to deliver patient services for both treatment and diagnosis of medical conditions (Shi and Singh, 2014). Hospitals are commonly thought of as the facility in which inpatient care takes place, but they have broadened their scope to include a variety of services, some of which are outpatient and some of which are not located in the physical location of the hospital.

This chapter begins with a brief history of hospitals in the United States and an overview of the development of the hospital industry. This will inform the later discussion on structure and ownership patterns. A description of hospitals by form, function, and services is included in this chapter. Issues related to the organization and management of hospitals are described, as well as issues related to licensure and accreditation. Important issues of costs and cost control strategies are discussed here before concluding with several important policy issues.

## History

There were a great many hospitals in the colonial and early history of the United States, as noted in Chapter 7. These were small, proprietary, and mostly operated out of the houses of those who identified as being doctors.

Gradually, larger and more organized hospitals arose, mostly in urban areas where illness was often associated with poverty. Churches took care of poor people in larger homes known as almshouses. As poor people gathered in groups were likely to become sick, almshouses began to be known as hospitals. During this same period (mid-1800s), port cities experienced influxes of people who were sick, often with a contagious illness. Cities, with help from churches, identified separate houses for these sick people and located these well outside the cities. These pest houses quarantined people just off ships to prevent illnesses such as measles and smallpox from spreading to the community (Sultz and Young, 2014). It did not take long for two separate groups to develop: the poor and sick, taken care of by the church; and the contagious, taken care of by the local government. A third group that needed some type of institutional care consisted of those who were not able to function within the social structure of the day. This group today is understood to have mental illness, but at this time they were viewed as a danger to the community (Sultz and Young, 2014).

These two types of early hospitals took care of those who were undesirable in some way—because of poverty, infectious illness, or mental illness. Cities gradually began to tax citizens to help defray the cost of taking care of these marginalized people. Hospitals supported by these tax funds became known as public hospitals. Some of today's very well-known hospitals arose from this historical period, such as Bellevue Hospital, which was originally known as the Poor House of New York City. Another example is the Public Hospital of Baltimore, which in 1889 became Johns Hopkins Hospital (Sultz and Young, 2014). The medical school associated with this hospital was the model supported by Abraham Flexner, as described in Chapter 7.

More affluent people had no desire to go to a publicly supported hospital, because most of the patients were poor, very sick, and possibly contagious or mentally ill. By the late 1800s, several advances in medical sciences, such as anesthesia, made surgery more acceptable and safer; and x-rays were beginning to be used for diagnostic purposes. As allopathic doctors adopted these innovations, they preferred placing patients in their own private hospitals. As a result, a different type of hospital developed, one founded by allopathic physicians and funded by wealthy donors as well as by paying patients. These hospitals were known as voluntary hospitals because the donors willingly made financial donations. Some services were provided to poor people who were noncontagious or not mentally ill, but they primarily cared for more affluent patients who could pay for services as well as make charitable contributions to the hospital. After the Flexner Report criticized

for-profit hospitals and medical schools, these private hospitals were organized into structures of nonprofit organizations, including requirements such
as a Board of Trustees, upon which the wealthiest contributors would sit.

These two terms for hospitals—public and voluntary—mean slightly different things today, but this history has negatively impacted the public's perception of hospitals. Public hospitals are still viewed as primarily associated
with caring for the poor, although many public hospitals today are associated with academic teaching centers, as will be seen later in this chapter.
All nonprofit hospitals must take care of uninsured people, but it is true that
public hospitals—supported by city, state, or federal tax monies—are viewed
as the safety net hospitals. Some of the most well respected hospitals in the
nation, including Mass General in Boston and Cook County Hospital (now
known as the John H. Stroger Hospital) in Chicago, are public hospitals
(Kovner and Knickman, 2011).

## Development of the Hospital Industry in the United States

The development of the hospital industry is marked by cycles of growth and
subsequent regulations to slow expansion. There were 178 hospitals in the late
1880s, and 4300 by the time the Flexner Report came out in 1910 (Sultz and
Young, 2014). This growth continued until 1929 when there were 6665 hospitals
(Shi and Singh, 2014). Although the relationship between supply and demand
was not part of formal policy analysis at the time, this expansion of hospitals led
to one of the most famous sayings in health care: "…a built bed is a filled bed."
A more popular version of this is known as Roemer's law, which states: "If you
build it, they will come" (Roemer, 1961; Shi and Singh, 2014).

By 1937, the number of hospitals had dropped to slightly more than 6000,
partly in response to the economic situation in the United States, especially the 1929 depression. Not only did patients have less money to pay
for needed medical care, the wealthy donors who financially supported the
voluntary hospitals had also lost money (Shi and Singh, 2014). This created
the first cycle of merging and reorganizing into larger organizations, resulting in fewer hospitals. Shortly after World War II, policy analysts tried to
predict the number of hospitals needed, and realized that counting hospitals was not useful, because the size varied so much. A far more sensitive
estimate is the number of hospital beds/population, which is the indicator
used today for planning purposes. In 1946, it was estimated that there were
3.2 hospital beds per 1000 people, but it was felt that was not enough. The
Hill–Burton Act was passed in 1946 to support the growth of the hospital

industry throughout the 1950s and 1960s. This Act was terminated in 1974, but its impact continued to be felt throughout the 1980s, when the goal of 4.5 hospital beds/1000 was attained (Shi and Singh, 2014).

The Hill–Burton Act is the only time that federal monies have been directly given to hospitals. Both Medicare and Medicaid, which were passed in 1965 (Chapters 18 and 19), created increased demand for hospital services by improving financial access for the elderly and the poor. Although indirect, the impact of these two programs on hospitals is very significant. The consequence of this improved access showed up in increased occupancy of hospitals, which provided financial support to continue the hospital expansion phase.

The Hill–Burton Act also reinforced the Flexner Report in terms of pre-ferred structure for hospitals. The newly created hospitals were termed community hospitals but were based on the model of voluntary hospitals, which were nonprofit organizations and thus tax exempt. One piece of this legislation was to link nonprofit tax structure to a requirement for caring for a certain number of people each year who did not have insurance. As will be seen later, this was very important.

Part of Roemer's insight is that sometimes supply creates demand when there might be other ways of meeting health needs. The expansion phase of hospitals increased capacity in the most expensive part of the U.S. health care system. Medicare and increased private health insurance created a group of people who could afford these services, and also created economic incentives for the development of still more services to be delivered within the hospi-tal setting. As might be expected, spending in the hospital sector increased, which in turn increased overall medical care spending. By the late 1980s, the policy discussion turned to methods of controlling both growth and costs in the hospital sector. Part of this discussion was a significant change in how Medicare paid for hospital services, which will be described in a later section of this chapter. The overall impact on hospitals was a decrease in revenues.

The result was a significant downsizing of the hospital industry, espe-cially of smaller and rural hospitals. Small rural hospitals did not have the population to support increasingly technological and expensive hospital-based services. The number of hospitals declined, occupancy rates declined, and the time that people stayed in the hospital (length of stay) also declined. By 2004, the number of hospitals had fallen to about 4900 hospitals (Kovner and Knickman, 2011), and the number of hospital beds per population had declined to 2.8/1000. Occupancy rates, which had been about 75% in 1980, declined to 64%, and length of stay declined from 7.5 days in 1980 to 4.8 days in 2004 (Shi and Singh, 2014).

# Classification of Hospitals

There are 5723 hospitals as of 2013 (AHA, 2014), which translates to 2.8 hospital beds/1000 population (World Bank, 2015). There are many ways of categorizing these hospitals, several of which are not mutually exclusive. For example, a hospital may be described as short-stay, general, community, and proprietary. Depending on the purpose of the analysis, one of these categories may be more appropriate than another, and they are all used depending on the purpose of the analysis. Some of the most commonly used terms in classifying hospitals are shown in Table 8.1.

**Table 8.1   Ways of Classifying/Describing U.S. Hospitals**

| Category | Description |
|---|---|
| **Location** | |
| Urban | *Urban* hospitals are located in an area defined by the U.S. Census Bureau as being in an area that is defined as a Metropolitan Statistical Area (MSA), which contains about 50,000 residents. |
| Rural | *Rural* hospitals are defined as being located in a non-MSA. About 17% of the U.S. population lives in an area defined as being rural. About 40% of hospitals are located in a rural area, but rural hospitals only account for about 12% of all hospitalizations. Patients in rural hospitals are more likely to be older, and are also more likely to be discharged to another facility. The average size of rural hospitals is also smaller than urban hospitals. |
| **Size: Number of Beds** | |
| 6–99 | This category is used to describe single hospitals, not networks of hospitals. The categories noted here are commonly used ones, but many others are also used. |
| 100–199 | About half of all hospitals have 100 beds or less, and only 5% are more than 500 beds. The largest single hospital is New York Presbyterian, with 2236 beds. |
| 200–299 | In the hospital sector, hospitals larger than 100 beds are more expensive to operate, unlike other sectors of the economy, where larger organizations are more efficient. This is primarily because of the need for larger hospitals to have a more extensive array of sophisticated technological equipment for both diagnostic and treatment procedures, with the accompanying increased labor costs. |
| 300–399 | |
| 400–499 | |
| 500+ | |

(*Continued*)

**Table 8.1 (Continued)   Ways of Classifying/Describing U.S. Hospitals**

| Category | Description |
| --- | --- |
| **Level of Care** | |
| Secondary | As explained in Chapter 6, all hospitals provide at least *secondary* care. This means that the hospital can do all routine acute care and surgery. These services are dictated by accreditation standards. |
| Tertiary | More specialized and/or technologically demanding services are frequently triaged to what is known as a *tertiary* care hospital. This hospital is larger and has more diagnostic and specialized equipment available. It is almost always associated with a teaching hospital. Tertiary care hospitals also have all levels of trauma care in their ER. |
| **Duration of Care** | |
| Short stay (acute) | *Short-stay* hospitals are the ones in which the ALOS is less than 25 days. This category includes nearly all hospitals, since only about 2% of hospitals are long term, although this category of hospital is slowly increasing. |
| Long term (chronic) | *Long-term-care* hospitals (LTCH) are not nursing homes; but they are often specialized. They include state-run as well as private hospitals, and also psychiatric hospitals, as well as chronic diseases, including tuberculosis, hospitals. A substantial proportion of patients are the ones that are dependent on breathing assistance, such as ventilators, which have come from short-stay hospitals. |
| **Specialty Status** | |
| General acute care | The term *general* hospital does not mean that the medical care is any less effective; rather it means that more different services are offered. This hospital is more comprehensive than any of the *specialty* hospitals and includes over half of all hospitals, regardless of size. |
| Specialized | *Specialty* hospitals offer medical and diagnostic care to people with specific types of diseases, or to only a specific target population. The two best examples include children's hospitals and rehabilitation hospitals. Also included in this category are burn hospitals, as well as cancer hospitals. |

*(Continued)*

**Table 8.1 (Continued)   Ways of Classifying/Describing U.S. Hospitals**

| Category | Description |
| --- | --- |
| **Specialty Status** | |
| Psychiatric | *Psychiatric* hospitals, which include substance abuse treatment, are considered to be in their own category, and as such, they represent 7% of all hospitals. |
| Teaching hospital | A *teaching hospital* must have at least one graduate medical residency training program. Teaching hospitals are always tertiary care hospitals and, as such, attract patients with more complex illnesses. About 20% of hospitals are associated with a residency training program. |
| **Government Status** | |
| Federal | By far the largest proportions of hospitals are *nongovernmental*. Although hospitals receive indirect subsidies from all levels of government through the tax structure, it is rare for these to be so direct as to be considered *owned* by the government. For example, only 4% of all hospitals are actually considered to be federal. The largest category of federal hospitals is associated with the VA and will be discussed in Chapter 10. About 18% of hospitals can be considered to be *state* or *city* or *county*. Most of these are specialized hospitals, frequently including tuberculosis or psychiatric hospitals. |
| State/local | |
| Nongovernmental | |
| **Ownership Structure** | |
| Nonprofit | Between 50% and 70% of hospitals are *nonprofit*, depending on the exact organizational structure of the hospital. |
| Proprietary/investor Owned/for-profit | About 18% of all hospitals are *for-profit*, although they are not distributed equally throughout the country. |
| Public | *Public* hospitals are those that receive enough direct tax subsidies to be considered as *owned* by whichever level of government makes the most contribution. Since they must provide care for all regardless of insurance coverage, they are also known as *safety-net* hospitals. |
| **Networks** | |
| Sole community hospitals (SCH) | *SCH* are those that are the primary source of inpatient care in a designated market, and those hospitals that operate independently of other hospitals. |

*(Continued)*

**Table 8.1 (Continued)   Ways of Classifying/Describing U.S. Hospitals**

| Category | Description |
|---|---|
| **Networks** | |
| Proprietary networks | *For-profit* hospitals are increasingly in networks, owned by one company. |
| Religious networks | The biggest *religious* network is that of the Catholic Church, which owns and operates several networks of hospitals throughout the nation, accounting for 12% of all nonprofit hospitals. Almost half of all hospitals today are in some sort of a network. |

*Source:* Data from American Hospital Association. Fast Facts on US Hospitals. Available at: http://www.aha.org, 2014, 2012 ; Shi, L and Singh, DA, *Delivering Health Care in America: A Systems Approach*, 6th edition. Burlington, MA: Jones and Bartlett, 2014; Sultz, HA and Young, KM, *Health Care USA: Understanding Its Organization and Delivery*, 8th edition. Burlington, MA: Jones and Bartlett, 2014; Barton, PL, *Understanding the US Health Care Services System*, 3rd edition. Chicago: Health Administration Press, 2007; Kovner, R and Knickman, J, *Jonas and Kovner's Health Care Delivery in the United States*, 10th edition. 2011.

One of the most important ways of classifying hospitals is by ownership status, which includes three different categories: *nonprofit, proprietary*, and *public* (Table 8.1). The majority of hospitals are nonprofit—meaning they have a social mission, which may be secular or religious, because religious organizations are also nonprofit. However, it is not true that they do not make a profit. All organizations attempt to take in more money than they spend, but nonprofit organizations use the excess revenues to support their social goals. Nonprofit organizations do not have to pay any federal, state, or local taxes. However, this advantage does not come without some obligations. For example, a nonprofit organization must demonstrate that its service provides a benefit to the whole community. For the nonprofit hospital, this is mostly demonstrated by caring for people without health insurance. By doing this, nonprofit hospitals provide medical care that would otherwise require tax revenues from the community. All nonprofit hospitals are required to do a certain percentage of what is known as uncompensated care, depending on the size and location of the hospital (Owens, 2005). Another important requirement for nonprofit status is that any excess monies (i.e., revenues over expenses) cannot be distributed to individual stockholders, but rather must be invested back into the hospital. Other requirements include limits on administrative salaries so they are in line with industry standards, and meeting performance and quality standards (Newman, 2001).

If a hospital meets the standards for being a nonprofit organization, as set by the Internal Revenue Service (IRS), they do not have any federal, state, or local tax obligation. This is especially important to those hospitals that are located in urban areas, often on land that is very highly valued and therefore highly taxed. Not surprisingly, the IRS monitors hospitals closely to make sure they adhere to these expectations. As will be seen in the next section, hospitals are complex organizations and frequently restructure to maintain financial stability. Sometimes hospitals acquire some for-profit companies under the overall nonprofit structure of the hospital. This is called vertical integration and usually involves services such as laundry, food, or cleaning services. This can be accomplished while still maintaining a nonprofit tax status, as long as it is done within the IRS standards.

There is a strong philosophical attachment to the nonprofit structure for hospitals, dating back to the Flexner Report, when Flexner recommended that all hospitals be nonprofit. This recommendation, along with the development of nonprofit voluntary or community hospitals, meant that essentially all hospitals in the United States were nonprofit until the 1980s.

Since then, there has been a slow but steady increase in hospitals that were first known as investor-owned, a euphemism for a *for-profit* ownership status. This is still a relatively small category, because slightly less than 20% of all hospitals fall in this category, as Table 8.1 shows. There is a strong regional bias in location of for-profit hospitals, with Nevada, Florida, and Tennessee having almost half of their hospitals being for-profit. Other states such as Minnesota, Iowa, Montana, and Connecticut have less than 3% of their hospitals in the for-profit structure (KFF, 2010a). The for-profit ownership category is steadily growing, whereas the nonprofit, smaller hospitals are closing and/or merging with larger hospitals. For example, the number of nonprofit hospitals has decreased every year since 2002, whereas for-profit hospitals have increased by slightly more than 10% (Selvam, 2012).

Because nonprofit hospitals struggle to maintain financial stability, it is interesting to postulate why for-profit hospitals might be more financially successful than nonprofit ones. Some argue that because for-profit hospitals are not required to provide medical care for uninsured patients, they can accept patients from a more affluent fully insured group. In 2003, the Congressional Budget Office examined for-profit and nonprofit hospitals in five states—California, Florida, Georgia, Indiana, and Texas. They found that, on average, nonprofit hospitals provided more uncompensated care compared with for-profit hospitals (CBO, 2006). Another important factor is that a nonprofit community hospital is required to offer comprehensive medical services, some of which lose money. A for-profit hospital may be a specialty hospital, which concentrates only on those services that are profitable.

Those that support the increase in for-profit hospitals allege that these proprietary hospitals are more efficiently managed by those trained specifically in business, not health care. Essentially all for-profit hospitals are members of multihospital chains, called *networks*, as noted in Table 8.1. For example, Hospital Corporation of America, Community Health Systems, and Health Management Associates own more than 400 hospitals. One of the other large for-profit companies is Tenet, which is in the process of buying Vanguard Health Systems, which will create an even larger company (Herman, 2013a; Moody's Investor Service, 2014).

About 65% of all nonprofit hospital beds are also in multihospital chains, with 25% of these beds being in hospitals sponsored by the Catholic Church (Shi and Singh, 2014). This religious sponsorship significantly impacts the nature and types of medical services offered to patients, especially end-of-life services and reproductive services offered to female patients. The independent, nonprofit general hospital classified as the *sole community hospital* (SCH) serving one community or region has become increasingly rare (Table 8.1).

The final ownership classification category shown in Table 8.1 is *public*, which involves a direct taxpayer-funded subsidy. Many of these hospitals are associated with medical schools and are also *teaching hospitals*. Public hospitals are usually larger than other hospitals in their market area. They also typically have large, busy, and highly rated emergency rooms, which provide all levels of trauma care (Kovner and Knickman, 2011). As noted previously, they are also referred to as safety-net hospitals, because their mission is to care for the uninsured, which is why they receive direct tax subsidies. The *public* classification includes *federal*, but the only truly federal hospital is the Veterans Administration system, which will be described in Chapter 20.

# Organization and Management of Hospitals

Hospitals—even small ones—are very complex organizations with a defined governance structure and a structured, hierarchal organizational structure. This section will give a brief overview of some of the most important features of the organizational structure of the hospital. Each hospital's structure is unique, but they do share many features, which are shown in Figure 8.1.

*Governing Boards.* The origin of the governance structure of the non-profit hospital comes from the voluntary hospital model, when the founding financial donors were on an advisory board called the Board of Trustees. The main responsibility of these governing boards is to respond to the many different stakeholder groups of the hospital, including citizens, businesses, human services organizations, as well as professional organizations and insurance companies, both public and private. Governing boards have significant power and authority, including appointing physicians who will be able to admit patients to the hospital, but the day-to-day operating authority rests with the hospital administrators, who have specialized training in managing large, complex organizations.

Each hospital has a group of top-level, executive officers, each of whom is in charge of a separate aspect of the hospital. The top administrative officer, known as the *chief executive officer*, is analogous to a corporate president. There are at least four other high-level administrative officers, usually considered to be analogous to corporate vice presidents. Two of these are responsible for important systems within the hospital. The *chief financial officer* has the overall responsibility for financial matters, and the *chief information officer* is responsible for the management information system. The

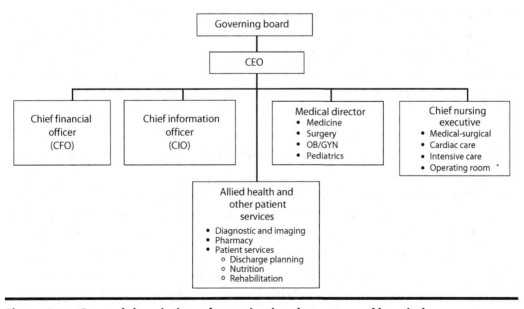

**Figure 8.1    General description of organizational structure of hospitals.**

other two are responsible for the direct care staff: the *chief nursing executive* and the *medical director*. These highest level executive administrators are responsible not only for the oversight of the various departments but also for strategic planning.

Only a physician has the authority to admit a patient to the hospital and only physicians who have admitting privileges granted by the Board of Trustees can admit patients to that particular hospital. This medical staff is organized into large groups (sometimes called Divisions) by medical specialties, such as medicine, surgery, obstetrics/gynecology, and pediatrics. In large hospitals, there are administrative divisions by subspecialties of internal medicine such as cardiology, gastroenterology, pulmonary medicine, and endocrinology. The medical staff also have their own executive committees, such as the medical records committee, the infection control committee, a quality improvement committee, and the credentialing committee, which acts to review those who have applied for admitting privileges.

One of the unique aspects of a hospital's organization is that not all physicians are formal employees of the hospital. Many physicians have their own individual or group practices with admitting privileges to various hospitals. One of the more recent subspecialties of internal medicine is the hospitalist, which is an employee of the hospital. This physician basically serves as the primary care provider by being responsible for coordinating all the medical care while a patient is in the hospital (Glabman, 2005).

The largest single component of the hospital is the *nursing division*. Like the medical staff, this division has administrative leaders (nurse administrators, head nurses, nurse managers) and is also divided into smaller, more specialized units for easier management. The administrative subdivisions in nursing are usually by type of services needed, such as medical–surgical, cardiac care, or intensive care. Nurse staffing is a critical aspect of the hospital, because there must be adequate nursing staff around the clock. Nurse staffing is often a point of controversy, especially as registered nurses become replaced by lower-level nurses such as licensed practical nurses, as discussed in Chapter 7.

These three large components of the hospital—the executive administrative staff, the medical staff, and the nursing staff—comprise the bulk of the organizational structure, but there are many other very important services and personnel, all of whom have their own departments and management. For example, every hospital has a division of *allied health professionals*, which include various technicians as well as many others who interact directly with patients, such as nutritionists, counselors, and social workers. Also included in this group are the several types of administrative staff that interact with patients, including discharge planners. As noted in Chapter 7, the biggest growth in hospital personnel has been in this group of allied health professionals.

There is also usually a department involving *diagnostic services*, which includes radiology, as well as laboratories such as pathology, which assists in analyzing various body tissues. Hospitals maintain a *pharmacy*, which is in charge of ordering and keeping track of all medications administered within the hospital. There is often a specific department entitled *patient services*, which includes discharge planning, social services, nutritional services, and sometimes rehabilitation services. Finally, there is a department of *hotel services*, which include functions related to building maintenance, laundry, room cleaning, and telephone services. These are the services that are frequently most important to patients.

## Licensure, Accreditation, and Regulation

Hospitals are highly regulated organizations. There are three methods of regulations: licensure, accreditation, and certification. Each serves a different function and is the responsibility of a different organization. *Licensure* is the responsibility of the state government. Each hospital must be licensed by the state in which it is located, with variations by state. Most of the licensure standards focus on the physical safety of the building, including building codes, establishing fire safety routines, and ensuring adequate space for each of the services delivered. Quality of care is not part of the licensure standards. A licensed hospital is not necessarily a certified or accredited hospital.

The term *certification* specifically refers to the fact that a hospital is able to admit and receive payment for patients who are on either Medicare or Medicaid. These standards are enforced by the federal government (specifically the Department of Health and Human Services). These standards relate not only to patient safety but also to quality of care, especially to outcomes of care. These quality and outcome standards are reviewed yearly, usually by the state health department.

Both licensure and certification are regulations that are governmental: licensure at the state level and certification at the federal level. *Accreditation*, however, is nongovernmental, and is under the responsibility of a nonprofit organization called the Joint Commission on Accreditation of Healthcare Organizations (JCAHO). The Joint Commission sets separate quality standards for each type of health care organization. The accreditation process includes the hospital receiving the quality standards, preparing a self-study report, and then having a periodic unannounced visit for the accreditors to inspect how successfully the hospital meets the quality standards.

## Hospital Finance and Controlling Costs

Financing hospital care includes who pays for care as well as controlling the cost of care. This is a very complex topic, so this section will provide only a big picture level of understanding, starting with how money comes into hospitals. Even this broad description of revenues depends somewhat on the type of hospital. Chapter 15 describes this in more detail.

The major source of revenue for most hospitals is private health insurance. In most nonprofit hospitals, nearly 40% of all revenues are from private insurance (Barton, 2007). Medicare (described in Chapter 18) generally provides about 30% of hospital revenues and Medicaid (described in Chapter 19) provides about 20% (Barton, 2007). Public hospitals are also organized as nonprofit organizations, but because their mission is usually to care for less affluent populations, a higher proportion of their revenues tends to be from Medicaid and a lower amount comes from private insurance (Kovner and Knickman, 2011).

One of the most significant financial problems faced by nonprofit hospitals is uncompensated care, or care provided for people who have no insurance of any type. All nonprofit hospitals are required to provide medical care to patients who seek care from the emergency room, regardless of their insurance coverage or their ability to pay for the care. This makes medical care quite different from all other consumer services, as will be demonstrated in Chapter 11. Hospitals may transfer patients without insurance to a public hospital, but only after the person is treated and stabilized. The burden of uncompensated care (sometimes called charity care, free care, or bad debts) varies depending on the location of the hospital, but it is at least 5% of all discharges nationwide (Barton, 2007). This seems like a small percentage, but in 2005 the total amount of uncompensated care that hospitals had to absorb was $25 billion (Weissman, 2005). Urban hospitals and teaching hospitals have a much larger proportion of uncompensated care, as do public hospitals. This is why public hospitals receive tax subsidies, but these are usually not enough to cover the cost of people who receive medical services without paying. Medicare and Medicaid do provide some additional funds to specific hospitals that have a disproportionate burden of uncompensated care, including paying for care for undocumented people, as described in Chapter 5. Additionally, sometimes Congress allocates specific lump sums to assist hospitals with large amounts of such charity care (Barton, 2007).

As might be expected, the problem of providing medical services to uninsured people causes much conversation among hospitals and various policy makers, at all levels of government. Hospitals typically operate on a very narrow revenue margin, so the burden of uncompensated care is very important in determining whether a hospital can maintain its solvency. A particular point of contention is whether for-profit hospitals provide medical care to uninsured people. There are no tax regulations to force them to do so, as there are for nonprofit hospitals. Because of the lack of transparency of information from for-profit organizations, it is difficult for policy analysts to determine the extent of uncompensated care among for-profit hospitals.

## Controlling Hospital Costs

Hospitals—including emergency rooms—are the most expensive site in which medical care services are provided. Because of this, as well as the burden of uncompensated care, hospitals have always been in the forefront of efforts to control costs. There are three major efforts at cost control in the hospital sector: methods of insurance reimbursement, clinical practice protocols, and oversight of resource utilization within the hospital setting. These strategies have been variously enacted over the years, sometimes by the federal government, but in other cases by certifying or accrediting organizations. This is also a very complicated topic, so this section will give one example of each strategy.

The best-known strategy of controlling cost by *changing methods of insurance reimbursement* is Medicare's adoption of a different way of reimbursing hospitals for the cost of inpatient care. Insurance policies typically reimburse hospitals using a fee-for-service method involving a cost-plus retrospective method of reimbursement. This means that reimbursement occurs after the care has been provided (retrospective) and includes overhead costs and a profit margin (cost-plus). Each insurance policy has its own method of reimbursement schedules, with some reimbursing based on a daily cost or a length of stay, whereas others reimburse by specific fees for procedures. Some allow all overhead costs to be included, whereas others allow only some or no overhead costs. Even with restrictions, this method of reimbursing hospitals is financially beneficial to the hospital and creates economic incentives for possibly excess care to be provided because hospitals can earn more money by keeping patients longer and providing more services.

After an extensive study, the Medicare Administration decided to change the way hospitals are paid for medical care provided under the Medicare program. They changed to a prospective system, called Prospective Payment System (PPS), and they based the reimbursements on diagnosis, not length of stay. To create the payment mechanisms for the diagnosis, panels of physicians created what are known as Diagnosis-Related Groups (DRGs). Hospitals predict how many patients and which diagnoses they will treat in a 1-year period. The Medicare Administration gives the hospital this amount, and they must stay within this budgeted amount. The impact of this switch to prospective payment based on DRGs was significant. Occupancy rates, length of stay, and number of inpatient days all declined, significantly reducing hospital revenues (Barton, 2007). Under this system, hospitals do everything they can to stay within the reimbursement parameters of DRGs. This method of cost control clearly demonstrated the importance of economic incentives to clinical practice patterns within the hospital setting.

A second major attempt at controlling costs and improving quality is using *clinical practice protocols*. Improving the quality of medical care delivered in the hospital setting is a major concern of patients and doctors, and also by the JCAHO. The accreditation standards require that a hospital conduct a routine review of the quality of care delivered to hospital patients. One of the several standing committees that directly address this issue is the infection control committee, which assesses and analyzes infections that occur in hospitalized patients.

The third method of cost control is related to managed care techniques, which will be discussed in Chapter 9. *Oversight of resource utilization* is one of these techniques. The major focus of most reviews is whether appropriate and cost-effective technological resources within the hospital were utilized for a patient. The focus of these utilization reviews is to ensure that only medically necessary care is given to a patient. Although this improves quality, it also saves money. A second example of this method of cost control is the presurgical review that every insurance company now requires.

Although many patients view this as a delay in obtaining care, this method of presurgery review reduces unnecessary surgery, the consequence of which is increased costs as well as exposure to unnecessary risks.

## Summary and Policy Issues

This chapter has presented some of the most important characteristics of the hospital sector in the U.S. health care system. Many important issues have been left out, including how to ensure quality of care, especially by reducing medical errors. Another very significant area of concern involves ethical issues that arise when treating very severe illnesses. One additional policy issue will be mentioned here, which is the geographical distribution of hospitals, before we conclude with some thoughts about the changing organizational structures of hospitals.

### *Geographic Distribution of Hospitals*

One of the more perplexing policy issues is how to maintain an adequate number of hospital beds for rural areas. All of the financial pressures described in this chapter are worse for rural hospitals, which tend to be smaller, less well equipped, and sometimes less utilized. It is more difficult for rural hospitals to attract and retain all types of health care providers. The level of equipment for both diagnosis and treatment is also more difficult for rural hospitals to acquire and maintain. Yet, in some rural areas, the hospital is a center for the community and may be one of the only places to receive medical care.

There are many policy efforts aimed at maintaining rural hospitals, ranging from the establishment of telemedicine to increasing payment from Medicare and Medicaid to rural hospitals. Examples of the policy efforts to support rural hospitals include several pieces of federal legislation. For example, the Balanced Budget Act of 1997 reduced Medicare payments to all hospitals as part of a general cost-control measure. Two years later, Congress corrected this by restoring some of the money to rural hospitals, especially those that are the primary source of medical care for a region. These were designated as Critical Access Hospitals, which enabled them to receive cost-plus reimbursement from Medicare, instead of reimbursement by the PPS method described here. In 2003, another piece of legislation (Medicare Reform Act of 2003) further increased reimbursements to rural hospitals, and also included funds to encourage rural hospitals to develop telemedicine with regional teaching hospitals (Kovner and Knickman, 2011).

## Reorganization of Structure of Hospitals

The past 15 years have seen increased reorganization of hospitals, as they respond to changing patterns of reimbursement. As has been noted in this chapter, one important result of this has been the merger of smaller hospitals into larger hospitals. After holding steady for much of the 2000s, the number of mergers has steadily risen. In 2012, there were 105 mergers in comparison to 50 in 2009. Of those 105 mergers, about 65% were among nonprofit hospitals (Creswell and Abelson, 2013).

This has especially impacted small hospitals in rural areas, as described above. Even for slightly larger, nonrural hospitals, the result is a more complex, vertically integrated organizational structure that may not have a close relationship to the communities in which they are located. Many communities feel strongly the loss of their independent SCH, as described in Table 8.1.

There is constant pressure to spend less on hospital care, with policies reducing what public insurance will pay. As a result of this loss of revenue, hospitals have expanded their services to include not only classic inpatient care, but also other sorts of care, including subacute care. This level of care is a mixture of rehabilitation and convalescent services with longer stays, usually about 10 days. The reimbursement for this is generally higher in a hospital setting than in a nursing home, which has encouraged hospitals to set aside beds for this purpose (Sultz and Young, 2014).

At the other end of the spectrum of care, hospitals are also starting to develop more settings for ambulatory care, including urgent care centers to take the pressure off their emergency rooms, as will be described in the next chapter. In some cases, for-profit hospitals and other for-profit corporations are establishing free-standing urgent care centers to establish a presence in neighborhoods, whereas nonprofit hospitals are more likely to retain these functions as part of their physical location.

Although the overall percentage of for-profit hospitals remains small, their impact on the hospital sector is very significant. This ownership structure provides competition for nonprofit hospitals, because they do not have to provide comprehensive services nor do they have to provide as much uncompensated care. The for-profit ownership structure also provides a focal point for the continuing philosophical debate about the nature of medical care services. As will be seen in Chapter 11, health care services can be viewed as a typical market good, ruled by competitive forces, or they may be viewed as a social good that should be distributed outside the influence of the market. The growth and development of the hospital industry is controlled by regulation that reinforces it as a social good, but the slowly increasing for-profit sector is primarily governed by competitive forces. Those who argue that health services are social goods view this as unfair, whereas those who view medical services as market goods view the nonprofit organizational model as not providing enough services to the community to deserve the tax breaks they receive. This philosophical conflict will only grow larger as economic pressures continue to restrict hospital revenues. This same philosophical conflict has become even more significant in the ambulatory care setting.

## Acknowledgments

The following people made significant contributions to the content of this section, including gathering material and references, as well as writing and analysis: Halicia Lyttle, Tiphanie Jones, and Sam Taylor. A special note of thanks goes to Halicia Lyttle for her work on tables and references. This chapter was significantly improved by the comments and suggested revisions of Julie Minnisch and Jonathan Rosenblatt. Julie reformatted Table 8.1 and Jonathan constructed Figure 8.1.

*Chapter 9*

# Ambulatory Care: Functions, Structures, and Services

Every year, nearly three-fourths of the U.S. population sees some sort of health care provider on an ambulatory or outpatient basis, whereas during that same year, about 10% uses a hospital. This chapter begins with a description of the scope and extent of ambulatory services in the United States, including some ambiguous nomenclature. Primary care is one type of ambulatory care, but it is also an important conceptual model for both medical care and cost control. The managed care model is based on primary care, so the concept of managed care is introduced here, with a more specific description of this as a form of insurance given in Chapter 14. This chapter concludes with a discussion of several policy issues, especially regarding the supply of primary care providers.

## Settings for Ambulatory Care Services

Ambulatory and outpatient care are commonly used interchangeably, although these terms have slightly different meanings. Ambulatory care means the patient walks in to the medical care facility, whereas outpatient care technically means any medical care received without spending the night in some facility. Both terms are used interchangeably to include all diagnostic services and treatment of any medical condition that does not require an overnight stay. Both terms are used to describe the function or level of care as well as the facility or physical site of the care. In many situations, the physical location of the medical care is determined by economic incentives as well as clinical considerations. For example, secondary care such as a simple surgical procedure is increasingly performed in an outpatient setting because the reimbursement pattern is more favorable to the hospital. Primary medical care services are always provided in an outpatient setting, although some people inappropriately use emergency rooms (ERs) for this purpose. Tertiary care is always delivered in an inpatient setting. The first section of this chapter describes the range of services that are considered ambulatory care, excluding primary care services (which will be the focus of the next section).

Table 9.1 shows the four major categories of ambulatory services, along with several examples of each category. The majority of outpatient services involve medical, nonsurgical services, which includes both *general* and more *specialized* medical treatment. The physical location of general medical treatment is often the ER of the hospital. ERs see patients who are categorized as needing one of three categories of care, the first of which is emergency care. This represents a serious and often life-threatening situation requiring immediate attention. Examples include accident victims, patients with serious chest or abdominal pain, as well as victims of drug overdose.

The second category of care delivered in the ER is known as urgent care. These health conditions require medical care soon, but not immediately, and

**Table 9.1   Examples of Outpatient Medical Care Services**

| Type of Outpatient Service | Examples |
|---|---|
| 1. General medical services | • Emergency rooms in hospitals<br>• Urgent care centers, which may be in hospitals or free-standing |
| 2. Specialized medical services | • These may be in a hospital or free-standing<br>• Includes a wide range of services, such as cancer treatment (both chemotherapy and radiotherapy), renal dialysis centers, pain management, sports medicine, and various clinics related to organ systems such as dermatology or gastroenterology |
| 3. Diagnostic centers | • Includes all types of diagnostic imaging such as x-rays, magnetic resonance imaging, computed tomography scans, ultrasound, mammography<br>• Also includes screening for cardiac diseases |
| 4. Surgical centers | • May be associated with hospitals or free-standing<br>• Usually specializes in minor surgical procedures or arthroscopic and/or laparoscopic techniques |

are conditions that are not life-threatening. It is often difficult for a patient to decide whether their symptoms represent a true emergency or a condition that could be treated in a less intensive care setting. This is widely acknowledged as mostly something that cannot be helped much.

The use of the ER that is most frustrating is for nonurgent care, which is a routine acute medical problem that is easily resolved. Treating such illness episodes in the ER is a misuse of this expensive resource, and leads to dissatisfaction for both patients and physicians. Patients without health insurance and without access to primary care are most likely to use the ER for nonurgent problems. In order to solve this problem, some hospitals have established urgent care centers, so nonurgent cases can be triaged to this less intensive site for outpatient care. Urgent care centers are also frequently located as independent structures, owned and operated by large for-profit companies.

Another significant category of outpatient care services is more specialized, as shown in Table 9.1. Hospitals frequently organize and schedule specialty clinics, structured around a particular organ system (e.g., dermatology or gastroenterology) or a particular medical problem such as wound care or pain management. These provide secondary medical care services and are convenient for the hospital in terms of staffing.

Specialized medical care services are also offered by free-standing clinics, including cancer treatment clinics that utilize both chemotherapy and radiotherapy. These are often independent for-profit clinics. Another example of free-standing specialized outpatient services clinics are renal dialysis centers, which are also usually run by a for-profit company.

Diagnostic services include imaging technology of various sorts, such as magnetic resonance imaging, but also more accessible services such as screening for cardiovascular diseases. Diagnostic centers are increasingly free-standing and owned by a for-profit company or a group of physicians (Inglehart, 2006).

The last category of outpatient care shown on Table 9.1 involves same-day surgical procedures. These may be owned and operated by the hospital, but many are owned and operated by a for-profit company, or by a group of physicians. Same-day surgeries have dramatically increased so they now account for almost 70% of all surgeries performed (Jackson, 2002). The number of surgeries performed on an inpatient basis in community hospitals has shown a steady decrease for many years. For example, in 1980 only 16% of all surgeries performed in community hospitals were on an outpatient basis, but by 2004 nearly 65% of all surgeries performed in community hospitals were done in an outpatient setting (Shi and Singh, 2014). This shift in location for simple surgical procedures has been caused by technological innovations and changing economic incentives. Technological advances in arthroscopic and laparoscopic techniques have made many surgeries less risky. However, hospital cost control attempts described in Chapter 8 have also had a significant impact on this shift. Some of these cost-control efforts lowered rates of reimbursement for inpatient procedures, but not for outpatient services. Hospitals have been able to make up for lost revenues by switching routine, lower-risk surgeries to same-day procedures. Space constraints in hospitals often limit the volume of procedures, so physicians developed free-standing ambulatory surgical centers. Today, nearly all of the free-standing ambulatory surgical centers are owned by groups of physicians (AAASC, 2012).

All four categories of outpatient services shown in Table 9.1 were initially developed and provided by hospitals, mainly to provide alternative sources of revenue, as noted above. However, for-profit companies and investor groups of physicians also began developing these resources independent from the restraints of a hospital bureaucracy. Today, the vast majority of all free-standing outpatient medical treatment centers, including all four categories shown in Table 9.1, are for-profit, either owned and operated by a large corporation or by a group of physician investors. For example, 90% of the free-standing ambulatory surgical centers are owned by physician investor groups. A large majority of free-standing diagnostic imaging centers are also owned by physician investor groups, although the imaging technicians may also be part of ownership (Strope et al., 2009). Almost 75% of the renal dialysis centers are for-profit and owned by groups of physician investors (Schlesinger et al., 1989). About 50% of free-standing urgent care centers are owned by large corporations (Spotlight, 2014).

Each of the free-standing service sites described in this section must be licensed by the state in which they practice. Additionally, each must be certified if they wish to be reimbursed by Medicare or Medicaid. Each must also be professionally accredited by the Joint Commission on Accreditation of Health Care Organizations, which enlarged its professional scope to include such free-standing outpatient medical care sites.

These free-standing outpatient centers are in direct competition with hospitals, which offer many of the same services. Economic theory predicts that increased competition results in lower costs, but as Chapter 11 demonstrates, unlike other sectors of the U.S. economy, competition does not decrease costs in the health care field.

A final issue is how patients are referred to these for-profit settings for outpatient care. Traditionally, it was viewed as unethical for a physician to refer his/her own patients to any for-profit center in which they have a substantial ownership share (Kouri et al., 2002). However, as the for-profit presence has increased in the medical care sector, this perspective is diminishing.

# What Is Primary Care?

Primary care services are a subset of outpatient care services, but the term primary care also describes a theoretical framework for providing all medical services needed by an individual. As noted in Chapter 6, primary care services are considered part of both medical care and public health. Primary care services are the cornerstone of all health care delivery systems.

The concept of primary care has been addressed by both the Institute of Medicine (IOM) and the World Health Organization (WHO). In 1978, the WHO identified primary care as essential medical care (WHO, 1978). This designation was linked to their famous Alma-Ata Conference on Primary Care, which identified the importance of Community-Oriented Primary Care (COPC). This approach recognizes community-oriented health promotion activities as an important part of the primary care system (Minkler, 1992). A second important part of the COPC model stresses access. Medical professionals, as described in Chapter 7, provide primary care, but in less affluent countries community-based lay practitioners and other culturally based healing approaches are very important parts of the primary care system.

Many countries with fewer resources orient their entire health care systems around primary care, and this strategy seems to work, as countries whose health systems are so oriented seem to have better health status for less money (Starfield, 1994; Shi and Starfield, 2000, 2001). Even within the United States, those states with more primary care physicians per population have better health outcomes, as shown in Figure 3.4.

In 1996, the IOM defined primary care as "the provision of integrated, accessible care services by clinicians who are accountable for addressing a large majority of the personal health care needs, developing a sustained partnership with patients, and practicing in the context of family and community" (IOM, 1996). It is this definition that is primarily used in the U.S. medical care system.

## *Functions of Primary Care*

Figure 9.1 shows seven important functions of primary care, four of which are essentials of patient care. The patient care functions include providing all three

| Patient care | System management |
|---|---|
| • Preventive care services | • Point of first contact for patient |
| • Diagnosis | • Gatekeeper |
| • Treatment of acute illness | • Coordination of needed services |
| • Management of chronic illness | |

**Figure 9.1   Functions of primary care.**

levels of prevention mentioned in Chapter 1. Diagnosing and treating acute illness and diagnosing and managing chronic illness are also essential functions of patient care. Treatment and diagnosis sometimes involve other levels of care (Chapter 6), and other more specialized health care providers. This involves coordinating care for each patient, one of the systems management responsibilities.

This coordination role is an essential hallmark of good primary care. It is not enough to simply refer a patient; rather, the patient needs to come back to the primary care provider for follow-up and continued monitoring. Ideally, the primary care provider acts as the central hub for patients with complicated illnesses. This includes managing all communications between physicians and ensuring the patient is receiving continuous, longitudinal care. In an ideal health system anchored in the primary care model, all secondary and even tertiary medical care is integrated with primary care through the primary care provider.

Acting as the point of first contact and the gatekeeper are interrelated systems management functions (Figure 9.1). Having one health provider act as the point of first contact increases ease of access. The idea of first point of contact has always been popular, because this is the family doctor, who knows each patient well. Less popular is the related function of the primary care provider acting as the gatekeeper to the rest of the health care system. Patients do not visit specialists, or get admitted to a hospital, without first seeing a primary care provider. Some of the most efficient health care systems in the world strongly emphasize this gatekeeper role, as discussed in Chapter 22. Some people feel this is a waste of resources because it requires an additional doctor when they "know" they need some sort of more specialized care. The gatekeeper function is an essential part of the system management responsibilities and saves money, because it protects patients from unnecessary procedures and often duplicated expensive medical examinations.

The primary care model provides optimal medical care, with each patient having one significant contact for all health problems, and more specialized care being coordinated by the primary care provider. This creates continuity of care, reduces the risk of too much medical care, and uses medical specialists appropriately for more narrowly defined medical problems. The purpose of the more comprehensive specialty training of the primary care provider is to enable them to recognize the health of the whole person rather than a specific symptom.

There are two distinct barriers to fully implementing this model in the U.S. health care system. The first relates to health care financing. Controlling the use of multiple resources in caring for complex medical problems is difficult in the competitive multipayer financing method used in the United States, as will be described in Chapter 15. Second, primary care-based health care systems require a substantial proportion of the physician work-force be involved in primary care. As noted in Chapter 7, only about 30% of U.S. physicians are employed in primary care.

In the United States, the primary care model is best implemented in a managed care model, where there is better control over use of resources. The managed care model is used in other countries with more universal and less targeted health care systems (Chapter 22). This is why a description of the concept of managed care is included as part of this chapter.

## *Settings for Primary Care Services*

Table 9.2 shows six different sites where primary care services can be obtained. About 80% of primary care services are obtained in some type of formal office practice (Shi and Singh, 2014), which may be a solo or group practice, including a managed care practice.

Solo practice is one physician providing all needed care for one group of patients. This is a nostalgic and romanticized idea of the family doctor, who was always available to his/her patients, and who knew them all well. This was the predominant practice model in the United States for many years, one that was highly supported by the American Medical Association (AMA), because it was viewed as the practice structure that provided the maximum professional autonomy of the physician. However, there are many disad-vantages for the physician, primarily in terms of personal lifestyles. Also, as insurance increased, the paperwork and business demands of a medical practice are more time-consuming.

The obvious solution was for physicians to establish group practices, which are defined as three or more physicians in one practice setting. This is the predominant model of today, with over three-quarters of all physicians involved in this structure (Hing and Burt, 2007). Group practices may be the same specialty or different ones. They may be a truly collaborative prac-tice with shared patient responsibilities or more independent practitioners

**Table 9.2   Settings and Ownerships for Primary Care Services**

| Setting for Primary Care Services | Ownership |
|---|---|
| Private, office-based<br>  Solo<br>  Group practice | Usually owned by the individual physicians involved in the practice. Organized as a small for-profit business. |
| Managed care (health maintenance organization) | Always a group practice of diverse specialties. May be nonprofit if associated with a hospital. Most for-profit health maintenance organizations (HMOs) are owned by large corporations. |
| Retail clinics | For-profit; mostly owned by large health care corporations and placed in stores that have a pharmacy. |
| Community health centers | Public; based on a federal initiative to increase access of primary care services to underserved communities. |
| Voluntary organizations<br>  Planned Parenthood<br>  Free clinics | Nonprofit; supported and run by nonprofit organizations. |
| Public health clinics | Public; supported, staffed, and run by state public health departments, using tax funds of the state. |

sharing an office space. The term private practice is used to refer to both solo and group practice. This term implies that the practice is independent rather than being part of a larger corporate structure.

A special type of group practice is a health maintenance organization (HMO), which is a type of managed care practice. An HMO is a group practice that provides all levels of care from primary care to tertiary care, and is an example of a more structured practice setting. Managed care is a very important topic that relates to the provision of medical services, not just primary care, but all necessary medical and health services. It is an important determinant of how physicians are paid for their work. It is also a very important insurance model and a mechanism of cost control because of how the economic incentives are designed. Because of its relationship to many topics, it will be discussed in several places in this book, the first of which is to contrast it to private practice here in this chapter. A description of the concept of managed care will be described in the next section of this chapter. The role of managed care and the HMO in terms of insurance will be more fully explained in Chapter 14.

One of the newer and rapidly expanding sites for primary care services are retail clinics. These are primary care clinics that focus more on the patient care functions than on the system management functions shown in Figure 9.1. The clinics are primarily set in retail stores that also have pharmacies, such as Walgreens and CVS, although they have now expanded into Walmart and Target stores. These originated in 2000 in Minnesota, with the first ones located in grocery stores (Sultz and Young, 2014). As with other for-profit models of medical care services, these grew first in the southern and western states. The names of these clinics reveal their objectives. For example, one of the earliest and still prominent chains is "MinuteClinic," whose slogan is "You're sick, We're Quick" (Sultz and Young, 2014). This chain has grown quickly, and has now spread into most states, including New England, which is the part of the country most resistant to for-profit medical care. There are 12 different corporations that own various clinics. States have to approve the establishment of these for-profit clinics, and each clinic has to be accredited and licensed.

Response to these clinics is varied, both for patients and for physicians. Many patients like the convenience of them, especially for routine acute illnesses. No appointment is needed and the clinics are open as long as the store is open. Because the clinics are located in retail stores with pharmacies, obtaining prescribed drugs is easy. These clinics are often cheaper than any other types of primary care, primarily because of low overhead and limited services, as well as the fact that care is provided by mid-level providers, not physicians. Many people like the idea of being able to get care quickly without an appointment. For those without a primary care doctor, this is preferable to an ER. Most insurance companies reimburse care delivered in these clinics and some insurance companies openly encourage utilization by waiving the copayment for care received in a retail clinic (Kowalczyk, 2014).

Response from the medical community is more mixed. One limitation is the inability to adequately follow up subsequent care. Although electronic medical records are increasingly being used, communication between different companies and software packages has not been smooth. Stores in which these clinics are located have increased prescription drug sales, which has caused the AMA to suggest investigating these companies for possible conflict of interest issues (Sultz and Young, 2014).

The care offered in these clinics does meet the conceptual framework of the primary care model, as shown in Figure 9.1, especially with respect to the management of chronic diseases, which frequently involves more system management responsibilities. One corporation (Quadmed) is now working with Walmart to establish Primary Care Centers, which focus on coordination of care for patients with chronic diseases. Six clinics have been established in South Carolina and Texas, with others planned (Abrams, 2014). One of the challenges is coordinating care with hospital services, because the mid-level providers that staff these clinics cannot admit patients to a hospital.

At the other end of the spectrum of primary care services are Community Health Centers (CHCs). These are specific federally funded outpatient clinics that provide health and medical services to medically underserved populations. They focus on provision of primary care services and prevention services. These clinics arose from Johnson's War on Poverty, which passed the Office of Economic Development Act of 1964. This topic will be described in Chapters 17 and 20. CHCs are funded directly by federal grants but also receive reimbursement from Medicaid for care provided (Chapter 19). They are located in federally designated medically underserved areas, which are geographic regions of the country identified as lacking in medical resources and which also have low population health status indicators such as those discussed in Chapter 3. They may be either rural areas or urban areas, but are always less affluent communities, and often include areas with a large proportion of minorities (McAlearney, 2002). They are technically nonprofit organizations, but in Table 9.2 they are noted as being public because of the federal subsidies that completely fund them.

CHCs are primarily staffed by teams of primary care physicians as well as mid-level providers. They also include dental care, and often have education services as well as community outreach workers (Shi et al., 2007; Sultz and Young, 2014). They are the safety net of primary care services, because most of the patients are uninsured.

Another setting for primary care services for those with no insurance are several voluntary sites, which include clinics established and funded by nonprofit organizations. A prominent example are the clinics run by Planned Parenthood Federation, which provide not only contraceptive services but also basic primary care with an emphasis on reproductive health and more general preventive services. Also included in this category are settings termed free clinics. These are exactly what the name implies: a place where people with no insurance can receive primary care and preventive services free of charge. These clinics are frequently staffed by volunteers, and are funded by churches or nonprofit organizations, or sometimes hospitals (Felt-Lisk et al., 2002). There are not many of these in the United States, but the number seems to be growing, and they represent another part of the safety net for primary care.

The final setting for primary care services shown in Table 9.2 are public health clinics. These are clinics funded and operated by state or local public health departments. They are categorical, or what is being termed "targeted" in this book. This means they are designed to provide preventive services to a particular group, such as low income women, homeless people, or incarcerated individuals (prison clinics). This is another part of the safety net for primary care services.

## *Utilization of Primary Care Services*

Having access to primary care has an important impact on the health of a community, but it is also a cost savings technique. Providing primary care, including preventive health services, reduces the total cost of more expensive medical care, at least on a population basis. This requires sufficient primary care availability and also financial access. Monitoring primary care utilization is one way to determine how accessible these important basic services are. For example, the average number of physician visits for primary care per year made by each person is about four (DHHS, 2005a). Women tend to visit physicians more often than men; older people have more primary care visits than younger people; and African-Americans of all ages have fewer visits, which is widely interpreted as evidence of a lack of access (Chapter 21).

Utilization of primary care services is highly related to financial access, as demonstrated repeatedly after the passage of programs to increase financial access. For example, within 2 years of the passage of Medicaid, the number of ambulatory care visits increased dramatically. The trend of increased utilization associated with both Medicaid and Medicare (Chapters 18 and 19) has remained steady (Kovner and Knickman, 2011).

# Managed Care Concepts

Managed care has profoundly changed both the financing and the delivery of all medical care services, including primary care, but precisely defining it is a challenge. The most accurate quote about managed care is this:

"Managed care is used so promiscuously as to have no meaning at all" (Mechanic, 1994). It is both a delivery system that integrates all levels of care and a financing or insurance system. At the core of the managed care model is the idealized concept of primary care described in this chapter, although managed care includes all levels of care needed by the patient, including secondary and tertiary services.

Managed care is not about managing medical care, but rather managing costs of medical care. It accomplishes this in three specific ways. First and very importantly, the organization that provides or delivers care and the organization that finances care is the same. This integration of delivery and financing creates economic incentives to provide care more efficiently, although it can also create incentives for restricting care. Second, reimbursement of care is moved from fee-for-service to prepaid, which also encourages more cost-efficient medical care. Finally, medical care is arranged around the concept of primary care, with special emphasis on preventive care and the systems management functions of the primary care provider shown in Figure 9.1.

By definition, managed care organizations are a type of group practice that includes all specialists that might be needed to care for patients in a network of providers. The network of providers may be all in the same physical location, or the relationship might be through contracts and subcontracts with a financing organization, usually an insurance company. All physicians in the network agree to similar reimbursements, and larger physician networks create enough volume to allow for lower individual reimbursement levels.

One of the controversial aspects of early managed care organizations was the method of setting physician reimbursements. Traditional insurance allowed the physician and the hospital to charge a separate price for each and every service delivered to a patient. The more medical care received by a patient, the more money received by the physician and/or the hospital. This fee-for-service system encouraged medical care treatment and procedures, some of which may be unnecessary. HMOs developed a method of payment for patients that was based on predicted costs of care, rather than prices per services. This prepayment method meant that the insurance premium is paid for all needed services, without many of the other methods of cost sharing used in traditional insurance policies, which will be described in Chapters 13 and 14. Doctors were also paid differently, usually by salary for all care delivered to patients as opposed to fees for each service. Before the legislation that actually created HMOs, a few group practices experimented with these alternative payment methods. The AMA formally opposed these, but was found guilty of violating the Sherman Antitrust Act (Shi and Singh, 2014). Some of the early group practices that experimented with alternatives to fee-for-service reimbursement include Kaiser-Permanente in California, the Group Health Cooperative of Puget Sound in Washington, the Health Insurance Plan of Greater New York, and the Group Health Plan of Minneapolis. These organizations also experimented with integrating the clinical and financial aspects of medical care (Shi and Singh, 2014).

Increased acceptance of this model and concern about steadily increasing costs in the health care sector led to the 1973 legislation by Nixon formally establishing HMOs. Inherent in this Act is the belief that prepaid medical care placed the economic incentives in the right place for just the right amount of medical care; and that if there were an increased number of HMOs, there would be increased competition and thus costs would drop (Shi and Singh, 2014).

The HMO model emphasizes the system management part of the functions of primary care shown in Figure 9.1. There is variation today across many different managed care organizations, which will be described in Chapter 14. The core of the original managed care concept is the primary care physician: this health provider is the point of first contact and the gatekeeper to the rest of the network of health care providers and services. A patient could see other specialists only if the primary care physician did a formal referral, with the referral to an approved network of other physicians, each of whom had agreed to the reimbursement structure of the HMO. In this function, the HMO also acted as the insurance company. The HMO required utilization review of all care referred to specialists, which was meant to control unnecessary care and to better coordinate services. This function of utilization review is a specific way to reduce utilization of more expensive health services, such as surgery.

The original HMO concept rested on the idea that encouraging utilization of primary care, especially preventive services, would reduce overall costs. This was done by reducing the cost of preventive services to patients, as described in Chapters 11 and 13. However, it was also accomplished by putting some controls on the patient care functions of primary care shown in Figure 9.1. For example, primary care physicians were encouraged to emphasize preventive care, often through salary incentives. Also, clinical protocols for primary care were introduced in an effort to standardize the medical care process, thus making costs more predictable. These clinical cost controls were only possible because the organization that provided the medical care was also the organization that paid for the medical care. More details about these methods of cost control will be given in Chapter 14.

The HMO Act of 1973 included federal subsidies to the early HMOs so the premiums for these plans were lower than the traditional, fee-for-service indemnity plans offered at the time. The growth in HMOs was slow but steady, and today most people have health insurance plans that can be characterized as managed care, although it is worth remembering what Mechanic said, because there is wide variation among current managed care plans. Although all HMOs are examples of managed care organizations, not all managed care organizations are HMOs, as will be seen in Chapter 14. All managed care organizations maintain the primary care model at the core, especially the reliance on the primary care specialist to provide ample primary and preventive care services, and to act as the gatekeeper to more expensive services.

## Summary and Policy Issues

Primary care is an important conceptual model utilized around the world by health care systems to ensure that everybody receives basic and essential medical care services. Sometimes overlooked is the fact that population-based utilization of primary care services is also the major way in which other developed countries control the costs of their health care systems.

The United States comes closest to the concept of a primary care model in a managed care setting, which magnifies the current shortage of primary care physicians. HMOs work best to control costs with enough primary care physicians to serve as gatekeepers to other services. In HMOs with a strong primary care function, there is a reduced need for secondary medical and surgical specialties (Weiner, 2004). As will be seen in Chapter 17, the Affordable Care Act (ACA) requires more primary care providers and also encourages the cost control strategies of the managed care model.

Even though many policy initiatives have encouraged the implementation of the managed care model, there is no universal support for this model among either physicians or consumers. An issue that repeatedly arises is whether HMOs manage care too much, meaning that decisions about medical care services are made based on financial concerns instead of clinical ones. Finances and clinical decision have always been very closely intertwined, but in the managed care setting, this relationship is magnified. However controversial, it must be acknowledged that other countries have health care systems that are largely based on the primary care model and the managed care model, where the delivery and financing of services is integrated and medical decisions are reviewed. Chapter 22 will describe these.

Complicating cost control efforts in the United States is the increasing influence of the for-profit sector in the U.S. health care system. This is a significant shift in values for the U.S. health care system, since the 1910 Flexner Report clearly identified the need for all hospitals and medical schools to have a nonprofit structure to increase quality of instruction and care. In 1973, the HMO legislation required federally designated HMOs to maintain a nonprofit organizational structure (Sultz and Young, 2014). Over the past 20 years, there has been a slow but definite shift toward more for-profit organizations in all levels of care, including HMOs. An unanticipated consequence of the ACA is the increase in independent, for-profit centers for ambulatory care—for both primary and secondary care. The ACA has created a group of people with health insurance in an environment where there are not enough primary care physicians, and a growing market for small, for-profit urgent care centers that are being built across the country. This will undoubtedly increase access for routine medical care, but not in the primary care-centered model that is designed to be the backbone of the medical care system, and allows for better cost control.

## Acknowledgments

I thank Nolis Espinal, who contributed source material for the ownership status of outpatient care services, and Chandler Kaplan, who contributed source material on community health centers. Reema Chapatwala, Jillisia James, Christopher Lukasik, and Renee Williams-Sinclair significantly improved this chapter with their careful review and comments. They also added references and source material. Jessi Duston constructed Figure 9.1.

*Chapter 10*

# Other Components of the Medical Care System

The two biggest topics in this chapter are two large and arguably independent subsystems of the health care system. The mental health care system and the long-term care system involve all eight levels of care, both inpatient and outpatient sites of care, and many of the health professionals already described. Two smaller topics involve two additional subsystems, both of which serve many people—dental care and vision care. One large system that is not included here is the Veterans Administration (VA), which is also an independent subsystem. However, it serves as a major example of a targeted system, so it will be discussed in Chapter 20.

## Mental Health Care System

Physical health is viewed by both patients and physicians as being more or less a continuum with the health care system structured to provide services at various stages of health. There are not equal resources devoted to each level of care as discussed in Chapter 6, and there is often poor communication between the various professionals involved in each level. In the mental health care system, there is no such continuum of levels of care, even conceptually. The organization of the mental health—or behavioral health—system is worse than fragmented: it is a set of independent, separately functioning components, each of which mostly deals with mental illness as an episodic illness. The most recent federal commission examining mental health services concluded that the mental health system of the United States is in "shambles" (White House, 2002).

Diagnosing and even defining mental illness is even more challenging than categorizing physical illnesses. A common definition of mental illness is a psychiatric disorder (Shi and Singh, 2014), but a more general definition is used by the National Alliance on Mental Illness (NAMI), which defines mental illness as "a medical condition that disrupts a person's thinking, feeling, mood, ability to relate to others, and daily functioning" (NAMI, 2014). Services to deal with mental health issues fall under the medical care sector, and—as will be shown here—are increasingly part of the primary care provider's responsibility, as opposed to a more specifically trained mental health specialist.

The history of mental health services in the United States is long, complicated, and not very pretty, but it is revealing in terms of understanding the complexity of treating mental illness.

## History of Mental Health Services

Mentally ill patients were usually cared for in early hospitals or almshouses, as described in Chapter 9. At this time, there were two schools of thought about caring for the mentally ill. The first viewed mental illness as not treatable, so the goal was to separate the person from the rest of society. Many mentally ill people were in jails, and there still is an unfortunate overlap between mental illness and the criminal justice system. Besides jails, there were also specific hospitals for the mentally ill, often called lunatic asylums. These institutions were all tax-supported, at first by local towns, then by states. By the early 1900s, every state had at least one state-funded insane asylum where the mentally ill were housed, often for their whole lives. Dorothea Dix visited many of the mentally ill in these publicly funded institutions, and fought for many years for better treatment. Despite Dix's activism, the goal of these institutions remained custodial, and living conditions, although somewhat improved, remained much less than what she advocated (Glied and Frank, 2009; Levin et al., 2010).

The second school of thought arose in Europe, based on the work of a French psychologist who viewed the mentally ill as treatable. This method of treatment also relied on hospitalization, but also included some sort of treatment. These small private hospitals provided a much better living experience, and often included work, at least as far as the patients were able. Naturally, these institutions cost money, and only the relatively affluent could afford them (Moniz and Gorin, 2007; Levin et al., 2010).

By the early 1950s, psychiatric care still remained mostly inpatient-based and custodial, although psychoactive drugs, electroshock therapy, and other psychosurgical techniques such as lobotomies were increasingly used (Levin et al., 2010; Sultz and Young, 2014). Mental health activists continued to highlight the poor living conditions and the lack of effective treatments, causing a 1955 federal commission to study the quality of care of state institutions (Levin et al., 2010). Ten years later, the first legislative act dedicated to putting resources specifically into the mental health system was enacted. These resources came from Medicaid and Medicare programs (described in Chapters 18 and 19), as well as special funds made available under the Social Security system. The federal commission also recommended that noninstitutional care settings be developed (Sultz and Young, 2014).

These resources, along with the changing ideas about treating mental illness, had a profound effect on the types of treatment available. In about 20 years, the entire structure of mental health services went from state-operated large institutions to a group of independent small, community-based treatment facilities, some of which were still publicly supported, but many of which were privately funded. In 1955, almost 80% of patients with mental health illness were treated in an inpatient setting. By 1990, only 21% were treated in an inpatient setting (Sultz and Young, 2014). The number of psychoactive drugs available for treatment of both major and less severe mental illness also greatly increased, and the length of hospitalization significantly decreased.

This movement is termed deinstitutionalization, but that is not quite accurate. Many patients were moved from the large state mental institutions to community-based settings. Not all patients could be moved into less restrictive care settings, so they were transferred into other health care institutions, mostly to nursing homes. For example, between 1960 and 1970, the number of people in nursing homes almost doubled, mostly paid for by Medicaid (Levin et al., 2010). Costs of care increased as patients cycled between community-based care settings and institutional settings. There was little regulation on the community-based settings, so there was a wide variation in the quality of services available. There was also an increase in the homeless, as well as increases in the number of people in jails (Thornicroft and Tansella, 2009).

The prevailing concept in the mental health field remains that the best treatment takes place in the least restrictive setting. Although there is wide agreement with this, it is also acknowledged that this concept is not without disadvantages. For example, people with mental health issues must take a strong consumer role in order to find an appropriate place to receive services. As will be seen in the next section, there are many treatment settings, most of which are small, all of which are independent, and many of which are for-profit. Although health insurance covers mental health services, there are many limitations. Many worry that the current system is too decentralized and fragmented so that only those with strong family advocates and adequate wealth can obtain the type of care needed (Levin et al., 2010). As with earlier times in history, activists continue to draw attention to the needs of the mentally ill. Today, this comes mostly in the form of professional groups including the NAMI, which continues to propose policy initiatives that they believe improve the availability of treatment, especially for serious mental illness.

## Need for Mental Health Services

About 26% of the U.S. population over the age of 18 (about 58 million people) has some sort of diagnosable mental disorder that requires treatment (Kessler et al., 2005; NIMH, 2013). This includes disorders ranging from mild and situational anxiety and/or depression to severe, disabling psychotic diagnoses including schizophrenia. The most common diagnoses are phobias, substance abuse (both alcohol and drugs), and affective disorders such as anxiety and depression. More severe mental illness is diagnosed less often. For example, schizophrenia is diagnosed in about only 1% of the U.S. population over the age of 18; only about 6% of the total population has some mental health condition that is considered to be severe and/or chronic, requiring continuing care for more than 12 months (Kessler et al., 2005; NIMH, 2013).

Mental health disorders are the leading cause of disability, exceeding all other chronic illnesses and are responsible for more than $300 billion in expenditures each year, including the cost of treatment, as well as disability payments, and lost earnings (Kessler et al., 2005). Mental illness is also a known risk factor for many chronic illnesses, including cardiovascular disease and cancer (NIMH, 2013). More women than men seek care for mental health disorders; poverty is also related to a higher prevalence of mental health issues, and diagnosable mental health disorders seem to be more prevalent in the age group 45–54 years (NIMH, 2013).

Not all who need treatment necessarily receive what is needed. For example, in 2011, 18% of the U.S. population received a psychiatric diagnosis, and an additional 17% met the criteria for substance abuse, with no underlying mental illness. Of the approximately 45 million people diagnosed with a psychiatric disorder, only 38% received treatment. Of those who were treated, 12% were treated by a psychiatrist, implying they received some medication. Other sources of treatment included 16% being treated by a mental health specialist who could not prescribe medication; 23% were treated by a primary care provider, 8% were treated by someone in the human services system, and about 7% were treated by an alternative or complementary care provider (Wang et al., 2005). In this study, only 60% of those with a diagnosis of a severe mental illness received any treatment at all (SAMHSA, 2014).

Other studies have focused on untreated mental illness among veterans returning from Iraq and Afghanistan. Most estimates indicate that more than half have some type of mental health illness, and only half of them seek treatment, either within the VA or outside the VA (Hoge et al., 2004; Vogt, 2011). A substantial category of untreated mental illness occurs in substance abuse, which is frequently a comorbidity with a psychiatric diagnosis. The presence of substance abuse in those with some psychiatric or behavioral diagnosis ranges from 23% to 80%, depending on the diagnosis (SAMHSA, 2014).

All of these trends combine to what is identified as a large and growing unmet need for mental health services.

## *Organization of Mental Health Services*

Mental health services are provided in a variety of ways. Sultz and Young (2014) describe four components of services. These components are shown in Figure 10.1.

The first component is the only one that can be clearly characterized as being specifically focused on the diagnosis and treatment of mental health problems. As can be seen in Figure 10.1, this includes both inpatient and outpatient care. Inpatient settings are reserved for those with a diagnosis of a severe mental illness, but nearly all inpatient treatment beds are for short-term use. The only long-term residential care available is in nursing homes, and this is usually for very disabled adults. About 12% of all inpatient beds are in a defined psychiatric hospital, with half of those being in a public facility supported by either a state or a county (Barton, 2007). About one-third of inpatient treatment occurs in general, nonprofit community hospitals in a unit specializing in psychiatric care. Besides community hospitals, there are some specialized psychiatric hospitals, some of which are contained

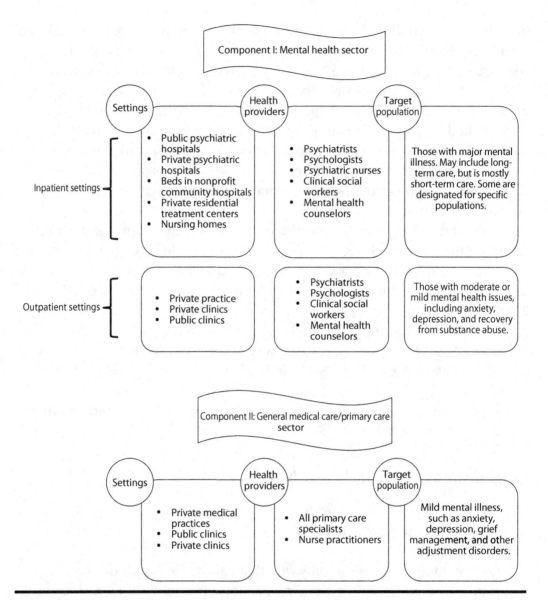

**Figure 10.1 Organization of mental health services.**

*(Continued)*

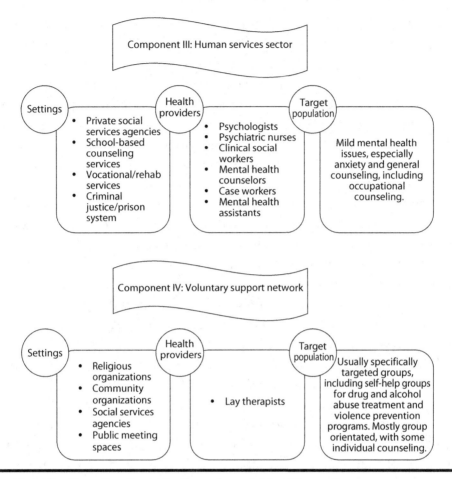

**Figure 10.1 (Continued)   Organization of mental health services.**

in the VA system, which will be described in Chapter 20. The rest of the inpatient treatment occurs in residential treatment centers. These tend to be smaller than hospitals; many are specialized and are increasingly for-profit.

The majority of treatment for mental health problems occurs in an outpatient setting. As can be seen in Figure 10.1, there is a wide range of possible ambulatory settings for diagnosis and treatment of mental health disorders. This treatment setting is generally used for those with moderate to mild mental health problems. The type of care a patient receives is determined by several factors such as insurance coverage and willingness to be treated for a mental health illness. The providers all have specific training in treating mental health problems.

The second component of the mental health care system involves providers who do not necessarily have specialized training in mental health care.

Many people choose to seek care for mental health issues from their primary care provider. Some primary care providers will provide treatment in the form of medication; some will refer more serious symptoms to a mental health specialist, whereas others refer the patient to a source of care outside the medical system. Because of the increasing number of people turning to their primary care providers, some conflict has arisen between primary care providers and more specifically trained mental health specialists about appropriate referring guidelines (Russell, 2010).

An important resource for diagnosing and treating mental health illness lies outside the medical sector, although it does involve specifically trained mental health professionals. Figure 10.1 shows this third component as the human services sector. This includes mental health services delivered in formal organizational settings, such as schools, vocational centers, and prisons. The mental health providers are specifically trained, but are frequently mid- and lower-level mental health professionals working under psychiatrists or psychologists, who will be described in the next section.

Figure 10.1 includes a fourth component, one that is usually not included when describing mental health services. All of the treatment in this component is by individuals who are *lay therapists*. Some of these have some limited training in counseling such as religious leaders of congregations. Others have no specific training, but help others through their own personal experiences, usually in some sort of group setting. Many people receive treatment through one of these self-help groups, especially for various addictions, including alcohol, drugs, and overeating.

## Mental Health Care Providers

This section describes the various health professionals who have specific training in mental health treatment. Even though primary care specialists are increasingly diagnosing and treating mental health disorders, they are not usually included when estimating the mental health care workforce. This is ironic because they are able to prescribe psychiatric drugs, when many of the more specifically trained mental health professionals described in this section cannot.

The only mental health professionals who can actually prescribe psychiatric drugs are those trained in psychiatry (which is a medical specialty), medicine itself (which does include primary care specialists), or psychiatric nurses. Table 10.1 shows seven different types of mental health providers. This section will describe some of the most important characteristics of

**Table 10.1 Mental Health Care Providers**

| Provider | Education/Training | Licensure/ Certification | Prescribe Medication | Average Income ($)[a] | Percentage of Mental Health Workforce[b] |
|---|---|---|---|---|---|
| Psychiatrist | MD or DO Residency | Yes/Yes | Yes | 185,000 | 6% |
| Clinical psychologist | PhD or PsyD | Yes/Yes | No | 89,000 | 15% |
| Clinical social worker | Master's degree | Yes/Yes | No | 45,000 | 40% |
| Psychiatric nurses | RN with specialized training | Yes/Yes | Yes | 88,000 | 10% |
| Mental health counselors | Master's degree | Yes/Yes | No | 42,000 | 15% |
| Caseworkers/mental health assistants | Bachelor's degree | No/No | No | 25,000 | 14% |
| Lay therapists • Alt. care • Religious • Self-help | Varies: some specific training; some theological counseling; personal experience | No/No | No | NA | NA |

[a] Data on average income is from Bureau of Labor Statistics.
[b] Percentages based on estimates from Bureau of Labor Statistics, by major responsibilities.

each. There is considerable confusion between the first two: psychiatrists and psychologists, so they will be described in the most detail.

## Psychiatrists

Psychiatrists are physicians who hold either a Doctor of Medicine (MD) or a Doctor of Osteopathy (DO) degree. They are usually categorized as one of the primary care specialties, but their focus is exclusively on diagnosing, treating, and, increasingly, managing psychiatric medications. Psychiatrists are the highest paid of all the mental health professionals, but they represent only about 6% of the total mental health workforce. About half of all psychiatrists work in a private practice setting (APA, 2014).

As shown in Table 10.1, psychiatrists are one of only two mental health professionals that can prescribe medications. The traditional method of therapy for mental illness has always been talk or behavior therapy, where a therapist spends 50–60 minutes per session with a patient. The increasing use of psychiatric medications has changed the nature of psychiatric practice. The practice pattern of most psychiatrists has shifted to a more common primary care model of 15-minute visits, with the major purpose being the prescribing and monitoring of several psychiatric medications (Antonuccio et al., 2003; Harris, 2011). If a patient wants—or needs—both talk therapy and medication, it now usually involves two different mental health professionals, one of which is a psychologist.

## Psychologists

Psychologists have one of two doctoral level degrees: either a PhD, or a Doctor of Psychology (PsyD), which is a clinical, professional degree. Psychologists are nationally certified and licensed at the state level. There are 13 designated board-certified specialties (APA, 2013). Psychologists are specifically trained in methods of understanding behavior, how behavior interacts with brain function as well as the environment, and various models of behavior therapy. Only two states permit psychologists to prescribe medications (APA, 2013).

Psychologists primarily care for patients in outpatient settings and work with psychiatrists when patients are hospitalized. They also work in several institutional settings, where they do individual counseling as well as administer and analyze diagnostic psychological tests. The increased use of psychotropic medications has limited the scope of practice of psychologists and has also shifted the responsibility for routine mental health care to primary care physicians (Levin et al., 2010). Incomes vary somewhat by region of the country, but are lower than those earned by psychiatrists (BLS, 2012).

## Clinical Social Workers

The largest category of mental health professional is the clinical social worker (CSW), which is a specialized type of social worker. A CSW is licensed and certified to treat mental illness in a variety of practice settings, most commonly in an outpatient setting. The degree for this level of mental health care professional is the Master of Social Work (MSW), which allows for reimbursement from an insurance policy as an independent therapist (NASW, 2005). A CSW may also treat groups of patients in institutional settings. Many develop their own specialty practice, such as couples counseling and substance abuse counseling. They usually have independent practices, but they also frequently work in other client-centered settings such as health centers, human services programs, and ambulatory care practices. The therapeutic framework for social work is different than that used by psychologists or psychiatrists, and often involves more analysis and reflection on interactions between the person and important peer groups, such as friends and families.

## Psychiatric Nurses

Psychiatric nurses hold an Advanced Practice Registered Nurse degree, as described in Chapter 7. In this case, the specialized training is in psychiatry and is at the master's degree level. Some psychiatric nurses are also nurse practitioners. As shown in Table 10.1, they are able to prescribe medications within the practice guidelines of the state in which they practice.

## Mental Health Counselors

This category of mental health professionals are sometimes termed Clinical Counselors or Mental Health Counselors. They hold a master's degree, generally in psychology, and have 1 or 2 years of supervised clinical training. This profession serves similar clients as CSWs, but their orientation is psychoanalytical. There is a separate national certification board for this group of mental health providers (AMHCA, 2013). Within this field is the specialty of marriage and family counseling, which has a separate specialty board certification process.

## Caseworkers/Mental Health Assistants

This category of mental health providers works under the supervision of the independently practicing mental health professionals. Although they do not work independently, they interact individually with patients in a counseling role, often in the context of a treatment team in an organization. They work in both outpatient and inpatient settings.

## Lay Therapists

This is a group that is primarily nonprofessional, but because these individuals provide an important range of mental health services, they are included to complete the description of the full range of mental health resources. There are three distinct groups included here. The first can be categorized as alternative healers doing individualized therapy for emotional and mental illnesses, especially anxiety disorders. Among the alternative healers discussed in Chapter 4, Reikki therapy is often used as a method of coping with anxiety and depression, as well as stress.

The second group of lay therapists also provides individualized mental health services. These are various religious leaders who serve a congregation. Many of the various forms of religious and theological training include training in counseling, which generally focuses on family and marriage therapy. These services are directed at a self-identified group of people— that is, those who are part of their religious communities—and also have a spiritual dimension.

The most well known of the lay resources are the third group, which are self-help groups. These include Alcoholics Anonymous, Narcotics Anonymous, and Overeaters Anonymous. The leaders of these groups are not professionally certified, but some have specific training for their particular specialty, mostly through a peer model. It is also very common that the people leading and/or organizing these self-help groups have had some personal experience with the issues being addressed by their group.

It might be argued that this description of mental health providers is too inclusive, especially as the last category depends on self-diagnosis and self-referral. However, self-referral is how nearly everyone accesses the medical care system, both for physical and mental health symptoms. Which provider one chooses is a matter of culture, self-diagnosis, and access. Although these are important issues when discussing access to medical care for physical symptoms, they are even more critical to understanding access to mental health care services. The next two sections discuss two important aspects of access to mental health services.

## Access to Mental Health Services: Financial Issues

The treatment of mental disorders is costly both to individuals and their families, but also to the overall health care system. Part of this cost is emotional and social, but this section focuses on the financial cost. The total cost of diagnosis, treatment, and rehabilitation of mental illness to the entire health care system is estimated to be about $148 billion; however, this does not include the loss of productivity, which by some estimates is another $80 billion–$100 billion (NIMH, 2013; NAMI, 2014). Although the treatment of mental illness has a strong publicly funded component, more than two-thirds of the amount of money spent on diagnosis and treatment today comes from private sources. Unlike the treatment of physical illness, this split between private and public sources for care results in two very different levels and type of care, so much so that source of payment is considered as defining two separate subsystems (Shi and Singh, 2014). This section will briefly summarize some of the most important issues related to each method of payment.

### Public Funding of Mental Health Services

Those who are uninsured receive inpatient mental health care from a variety of sources including state and county mental health institutions and clinics specifically designated for this population. The two public health insurance programs—Medicare, but especially Medicaid—pay for short hospitalizations in hospitals, depending on the availability of psychiatric beds. Medicaid also pays for longer, more custodial care in a nursing home setting, including care for dementia patients as well as people with chronic mental and/or emotional disabilities. Publicly funded mental health services are provided by the VA, but only to the eligible target group, which will be described in Chapter 20.

Availability of outpatient care for uninsured people is very limited. As will be shown in Chapter 19, Medicaid will provide some outpatient services for mental illness, but primarily to children to prevent disabilities. Medicaid prohibits any treatment for substance abuse unless it is specifically linked to an existing mental illness diagnosis.

## Private Health Insurance: Parity of Coverage

One of the purposes of health insurance is to increase financial access to health services, especially those that are unexpected and expensive. Health insurers have always viewed treatment of mental health illnesses as unpredictable and unreliable, making it difficult to predict costs of treatment. Because of this, health insurance companies frequently limited their coverage of mental health services to inpatient settings. Most health insurance policies had limits on coverage, expressed as number of days hospitalized per year, which people with severe mental illness routinely exceed. Gradually, health insurance policies began to cover outpatient mental health services, with various measures requiring policyholders to share the cost of outpatient mental health treatment. These cost-sharing measures included large copayments for each visit as well as limits on the number of outpatient visits permitted each year. Because state legislatures ultimately control insurance coverage, there was great variation in coverage of outpatient mental health services. For example, in several states, copayments for mental health services are 50% of the cost of the visit. Health insurance companies are also allowed to charge a separate deductible for any mental health coverage at all (Cauchi et al., 2014).

Mental health activists have been working for many years to require all health insurance companies to cover mental health visits in the same way that visits for physical symptoms are covered. Several pieces of legislation in the 1990s attempted to achieve parity of coverage, but it was not until the passage of the Mental Health Parity and Addiction Equity Act of 2010 that the concept of parity seemed to finally gain acceptance. Although this Act establishes the principle of parity, it did not require all health insurance companies to actually cover mental health services. Health insurance companies that did not want to fully cover mental health care simply dropped it from their policies. Additionally, some states passed legislation that required health insurance companies to only cover mental illnesses that could be demonstrated to have a biological origin (Cauchi et al., 2014; SAMHSA, 2014). Also, this Act was not applicable to either Medicare or Medicaid (SAMHSA, 2014).

The Affordable Care Act (ACA; described in Chapter 17) provides significant expansion of coverage and resources for mental health care (Munoz,

2014). Under the ACA, no health insurance company will be able to limit coverage for treatment, either for physical or mental ailments. Health insurance companies are no longer allowed to deny coverage for preexisting conditions, and the ACA specifically includes mental illness as one of the preexisting conditions. The ACA requires all health insurance companies to provide preventive care with no copayments. This includes several mental health measures, including depression screening for adults and behavioral assessments for children. Finally, all health insurance companies are required to cover mental health and substance abuse services and are prohibited from differentiating between coverage for physical and mental health ailments (Cauchi et al., 2014).

As costs continue to increase for mental health care, the health insurance industry has turned to managed care organizations to help control the costs of mental health care. Mental health benefits for both private and public insurance programs, such as Medicaid, are now almost exclusively administered by managed behavioral health care organizations, most of which are for-profit companies. These companies reduce costs by closely monitoring utilization of all mental health visits, both outpatient and inpatient. They also utilize case management services, which are usually provided by the lower-paid providers shown in Table 10.1. Employers contract with these managed care organizations for their mental health services, which allows them to escape the requirement of parity of coverage. For example, many behavioral managed care companies offer a basic contract that limits outpatient coverage to 20 visits per year and inpatient coverage to 30 days of hospitalization. If a consumer wants higher levels of coverage, a higher annual premium is charged (Cauchi et al., 2014).

The goal of covering mental health illness in the same way that physical health is covered is shared by a great many people in both the medical field and the public health field. All recognize the importance of eliminating the barrier of finances for access to mental health services. However, there are additional factors related to barriers to adequate access, which will be addressed in the next section.

## *Access to Mental Health Services: Sociocultural Issues*

Because some mental illnesses result in inappropriate behavior in social situations, the general public is confronted with mental illness in a different manner than with somatic illnesses. A person may be in pain, or even contagious, but if they are acting in a socially appropriate manner, no one is aware of their health status. The mentally ill are often viewed as being dangerous, even violent. Although this is not accurate, it is true that untreated severe mental illness often leads to interactions with the criminal justice system. Mental health researchers view this primarily as a result of inadequate resources and poor access (Norman, 2011).

There is widespread agreement in the health field that there are not enough resources to meet the need and demand for mental health services. There are shortages of all the providers who can prescribe medications at a time when medication use is increasing (NAMI, 2014). There is also an emerging shortage of both CSWs and mental health counselors, both over the issue of the low salaries made by these two groups (Levin et al., 2010). There is also a well-documented shortage of inpatient beds, either in community hospitals or in private residential facilities (NAMI, 2014). The result is a shortage of resources for all levels of behavioral issues.

Access to available resources is limited by financial issues, as noted above. However, much attention is also paid to other social and cultural reasons for limits on access, mostly having to do with the continuing stigma related to mental illness. Mental health activists view this as the most important reason why people do not receive needed services. A recent Rand-supported survey revealed that nearly one-third of Americans erroneously feel that schizophrenia is related to having a bad character, and that mental illness is linked to violent behavior (Collins et al., 2012). Media coverage of those with mental illness who do commit crimes perpetuates the fear felt by the public and contributes to the stigma (Wahl, 1999). Another erroneous public perception concerns whether the mentally ill can control their symptoms themselves, without any professional intervention (Pinto-Foltz and Logsdon, 2008). There are also many misperceptions about the effectiveness of treatment for the mentally ill (Corrigan, 2004).

These public views of mental illness contribute to a reluctance to seek treatment, which leads to untreated mental illness, resulting in more socially inappropriate behavior, thus reinforcing the stigma (Sirey et al., 2001; Corrigan, 2004). Some studies indicate that even medical and mental health professionals sometimes have a negative view of treatment, especially in predicting positive outcomes (Wahl, 1999; Corrigan, 2004). Of the several research and policy issues in this field, many identify the reduction in stigmatization of mental illness as the most important (Angermyer et al., 2004; Norman, 2011).

## Reforming the Mental Health Care System

Not surprisingly, there are many calls for reform in the mental health system. Many feel that the ACA's more stringent regulations on health insurance companies for parity of coverage of mental health services will help in terms of financial accessibility, although not in terms of actually increasing physical resources and the mental health care workforce.

In 2002, when the Bush Freedom Commission on Mental Health labeled the mental health care system a shambles, they identified six goals for reforming this system. They include working to increase the understanding of the public about the complexities and realities of mental illness; reducing disparities in mental health services; providing early mental health screening; reforming mental health services so they are consumer-driven; providing excellent quality services when they are needed; and using technology to share information across all sectors that provide mental health services (White House, 2002). Although these goals are far from met, an important shift in treatment has occurred as a result of this report. Increasingly, the orienting concept is creating Recovery Oriented Systems of Care (ROSC), which are designed to help individuals pursue a fulfilling life, even in the face of mental health and/or behavioral issues. These ROSCs are an attempt to shift from episodic care to a continuum of care that involves a variety of care providers, ranging from mental health specialists to lay people (DHHS, 2005b). This supports the idea of integrating the primary medical care system with the more specifically identified mental health system.

# Long-Term Care System

This section focuses on services delivered to the elderly, although many of the same types of services are utilized by others with medical needs. Almost 13% of the whole U.S. population today is older than 65 (Sultz and Young, 2014), and nearly 70% of people over the age of 65 are predicted to need some type of assistance with activities of daily living, although most of these can be provided in the person's home (Shi and Singh, 2014). By 2030, it is estimated that 20% of the U.S. population will be older than 65, and 12% will be older than 85. In fact, it is the over-85 age group that is currently the fastest growing, and this is expected to continue (Shi and Singh, 2014). Of course, not everybody over the age of 65 needs long-term care services. In fact, less than 20% of this group will need institutional care, such as a nursing home (AARP, 2014).

The traditional pattern of caring for the elderly has been in the home environment, utilizing unpaid family and/or friends, and predominantly female caregivers. Some of the early almshouses provided custodial care when families could not, evolving into old age homes or rest homes. As with mental institutions, these early nursing homes soon gained a well-deserved negative reputation. Many of the elderly had physical and cognitive deficits and were cared for in institutions with insufficient, poorly trained, and low-paid staff, leading to increased use of physical restraints and medication to control behavior.

Legislation was passed to provide better care for the elderly, beginning with the 1935 Social Security Act, which provided financial assistance for older Americans as well as those with disabilities (Shore, 1994). In addition to providing income, this Act created funding for nonprofit organizations to organize nursing homes. Further funding for elder care services was provided by the passage of Medicare and Medicaid in 1965, which will be described in Chapters 18 and 19. This funding created a market for nursing homes, which coincided with an increasing number of women working outside the home, as well as increasing life spans. For-profit organizations rapidly entered this market, and today, most of the institutions that care for elders are for-profit. Reimbursement using public funds is linked to higher standards for care, including staffing ratios, cleanliness, and frequency of services. These standards gradually improved the quality of care in nursing homes and caused some of the lower quality nursing homes to close.

## Organization of Long-Term Care Services

There is a wide array of services that fit under the category of long-term care. These range from formal institutions with skilled health care professionals to home-based personal assistance services provided by family members or community groups. Table 10.2 shows six categories that capture the range of these services, and each will be briefly described here.

### Nursing Homes

This is the most visible facility in the long-term care system and is also the most expensive. The national average cost of a nursing home bed is $90,000 per year for a private room and $80,000 for a semiprivate room (CMMS,

**Table 10.2   Types of Long-Term Care Services (LTCS), Ownership Models, and Method of Payment**

| Type of LTCS | Ownership | Payment Pattern |
| --- | --- | --- |
| Nursing homes<br>  SNF<br>  "custodial" | 67% for-profit | • 55% Medicare/Medicaid<br>• 30% personal<br>• 9% private LTCI<br>• 6% other insurance policies |
| Assisted living/<br>  residential care<br>  facilities<br>Social and supportive<br>  services | 80% for-profit | • Almost all private pay<br>• Medicare/Medicaid may pay<br>  for part of some costs<br>• Some LTCI policies will cover<br>  this setting |
| Adult day care services<br>Social as well as some<br>  specialized medical<br>  services | 40% for-profit | Almost all private pay.<br>Medicaid will cover some medical<br>  services. |
| Home-based care<br>Includes agency-<br>  based as well as<br>  family members | Agencies are 80%<br>  for-profit<br>Family members are<br>  unpaid | 81% of the services that are not<br>  delivered by unpaid family and<br>  community members are paid for<br>  by Medicare and Medicaid. |
| Respite care<br>  In-home services<br>  Out of home services | 80% of agencies are<br>  for-profit | Almost all private pay. In some<br>  cases, Medicaid will cover<br>  expenses. |
| Hospice care<br>  Home-based<br>  Institutional | 60% for-profit | Mostly private pay.<br>Some Medicare and Medicaid<br>  payment. |

*Note:* LTCI, long-term care insurance; SNF, skilled nursing facilities.

2011), a very substantial economic burden for most people. As shown in Table 10.2, a little more than one-half of the cost of nursing homes comes from public sources, with one-third coming from Medicaid alone (CMMS, 2011).

Nursing home residents may be of any age, although 86% are over the age of 65, and 45% are over the age of 85 (NCEA, 2012). The length of stay varies, depending on the level of care required. A patient in a *skilled* nursing bed requires the services of a registered nurse or another category of a skilled nurse. This reflects a medical condition requiring medical or nursing care, or skilled rehabilitation services. Medicare pays for 100 days annually of this level of care. Patients may not be able to care for themselves, but have no specific medical issue. Examples of this type of patient include dementia patients and chronically disabled individuals. The level of care for these patients is *custodial*: Medicaid pays for this, as long as the person meets income requirements, as described in Chapter 19. Medicare does not cover this level of nursing home care.

A single nursing home typically has a mixture of both skilled and custodial beds, and patients are moved between these beds as their medical needs change. Nursing homes typically have a patient mix involving a range of payment methods, including Medicare, Medicaid, private long-term care nursing home insurance (which will be described below), as well as private pay patients. Just as patients are moved between beds by level of care needs, they are also moved by payment methods, because each payment method has slightly different requirements for the type of care that must be provided. Hospitals have also established sections of their inpatient units that are designated as skilled nursing beds. These are often used for rehabilitation of patients recovering from joint replacement surgeries.

## Assisted Living/Residential Living Facilities

Residential care facilities, also known as assisted living, provide a living environment for those who need some minor assistance and/support in daily activities. Assisted living facilities vary widely in size, ranging from a large house split into rooms to a large apartment complex with individual apartments. Residents typically have their own private apartments, most with small kitchens. Services include congregate meals, recreation opportunities, housekeeping, and 24-hour monitoring for emergencies. Most also allow residents to make individual arrangements with home health care services for additional personal assistance. There are about 6300 residential facilities nationwide, with a total of 475,000 apartments (ASLF, 2012). There is no certification or licensure for these facilities, other than meeting general building safety and public health guidelines.

The cost of assisted living facilities varies regionally, with those in the Northeast more expensive than those in the southern and southwestern regions of the country. Also, not surprisingly, those that provide more services are more expensive. One industry estimate of the national average is about $3300 per month (MetLife, 2012). Neither Medicare nor Medicaid will pay for this residential living arrangement. Some facilities have some apartments set aside for those with government-funded rent assistance for low-income residents, but this part of the long-term care system is exclusively free market oriented, with consumers paying for what they receive in services (Chapter 11).

## Adult Day Care Services

Adult day care services are designed to provide social opportunities for an individual who is being cared for at home, hopefully reducing social isolation. Some programs include medical assistance, and have nurses, occupational and physical therapists, as well as recreation therapists. Some adult day care programs focus on specific groups of patients, such as those with dementia, or a specific disability such as blindness.

These programs are licensed by the states in which they are located, but the regulations vary depending on whether they follow a medical or social model more closely. For programs following a social model, the regulatory agency is the same as those that licenses child care facilities. Day care programs that include medical assistance are licensed as a health care facility.

Many of the adult day care programs are run and/or managed by for-profit organizations, just as child care facilities are—with the individual paying for services. Some of these facilities are community-based nonprofit organizations that provide services on a sliding scale fee so low-income residents can also take advantage of them (NRRC, 2010).

This level of care is thought to help prevent institutionalization by allowing people to remain in their homes or their families' homes, and providing opportunities for increased social interaction. In general, this is viewed as being a more cost-effective way of allowing people to age in place, as long as they can perform most of their activities of daily living. These programs also provide what is known as respite care.

## Respite Care

Adult day care services are one form of respite care, but this category includes a much larger range of services. Respite care includes any services that provide relief for family caregivers of elderly people. This includes non-paid friends and volunteer community members, as well as paid individuals who work for respite organizations. Respite care is meant for short-term services, including overnight stays. Although many services occur in the home environment, respite care may also take place in an institution such as a day care program, or perhaps an overnight stay in an institution designed for that purpose.

Respite care is typically viewed as not medically necessary, so neither Medicare nor Medicaid or other private long-term health insurance policies cover it. People who are able to live in their own homes—or the homes of their families—are less costly to care for, but also have a much better quality of life. Respite care is an important part of the services required for continued home care. The Lifespan Respite Care Act of 2003 provided almost $3 million over the course of 5 years to enable states to develop publicly funded nonprofit organizations that would provide respite services to all families who need them (MHANY, 2007).

## Home-Based Care

Home-based care includes all the services—both medical and custodial—that enable a person to remain in either their own home or to stay in a family member's home. As is obvious from the discussion about respite care, home-care services is a component of the long-term care system that is underappreciated and undervalued. This is the most common method of providing assistance to the elderly: more than 80% of the elderly who require assistance are given that care by family members. Most of the caregivers are women, and more than 75% of them are also employed outside the home (Sultz and Young, 2014).

This part of the long-term care system is typically viewed as free. However, this understates the pressure on family caregivers, who are usually women also caring for children. The term sandwich generation is often used to describe their situation (Pierret, 2006). This pressure translates into increased physical and mental health illnesses, which are costly to the health system, as well as to the overall economy. It is estimated that the annual cost of work lost attributable to such caregiving demands exceeds $34 billion (MetLife, 2012). The economic contribution to the economy of unpaid workers for home care services is more than $450 billion per year, which is actually more than double of all the expenditures for nursing home care (Feinberg et al., 2011). Without the contribution of these unpaid family members, the economic burden on taxpayers would be very significant. This research and the general reassessment of the importance of family care providers has led to several policy and legislative changes, one of which was to recognize the importance of respite care, as noted above.

Another change was to allow Medicare and Medicaid to pay for some of the medically necessary services that are provided in the home environment. When this change was originally enacted in the 1980s, it caused an increase in home-care agencies, almost all of whom were for-profit companies. As these were poorly regulated, there were allegations of poor care and fraud that caused public reimbursement to be severely restricted, resulting in a reduction in the number of home care agencies. In the 1990s, reimbursement changes once again allowed for payment of more home-based medical services, resulting in another increase in for-profit home care agencies. This time, however, there is regulatory oversight to correct previous problems (NAHCH, 2010; Sultz and Young, 2014). In 2011, there were more than 12,000 formal home health care organizations, and more than 2 million people received care from one of them. As can be seen in Table 10.2, almost all of the home-care services not provided by family members are paid for by either Medicare or Medicaid (CMMS, 2011).

## Hospice Care

Hospice care is a philosophy of care provided to people who have a terminal illness with no effective medical treatment available, irrespective of age. This model originated in England in the 1960s and was introduced into the United States by a grassroots movement of consumers. Hospice services are also known as palliative care and are meant for those who have a life expectancy of 6 months or less. Under this model of care, the goal of treatment is comfort, pain relief, and emotional support, not curative treatment. Hospice services are delivered by a treatment team that includes physicians, nurses, pharmacists, physical and respiratory therapists, and grief counselors. These services are very commonly delivered at home, but there are also hospice facilities available in many states. Additionally, some nursing homes and some hospitals have set aside some beds designated as hospice care.

As with home care agencies, changes in Medicare reimbursement practices led to a rapid increase in hospice organizations, the majority of which are for-profit. Despite the prevalence of this for-profit structure, hospice also emphasizes the importance of volunteers in delivering care. In order for a hospice organization to be certified to receive funds from Medicare, the organization must demonstrate that it has at least 5% of its total patient care hours delivered by volunteers (NHPCO, 2012). Another basic belief in the hospice concept is that these palliative care services should be available to everyone regardless of their ability to pay. This has led many hospice organizations, including those that are for-profit, to offer service on a sliding scale if the person does not qualify for either Medicare or Medicaid. In some states, licensure is linked to the ability to demonstrate contribution of services to low-income people.

Hospice care has many advantages, including the fact that it is a much more cost-effective way of caring for people at the end of their lives. The level of acceptance of hospice care has been slow, however, among both physicians and patients. In the United States, physicians are trained to view death as a failure. However, acceptance of this model has increased as more people have experienced painful, intervention-intensive hospital deaths. By 2011, there were about 5300 hospice organizations, and 44% of all deaths occurred while being treated under the hospice model (NHPCO, 2012).

## Financing Long-Term Care Services

Formal, institutional long-term care is expensive with the total cost of all paid long-term care services about 9% of the total health care budget. This is about the same percentage as that spent on prescription drugs (AARP, 2014). Most elders will never need a nursing home, especially a long-term stay. Only 14% of Americans over the age of 85 are in nursing homes (AARP, 2014). Much of the assistance is by unpaid friends and family members, the economic value of which is overlooked. There are three methods of paying for long-term care services, one of which involves public funds.

Both Medicare and Medicaid do cover some of the expenses of long-term care, although Medicare pays for only about 14% of nursing homes (Shi and Singh, 2014). This is because of the nature of coverage of these two programs, as has been mentioned previously. A more complete description of this is in Chapters 18 and 19. Over time, the balance of coverage between these two public programs has resulted in some perverse economic incentives. Medicaid only covers low income people, so individuals sometimes spend down their assets in order for custodial long-term care to be paid for. The result is that almost two-thirds of all long term is paid for by Medicaid (Sultz and Young, 2014). As will be seen in Chapter 19, the original concept of Medicaid was to provide comprehensive services for young families with children, not to provide long-term care for the elderly.

The second method is through self-payment by individuals. As can be seen in Table 10.2, this is a very common method of payment, especially because many of the agencies and organizations providing long-term care services are for-profit organizations. Nationwide, over one-third of all costs in nursing homes are paid by individuals (Gleckman, 2009). This is a large economic burden to a family, which leads to the third method, which is an insurance policy.

General health insurance policies, either through an employer or purchased individually, do not cover components of long-term care, especially nursing home expenses. There are, however, specific policies for various components of long-term care. These were originally only designed for covering nursing home stays and initially they were marketed only to the elderly population. After quite a lot of regulatory efforts to control uneven coverage and poor benefits, long-term care policies began to cover a full range of services, including—but not limited to—nursing homes. For example, some will cover the costs of an assisted living or other residential facility. These policies are still marketed to the over 65 age group, but they are also now available to younger people, especially as part of group health insurance offered by employers. As shown in Table 10.2, only about 9% of nursing home costs are paid by a long-term care insurance (LTCI) policy.

This is primarily because these policies are a very complicated purchase. There are a wide variety of policies with many restrictions limiting benefits. For example, many policies have limits on future payments because of inflation in the economy, whereas others have specific limits on various types of services. Others have lifetime caps on benefits, have limitations on renewal, and also some require prior hospitalization before covering services. Most provide only partial coverage. This confusion has resulted in only the more educated and affluent having nursing home insurance. Premiums themselves are low for younger consumers. For example, a 60-year-old pays on average $1000–$2000 per year in premiums. This buys between 2 and 4 years of partial coverage of nursing home expense. Premiums for older people are higher. A 75-year-old can expect to pay about $6000 per year for a similar level of coverage (AARP, 2013). Coverage can be denied based on preexisting conditions. About 15% of those applying for LTCI are rejected (Shi and Singh, 2014).

## A Few Final Thoughts on Long-Term Care

The long-term care system includes a full range of services and a wide array of people delivering these services. Some are highly skilled, licensed and certified, and expensive—such as doctors and nurses. Others have some training, perhaps even certification, and are less expensive. However, a great many are family and friends, with no training. Although these caregivers do not add to the formal direct cost of long-term care, their contributions need to be included when estimating the overall cost of providing care to the elderly.

The great majority of people prefer to age in place, which means remaining in their own homes as long as possible. This has presented problems in deciding how to use public funds to pay for care that is not specifically related to skilled medical or nursing services.

The predominant model of ownership in the long-term care system is for-profit organizations. Although long-term care services are highly regulated, it is also the sector of the health system that is primarily based on individuals directly paying for services. The consequence of this is that access is primarily determined by income and other personal resources, including unpaid caregivers. Does it matter if long-term care facilities are mostly for-profit? This is a question that is a point of discussion and research. As will be shown in Chapter 11, this is partly philosophical, and related to the framework of market and social justice discussed in Chapter 5. Some of the research points to some disturbing differences. First of all, at least for the largest of the for-profit chains, nurse staffing levels are much lower than in analogous nonprofit facilities (Harrington et al., 2012). A Government Accounting Office study did a more comprehensive analysis of these 10 large chains and noted the low staffing levels. This report also noted a higher number of deficiencies in quality standards used by Medicare and Medicaid. The deficiencies noted were ones that were more likely to be significantly related to increased harm to residents as well as poor quality of care (CMA, 2012).

Many activists have supported the development of a publicly subsidized national long-term care insurance program to make long-term care services more accessible to all income levels. Others oppose this saying that family caregivers would be less responsible for providing care, which now does not cost anything, at least in terms of money. The ACA initially included a national voluntary long-term care insurance program by using a payroll deduction program matched by federal contributions. However, criticism of various aspects of the plan were so extreme, it was dropped before it was implemented (Sultz and Young, 2014). There is no easy solution to this issue.

## Dental and Vision Care Systems

Dental care and vision care services have many things in common. First, both are well utilized, and second, most of the costs are paid by the consumer instead of a health insurance company. For both fields, there is some insurance coverage, but not comprehensive or complete coverage. Although both dental and vision services are necessary to health, the symptoms that lead people to seek care are not viewed as being part of the Biomedical Model, which is the conceptual basis for health financing. Also, although these services are not cheap, they are not nearly as expensive as major medical procedures, which were the impetus for developing health insurance.

This section will only briefly summarize some salient aspects of each of these components, including the hierarchical professional structure of each field, and a description of how these services are financed.

## Dental Care System

Dentistry was originally a branch of medicine, with dental surgery being the first specialization in medicine (Suddick and Harris, 1990). Dental extractions were used as a method of improving health or curing specific medical conditions as well as being used to relieve oral pain. During the late 1600s, dentistry developed into a field separate from medicine, with several schools and textbooks available in England and Europe by the late 1700s and early 1800s (Gelbier, 2005). Today, dentistry is a well-developed medical profession, with educational requirements, as well as professional certification and licensure requirements very similar to those in the medical field.

### Providers, Education, and Regulation

As with medicine, dentistry is a hierarchical profession, with the dentist having the most education, the most responsibility and the highest income. Dentists have one of two doctoral degrees: a Doctor of Dental Medicine (DMD) or a Doctor of Dental Surgery (DDS). There are 64 professionally accredited dental schools in the United States, each of which involves 4 years of training past the undergraduate level. Additionally, there are residency programs in one of the nine recognized specialties, including oral surgery, orthodontics, and endodontics (Edelstein, 2010). Unlike medicine, the vast majority (83%) of dentists maintain general practices (BLS, 2012). Most general dentists perform treatments such as restorations, including crowns as well as routine fillings; endodontic procedures such as root canals; oral surgery such as extracting teeth or doing dental implants; and periodontal therapy, which involves treatment of gum disease. However, because there are also recognized specialties in each of these areas, some general dentists will refer complicated cases to more specialized dentists. In oral surgeries, some periodontal treatments, and some restorations, dentists use a variety of anesthesia techniques. They also have some prescription rights, including antibiotics, painkillers, and other sedatives used in the treatment of pain related to dental work. Dentists are both professionally certified by one of several professional boards and licensed by the state to practice. They also have continuing education requirements to maintain their professional license to practice.

Dentists are primarily white (86%) and male (65%). Their incomes vary according to specialty and region in which they practice, but the range of salaries for general dentistry is from $75,000 to $187,000. Salaries for more specialized dentists are higher, with an average of $150,000 and a range from $122,000 to 287,000 (Dental Salaries, 2013; BLS, 2013).

In most general dental practices, there is also a dental hygienist. The educational requirements for dental hygienists vary from a 2-year certificate program to a 4-year baccalaureate program, as well as a master's program. Dental hygienists are both professionally certified and state licensed. Although they are under the general supervision of the dentist, they also have independent interactions with patients, and have regularly scheduled routine visits with patients as part of the preventive care function of a general dental office.

A fairly new dental profession has become more common. The oral preventive assistant (OPA) was originally suggested as a way to increase the professional opportunities for dental assistants, and to improve access to simple dental care including restorations such as fillings. The OPA has additional training and additional professional certification, and is conceptualized as a mid-level provider in dentistry (Edelstein, 2010).

## Changes in Dentistry Practice

For many years, one of the prime responsibilities of a general dentist was to perform simple restorations such as fillings, especially in children. When teeth became too heavily decayed, general dentists extracted teeth and fitted people for false teeth. Two separate advances have significantly changed this dental practice. One is highly technological, and the other involves primary prevention.

The primary prevention activity is the increased recognition that childhood cavities can be largely eliminated by the use of fluoride. When added to a public water supply, fluoride is a very effective primary prevention method. However effective this may be, there are several sources of opposition to this action. One is that adding a chemical to the water supply is a form of mass medication that does not allow people to opt out. Other opposition centers on a mistrust of government, viewing this action as communist. However, as the community-based public health programs involving adding fluoride to the water supply have increased, childhood cavities have become significantly more rare.

The very significant reduction in childhood cavities required the dental profession to develop other types of treatment. One of the most important is the technological advances—where the focus is on saving teeth instead of pulling them, with increased root canals and crowns being performed. However, even more significant is the successful development of dental implants. The general dental office is now focused on various preventive procedures, including routine visits with dental hygienists, and restorative care for adults, with emphasis on saving teeth.

## Financing

Most people view it as an oddity that dental services are not included in health insurance plans. At the time that health insurance policies were being developed, dental services were cheaper and more predictable, so were not viewed as being necessary for inclusion in health care insurance policies. As more technological advances both improved dentistry and increased the cost of these services, consumers began to demand insurance coverage for dental procedures. Dental insurance has slowly developed into a separate program of insurance policies. This market is dominated by what are known as consumer-driven policies, purchased by individual consumers, although some group policies are also available through employers (see Chapter 13). Medicaid covers routine and preventive dental care for children, but Medicare does not cover dental services of any kind.

## Vision Care System

Vision care services has confusing terminology, some of which comes from historical development of the field, and some of which comes from two competing professions, each of which use the title Doctor. One of these is a medical doctor, holding either an MD or a DO degree. This professional is called an *ophthalmologist*, although the term oculist is also sometimes used.

The term oculist is also used to refer to the other major eye care professional: the *optometrist*. An optometrist holds a degree Doctor of Optometry (OD), which is a 4-year graduate program beyond the undergraduate level, and an internship that is generally 1 or 2 years. There are 20 schools of optometry in the United States, all of which are professionally accredited. As with all independently practicing health providers, optometrists are both professionally certified and state-licensed (AOA, 2012).

Defining the difference between these two is not easy, as there is considerable overlap in terms of what they actually do. Both administer eye examinations and prescribe corrective lenses—both glasses and contact lenses; both do screening for eye diseases; both diagnose eye diseases; and both do routine treatment of eye diseases, such as involving topical or oral medications. However, only ophthalmologists can do surgery, although some states do allow optometrists to do laser surgery. Some states allow optometrists to do injections into the eye, although that is primarily performed by ophthalmologists (AOA, 2012). If an optometrist discovers an eye disease that requires more invasive treatment, the patient is referred to an ophthalmologist.

There is some competition between these two professionals, especially for vision correction. Ophthalmologists make significantly more than optometrists do, and their prices are somewhat more expensive for patients for routine eye care. Income for optometrists ranges from $93,000 to $145,000, depending mostly on the region of the country in which they practice (Optometrists Salaries, 2013).

Most private health insurance policies, as well as Medicare, will pay for one routine eye examination each year, but will not cover the cost of either glasses or contact lenses. In most states, Medicaid will cover the cost of both the examination and glasses. Health insurance policies—and Medicare—will cover the cost of medical treatment of eye problems, such as cataract surgery, but not laser surgery to correct routine vision problems.

Other professions work within the vision care field. These include *orthoptists* and *opticians*. Orthopists work closely with ophthalmologists to train patients in eye movement after surgery. This involves a 2-year training program after the undergraduate level. An optician specializes in the fitting and fabrication of corrective lenses, both glasses and contact lenses. The optician can make the correct lens, based on the prescription given either by an optometrist or ophthalmologist. An optician may work independently, often as part of a for-profit company, such as Pearl Vision; however, both optometrists and ophthalmologists also employ opticians in their practices so they can provide a full range of services for their patients.

The vision care system and the public health system have a significant level of interaction, especially in secondary prevention. Routine vision screening of children occurs in most public schools under the direction of a school nurse or a public health professional. For many families, this is the first indication of a vision problem, which might negatively impact a child's educational progress. However, there is a significant lack of access to glasses, because most health insurance policies do not cover the cost of eyeglasses. Vision changes frequently during childhood, requiring new glasses.

## Summary

This chapter describes some of the most important aspects of four different and very important subsystems of the U.S. health care delivery system. These systems—mental health, long-term care, dental care, and vision care—are utilized by millions of Americans, but are frequently not included when describing the U.S. health care system.

For both mental health care and long-term care, utilization is not equal to the need, for very different reasons. In long-term care, access is limited by personal resources. For people with mental health or behavioral issues, a substantial part of the problem is not only money, but a stigma associated with mental health. Most vision services and dental services are paid for by the individual consumer. From the view of the public health field, there are access problems in each of these important subsystems.

## Acknowledgments

The following people made significant contributions to the content of this section, including gathering material and references, as well as writing and analysis: Tia DiNatale, Avery Hennigar, Ariana Lymberopoulos, Alexandria McGowan, Laura Norton, and Sheighlyn Knightly. Jennifer Salop, Sydney Leone, and Rashinda Key improved the content of this chapter through their careful review and comments. Rashinda designed Figure 10.1 and Jonathan Rosenblatt constructed it.

# POLITICAL AND ECONOMIC VALUES AND HEALTH CARE FINANCING

The first two chapters of Section III are directly concerned with the political and economic environment of the United States. This environment is substantially responsible for the manner in which the U.S. health care system operates, including how health services are financed. Many of the disagreements about health care policies are based on differences in political and philosophical perspective, so it is important to fully understand these.

Chapter 11 (Health Economics 101: Do Health Care Goods/Services Follow Standard Economic Rules?) describes the guidelines used by economists to determine situations in which the free market approach using competition can result in lower prices for goods and services. The purpose of this chapter is to explore whether the market justice model can be used to allocate health care goods and services. Chapter 12 (From Economics to Health Policy and Regulation) builds on this and compares several different policy suggestions for financing medical care services, focusing on the political values underlying these ideas. This chapter also considers the role of regulation and the scope of the federal and state governments in the health care system. These two chapters, taken together, provide insight into the market justice and social justice perspectives on various health policy initiatives.

The next three chapters focus more specifically on medical care financing, beginning with Chapter 13 (Health Care Financing: Health Insurance), which provides an overview of health insurance, including how premiums are determined, types of health insurance, how people in the United States get access to health insurance, and whether it matters to have health insurance. Chapter 14 (Health Insurance: Two Conceptual Models) is a more focused analysis of two general models of health insurance, including the managed care model, which has been described conceptually. This chapter now presents the financing of this model. Chapter 15 (The Payment Function: Money Moving through the System) presents a comprehensive overview of the payment function, the process by which health care providers are paid.

Section III concludes with Chapter 16 (Why Does Medical Care Cost So Much and What Can We Do About It?) and a return to broader policy issues, this time focusing on why medical care services cost so much and the various policy efforts to control these increasing costs.

*Chapter 11*

# Health Economics 101: Do Health Care Goods/ Services Follow Standard Economic Rules?

The field of economics focuses on how goods and services are allocated in society. The simplest view of this allocation or distribution of goods and services is that people with more money have increased access to more and/ or higher quality goods and services. This is commonly called the free or private market system, which is the foundation of our capitalistic economy. This method of allocation based on money involves both an economic and a philosophical perspective. This chapter focuses on the economic perspective, but as will be seen, the philosophical perspective determines the structure of the allocation system and our perception of how well it works. This chapter analyzes whether this allocation method is applicable to the health field, where goods are things we use such as wheelchairs, glasses, and prescription drugs, and services include both diagnostic and treatment activities of some type of health care provider.

Systems of allocation are especially important when goods are scarce. If there were an adequate supply of goods and services, then it would be easier for people to have access to them. We do not like to think of scarcity of resources when thinking about health care goods and services, so frequently people will reject economic analysis as being relevant to the health field. However, scarcity is very common in the health care system. Organs available for transplantation are an example of extreme scarcity in medical care. Coming up with an allocation scheme for organs that is independent of money and fair has been very challenging. Scarcity is present in many other aspects of medical goods and services. When there are not enough primary care providers, for example, who determines where they should practice? If there is not enough influenza vaccine, who determines who has access first?

Although medical need is clearly part of the way health care goods and services are allocated, financial access is just as important a determinant of who receives medical care services (Santerre and Neun, 2004; Shi and Singh, 2014). Shi and Singh (2014) did not invent the term market justice, but their use of it in the context of the health field has led to a greater appreciation of this as a method of allocating health care goods and services. The term market justice makes clear something that is implicit in the free market orientation. This free market orientation in its purest form implies that giving people a good or a service they cannot purchase themselves is wrong, both economically and philosophically. Following from this thought, distributing health care goods and services through the private market is a just or equitable way of allocation.

This position is based on several assumptions, one of which is important to this discussion. This is whether health care goods and services are just like all other commodities that are distributed by this free market, such as bread, jeans, cars, or cellular phones. This is a spirited debate in the field of economics, with most—but not all—economists viewing health care goods and services as being very different from these other commodities we purchase. The public shares this hesitance of viewing health care goods and services as being the same as other goods. For example, people will fairly often make a contribution to a fund to pay for some very expensive medical procedure that a family cannot afford, but not to purchase a car. Hospitals routinely provide care to people who cannot pay, but grocery stores do not give bread to people who cannot pay.

When the free market does not work to fairly allocate goods and services using money, it is labeled as a market failure. The most common reason for such a failure is when the free market does not distribute goods equitably or fairly. Under the ideas of market justice for nonhealth care goods, it is viewed as equitable that people with more money have increased access to goods. However, medical goods and services are viewed differently, primarily because of this idea related to medical need. Many in the fields of medicine and public health strongly prefer an allocation system designed around the concept of medical need rather than ability to pay. This model of allocation is part of what is termed the social justice model, which will be more completely described at the end of this chapter.

When a market fails, the primary result is some sort of governmental action. In the health field, this is usually a regulation in which those who do not have fair access are helped. Most of the examples of health care reform in Chapter 17, including the Affordable Care Act, are trying to correct an unfair allocation of health care goods and services. This means the allocation method is moved from one following market justice to one closer to social justice guidelines.

One of the basic assumptions of the free market is that competition acts to lower prices. This is true in what is called a perfectly competitive free market, where the supply of the good at a specific price is equal to the demand, reducing scarcity. There are several guidelines to determine whether the market situation is perfectly competitive, so this relationship between increased competition and lower cost can exist. The farther away from meeting these guidelines, the less perfectly competitive the market is, and the more likely it is for the market to fail. The next section of this chapter describes six guidelines that capture most of what economists use to characterize a perfectly competitive free market.

# Very Simple Health Economics Guidelines

One of the most common policy suggestions made in the health field involves increasing competition to lower prices. However, if health care goods and services do not follow the guidelines for a perfectly competitive market, then competition will not lower costs. It is very important to understand whether these guidelines are met by health care goods and services, so this section will describe and analyze these in the context of the health care system. This analysis is not an either–or situation. Rather, it is a spectrum, because some of these guidelines will come closer to being met than others. They are not presented in any order of importance. All need to be met in order for increased competition to substantially decrease costs.

## Free and Easy Entry into the Market for Producers

This first essential guideline relates to having enough supply. In this context, producers include all those who provide either goods or services in the health care field. This includes all the health care professionals described in

Chapter 7. It also includes facilities where care is given, ranging from free-standing clinics to hospitals, as well as nursing homes, residential facilities for mental health, and physician offices. Also included in the category of producers are pharmaceutical companies, as well as manufacturers of medical equipment (e.g., crutches and dialysis machines) and diagnostic imaging technologies.

The term free and easy means that there are few barriers to becoming a producer of health care goods or services. Easy entry into the medical field means a larger supply, which allows consumer choice and increased competition. There are minimal barriers to producers in the nonhealth care sectors of the economy to enter the market, depending on what one wishes to produce and where. For example, handmade crafts can be sold on several websites with few barriers to participation. Selling the same handmade crafts in a physical store involves more barriers, primarily in zoning ordinances of towns. There may be more significant barriers to owning a franchise of an existing company, which may be determined by the corporation to protect against a potential oversupply, reducing the profits for each franchise.

How easy is it to enter the health care market? A moment's reflection on Chapters 7–9 results in acknowledging that becoming a producer in the health field is very difficult. Barriers include extensive and expensive educational requirements, professional certification, state licensure, and meeting governmental regulations for receiving public funds. The difficulties arise from several different factors, each of which results in a variety of barriers. It was much easier to become a health care producer shortly before the Flexner report came out (Chapter 7). Between concerns for patient safety and protecting the rights and incomes of professionals, consumer choice became significantly limited, as it remains today. When choice is limited, competition is not able to lower prices. The link between professional education, state licensure, and quality is very well accepted by all, and not likely to be weakened, even by those who favor increased competition.

A similar narrative describes other more institutional producers in the health field, such as hospitals. When public money is used to pay for services, additional certification procedures are used to protect the public interest. This is especially true in the long-term care industry, where nursing homes have to meet certification for Medicaid reimbursement. As more free-standing for-profit facilities develop, is this public safety responsibility diminished? It is certainly easier to establish a single-purpose urgent care center or an ambulatory care center than a full hospital, but even these are reviewed by both state officials and public health authorities to make sure they meet quality guidelines. These quality guidelines relate not only to the facility itself, but also to the health providers who practice in the facility.

Meeting this guideline returns us to the era before the Flexner report where there were many different producers, significant consumer choice, and consequently, lower prices. However, the technological demands of this particular era were significantly less.

## Many Producers/Sellers and Consumers/Buyers Interacting Freely

This criterion is closely related to the first one, because it assumes the presence of many producers and/or sellers. However, the most significant aspect of this criterion is the phrase interacting freely. In a perfectly competitive market, consumers have the ability to decide for themselves what they wish to purchase. There are few barriers involved in the process, except those related to public safety or other public interests. For example, consumers have free choice of restaurants, although each restaurant is inspected and meets some level of food safety expectations. Consumers also have free choice between products, such as brands of sneakers or jeans.

There is not an equivalent ability of consumers to freely choose the health care goods or service they want to receive. For example, it is not the patient who determines the medical service they receive—it is the health care provider. Consumers may—and do—present demand to health care providers, especially related to prescription drugs that are marketed directly to consumers. However, the consumer cannot directly purchase that drug without the agreement of the physician. If a patient has to be hospitalized, it is the physician who dictates that choice, not the patient. Physicians must have staff privileges at hospitals, and they typically do not have such admitting privileges at all hospitals, as described in Chapter 8.

Other limitations on consumer's interactions with health care providers relate to restrictions from health insurance policies. Consumers receive medical care at least partly based on the type of health insurance coverage they have. For example, if they have a managed care plan, as discussed in Chapter 9, they are limited to a specific network of physicians.

Based on all these limitations, it is clear that consumers do not have either the range of choice or the freedom to make their own decisions required by the competitive free market.

## Separation of Supply and Demand

Competition can decrease prices most effectively when there is no collusion between those who supply the goods and those who buy them. Consumer demand is the driving force behind the perfectly competitive market. Suppliers are more likely to maximize their profits if they make more of what consumers want and/or demand. Although this is a very important guideline, this relationship is not always strong in other parts of the U.S. economy. For example, most consumers are very dependent on an auto mechanic to correctly diagnose and correct problems related to their car. Consumers start the demand process, but we usually do not know exactly which service and/or auto part we need. More generally, the entire advertising industry is based on the premise of telling consumers what they want, rather than companies producing goods that consumers demand. This is clearly a somewhat ambiguous criterion in the general U.S. economy.

However, it is even more problematic in the health care sector, because—as with the car—the consumer only begins the demand process by presenting a symptom to a physician. It is the physician who then determines what services—either diagnostic or treatment-based—are appropriate. No matter how relevant a patient might think a magnetic resonance imaging is for a particular symptom, it is only the physician who can provide access to that. Physicians create demand and, in a for-profit or physician-owned practice, the physician also owns the supply. This is one of the reasons for the controversy surrounding physician-owned imaging companies in particular, as discussed in Chapter 9.

Insurance companies act as brokers in this buying relationship, as will be described in more detail in the following discussion. Some consumers exercise a direct choice in selecting an insurance company, but many others are limited to those offered by their employers.

This criterion is one that is somewhat controversial in the larger economy, but which is certainly not supportive of the competitive free market reducing prices for consumers with respect to health care goods and services.

## The Product Being Purchased Is Homogenous

One of the assurances the consumer has when making a free choice of a good to purchase is that the one purchased is just like all the others. This means that we do not have to know about each and every pair of jeans.

We can be assured that the one we select from the stack of jeans in the store is of the same quality as all the others. Various state-based lemon law legislation provides specific protection for consumers in the case of large purchases, such as cars. Homogenous products ensure a lower price for that product, as opposed to a custom-designed, individually made product. Handmade products take more time, and their higher price reflects a value for that time and skill.

This criterion is interesting when applied to the health field. One of the ways in which health maintenance organizations (HMOs) and other managed care organizations control costs is by incorporating the concept of homogenous products. For example, having physicians follow treatment protocols that dictate certain procedures or time lines is an effort to reduce costs by reducing physician practice variability. One of the earliest examples of this was when HMOs first required physicians to obtain throat cultures before prescribing antibiotics for a possible diagnosis of strep throat. Initially, physicians resisted this as an intrusion on their clinical autonomy. It is widely recognized now as not only cost saving, but also helping in reducing the amount of antibiotics that people are exposed to.

The major problem with the widespread application of this principle is that medicine itself is not standardized, but an essentially individualized product. Two people with exactly the same symptoms may very appropriately be treated differently depending on factors unrelated to the symptoms, including age and other health conditions. Although this increases costs, each patient wants to be treated as an individual.

## Consumer Has Full/Complete Knowledge That Is Available and Understandable

This is one of the most important assumptions of the perfectly competitive free market. From among the many producers/suppliers, the consumer buys the desired product at the lowest price they can find. This purchasing decision is the very foundation of the entire free market model. However, it is based on the assumption that the consumer has enough knowledge to select one product from among several. In the general economy, consumers learn about products and brands in many different ways. This includes asking friends, seeing advertisements, consulting salespeople, as well as seeking more independent information such as internet sites and formal consumer ratings organizations.

Whether a consumer can have full and complete knowledge with respect to making purchasing decisions for health-related goods or services has always been a point of controversy. The original controversy had two components. The first concerns emotion. Economists envision a rational decision-making process, but illness often reduces this ability. Of course, not all health-related purchasing decisions are made in the face of urgent medical conditions, but many symptoms are distracting, at the least.

The second issue is the highly technical nature of knowledge required to completely understand a medical condition, and its treatment options. Few consumers have access to this level of knowledge and would not be able to understand it in any case. The increasing presence of many medically oriented websites has considerably reduced this concern. Medical information is now easily available and understandable, although accuracy depends on the source. Consumers today have a much higher potential of gaining the knowledge necessary to participate in the medical decision-making process than ever before. Besides more easily available medical information, there are now several easily available sources to provide quality ratings of physicians as well as hospitals.

However, there is another, very important part of the purchasing decision that is not available to consumers: the price or cost of a service. There is almost no information available for consumers to do the price comparison required of the competitive model. Even health care producers are unable to help in this part of the decision-making process, because they themselves do not know what things cost. Reasons for this are explored in the last guideline.

Of course, even if a consumer had enough medical knowledge and also had full access to price information, most of the medical services and many health-related goods still require the authorization of a physician for access, as well as the approval of an insurance company for payment. Nearly all economists agree that this limited information on both what goods and/or services are needed as well as what they cost creates a situation that severely limits the ability of the free market to effectively distribute health care goods and services.

## Consumers Pay for Goods/Services They Purchase/Consume

At the very heart of the perfectly competitive free market is the idea that consumers, based on the knowledge they have about the several products available, reveal their values and choices by committing their own personal money. Because everybody understands that money is valuable and has required personal effort to be earned, this is a significant choice. For Americans, there is a whole cultural value around this buying process, represented by the parental phrase that we value most the items bought with our own money. The simplest expression of this is paying cash at the time of purchase. Credit cards do create a distance between the purchase itself and the time of the payment, but personal funds are still required.

However, in the health care field, very few purchases are actually paid for by the consumer. In fact, of all the money spent on medical care in the United States, only about one-third comes from out-of-pocket expenditures, meaning the consumer pays the cost (Hancock, 2013). The great majority of money spent on medical care services in the United States are paid by third-party payers. This includes private employment-based group health insurance policies, private individual health insurance policies, and public sources of health insurance, including Medicare, Medicaid, and Veterans Administration.

Health insurance evolved to help people pay hospital bills that they could not afford, as will be explained in Chapter 13. Without health insurance, there would be much less medical care delivered. The strong presence of health insurance acting as a broker in the purchasing decision is a powerful limitation on the perfectly competitive free market's ability to control prices through competition. Consumers do not make the final choice of service, either the physician or the health insurance company does. In terms of the second guideline, producers and consumers do not interact freely: insurance companies have significant input into which good and/or service will be paid for, thus determining which good and/or service will be provided.

Additionally, the price side of the market is controlled not by what any good or service costs to produce, but rather what any health insurance organization will reimburse for it. This includes both private health insurance companies, as well as the public sources of health insurance—Medicare and Medicaid. Physicians know what one particular health insurance organization will pay for a service, but they do not know what that service costs to produce. As will be shown in Chapter 13, different health insurance organizations pay very different amounts for the same service, so the principle of homogeneity is violated on the price side as well as the supply side.

When consumers do not pay for what they consume, economists worry that people will get too much of a good. The best example of this is the all-you-can-eat buffet, or an open bar, where people consume too much. When consumers utilize more services because of lower prices, economists call this moral hazard. Economists have been arguing about moral hazard in health insurance since the 1960s (Arrow, 1963; Pauly, 1968). Some economists argue that insurance lowers the price of medical services enough so that people consume more medical services than if they were directly paying for them. Others are more dubious, noting that there are many associated costs of seeking medical care, including the time required to consult a health care provider, as well as the pain and discomfort of many procedures. This argument about moral hazard has many facets that involve both cultural and philosophical values. The United States is the only health care system worried about increased utilization because of moral hazard, as will be shown in Chapter 22.

For now, we need to summarize this discussion related to whether health care goods and services can be allocated by the free market. As can be seen by reviewing these six guidelines, none of them are met even partially. This has several important policy implications, one of which is that increasing competition is actually unlikely to decrease prices. The other is that, in fact, health goods and/or services are not like all others, and therefore are not likely to be distributed either efficiently or equitably by the free market. If health care does not meet the guidelines for being a private market good, is it instead a public good? The next section explores this idea.

## Are Health Care Goods and Services Examples of Public Goods?

Economists have several criteria for a good being defined as public, just as they have guidelines for defining a good as private. There are two major criteria that will be briefly discussed here. The first is termed *nonrival*, meaning that one person using it does not diminish another's use. The classic example of this is a public park, where many people can enjoy it at the same time. The second criterion for being classified as a public good is whether usage is *nonexclusive*. This means that it is too difficult to restrict the use of the good to only those who paid for it. The classic example of a public good is national defense, although roads and highways are also good examples (Santerre and Neun, 2004). In both cases, public tax funds are used to pay for these services.

On the face of it, health care goods and services do not seem to fit either of these criteria, especially the conditions related to a good being *nonrival*. As noted in the beginning of this chapter, there is scarcity in health-related goods and services, so one person's use might in fact diminish another's access. Medical services also do not easily fit into the *nonexclusive* criterion, because the ethical perspective of health care providers is to give medical services based on need, not money. This ethical perspective is one of the primary reasons that medical services are not the same as other commodities, as noted in the discussion in the beginning of this chapter.

Many public health services are closer to the criteria for a public good. This includes many of the activities included in the three levels of care identified as public health in Figure 6.3: health promotion, health protection, and community-oriented prevention activities. Activities funded through public tax dollars are often thought of as contributing to the overall health and well-being of a whole population, and thus are nonexclusive.

The conclusion of this discussion is that health care goods and services are not good examples of private goods. This has several important implications, including that one of the favorite policy suggestions of increasing competition to lower prices does not work in the health care field. Public health activists frequently describe health care goods and services as public goods, but as shown here, health care services do not completely meet the economic definition of a public good. Viewing health care as a right does express the philosophical perception of the social justice model as the best way to allocate health care services instead of the market justice model of increased competition. Before we proceed to a more detailed discussion of these two models of allocation, one more important economic concept needs to be described.

## An Important Economic Concept: Elasticity

One of the acknowledged limitations of the ability of competition to lower prices, even in a perfectly competitive free market, is whether the good or service is one that consumers identify as something they actually need or simply want. Goods that are perceived as being necessary are not as likely to have their prices lowered by increased competition, whereas goods that are desired, but not necessary, are far more likely to have their demand influenced by price. Although it is fairly easy to identify some categories of goods as necessities, such as food, the definition of what is necessary is at least partly dependent on an individual's perceptions. For those who use tobacco products, this good become a necessity, for example. For most people, gasoline is an essential good. A more trivial example can be found using sneakers, where prominent sports figures are associated with certain brand names. These sneakers are much more expensive than other, nonbranded sneakers for a closely equivalent quality. People who care about brand names will pay more for sneakers than those who do not. Economists recognize that as prices increase, some people may substitute cheaper brands for their favorites, or perhaps modify their behavior.

When the demand for a good is not much impacted by price, that good or service is said to be *price-inelastic*, which means that a cigarette smoker will pay continually increasing prices, because they identify cigarettes as something they need. If increased prices cause the demand for a good or service to decrease, that good is said to be *price-elastic*. The demand might decrease because the consumer decided they could do without the good, for example, not going out to eat. Or consumer behavior might change, as a person substitutes a nonbranded item of clothing for the more expensive branded one that they prefer. Goods that are price-inelastic are viewed as more necessary, because consumers will pay higher prices for them. Inelastic goods are much less likely to have their demand influenced by lower prices (Teitelbaum and Wilensky, 2013).

The concept of elasticity has several different and very important applications to health-related goods and services. First of all is the complex problem of determining the difference between a medically necessary treatment and a desired treatment. As one example, a lifesaving surgical procedure is clearly necessary, but many purely cosmetic surgeries are not. This distinction is important because health insurance covers medically necessary procedures, but not cosmetic procedures, unless there is an underlying medical problem. Reconstruction surgery after a breast is removed for cancer is an example of a procedure that is now viewed as a necessary part of recovery and is therefore covered by most health insurance policies.

The development of health insurance will be more completely described in Chapter 13, but the relationship of what is covered and the concept of elasticity must be considered here. Early health insurance policies developed primarily to help hospitals succeed financially, especially as hospital-based services became more expensive (Shi and Singh, 2014). Hospital services were universally viewed as medically necessary, and they were also the most expensive of all health services. Insurance is designed to reduce the risk from large and unexpected expenses, as will be described in Chapter 13, so these early policies did not cover less expensive services, such as care for acute illnesses provided in a primary care setting. This created an economic incentive for medical care to be located in the most expensive sector of the health care system: the hospital.

Unfortunately, this also created the view that less expensive services might not be as medically necessary. Certainly, outpatient care for acute illnesses (described in Chapter 9) is less urgent than hospital-based care, but still medically needed. However, as discussed in Chapter 9, primary care also includes many preventive services, ranging from routine well child examinations and vaccinations to screening for many different chronic illnesses. Health care professionals—both medical and public health—view these services as necessary, but many patients do not. People with no physical symptoms are not as likely to pay for services to maintain their health status, especially as prices for these preventive services rise. The best example of this is childhood vaccinations, which are very price-elastic, meaning that when people have to pay for these themselves, consumption drops, despite the urging of health professionals (Santerre and Neun, 2004).

By the 1970s, economists and other health policy analysts felt the health care financing system was creating perverse incentives, meaning that health care providers and hospitals made more money if people were sicker, but no money for keeping people well. The HMO legislation of 1973 (described in Chapter 14) was based on the idea that a different economic incentive was needed: one that would encourage the use of primary care, and especially preventive care. It was also anticipated that increased utilization of these lower-priced services would prevent the future need for more expensive hospital services. This legislation was the first to clearly understand the concept of elasticity in terms of health care services. Expensive and necessary (price-inelastic) hospital-based services needed to remain covered, but primary care and especially price-elastic preventive care also needed to be covered in health insurance policies. This led to a different sort of health insurance policy, one that encouraged more utilization of lower-priced primary care services in the hopes that utilization of expensive hospital services would be reduced. As might be expected, some economists worried about moral hazard—that is, people utilizing primary care services too frequently. As a result, most of the early HMOs charged a low copayment for each office visit to control for overutilization without interfering with the economic incentive to utilize more primary and preventive care services.

This chapter demonstrates that it is more complex to allocate health goods and services than any other types of goods and services in the U.S. economy. Medical care services do not completely fit the guidelines for either private or public goods. We have strong cultural values about the availability of health services for those who have limited financial access through no fault of their own. We also have strong cultural values about the importance of an economic system based on competition.

The economic concept of elasticity demonstrates how important the type of financing method is in influencing personal utilization of all types of health care goods and services. The financing system that depends on trying to fit health care goods into the free market model is market justice, and its assumptions have been described in this chapter. The alternative allocation system is based on viewing health goods as closer to public goods, and is called social justice. This model will be described in the final section of this chapter.

## Market Justice versus Social Justice: Where to Go Next?

A financing method that depends primarily on market justice tries to incorporate as many dimensions of the perfectly competitive free market system as possible. This is the conceptual model that has just been presented. The alternative model is called social justice, which is a concept that was first widely described in the mid-1970s (Kristol, 1978; Beauchamp and Childress, 2001). This is based on the philosophical notion that a just or good society is one in which it is a basic responsibility of society—or more properly, government—to equitably distribute all goods in society, determined on the basis of who needs them. Under this concept, health care is viewed not as a commodity to be purchased, but rather as a human right. Access to this right should not be by purchasing it on an individual basis; instead, access should be collectively assured. Under social justice, if one cannot have access to medical care because of lack of funds, this would be labeled as unfair, unjust, and also unethical. Under social justice, access to medical care is based only on medical need. Shi and Singh (2014) have expanded the application of these two models of allocation to the health care system. This section further expands this into policy considerations and also relates this to the field of public health.

Table 11.1 compares the significant features of each of these two allocation models. The market justice system is based on a politically conservative value system, one in which the individual has primary personal responsibility, both for individual lifestyle decisions, as well as purchasing any needed

**Table 11.1  Characteristics of the Market Justice and Social Justice Allocation Models**

| Characteristic | Market Justice Model | Social Justice Model |
|---|---|---|
| Nature of health care goods/ services | Commodities to be produced and sold based on demand | Services allocated based on medical need as basic human rights |
| Health Status | Primarily determined by individual determinants of health | Primarily determined by social determinants of health |
| Role of government | To ensure basic public and consumer safety | To ensure public and consumer safety and to provide equitable access |
| Financing | Primarily based on individual purchase, either directly or through health insurance | Financing shared by all in society through taxes |
| Concerns/fears | Denies needed care to people not responsible for their situation | Providing health care services to all is expensive |
| Political position | Conservative | Liberal |

*Source:* Adapted from Shi, L. and Singh, D. *Delivering Health Care in America: A Systems Approach*, 6th edition, Jones and Bartlett, Burlington, MA, 2014.

health care goods and services. The role of the government is very limited in this allocation system. Social justice is based on a more politically liberal position, one that argues that health is not mostly related to individual responsibility, but rather is based on social determinants, as discussed in Chapter 2. Ensuring good health and access to needed health care goods and services is a collective responsibility, and the role of the government is not only one of protection, but also of ensuring access to needed health care goods and services.

Table 11.1 represents what might be called the most pure—or perhaps extreme—representation of these two different allocation models. The current distribution system used in the U.S. health care system is a blend of both allocation models. Some goods/services are allocated by economic ability to pay, rather than simple medical need, as indicated by the very close association of health insurance coverage and utilization of health care goods and services. For example, employer-based insurance coverage went down significantly during the recession of 2007–2009, and utilization rates for all medical services also decreased (Holohan, 2011).

However, even under an extreme market justice model, the role of government is profound and influences all aspects of the system, beginning with extensive professional certification and licensure. In addition to this role of public safety, there are several programs that provide access to specific groups with inadequate access, which is a hallmark of the social justice system. Both Medicare and Medicaid represent an allocation method with some dimensions of a public good, although to a defined, targeted population. The Medicare program also incorporates a great deal of the private market system, as will be discussed in Chapters 13 and 18. In the end, even the most conservative analysts admit that allowing poor health to exist costs society more, primarily because health care professionals provide services to everybody with urgent medical needs, irrespective of their ability to pay. As will be shown in Chapter 15, this cost is passed on to everybody.

There are substantial concerns with following either of these two distribution models exclusively, as shown in Table 11.1. For example, the major weakness in the market justice model is that because health goods and services do not meet the demands of the competitive market, people who need necessary health care may not receive them. This is especially challenging when the group is viewed as innocent, as noted earlier. The biggest fear in a medical care system based on medical need is that it would cost too much, although this is how the countries described in Chapter 22 organize their health care systems for less cost and better outcomes. There is also a fear of lower quality associated with a completely public health care system, although this is also not true in the countries described in Chapter 22.

As might be expected, these two concepts of how to best allocate medical care services lead to very different sorts of policy suggestions in the health care field, including identifying the most appropriate role of the government in the health care system. The health care policy suggestions are very frequently anchored in the philosophical and political values expressed in Table 11.1, although they are infrequently labeled as such. The next chapter clarifies the link between philosophical and political values and various policy and regulatory actions.

# Acknowledgments

This topic owes its place in my class and this book to Dr. Bob Gage, the former director of University Health Services and Professor of Public Health at the University of Massachusetts. Dr. Thomas Duston made several important contributions to my overall understanding of medical economics over the years. He also provided important specific comments on this chapter. Annie Beach and especially Elyssa Williams provided very helpful feedback to both the content and readability of this chapter. Elyssa's notes as she outlined this content were very helpful in the revision process.

## Chapter 12

# From Economics to Health Policy and Regulation

This chapter builds on the previous one by linking the allocation models of market justice and social justice to health policy and regulation. Health policies and regulations are always accompanied with controversy, and it is often quite difficult to interpret the discussion. The assumption of this chapter is that all policy is political, and should first be assessed by linking it to the allocation model to understand the intention of the policy or regulation.

Any discussion about policy and regulations brings up the role of government in health care. This is a frustrating topic, because all levels of government are intricately and significantly involved with every single aspect of the health care system, including financing and delivery issues. If the influence of the government were removed from any health care program, it would drastically change the very nature of the program and of the U.S. health care system itself. As has been shown several times in earlier chapters, many of the regulatory activities focus on public and consumer safety. These are less controversial than the policies that address inequitable access, although both are strongly anchored in the social justice framework.

This chapter demonstrates that this dichotomy is not necessary, although it does require more of a bipartisan political atmosphere than currently exists. There are many policy suggestions that use the strengths of the market justice model and combine them with the assurances of the social justice model. Before presenting some examples of health policies that range along the spectrum, this chapter will first briefly describe the nature of health policy, including the process of identifying and implementing policy suggestions. This, of course, goes right into the topic of how various levels of government are involved in the regulation of the health care sector. This is a complex topic, and will be only briefly described here. The chapter concludes with several actual and suggested policy initiatives, and how they relate to the two models of allocating resources—market justice and social justice.

## What Is Health Policy?

A policy is any sort of an authoritative decision or guideline that "directs human behavior to a certain goal or end, either in a private or public sector" (Hanley, 1998). The focus in this book is on health policy, but it is often impossible to separate broader social policy from more specific health policy. One example of this is Social Security, a social policy enacted in 1935 that has important connections to both provision and financing of health care services (Shi and Singh, 2014).

A policy is directed at more than one person. For example, a primary care provider may strongly suggest that a patient quit smoking cigarettes, but this is not a policy, even if the physician says this to each patient. An antismoking policy includes a formal action directed at a group of people, such as banning smoking in public places. Policy is almost always thought of as involving some level of government. It is true that one of the primary roles of all levels of government is to create policy. However, private and/or professional organizations also engage in creating policy. Chapters 7 through 9 include many different examples of the role of professional organizations in the certification process. Policy is made by an authoritative organization, meaning one that has the power not only to create policy, but also to enforce it. Rules and regulations are the primary way in which policies are enforced.

Not all policies are based on regulations, in the sense that they impact a population without limiting or restricting behavior. These allocative policies are of two different types. The first are *distributive* (Longest, 2010). Examples of these sorts of policies include funding research and demonstration efforts through the National Institutes of Health. Although much of the biomedical technology is ultimately made and marketed by private, for-profit companies, most of the research leading to the development of the technology is funded by public tax funds. This distributive type of policy also includes establishing new programs, such as the health maintenance organization (HMO) legislation of 1973, mentioned previously (Shi and Singh, 2014).

A second category of allocative policies are called *redistributive*. They are designed to impact one specific targeted group that lacks access, with resources taken through taxes from another group to pay for the services. All of the welfare programs, including Medicaid, fall under this. Redistributive policies arise from the social justice model of allocation and act to correct failures of the free market that have caused an unfair distribution of health care goods and services.

Of course, there are many health policies that are overtly regulatory in nature, and these are called normative policies. These impact all parts of the U.S. health care system and all consumers. Some of these are enacted at the state level of government: for example, every state has regulations specifying what benefits/procedures health insurance companies must cover. Regulations on restaurants that were mentioned in Chapter 6 are also at the state level. Of course, many other regulations arise from the federal level, some of which states can modify. All health care institutions that receive any sort of public funds, from either Medicare or Medicaid, must meet federal standards, which states may add to, but cannot lower. All of the occupational safety standards are federal, which states may raise but not lower. It is these normative regulations that generate the most complaints. In almost all cases, these restrictions are enacted because of free market failures to adequately protect the safety of the public.

## Who Creates and Implements Health Policy?

Much of health policy is created by the government, at both federal and state levels. In both cases, health policy may originate either in the legislature or with the executive branch, the latter of which is the governor of a state or the president of the United States. The executive branch usually sets the policy agenda, with the legislative groups creating the specific policies. Much of health policy is in the form of legislation, so both executive and congressional branches must cooperate to pass policies that are consistent with the overall agenda.

At a broader level, health policy is heavily influenced by various stakeholders. Some of these are lobbying groups associated with professional associations such as the American Hospital Association. Others are lobbying groups associated with corporate interests, such as the American Pharmaceutical Association. A very large and diverse group is the general public, whose influence is felt in one of two ways. First is through the idea of representative government, where politicians are supposed to represent the interests of their supporters. Even though this may be more theoretical than realistic, it is commonly stated by both the legislative and executive branches of government as reasons for either supporting or opposing various pieces of legislation. More realistically, consumer input is more effective, through organized, lobbying groups. There are many of these, such as the American Association of Retired People, which represents a large group, as well as those that represent more narrowly targeted groups such as Mothers Against Drunk Driving.

Not all stakeholders care about the same things, and frequently the major interests of one stakeholder group are in conflict with another's. Figure 12.1 shows the major groups of stakeholders and identifies some of the broad issues with which they are most concerned. Not only do each of the stakeholder groups included in Figure 12.1 have different goals, they frequently also have very different philosophical and/or political views of how health care goods and services should be allocated. Some are very closely allied with the idea of market justice, whereas others are closely allied with social justice. The result of this is a very slow change process in the health field, which will be described in Chapter 17.

Even the very brief description of the policy-making process included here is not complete without an even briefer note about the budget and how it relates to policy making. As each piece of health policy comes with a budget allocation, the budgeting process at both the state and federal levels is intricately involved in the policy making process. It is extremely common for legislation expressing policy to be dramatically altered because of budgetary constraints. At the federal level, the Office of Management and Budget (OMB) has a central role to play in the implementation of health policy. The OMB analyzes the cost of policy options and compares them to the overall agenda of the president. It also predicts the cost of the regulatory infrastructure needed to implement a policy, as well as estimating the cost of the policy itself.

Once passed by the Congress and signed into law by the president (or governor, if at a state level), a piece of legislation frequently undergoes a period of specification. The legislation goes to a committee appointed by the executive branch, which includes all relevant stakeholder groups. The role of this committee is to translate the legislation into specific guidelines that can then be implemented (Teitelbaum and Wilensky, 2013). An example of this process occurred in 2013 with one part of the Affordable Care Act (ACA). Included in the legislation was the stipulation that all health insurance policies must cover

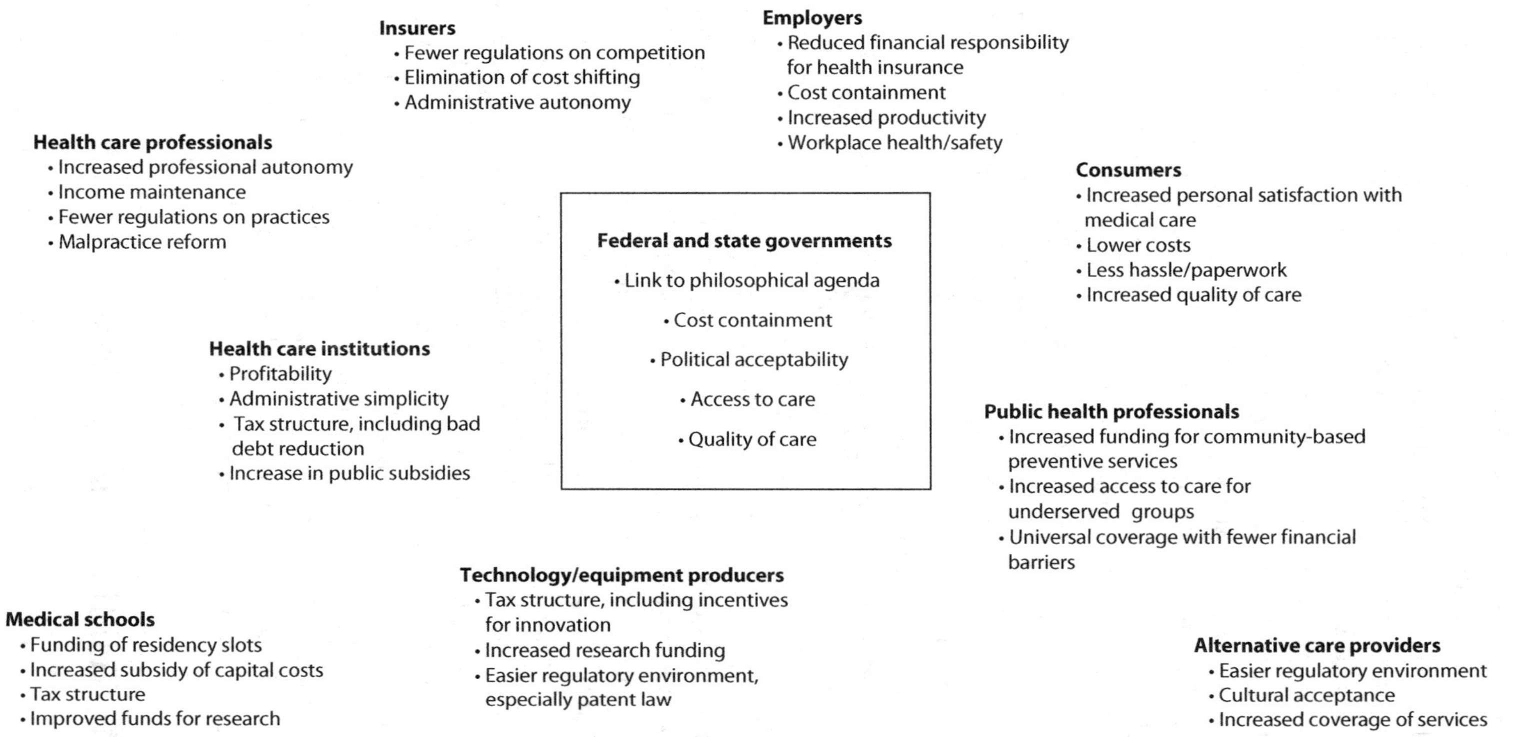

**Health care professionals**
• Increased professional autonomy
• Income maintenance
• Fewer regulations on practices
• Malpractice reform

**Insurers**
• Fewer regulations on competition
• Elimination of cost shifting
• Administrative autonomy

**Employers**
• Reduced financial responsibility for health insurance
• Cost containment
• Increased productivity
• Workplace health/safety

**Consumers**
• Increased personal satisfaction with medical care
• Lower costs
• Less hassle/paperwork
• Increased quality of care

**Health care institutions**
• Profitability
• Administrative simplicity
• Tax structure, including bad debt reduction
• Increase in public subsidies

**Federal and state governments**
• Link to philosophical agenda
• Cost containment
• Political acceptability
• Access to care
• Quality of care

**Public health professionals**
• Increased funding for community-based preventive services
• Increased access to care for underserved groups
• Universal coverage with fewer financial barriers

**Medical schools**
• Funding of residency slots
• Increased subsidy of capital costs
• Tax structure
• Improved funds for research

**Technology/equipment producers**
• Tax structure, including incentives for innovation
• Increased research funding
• Easier regulatory environment, especially patent law

**Alternative care providers**
• Easier regulatory environment
• Cultural acceptance
• Increased coverage of services

**Figure 12.1   Major stockholders in health policy and their main focus areas. (Adapted from Shi, L. and Singh, D.A., *Delivering Health Care in America*, 6th edition, Jones and Bartlett, Burlington, MA, 2014.)**

a standard package of preventive services without any deductible or copay, to eliminate financial barriers. The purpose of this was to increase access to preventive health services using the understanding of elasticity described in Chapter 11. The committee identified 15 separate services that they defined as preventive, and would therefore be provided with no consumer cost sharing. Some of these were expected and predictable, such as immunizations (Starr, 2011). The most surprising service to be included as one of the essential preventive services was contraceptives for women, a recommendation that was heavily supported by several consumer groups as well as public health professionals (APA, 2014). The negative reaction to this decision was by very conservative political and religious groups that do not support contraception. The opposition involved extensive media coverage, as well as several court cases, including the Supreme Court. The Obama administration eventually won all the arguments, but many compromises were made in the process, such as allowing religious groups exemptions so they did not pay directly for contraception (Teitelbaum and Wilensky, 2013; PPA, 2014).

Once all implementation details are specified, health legislation is then implemented by what is best termed the health bureaucracy. For example, at the federal level, there are three health agencies—each with very significant levels of responsibility for enacting health policies. These three are the Department of Health and Human Services (DHHS), the Department of Defense (DoD), and the Department of Veterans Affairs (VA) (Teitelbaum and Wilensky, 2013). Both the DoD and the VA are responsible for health insurance programs for both active and retired military, as well as research into relevant health-related issues. The DHHS has thousands of programs, including those that provide direct services, programs that sponsor basic research, and also demonstration projects for innovative ways to provide health care services. The DHHS has 12 separate agencies, each of which houses important regulatory agencies that protect the safety of the American public such as the Food and Drug Administration, the Environmental Protection Agency, and Occupational Safety and Health Administration (Teitelbaum and Wilensky, 2013). The everyday life of each American is directly impacted by more than one of these 12 federal agencies.

## How Can We Tell If a Policy Works?

Determining the effectiveness of specific health policies is a very complex and inherently frustrating process. Because of the political process of passing legislation, most health legislation is narrow in scope. Each piece of legislation is a result of compromise between the executive branch and the congressional branch, as well as the various congressional and budgetary committees that analyze and alter specifics, as described above. In general, more narrowly specified policies are more likely to make it through the political process. Frequently, one narrow policy is meant to fit in with another, previously passed policy in the hopes of achieving larger goals, such as lowering the cost of care, improving access to care, or improving health status.

Health conditions that policies are trying to remedy are very often related to larger social conditions that represent a basic feature of American life, such as income inequality. These social issues are all very slow to change. Also, because health policy is political, policies can often change as political parties change the level of power they have in both the congressional and executive branches. The result is often not enough time to determine the outcomes.

Despite this difficulty, there are several organizations dedicated to the analysis and evaluation of the impact of not only specific health policies, but also research in the health field. For example, one of the 12 agencies within the DHHS is the Agency for Health Care Research and Quality. The mission of this agency is to monitor and ensure the quality of health care delivered to Americans, irrespective of the funding source. This agency sponsors evidence-based research projects to determine the highest quality and most effective medical care. They also sponsor research into various models of delivering care that emphasize cost control (Teitelbaum and Wilensky, 2013).

Two other organizations are also significantly involved with assessing the effectiveness of health policies. One is the OMB, which has already been described. The other is the Congressional Budget Office (CBO). The CBO is an independent and nonpartisan office that provides advice and analysis to Congress and the president on economic and budgetary matters (CBO, 2011). Some of the most recent reviews have involved an analysis of the impact of the ACA on the overall budget and the federal deficit. In 2013, the CBO suggested 16 different health-related options for reducing the federal deficit, with an analysis of each one (CBO, 2013).

## Examples of Policies and Links to Models of Allocation

The philosophical differences between the two allocation models discussed in Chapter 11 are striking, beginning with how to describe the problem that a policy is trying to resolve. Table 12.1 shows the differences in how to describe and solve the general problem of the cost of medical care. The second part of this table shows different policy suggestions for some more specific problems including the price of prescription drugs, disease management, medical malpractice, and policy solutions for cigarette smoking. Each of the examples shown in Table 12.1 has been suggested by one of the two major parties. The Republican Party is the more conservative of the two national parties, and the right wing, commonly referred to as the Tea Party, is the group that holds most strongly to the market justice view. Libertarians also tend to be strong believers in the model of market justice, and are also considered politically conservative. Strong conservatives believe that consumers should be

**Table 12.1    Policy Ideas and Models of Allocation**

| Cost of Medical Care | Market Justice | Social Justice |
|---|---|---|
| Main problem | Medical care costs too much with less than acceptable outcomes. | Too many are uninsured, resulting in lack of access. This results in lack of care to many people, but also results in passing on the cost of caring for uninsured to others. |
| General ideas for policies to solve this problem | • Increase competition between health insurance companies.<br>• Increase personal responsibility.<br>• Encourage states to develop their own plans for maximum flexibility.<br>• Minimize role of federal government.<br>• Encourage establishment of for-profit retail clinics and ambulatory clinics to increase access and provide competition.<br>• Reform tax codes to provide incentives to businesses and individuals; use tax credits whenever possible.<br>• Cost savings through technology, especially electronic records. | • Make insurance available to all in order to spread out the cost over a larger group, and to increase access for everyone.<br>• Investigate social and environmental causes of poor health.<br>• Maximize role of federal government so all states provide same benefits to all. Encourage states to develop plans within a standard benefit framework.<br>• Cost savings through technology, especially electronic records.<br>• Reform tax structure to redistribute resources to fund more direct service programs. Use tax code to encourage more nonprofit organizations in direct care. |

*(Continued)*

**Table 12.1 (Continued)    Policy Ideas and Models of Allocation**

| *Examples of Other Specific Problems/Issues* | *Market Justice* | *Social Justice* |
|---|---|---|
| Prescription drugs are too costly | • Increase competition by allowing reimportation of drugs from selected countries for individuals to purchase.<br>• Encourage faster introduction of generic drugs.<br>• Speed up the FDA approval process for new drugs. | • Increase competition by allowing reimportation of drugs, under an inspection process to assure quality.<br>• Encourage faster introduction of generic drugs.<br>• Support the government buying selected drugs in bulk to resell at lower prices to consumers. |
| Disease management | • Establish Accountable Care Organizations to provide cost-effective care for chronic diseases.<br>• Use multidisciplinary teams of health care professionals that involve nonphysicians. | • Establish Accountable Care Organizations to provide cost-effective care for chronic diseases.<br>• Use multidisciplinary teams of health care professionals that involve nonphysicians. |
| Medical malpractice | • Tort reform to control the number of lawsuits against physicians and limit the settlement amount.<br>• Set up hospital-based systems to prevent errors and link payment to this. | • Promote new models that build on research identifying why physicians make errors.<br>• Set up hospital-based systems to prevent errors. |
| Cigarette smoking | • Work with businesses to increase accessibility to workplace smoking cessation sessions.<br>• Enforce age limits on purchase of cigarettes.<br>• Warning labels on cigarettes.<br>• Institute a fee for smokers on Medicare and Medicaid. | • Ban the sale of cigarettes.<br>• Eliminate federal tax subsidies to tobacco farmers.<br>• Warning labels on cigarettes.<br>• Ban smoking from public places.<br>• Taxes on cigarettes diverted into educational programs.<br>• Increase educational programs. |

closely connected to the goods we purchase, including health care goods and services. They feel that we should actually purchase what we use, that we should choose the product we want, that we are personally responsible for our health, and that increased competition is the best way to accomplish these ideals and reduce costs. Furthermore, they view government regulations as mainly restricting the ability of the market to allocate goods. This philosophical view translates into some of the policy positions shown in Table 12.1.

The most liberal philosophical position involves a strong belief in the model of allocation based on social justice. Under this model, the free market is thought to create unfair allocations and one of the major roles of government is to correct this inequity. The strongest advocates of this position support tax-based financing of the medical care system and are generally opposed to the existence of for-profit organizations in the health field. The Democratic Party is more liberal than the Republican Party, but only the left wing of the Democratic Party would agree to the most extreme version of social justice. Table 12.1 shows some of the policy positions that are supported by Democrats and others who support health policy being based on this allocation model.

Does this mean that we have only these two choices: that of a strong belief in market justice or an equally strong belief in social justice models of resource allocation? Policies anchored in an extreme model of market justice change the basic nature of our health care system, whereas policies arising from an extreme social justice model challenge our basic cultural and economic identity. A moment's reflection on the many examples of suggested—and enacted—health policy reveals that policies at either end of this spectrum are seldom actually implemented. Policies enacted by both political parties are more likely to be somewhere in the middle, and incorporate features of each allocation model, depending on the issue.

Figure 12.2 shows some specific examples of suggested and implemented policies for one of the biggest and most complex policy issues: how to finance medical care services. Not all possible policies are identified here, because the sheer number of policy suggestions do not permit that. The purpose of this figure is to demonstrate that it is better to consider these two allocation models as ends of a spectrum rather than dichotomous choices. By understanding the range of policy suggestions for financing medical care, it is easier to evaluate the policies. Each of the policies on this figure has actually been formally suggested by some portion of each national party, although not all have been implemented. For example, the extreme conservative position of eliminating all regulations on health insurance companies (#1) has been suggested only infrequently. The less extreme version of

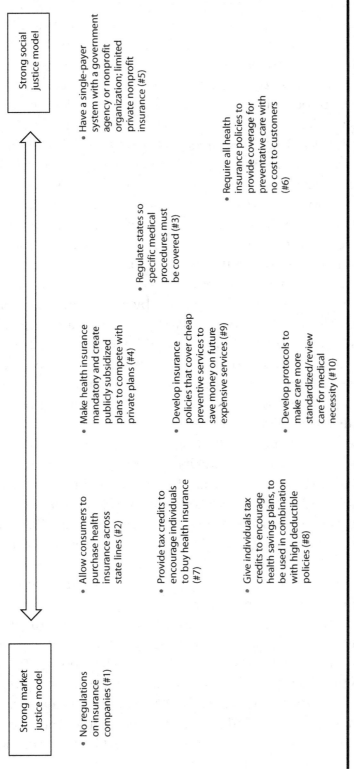

**Figure 12.2 Specific policy proposals for financing medical care services.**

loosening regulations on consumers' ability to freely purchase health policies (#2) was part of the Republican Party's presidential platform in 2008 and 2012. Each state regulates the insurance companies that operate within that state. This includes not only approving rates, but also the types of services that are required to be covered. States that require more covered services and higher levels of benefits have higher premiums. Under current policies, consumers are restricted to purchasing health insurance policies in the state in which they live. Limiting consumers in this way is justified as a consumer protection regulation, as having consumers make choices among policies with very different levels of benefits is widely viewed as being too challenging. The platform policy suggestion of the Republican Party loosening this restriction was based on the idea that consumers could have access to the required knowledge to exercise a choice. Under a strong belief in market justice, a consumer should have the freedom to make a choice to have less health insurance if they wished to pay less money.

Critics of this point out that a bad choice by a consumer has consequences not only for that person, but also for others. If a consumer purchases a health insurance policy with limited benefits, the cost of medically necessary care will be shifted to others. The result is increased premiums for those who have insurance, or increased taxes. Economists have a term for this issue: a free rider is someone who gets a benefit without purchasing it (Hanley, 1998; Feldstein, 2005).

There are several possible solutions to this issue, one of which is to require all states to offer similar benefits (#3). Another solution is to require or mandate every person to buy health insurance, within a standardized framework (#4). This, of course, is one of the central policies of the ACA, and one of the more controversial ones. As noted in Figure 12.2, this policy suggestion is actually close to the middle of the spectrum of values, meaning that this idea should have bipartisan support. The irony of the strong opposition is the original idea of mandating health insurance coverage was a conservative idea. Free riders weaken the strength of the market justice model of allocation. Conservative economists have always struggled with the issue of free riders and how to control this problem with a minimum of government regulation, which they also oppose. The Heritage Foundation, a conservative think tank, was the first to publish a strong opinion about requiring each individual to purchase health insurance as a measure of personal responsibility (Starr, 2011). This was the central feature of the Massachusetts statewide health care reform enacted by Governor Romney, who later as a presidential candidate opposed this feature of the ACA. The opposition to an individual mandate was not only from conservatives, but also from liberals operating under a strong social justice position. Their argument was that it was unfair to require individuals to purchase a product that was too expensive for them. This criticism led to the creation of subsidies for the purchase of health insurance.

The ACA will be more completely described in Chapter 17, but two features relevant to the philosophical discussion of this chapter need to be included here. First, the idea of subsidies comes from a social justice perspective of redistributing income. It is also an example of a redistributive policy, as discussed earlier in this chapter. The second feature in the ACA legislation relevant to this discussion created a marketplace where publicly subsidized health care plans compete against private health insurance plans. This policy suggestion (#4) is right in the middle of the value spectrum, although it is more strongly related to market justice than social justice. A marketplace is consistent with the ideas expressed by market justice, whereas creating subsidies for those who cannot afford this required product stems directly from the social justice allocation model. This was opposed by many conservatives as well as those who favor an allocation model more strongly based on social justice.

The strongest social justice position is shown on the far right side of Figure 12.2 (#5). This proposal eliminates the role of the free market in health insurance and creates a governmental or nonprofit organization to allocate medical resources based on medical need. This specific version of this idea is termed a single payer system, and will be described more fully in Chapters 17 and 22. This policy idea has been introduced several times in the U.S. Congress, but always defeated (Starr, 2011).

A strongly liberal policy included in the ACA is the requirement that health insurance policies be required to cover preventive care visits without any financial barriers (#6), as was discussed earlier. This is justified as a cost-savings policy, because it is widely believed that increasing participation in preventive activities will reduce consumption of more expensive, inelastic health care services later on.

Figure 12.2 shows other examples of both conservative and liberal policy suggestions. Conservative policies tend to be anchored in allocative policies, especially those that are distributive. Conservatives tend to most dislike policies that are based on income redistribution and support policies that establish economic incentives encouraging people to behave in certain ways. For example, most conservatives support people purchasing health insurance policies, as an expression of personal responsibility for the cost of their care. They support encouraging this behavior through economic incentives, such as tax credits (#7). A very popular conservative policy suggestion is tax credits to encourage Health Savings Accounts, which are coupled with purchasing of low premium health insurance policies with high deductibles (#8), as will be explained in Chapter 13. This policy suggestion is based on several of the economic guidelines noted in Chapter 11, especially the idea that consumers should pay for the medical services they utilize.

Democrats are more likely to support redistributive policies, including programs financed through the tax structure, such as Medicare, which will be described in Chapter 18. Many of the policy suggestions offered by Democrats are also normative, that is, based on regulations. Of course, there are many examples of this, many of which are also supported by more conservative Republicans. Many policies that are aimed at improving cost control fall under these normative, regulatory-based policies, several of which can be seen in Table 12.1. Figure 12.2 gives two examples of policies that create cost control mechanisms for medical care financing, both of which are used by the HMO model of health insurance, which will be more completely explained in Chapter 14. The idea that health insurance would cover the less expensive preventive services (#9) is central to the HMO model of health insurance. The idea of developing protocols to standardize treatment (#10) is also heavily used by HMOs and is directly drawn from the economic guidelines described in Chapter 11. Both of these cost control measures have bipartisan support.

Policies related to financing health care goods and services cover the range of philosophical and political values, from the most extreme support of the social justice model to the most extreme market justice model. However, as can be seen in Figure 12.2, the policies most likely to be implemented are in the middle of this spectrum, meaning they include components of both the competitive free market as well as the assurance of providing services to those who may not be able to purchase them. This latter idea of protection is central to the social justice model of resource allocation.

There is a very important aspect of health care goods and services that make this commodity unique. This was mentioned in Chapter 11, but bears repeating here. A person who cannot purchase any other commodity, even a good as necessary as food or housing, will not be given food, even if hungry; or shelter, even if homeless. There are a range of social agencies that attempt to meet these basic needs, but this depends on the ability of the person to connect with these resources. However, if a person with no insurance requires urgent medical care, the services are provided. The cost of this care is borne by others in several different ways (which will be described more completely in Chapter 15). This means that increasing health insurance coverage to all is not only a matter of social justice, but is also a matter of economic fairness, as is recognized by many other countries (Chapter 22).

## Summary

A basic assumption of this chapter is that all health policy has its origins in political and philosophical values. The effort to either evaluate or analyze any proposed health policy should begin with understanding the political and philosophical value in which the policy is anchored. Both this chapter and the previous one have used the idea of two different models for allocating resources to highlight the differences between policy suggestions. The market justice model of allocation is very closely related to the capitalistic basis of the U.S. economy and is based on a set of guidelines related to how well this model works. The social justice model is based on the idea that health care goods and services are very different from other commodities and therefore cannot be distributed using anything other than responding to medical needs. This approach further recognizes that medical care is unlike any other commodity, because people generally get needed health care even if they cannot pay for it.

The tension between a political and/or philosophical belief in market justice versus a belief in social justice can be seen in every aspect of the health care delivery system. For example, in terms of financing, which will be discussed in the next few chapters, a market justice perspective leads to a system in which every person is responsible for purchasing their own health insurance policy (or not) from a private, for-profit company. A social justice perspective leads to a policy where health care is financed by a general tax on all, and separated from actual use, as in most European countries, as will be noted in Chapter 22.

This chapter has demonstrated that most of the health policies regarding financing medical care include both perspectives. The idea that more money buys more and possibly better health care services is not a policy that most Americans can live with. For that reason, there are many principles of social justice built into the financing of medical care. Some policies establish specific programs directed at groups that are more vulnerable, including the poor and the elderly. Others are regulations aimed at protecting all consumers, such as requiring licensure to practice.

This dichotomy of philosophical perspective has produced a mixed model of allocation of health care goods and services in the United States.

This mixed model has produced mixed results, primarily because of the lack of central planning and/or cost control. As will be shown in Chapter 22, it is not unusual to have a mixed model of allocation, but the United States has a larger portion of health care goods and services allocated by the market justice model than any other country. There are several other models of resource allocation recognized by economists that do not involve perfect competition, as is assumed in the market justice model. Some markets are *monopolistic* if there is only one seller controlling the whole market (Feldstein, 2005). A market may also be *monopolistically competitive*. In this model, there are several sellers, although they are regulated. There are licensure and certification barriers to entering the market. Consumers do have access to information and some choice, but more limited than in the perfectly competitive model (Teitelbaum and Wilensky, 2013).

This is much closer to the situation in the health care market, even though the term monopoly seems to contradict the very idea of competition. However, other countries exert central regulatory influences that still allow competition, as will be described in Chapter 22.

It is within this mixed model of allocation and extensive but fragmented regulation that health care goods and services are financed in the United States. The next three chapters provide more detail about that, with Chapter 13 describing the nature of health insurance, Chapter 14 describing two basic models of health insurance, and Chapter 15 detailing how health care providers are paid.

## Acknowledgments

This chapter was significantly improved through the review and suggestions of the following students: Emily Assarian, Ryan Barry, Bianca Doone, and Nicolas Dundas. Dr. Thomas Duston made many important suggestions and observations about economics and policy; and specific suggestions on the table and figures. Emily constructed a draft of Figures 12.1 and 12.2, and Jessi Duston created the final version of these. Jonathan Rosenblatt served as the on-call person for final corrections.

# Chapter 13

## Health Care Financing: Health Insurance

The topic of health care financing is viewed by some as boring, by others as hopelessly complicated, and by everybody as frustrating. It is all of these things, but it is also essential to understand because financing is one of the most important determinants of access to medical care services. Both demand and supply of health care goods and services are significantly impacted by financing methods. Financing methods impact the amount of money spent in the health care system, as well as the many policies to control expenditures.

The U.S. medical care financing system is influenced by the philosophical tension between the two models of resource allocation that were discussed in the previous two chapters. As a result, the U.S. health care system has funding roles for both public and private financing, each with somewhat different government regulations. The result is a complicated, fragmented, and nontransparent pattern of financing. A particular complication is the lack of transparency for costs of services. The whole health insurance system runs on the basis of what different insurance payers will reimburse for a service, which is not based on actual cost.

The purpose of this chapter is to develop a basic knowledge about health insurance and its general role in the financing of medical care. This will begin with a general discussion of health insurance and how it developed in the United States. Exactly how insurance companies share costs with consumers is explained, as well as the different types of health insurance available in the United States. The United States has always been confronted with an unacceptably large percentage of uninsured, which has driven many health care reform efforts, as will be described in Chapter 17. The uninsured are described in this chapter and the impact of this group on the whole health care system is explored. The relationship of health insurance and health status concludes this chapter.

## What Is Health Insurance and Why Do We Have It?

Health insurance is a mechanism by which consumers have some financial protection from unexpected and expensive medical care services. A health insurance policy is a way in which consumers protect themselves from risk and uncertainty. This protection comes from pooling resources with a group of people so costs can be spread out over the whole group. Insurance is necessary because medical costs are not evenly distributed in the population. In the United States, about 20% of the population uses more than 80% of all health care dollars spent (Kovner and Knickman, 2011). Buying an insurance policy is different from buying an actual good or a service. Part of what is being purchased is a level of comfort that we are protected if we become part of the group that needs expensive medical care services. Insurance is buying access to health care services at some point in time in the future when the services are needed.

The idea of cost sharing across a large group is common to all forms of insurance, but there is one feature of health insurance that is unique, as has been noted previously. If a person loses either their house or car in an accident, they are financially individually responsible for recovering from that whole loss: no one helps to pay for either another car or a house. However, in the medical care world, hospitals treat everyone who shows up in their emergency room, even if they cannot pay for it. This free rider problem was identified in Chapter 11. As is true in most cases, there is no such thing as free. There are several ways for hospitals to recover the cost of this uncompensated care, which were identified in Chapter 8. One of these ways is cost shifting. This occurs when a hospital passes on to a private health insurance company part of the cost of care for a person insured under a public insurance program or a person with no health insurance. This eventually results in insured people experiencing increased premiums. It is this free rider problem that caused the Obama administration to mandate that each person must have some level of health insurance, as will be discussed in Chapter 17.

Throughout this chapter, the term group insurance will be used. Most people have insurance through some sort of a group. For employed people, this is an employment group. There are several targeted insurance programs in the United States. These are their own groups and include Medicare, Medicaid, and the Veterans Administration. These will each be described in more detail in Section IV of this book.

The general term used for all health insurance is third-party payer. The first two parties are the patient and the physician. The fact that insurance companies are viewed as a party to this medical interaction underscores the importance of the insurance function in the U.S. health care system as one that facilitates both supply and demand. Of all the money spent in the health care sector, almost 70% is from some sort of third-party payer (Teitelbaum and Wilensky, 2013). Having health insurance is one of the strongest determinants of whether and what type of medical care a person will have.

## Consumer Responsibilities: What Do We Pay for and What Does Health Insurance Pay for?

The consumer buys an insurance policy to reduce their personal risk for a large, unanticipated medical expense. The health insurance company is also trying to reduce financial risk by determining the appropriate price for its policies to cover the medical expenses of the entire insured group. This process is called *medical underwriting*. The risk of any specific individual experiencing some significant health problem is almost never predictable, but the risk of a larger group can be estimated by using population health estimates similar to some of the health status indicators described in Chapter 3. Insurance functions as a means of shifting financial responsibility for medical expenses from an individual to a whole group, so an individual does not pay entirely for the cost of their own care. Naturally, some people will pay more than the benefits they receive, whereas others will pay less than the benefits they receive. An important part of the medical underwriting process is not only to determine how much each person should pay, but also to identify what is an equitable loss for any one individual (Vaughn and Elliott, 1987).

A longstanding problem for health insurance companies is the tendency for healthy people to not buy health insurance coverage. This leads

| Premiums | Policy-specific cost-sharing methods |
|---|---|
| Experience rating:<br>If a person uses more services, their individual premium is increased, and if they use too many services, the insurance company could discontinue their policy. | Deductibles:<br>The amount of money that the insured individual must pay before the health insurance plan pays anything (typically an annual amount). |
| Community rating:<br>Each person within a group is charged same amount regardless of risk factors (incl. personal habits and occupation risk, age, gender, etc.). | Copayments:<br>Set fees that must be paid every time an individual uses a service. |
| Adjusted community rating:<br>Incorporation of both experience rating and community rating. Different groups charged different amounts by health insurance. Individuals within these groups pay the same. | Coinsurance:<br>The percentage of the cost of the medical care received paid by the insured individual. |
| | Catastrophic cap:<br>The maximum out of pocket costs a consumer has to pay in a single year (the rest of which will be covered by the insurance company). |

**Figure 13.1    Methods of cost sharing for health insurance.**

to what economists call *adverse selection*, when only mostly unhealthy people buy health insurance policies (Penner, 2004). When this happens, a health insurance company has to pay out a bigger proportion of their revenues in benefits to people, which in turn leads to increases in premiums for the whole group. It is in the best interest of both an insurance company and the consumer to have as large and as healthy a group as possible.

Part of this underwriting process is determining how many costs should be shared by consumers. Health insurance companies have two general ways of passing costs to consumers: one involves how much to charge each individual for the health insurance and the second is to determine what other cost sharing methods might be implemented once care is needed. These two categories are shown in Figure 13.1.

## Determining the Price of Premiums

Premiums are the annual cost each individual pays for their health insurance coverage. This is the most visible cost of health insurance, so the most competition occurs around the issue of the cost of premiums. Although this is an important cost, it is by no means the only one, as will be seen later. There are three different ways insurance companies determine how much to charge people. The first method is called experience rating and is how car insurance works. This is based on predicting how many services each person will use during the year, based on their health status and selected demographic variables. If a person uses more services, their individual premium is increased and if they use too many services, the insurance company could discontinue their policy. It is very labor-intensive to get health information from each individual, so health insurance companies predict utilization based on characteristics of the group they are insuring. This might include demographic characteristics such as age and gender, but also utilization rates from the previous year.

The health insurance company benefits from this method of determining premiums because it can more accurately predict the amount of money they will need to pay out for a group. Healthy individuals benefit from this method, because they have lower premiums. However, this method of pricing premiums penalizes sick people, and can cause very sick people to lose their insurance. Insurance companies are not allowed to charge for premiums using this method when they are insuring a group, but this method is still used when individuals are buying insurance independently.

The second method of determining the price of premiums is *community rating*. In this method, each person within a group is charged the same amount for a premium, regardless of risk factors such as personal health habits or age. If the group is large and relatively healthy, this produces relatively low costs to consumers and relatively high profits to the health insurance companies. This is the foundation for basing the group on employment, because it is assumed that people who work are healthy. As people utilize medical services, premiums go up for the whole group.

The third method of determining the appropriate prices of premiums encompasses both of these approaches to improve predictions of utilization. This is called *adjusted or modified community rating* (Teitelbaum and Wilensky, 2013; Shi and Singh, 2014). Under this method, health insurance companies charge groups different amounts for premiums, although each person within the group is charged the same amount. These differences can include demographic factors, such as age, gender, and family size, as well as geographic factors relating to the region of the country in which the group is located. This is the method used by the Affordable Care Act (ACA) to set premiums, as will be discussed in Chapter 17. Under the ACA, companies can adjust premiums for age, family size, geography, and tobacco use (Shi and Singh, 2014).

The problem faced by health insurance companies and consumers alike is that everybody wants to pay the lowest price possible for health insurance, but consumers want the maximum coverage when they need medical care, which is frequently unpredictable.

## Other Methods of Cost Sharing with Consumers

Figure 13.1 shows four other ways in which health insurance companies share costs with consumers. These costs are not as obvious as the cost of premiums, and are often part of the fine print that all consumers are warned to read carefully. These are not all used by all insurance policies, but every insurance plan uses at least one of these methods of cost sharing.

The most familiar method of cost sharing is also used in car insurance: the *deductible*. This is an annual amount of money that the insured individual must pay before the health insurance plan pays anything. In 2013, for example, nearly 80% of people with health insurance had a plan that involved meeting some sort of deductible first (Shi and Singh, 2014). Many consumers reduce the price of the premium for their car insurance by paying a high deductible amount. Until recently, this was not possible in health insurance, and deductibles were generally low (in the $250–$1000 per year range).

However, consumer demand for lower premiums for health insurance led the health insurance industry to develop a new type of health insurance plan called a high deductible health plan (HDHP). The premiums in these plans can be quite low, with high deductibles, such as $5000 or more. These plans first became available to individuals, but later also became available to groups, as long as they were associated with a Health Savings Account (HSA) of some sort. This is a market justice approach to health insurance, as noted in Figure 12.2. These kinds of insurance plans will be described in more detail later in this chapter.

Two other forms of cost sharing are *copayments* and *coinsurance*. These terms are frequently confused, but are quite different. Copayments are set fees that must be paid every time an individual uses a service. They may be set at different amounts, depending on which type of service is being utilized. For example, seeing a primary care provider usually involves a copayment that is less than seeing a specialist; utilizing an emergency room requires a higher copayment. Copayments are unique to health maintenance organizations, which will be described more fully in Chapter 14.

A more common form of cost sharing is *coinsurance.* This requires an insured individual to pay a percentage of the cost of the medical care received. A very common percentage is 20%, meaning that the health insurance company pays 80% of the cost of a medical service, after the deductible has been paid by the consumer. The consumer then pays the remaining 20% of the cost. This is a widely used method of cost sharing, and there may be different coinsurance rates for physicians and hospitals that are in different networks. This will be more completely explained in Chapter 14.

The last method of cost sharing in Figure 13.1 is the *catastrophic cap.* This was initially how insurance companies protected themselves from very large losses, by setting a maximum amount they would pay out for medical services. As technology improved and costs increased, health insurance policies began to offer a range of catastrophic caps, with lower ones being linked to lower premiums. Consumers pay more attention to premiums than other forms of cost sharing, and many people learned of this limitation only after they had exceeded the cap. One of the most significant restrictions on the private insurance industry from the ACA is the elimination of this type of catastrophic cap. Today, the concept of catastrophic caps has shifted from protection of the insurance company to protection of the consumer. The most common use of this term now is to represent the maximum out-of-pocket costs a consumer has to pay in a single year. Once this limit has been reached, the insurance plan has to pay all the remaining costs (Shi and Singh, 2014).

The primary reason for these types of cost sharing techniques is for the health insurance company to have some protection against paying out more money in benefits than they receive from premiums. The behavior these cost sharing methods are trying to impact is the decision that leads to a consumer using some medical service. From a conservative perspective, the very idea of health insurance increases moral hazard, because the medical service is no longer paid for by the individual. This means there need to be controls to limit utilizing too many services, and in the United States, a major way of controlling utilization is through economic incentives. This is also a method of rationing care. In other countries, utilization is controlled, but not primarily through economic incentives. Medical care is rationed by prioritizing urgent medical needs to receive care before less urgent ones. This is thought to cause longer waiting times for less urgent procedures, although—as shown in Chapter 22—this is not always true.

## History of the Health Insurance Industry in the United States

The method used in the United States to finance health care services has arisen in the context of our cultural, political, and philosophical values, especially in the tension between the assumptions of the market justice model versus the social justice model. The result is a system that is very different from that of other countries, as will be shown in more detail in Chapter 22.

Many of the national health care systems of other countries were devised in the late 1800s and early 1900s, which is when the U.S. system was starting to be more formally organized. The early systems that were of the most interest to U.S. politicians were those used in Germany, enacted in 1883, and in Great Britain, which was enacted in 1911 (Starr, 2011). In both of these countries, there was a focus on providing health insurance to workers and their families. This rested partly on a political goal. If there were more economic stability in workers, it was thought they would be less likely to vote socialist parties into power. Both of these early efforts were called sickness funds, and they were viewed as a way to increase the wealth of a country by encouraging a healthy and productive workforce. Although the focus was on workers and their families, both Germany and Great Britain made their systems nationwide and compulsory. In the United States, the Socialist Party, a fringe, third political party, was the first to endorse a national, compulsory health insurance plan. In 1912, the Progressive Party under Theodore Roosevelt had a platform in their party endorsing a publicly funded national health insurance plan. As noted in Chapter 7, this was opposed by physicians, industry and labor leaders, as well as the insurance industry, and failed (Starr, 2011).

In the absence of any sort of public insurance plan, several private insurance companies created some health plans. The earliest of these was in 1929, with the establishment of Blue Cross, created as a nonprofit organization so it would not conflict with the professional, financial, and ethical interests of physicians. This was opposed by most of the medical profession, which believed that people should pay directly for all their medical services

(Shi and Singh, 2014). During the years around the Depression, hospitals and physicians experienced increasing financial difficulties because people could not pay for medical services. Public interest in some type of national health insurance reemerged at this time. In response to the fear of a more central government role, physicians began a health insurance plan of their own: Blue Shield (Starr, 1982). This plan was limited to coverage of medical costs incurred in a hospital environment, and was supported by the American Medical Association as a way to keep medical decision making firmly in the hands of physicians (Shi and Singh, 2014).

World War II had a profound effect on the development of the private health insurance market in the United States. A loophole in the war-related wage freeze was that fringe benefits could be raised as long as they did not exceed 5% of total wages (Starr, 1982). This created an incentive for employers to offer health insurance as a fringe benefit. This was coupled with the growth of labor unions, which, after a long struggle, finally won the right to collective bargaining. More and more people gained health insurance, some through Blue Cross, some through Blue Shield, and some through one of the several new companies established to sell health insurance through employers. This was the beginning of the model of employer-based health insurance.

As the private health insurance market continued to grow, the political conversation about government-funded public or social insurance also continued. Between 1935 and 1950, several serious proposals for national health insurance were put forward, including one that was modeled after Great Britain's newly revised National Health Service. This effort was successfully fought by the AMA, which used the terminology of the emerging Cold War mentality to increase fears of socialized medicine. The defeat of the Wagner–Murray–Dingell Bill in 1949 was the last serious effort to create one national, universal health insurance program that would cover everybody in the United States (Starr, 1982).

An additional decision by the Internal Revenue Service in 1954 solidified the role of private health insurance provided through employment as the major way in which people had financial access to medical care services. It was decided that any contributions an employer made to the health insurance premiums for an employee were not taxable. This essentially meant an increase in salary that was not taxed and created an additional and strong incentive for larger companies to offer health insurance coverage as a way of attracting the best employees (Teitelbaum and Wilensky, 2013; Shi and Singh, 2014).

The model of employer-based health insurance was further strengthened by the creation of two public programs aimed at two separate groups that were left out of this employment-based health insurance. The poor who were not working were covered by Medicaid (Chapter 19) and the retired were covered by Medicare (Chapter 18). This was the beginning of the targeted insurance model that is the hallmark of the financing of the U.S. health care system.

It is interesting to note that other countries that began their system with an employment-based model, including Germany and Great Britain, moved away from that model into a national program that included everybody. One important consequence of this is that in other countries, when workers lose their jobs, they do not lose their health insurance, whereas in the United States, they do lose their health insurance. The targeted program model used by the United States involves additional administrative expenses, as will be discussed later in this chapter. Also, counterintuitively, the existence of several different private and public health insurance programs does not mean there is less government regulation in the U.S. health care system than in other countries. As has been demonstrated so far, there are many regulations and policies, all of which are based on the desire to control inequities resulting in the primarily market justice model.

Despite financial access to health care services being founded on employment-based health insurance, it is important to note that employers were never required to offer health insurance to their employees. Large companies did so primarily as a method of attracting and keeping workers, and also to compete with other large companies. Small companies usually do not offer health insurance to their workers, arguing that it is too expensive for them to do so. One of the several controversial features of the ACA is the requirement that all employers except very small ones offer health insurance to employees. Tax credits are offered to companies to help share the initial cost of this to the company.

As a result of this combination of cultural, political, and economic values, the U.S. health care system is a complex combination of private and public insurance plans. Each of these has its own guidelines for payment, for eligibility, and for cost sharing procedures for patients. This creates considerable difficulties not only for patients, but also for health care providers—both individual ones such as physicians and institutional ones such as hospitals. Each provider has to be able to process each individual health insurance company according to its own set of rules and guidelines.

# Types of Health Insurance

There are four general categories of health insurance: medical or health insurance, dental insurance, long-term care insurance, and prescription drug plans. These are very different types, and only medical or health insurance will be described here. There are two very large categories of medical/ health insurance: public and private. The focus of this chapter will be on private insurance, with public insurance (Medicare and Medicaid) mentioned only to clarify a point. These two programs are described in more detail in Chapters 17 through 19. Also described in more detail in Chapter 18 will be the specialized health insurance plans known as medigap plans, which are directed at a very specific market—those who are covered by Medicare, but wish to purchase additional private health insurance to cover what Medicare does not. This is necessary because Medicare is far from a comprehensive health insurance policy.

Private insurance is best described as involving nonpublic or nongovernmental health insurance. Another term that is appropriate is commercial insurance. Private health insurance may be offered by a for-profit or a nonprofit insurance company, although nearly all are for-profit. There are more than 180 companies in the United States whose major business is selling health insurance policies, but 25 of these account for two-thirds of the market. These include for-profit companies such as United Health, Humana Group, Aetna Group, Cigna Group, Kaiser Foundation Group, and Wellpoint Group, as well as nonprofit organizations such as Blue Cross and Blue Shield (Kovner and Knickman, 2011; Teitelbaum and Wilensky, 2013; Shi and Singh, 2014). Each of these companies is free to decide to offer a range of possible plans for consumers to select, and most of these companies offer many different types of policies.

These companies and organizations are all regulated by both state and federal governments. For example, states set standards for when insurance companies can reject an applicant, as well as setting rates for how much companies can charge for premiums. Nonprofit health insurance organizations such as Blue Cross and Blue Shield have additional regulations limiting their ability to exclude people, because they receive some public subsidies. Federal regulations include Health Insurance Portability and Accountability Act (HIPAA), which is well known for protecting patient privacy. However, this act also sets limitations on private companies' rights to exclude people from coverage, especially when they are in the process of changing jobs. An additional federal regulatory system is called Employee Retirement Income

Security Act (ERISA), which establishes national standards for employer-provided group health insurance plans. A third important one is Consolidated Omnibus Budget Reconciliation Act (COBRA). This requires employer-sponsored group plans to allow employees to continue their health insurance after termination of employment, paying the group rates instead of higher individual rates. All three of these federal regulations are directly anchored in the social justice model of resource allocation and act to limit the free market activity of insurance companies.

## Private Health Insurance

Within the private health insurance market, the majority of all policies are *group* insurance, or *employer-based* health insurance, as shown in Table 13.1. Health insurance is provided as a fringe benefit to employment, and the employer pays some part of the premiums. The percentage of the premium paid for by the employer has traditionally been 75%, although this percentage is part of labor negotiations, as employers try to shift more of the costs of the premiums to employees.

Group health insurance has always been viewed as an efficient way to provide health insurance, because the group is healthy enough to be employed, so their health risks are probably lower. Furthermore, premiums are set by community ratings in all group health insurance by federal law, so all individuals are charged the same amount. The larger the employer, the greater the bargaining power it has with an insurance company in terms of the price of premiums. In fact, some large employers do not use an insurance company at all, but instead self-insure, which means they create the insurance pool themselves and manage it. Slightly over one-half of all people covered by employer-based plans are covered by plans that are self-insured by their employer. Self-insured plans are exempt from several federal and state regulations, so premiums can be lower, but benefits are also frequently lower with these plans (Shi and Singh, 2014).

Because of the use of community ratings for setting premiums, the administrative costs of group plans tend to be lower than other types of private health insurance. As can be seen in Table 13.1, the average annual administrative costs of group health insurance policies range from about 12% to 23% (Litow, 2006). Smaller employers tend to experience larger administrative rates than larger groups. Also, administrative costs vary depending on the type of plan selected by the employee. Employers are required to offer a full array of plans, which will be described in Chapter 14.

**Table 13.1   Categories of Health Insurance Programs**

| Category of Insurance Coverage | Major Concerns | Average Administrative Costs | Range of Population Covered |
|---|---|---|---|
| 1. Insured by employer | • Cost of premiums increasing<br>• Underinsurance, resulting in increased medical expenses<br>• Loss of job leading to loss of insurance | 12–23% | 45–55% |
| 2. Consumer-driven: individually purchased | • Premiums increased by using policy<br>• Loss of insurance by using policy<br>• Hidden costs due to confusing plan details | About 30% | 8–10% |
| 3. Public insurance: Medicare | • Changes in federal policies that alter coverage<br>• Out of pocket expenses for uncovered expenses | 2–4% | 16% |
| 4. Public insurance: Medicaid | • State policies that limit coverage<br>• Continuing eligibility | 7% | 15–17% |

*Source:* Data from Litow, M.E., Medicare versus private health insurance: The cost of administration. Milliman Group, 2006. Available from: http://www.cahi.org; Kovner, A.R. and Knickman, J.R., *Health Care Delivery in the United States*, 10th edition, Springer, New York, 2011; Shi, L. and Singh, D.A., *Delivering Health Care in America*, 6th edition, Jones and Bartlett, Burlington, MA, 2014; Starr, P., *Remedy and Reaction: The Peculiar American Struggle over Health Care Reform*, Yale University Press, New Haven, CT, 2011.

Employees can choose to cover only themselves or their whole family. The national average for the cost of a group health insurance plan is $6000 for an individual, with the employer usually paying about $4500 of that. Cost for family coverage averages between $13,000 and $16,000 per year in terms of cost of premiums (KFF, 2013a). Plans vary with respect to other cost-sharing aspects such as deductibles, copayments, and coinsurance.

In the past 10 years or so, a new market for private health insurance has developed. This is called the *individual* market or sometimes the *consumer-driven* market (Table 13.1). It is called consumer-driven primarily because this is a market response to the many complaints about increasing premiums and to the decreasing number of employers who offer health insurance in the group market. This form of private health insurance is relatively small, only involving 8–10% of the private insurance policies, but it has been growing rapidly. Most health insurance companies sell both group and these individual policies, including Blue Cross and Blue Shield. This individual market is controlled by both federal and state regulations, but the regulatory environment is not as strict. Companies selling policies to individuals use experience ratings to set the price of premiums (Starr, 2011). Individuals apply for these policies online, answering a lengthy questionnaire, which includes providing access to personal medical records. Premiums are usually grouped into low, medium, and high risk, with the amount increasing as risk increases. Premiums can be increased if utilization is too high; the person can also be dropped by the insurance company. The consumer-driven market has been restricted in the ACA, which will eventually place these policies under the same regulations as those selling health insurance to groups of individuals.

Group health insurance policies are required to cover a fairly comprehensive set of services, which increases premiums. In the individual market, there is no such regulation, so there is a wider choice of policies, including those with lower premiums and higher deductibles—some as high as $5000/year. These policies are called High Deductible Health Plans (HDHPs). Many large employers now offer an HDHP insurance option as part of their group health plan choices.

The idea of high deductible, low premium plans, paired with HSA, is based on the market justice allocation model, as noted in Figure 12.2. This type of health insurance plan is based on the idea of increased personal responsibility because enrollees have an incentive to reduce their health care utilization. However, the person who is most likely to select this type of plan is both wealthier and healthier, leaving the less affluent and sicker to choose more comprehensive policies. This results in adverse selection for the more comprehensive policies, which then increases premiums, or perhaps leads employers to stop offering such policies, which will decrease access significantly (Davis, 2004).

As shown in Table 13.1, administrative costs are higher in these consumer-driven plans, primarily because of the cost of setting the premiums using the experience rating process. The cost of the premiums varies greatly depending on which plan is selected by an individual.

In 2004, about two-thirds of the U.S. population received health insurance from their employer, which includes the families of workers being covered also. This percentage has been slowly decreasing so that now only slightly more than one-half of the U.S. population are covered by private health insurance plans through employers, as shown in Table 13.1. Even though the percentage of people insured through their employer has steadily decreased, it is still a large group that is covered in this way. In 2011, 89% of all people under the age of 65 who had private health insurance had employment-based coverage. This makes employment-based health insurance the single largest source of health insurance (Kovner and Knickman, 2011).

Employment-based health insurance is susceptible to the business cycle, which has experienced significant challenges for the past 15 years, especially the 2007–2009 recession. Smaller businesses dropped health insurance and larger ones shifted as many costs to employees as possible. Because health insurance is linked to employment, people who lost their jobs also lost their health insurance. By 2013, nearly one-third of the U.S. population had health insurance through some sort of public program, as shown in Table 13.1. The major shift is an increase in those covered by one of the public health insurance programs, such as Medicare or Medicaid. The percentage covered by Medicaid went from about 12% in 2005 to almost 18% in 2012 (Shi and Singh, 2014). There is a fair amount of shifting between the types of insurance, especially between some form of employer-provided health insurance and Medicaid, which is why there are ranges provided in Table 13.1.

As healthy people leave a health insurance pool, premiums increase even more rapidly. As economic times worsen, health status worsens, so the result is more people needing health care with fewer people covered. Costs for caring for uninsured people are then shifted to a larger group— either through increased premiums for privately insured people, or through increased taxes to support one of the public health insurance programs. One of the primary goals of the ACA has been to reduce the percentage of uninsured, both through the private market and also by adding to the percentage covered by Medicaid. This will be explained in more detail in Chapter 19.

## What about the Uninsured?

The four groups shown in Table 13.1 account for about 80–85% of the U.S. population, leaving between 15% and 20% without health insurance, which is more than 50 million people. The size of this group has been significantly impacted by the ACA, because it is now reduced to about 9%, as will be described in Chapter 17. There are several misperceptions of this group, especially with respect to their work habits. Table 13.2 gives several variables that have been used to characterize this group.

Although many believe the most important descriptor of this group is that they are either poor or unemployed, this is not true. As shown in Table 13.2, 70% of this group work or live in a family with people who work, although they are more likely to be working in jobs that do not provide health insurance. Some people in this group are recently unemployed, which has caused them to lose their health insurance. Others are employed in low-wage jobs, often in the service sector of the economy, where health insurance is not as common (Teitelbaum and Wilensky, 2013).

Almost one-third of young adults are uninsured, which is twice the rate of the rest of the population. Some individuals in this group have jobs without health insurance, but many view themselves as not needing health insurance, and turn this benefit down at their jobs for the modest salary increase that usually accompanies this decision. Those who belong to a minority group or an immigrant group are more likely to be uninsured. There are also geographic differences, with residents of both southern and western states being more likely to be uninsured (Teitelbaum and Wilensky, 2013).

**Table 13.2  Characteristics of the Uninsured**

| Characteristic | Description |
| --- | --- |
| Income level | Rate of uninsured is twice as high among those classified as poor |
| Employment status | 70% of uninsured work or are in families with workers |
| Age | One-third of young adults are uninsured |
| Education | More than 50% of uninsured have high school education or less |
| Race, ethnicity | 12% of non-Hispanic whites are uninsured<br>32% of Hispanics are uninsured<br>21% of African-Americans are uninsured<br>17% of Asian-Americans are uninsured |
| Immigrant status | 34% of foreign-born residents are uninsured<br>14% of native-born are uninsured |
| Geography | Residents of states in the South and West are more likely to be uninsured than residents of states in the North and Midwest. |

*Source:* Data from Teitelbaum, J.B. and Wilensky, S.E., *Essentials of Health Policy and Law*, 2nd edition, Jones and Bartlett, Burlington, MA, 2013.

# What Difference Does Health Insurance Make?

Health insurance is a very important determinant of access to all types of health services, ranging from preventive care to more urgent care. Because of the ethics of the health care system, life-threatening or very urgent care is delivered to uninsured individuals if they seek care from an emergency room. However, preventive and routine care are frequently not obtained by those without health insurance, which leads to more severe illness, and ultimately, higher costs.

Table 13.3 summarizes some of the consequences of having no insurance. Not surprisingly, those who lack health insurance are more likely to not have a usual and customary source of care, which is where they can seek care for both preventive and routine care. This results in delaying care until the medical situation becomes more urgent (IOM, 2001a; Starfield and Shi, 2004; Teitelbaum and Wilensky, 2013). When care is delivered, those who are uninsured are less likely to be able to afford prescribed drugs (IOM, 2003).

Decreased utilization of primary and preventive care translates to negative impacts on the health of the uninsured. Those who are uninsured are more likely to be diagnosed at later stages of cancer than insured people and are more likely to die earlier (IOM, 2003). They are more likely to be hospitalized for an avoidable health problem (KFF, 2010b). The Institute of Medicine has estimated that having health insurance could reduce the death rate of the uninsured by 10–15% each year (IOM, 2003). In an initial expansion of Medicaid similar to that of the ACA, the newly insured group experienced

**Table 13.3   Selected Health Behaviors Impacted by Health Insurance**

| Health Behavior | Impact |
|---|---|
| No usual source of care | 55% of the uninsured<br>10% of those with any type of insurance |
| No preventive care | 42% of the uninsured<br>6% of those with any type of insurance |
| Went without care in last 12 months | 26% of the uninsured<br>8% of those with any type of insurance |
| Could not afford prescription drugs | 27% of the uninsured<br>10% of those with any type of insurance |

*Source:* Data from Teitelbaum, J.B. and Wilensky, S.E., *Essentials of Health Policy and Law*, 2nd edition, Jones and Bartlett, Burlington, MA, 2013.

increased utilization of primary care as well as lower death rates (Sommers et al., 2012).

The negative health impacts related to lack of insurance are the non-economic costs of the uninsured. However, it is equally important to consider the economic costs of this group. This is mostly captured in the cost of uncompensated care provided by nonprofit and public hospitals, as described in Chapter 8. In 2008, the dollar value of uncompensated care was $57 billion, with about 75% covered by federal, state, or city payments to hospitals (KFF, 2010b). Hospitals try to recover some of the remaining expense by negotiating higher reimbursement rates with some private insurance companies, so some of the uncompensated care costs can be shifted to them. Chapter 15 will describe this process further. Medical care given to those without health insurance is a cost shared by all, either through taxes or increased premiums for those with private health insurance.

Of course, the hospital does also attempt to collect the amount owed for uncompensated care by submitting unpaid bills to debt collection agencies. However, as shown in Table 13.2, people who are uninsured are more likely to be in lower-paying jobs, and thus are unlikely to be able to pay these bills.

## Summary

The method of providing financial access to people in the United States developed at about the same time that several other countries were designing their method of providing financial access. Each country creates a system that is consistent with its cultural, political, and economic values. European and Scandinavian countries chose to create a large group to take advantage of some of the principles of insurance discussed in this chapter. These countries also created a centralized financing system to increase both efficiency and access. In the United States, the focus was on creating a market-oriented system constructed around the philosophical values of the market justice system, with many regulations to control the inequities that are a result of this allocation method (Chapter 11). This created several different groups, under the assumption that each group had specific health needs that could be best met by different financing systems. The result is a complex and fragmented method of providing health insurance to the American public, using private and public methods of providing health insurance. Overlaying this fragmented system is a series of policies and regulations, enacted over time to solve specific problems. One result is a system that is difficult to describe or explain, much less actually try to navigate. Purchasing health insurance requires a considerable amount of attention by the consumer, because a poor choice cannot be reversed for a year.

Another consequence of this fragmented financing system is that consumers, health professionals, and health care institutions all think about the type and nature of their health insurance much more frequently than in any other country. Table 13.1 shows the concerns of each of the insured groups, including those who have group insurance through their employer. In many ways, this is the best way in which to get insurance, because this is usually the most comprehensive coverage for the lowest price. As noted in this chapter, employers try to shift the cost of premiums to employees, resulting in higher costs. An additional concern is underinsurance, which occurs when out-of-pocket or uncovered medical expenses exceed 10% of a person's income (Teitelbaum and Wilensky, 2013). Uncovered medical expenses occur in a variety of ways, including medical procedures that are only partly covered by an insurance policy, or extensive treatment that exceeds limits placed on specific expensive services. For example, high-dose chemotherapy is often limited to specified cancers, and sometimes limited to certain settings (Teitelbaum and Wilensky, 2013).

Uncovered medical expenses are the leading cause of bankruptcy in the United States, exceeding both credit card debt and unpaid mortgages. More than 60% of those who declare medical bankruptcy are those who actually have—or perhaps had—health insurance through their employer (Himmelstein et al., 2009). Bankruptcy due to unpaid medical expenses is a unique factor to the United States, because in no other highly developed country is loss of a job related to loss of health insurance.

Those who do not have private insurance through their jobs may choose to purchase a policy individually. Although a relatively small overall proportion of the whole private insurance market, this is a type of policy that is being more regulated by the ACA, as described earlier.

Almost one-third of the U.S. population receives health care under some sort of public insurance program, with the two largest being Medicare and Medicaid. Both of these groups have significant—but quite different—concerns, as will be explained in detail in Chapters 18 and 19. Those on Medicare are concerned about changes in the structure of Medicare because of political influences, but the most significant issue facing them are the many costs that are not covered by Medicare, which will be described in Chapter 18. Those who are covered by Medicaid are also concerned about political influences changing the structure of their program, especially at the state level.

Health care providers, both individuals and institutions, spend an inordinate amount of time thinking about various complications related to health insurance, as well as uncompensated care. Hospitals must deal with two major public forms of health insurance (Medicare and Medicaid), as well as literally hundreds of different private companies' policies. Each of these has slightly different guidelines for reimbursing, as will be discussed in Chapter 15. This creates a financing system that requires many different administrative layers. Table 13.1 captures some of the administrative costs of each type of insurance program. When analyzing the system as a whole, however, the best estimate of total administrative costs in the whole system is that about 31% of each dollar spent in the U.S. health care system goes to some type of administrative cost (Woolhandler et al., 2003). This is quite different from the estimate of administrative costs shown in Figure 6.2, which was limited to the costs related to the public insurance programs.

The ACA of 2010 is designed to fit in with the multiple payer design of the U.S. financing system. It does so by instituting many regulations on the current private health insurance sector, especially in the individual market, which is at the core of the proposed health exchanges. It also institutes the requirement that each person must have health insurance partly to increase the size and health of the insured group. The health exchanges are based on the idea that increased competition will create health insurance policies that are more affordable and attractive to consumers. One of the major goals of this insurance program is to reduce the number of uninsured from the current 50 million to somewhere about 30 million (Nardin et al., 2013). As will be shown in Chapter 17, this is being achieved.

Within the larger framework of health insurance are different types of policies, each with slightly different administrative requirements. These will be described in Chapter 14.

## Acknowledgments

This chapter has benefited greatly from the contributions of Dr. Thomas Duston, who read and commented on an earlier version. He has also found several important references for this chapter. Three students who reviewed this chapter made very helpful comments that made this complex process more clear: Diana Griggs, Alexandra Amaral-Medeiros, and Daphna Raz. They also found several important supporting references. Daphna also constructed Figure 13.1.

## Chapter 14

# Health Insurance: Two Conceptual Models

This chapter approaches health insurance from a slightly different perspective than Chapter 13, which focused on the general function of health insurance. This chapter describes two different models used to design health insurance policies. The first model is the conventional or indemnity model of insurance, which is the original model of insurance. The second model is based on the idea of managed care, and originated with the establishment of the health maintenance organization (HMO) model, which was described in Chapter 9. This chapter presents a description of these two models, and then describes the increasing trend toward managed care in all health insurance plans.

## Model I: Conventional Indemnity Health Insurance

The early history of health insurance in the United States described in the previous chapter is the description of indemnity insurance, which was based on the concept of recovering from a loss. The provider submits a claim for services provided to the insurance company, which pays the physician or hospital according to the rules of the policy. The health provider then sends the remainder of the bill to the patient.

Health insurance policies under the indemnity model commonly use a deductible as one method of cost sharing with the consumer after the cost of the premium. Once the deductible is met, indemnity policies generally also use coinsurance. These plans typically pay for 80% of the amount billed by the physician or hospital, with the understanding that the consumer is responsible for the remainder. These plans typically also involved an annual limit on what they would pay, known as the catastrophic cap, as discussed in Chapter 13.

A very important part of this model of insurance is the way in which physicians and hospitals are paid, which is by each service delivered. The fee-for-service (FFS) method of payment, discussed in Chapter 9, was more than a simple payment mechanism. It was also viewed as the way in which the physician–patient relationship was greatly strengthened and as the best way for patients and physicians to fit into the classic market economic model (Emanuel, 2014).

Linked to the early indemnity policies was the assumption that all covered medical services were provided in the hospital setting, although this model expanded to also cover medically necessary outpatient care. The idea of medical necessity did not include any medical encounter without a specific diagnosis, reinforcing the concept of illness based on the Biomedical Model, as described in Chapter 1. Preventive care such as immunizations and physical examinations, including screening procedures, were originally not included in the coverage. Also not originally covered in these indemnity plans were mental health services and prescription drugs.

This method of health insurance is generally blamed for the rapidly increasing costs of medical care, primarily because of the economic incentives of the policies. Patients had free choice of physicians, with no requirement for a gatekeeper to monitor the utilization of medical or surgical specialist. The insurance company had individual contracts with physicians, rather than with groups of physicians. A physician's income depended on the number of services provided to a patient, and a hospital's revenue from an insurance company depended on providing more and more services to a patient. Not only were incentives linked to quantity of care, financial incentives were also linked to the place in which care was provided: the hospital. This encouraged the development of increasingly technological and expensive treatment and diagnostic procedures. Additionally, all money was received from the health insurance company after the care was provided, in a system called retrospective reimbursement.

This is not to say that physicians—or hospitals—intentionally provide more medical care services than are actually needed. However, it is widely recognized today that this system does not encourage any economic incentives to curb any medical services, or to provide them in a less costly manner or in a less costly setting. Many health policy analysts identified both moral hazard and provider-induced demand as being the root causes of ever-increasing costs in the medical care system (Teitelbaum and Wilensky, 2013; Shi and Singh, 2014).

An additional consequence of the indemnity system of health insurance is a practical one related to the amount of administration necessary to identify charges related to each service. A complex and very specific accounting system integrated with individual diagnostic codes conveys charges to each insurance company. As will be discussed in the next chapter, each insurance company has slightly different guidelines for what they will pay, requiring health care providers and institutions to use sophisticated accounting systems.

This indemnity model of paying on an FFS basis, with incentives for increased utilization, especially in a hospital setting, was the predominant form of health insurance until the mid-1970s, when HMOs were introduced, as will be described next. However, this indemnity model of insurance is not limited to history, because two groups of people are still insured under this model. One of these two groups consists of those who receive medical care services under the Medicare program. This program was originally and still is based on this traditional FFS model, which still emphasizes acute medical care services. As will be shown in Chapter 18, the model has been adjusted to cover some screening procedures, and there are also some cost savings methods in reimbursing hospital-based care, as described in Chapter 8.

The second, smaller group are those who buy their own individual plans as opposed to being in an employment-based group. The health exchanges implemented by the Affordable Care Act (ACA) utilize the individual market, but the ACA is regulating them so these people's benefits will be similar to those provided by more comprehensive group policies. As just one example, the ACA requires that all insurance policies now cover 15 essential preventive services, with no cost sharing to the consumer. This will be described in Chapter 17.

## Model II: How to Control Increasing Costs—HMO Insurance Model

Between the economic incentives of the traditional FFS method of financing encouraging the utilization of more expensive hospital-based services and the entry of millions of people into the health care system because of increased availability of health insurance, costs increased rapidly. By the early 1970s, most health policy analysts agreed that several modifications were needed in how medical care was financed in the United States. There was wide agreement on four basic principles.

## Elasticity

Health economists realized that following the traditional view of elasticity encouraged utilization of the most expensive services located in the most expensive sector of the system, the hospital. Under the traditional view of elasticity, consumers purchased insurance coverage for the most expensive services, ones they would be most likely to receive anyway. Indemnity insurance policies did not cover less expensive costs because these were viewed as the responsibility of consumers. This model works well in other types of insurance, such as car insurance, but it is not as applicable to health care. As has been explained previously, medically urgent (and inelastic) services are provided to people even if they cannot pay for them. This payment arrangement prevented hospitals from losing money on uncompensated urgent care. Second, there is now a consensus that at least some utilization of more expensive services can be decreased by increasing the utilization of less expensive preventive (elastic) services. However, as the price of these elastic service increases, people will not pay for them, as was described in Chapter 11. It was widely recognized that health insurance policies need to encourage utilization of less expensive preventive services by covering them in a health insurance plan.

## Control Utilization

By the early 1970s, the association of increased utilization with increased cost was clearly established. The important issue was appropriate utilization of just the right amount of medically necessary services, with no duplication. Under the indemnity model of insurance, the consumer selects a physician based on their own perceptions of their medical problem. If a person had a stomachache, they could choose to see a surgeon first. If they were unhappy with the diagnosis, they could then seek another opinion from another physician. Not only is this costly, it was also thought to jeopardize a person's health by exposing them to duplicate and possible unnecessary medical services. The policy suggestion was to institute a primary care physician to be a gatekeeper to other more specialized physicians, and who would also coordinate all the care the patient received for several different specialists. Included at this time was the idea of reviewing suggestions for expensive care such as surgeries in order to ensure they were all medically necessary.

## Reduce Administrative Costs

Insurance companies are businesses that attempt to balance the money taken in by premiums and other consumer payments with the money spent in paying for benefits or claims. Under the indemnity model of insurance, consumers could consult as many physicians as they wanted, and physicians could charge the insurance company as much as they would like, with each individual service linked to both a diagnostic code and a price. One way to reduce administrative costs was to reduce the free choice of the consumer with respect to choice of physicians. This was accomplished by creating a network of physicians who would accept a lower level of reimbursement in exchange for a greater volume and more predictable supply of patients. A second way was to provide full coverage of all care without differentiating between each service. A third way was to integrate the provision of medical care with the financing of medical care, so the providers and the insurers were actually part of the same company.

## Pay Physicians a Different Way

The fourth principle was to reduce the economic incentives in the FFS method of paying physicians. It gradually became well accepted that paying physicians based on the FFS method encouraged utilization of services, some of which might be unnecessary or even harmful. Two other methods of paying physicians used in other countries were explored. One is capitation, in which the physician is paid a set fee for each patient in their practice. This amount is paid yearly, and the physician is expected to provide all necessary services to the patient within that amount. This is used by Great Britain, and is felt to be an important part of the cost control of that health system. Another method used to pay physicians is a salary that may be based on several factors, including hours worked, patients seen, or revenues generated.

Although there was widespread agreement at the theoretical level with these four principles, their implementation required that physician practices be more organized than the solo practices that were the norm at that time. The HMO Act of 1973 attempted to encourage the development of these group practices by providing federal funds for their establishment. Also included in this Act was the requirement for employers of more than 25 people to offer at least one HMO option as part of their group health insurance choices (Wilson and Neuhauser, 1985; Iglehart, 1994). The HMO Act failed to establish HMOs as they were originally conceptualized, but this Act has significantly changed the way health care is financed today by using many of the cost-savings principles noted here.

## From Conceptual Model to Early Implementation

The initial HMOs were established around the four theoretical principles described in the preceding section. An additional implementation principle was that each group practice offered a comprehensive set of services through one administrative organization, which both provided and paid for medical services. This administrative efficiency ensured the incentives for care were all in the same direction, and also created fewer levels of administration because there were no negotiations around reimbursement rates between doctors and insurance companies. The group or, later, network of physicians agreed to the insurance company's reimbursement rates for medical services, even though they were lower, because the physicians were guaranteed a more predictable volume of patients. Physicians practicing in the HMO model agreed to a salary instead of having their incomes determined by FFSs. Most salary arrangements were based on a capitated fee for each patient the physician cared for. Although this did result in somewhat lower incomes, physicians who agreed to this model of practice had the advantages of a group practice, with shared responsibilities for patients. They also had many fewer business responsibilities than in an individual private practice. Although all specialties are represented in this model, HMOs emphasized the use of primary care physicians as the point of first contact for each patient, and also as the gatekeeper for utilizing all other services.

HMO plans covered several types of medical services that were not commonly covered by traditional plans at the time. Preventive care services, including immunizations and well-child examinations, were not only covered but also encouraged as a strategy for reducing the need for more expensive services later on. The second innovation in coverage was prescription drugs, which were rarely covered by indemnity health insurance policies.

Prescription drugs were covered as part of the idea of completely covering all medically necessary care. There were no deductibles and no coinsurance used in the original HMO plans: approved medical services were covered at the 100% level. This meant no bills coming to the consumer, which was a significant attraction of the original HMO plans. The original HMO plans did not generally have a catastrophic cap, because their orientation was to pay for all approved services.

An important proviso for this arrangement was that only medical services provided by the approved network of HMO physicians were covered. In the original HMOs, any medical care provided by a nonapproved physician was not covered by the plan. As will be seen shortly, this has been modified quite a bit in current managed care plans.

The one consumer cost sharing mechanism used by HMOs was a copayment made at the time of any visit. This was one set fee charged for all visits. The purpose of this fee was treading the fine line between preventing overutilization (moral hazard) and encouraging increased utilization of less expensive medical services (elasticity) so more expensive treatments might be decreased.

HMO health plans made reimbursement agreements with hospitals that were similar to those used with plan physicians. Although the emphasis was on utilization of primary care services, HMO plans provided comprehensive care for enrolled members, including hospital-based care. The HMO policy was a contract between a consumer and the plan to provide all medically necessary and approved care.

## From HMOs to Managed Care Plans

Acceptance of this original HMO model was slow, for both physicians and consumers. From the physician's perspective, many aspects of this model were new and challenging, especially abandoning FFS as the method of payment. As noted above, HMO insurance required a physician to practice in a large group setting and to accept review by peers of previously unchallenged medical decisions. The result was a very different sort of medical practice.

Some consumers were very attracted to this HMO model, especially those with young children and chronic diseases. Each of these groups have heavy use of primary care visits not always linked to a specific diagnosis, so were often not covered by traditional health insurance. Also, these two groups had heavier use of prescription drugs, which were not included in any traditional health plans in the 1970s. Because premiums were subsidized, they were usually cheaper for consumers. However, many consumers did not want to give up their personal physician for an unknown network of doctors. The lack of choice was a serious limitation for many consumers. By 1976, only about 174 HMOs had been formed, which was only 10% of the target number of HMOs hoped for as a result of the 1973 HMO Act (Shi and Singh, 2014).

However, medical costs continued to increase into the 1980s, and traditional insurers began adopting several of the cost control mechanisms used by HMOs. These managed care models included two specific methods of cost control besides using a primary care physician as a gatekeeper. The first was to institute methods to review treatment decisions involving hospital-based services. One of the most common reviews involved preauthorization, meaning that another person reviewed and approved the expense before the patient received the services (Starr, 2011). This preauthorization method of controlling costs became ubiquitous, and remains an important feature of managing medical costs today. It is rare to find any health insurance policy of any model that does not require this.

The second method of managing costs included health insurance companies seeking selected contracts with individual physicians or networks of physicians, as well as hospitals. This is similar to the original HMO model, but it also allowed patients more choice, although higher prices were charged for patients using physicians from a lower tier of the identified network. This model led to what became known as a preferred provider organization (PPO), which will be described shortly.

An important organizational shift in managed care plans also occurred. The original legislation required HMOs to be structured as a nonprofit organization that managed costs by creating several mechanisms for its members spending less time in hospitals, thus saving the insurance plan money. However, PPOs are largely for-profit and managed costs primarily by negotiating discounts from both physicians and hospitals in return for volume of patients (Starr, 2011). Today, about one-half of consumers enrolled in a managed care plan are in a for-profit one (AAN, 2009).

These managed care plans were not universally liked. In fact, there was a fair amount of consumer distrust about whether PPOs and HMOs were managing costs so strictly that both quality and quantity of care was being threatened. However, premiums for the indemnity, FFS plans continued to increase, so consumers increasingly chose a managed care plan instead of an indemnity-type FFS plan. In 1978, 5 years after the establishment of the HMO model, 95% of employers offered FFS indemnity health plans to their employees. By 1988, only 61% of employers still offered this type of FFS health plan (Starr, 2011). During the 1990s and into the 2000s, the indemnity model of health insurance continued to decrease, so now very few of all employer-based group policies fall completely under this model (KFF, 2010c). Few employer-based group health plans fall under the classic HMO model either, because this limits consumer choice too much. The FFS traditional model of insurance is still dominant in the individual market, and, as noted, also remains the insurance model for Medicare. Medicaid programs are increasingly placed under a managed care model, in order to better control costs (Kovner and Knickman, 2011).

Today, the majority of employer-based group health plans are one of three different types of managed care plans (Teitelbaum and Wilensky, 2013; Shi and Singh, 2014). Table 14.1 shows these three types, along with a summary of some of the important characteristics of each. There are many variations among these three broad types, and insurance plans today do not fit easily into one category.

## HMOs

The classic HMO model is the most restricted in terms of consumer choice. This model follows the original concept by only covering services delivered by the defined network of HMO physicians. The model has a strong reliance on using a gatekeeper, and also uses utilization review, especially for expensive hospital-based services. This model of managed care remains the simplest in terms of financing. All covered services remain 100% covered: there are no coinsurances or deductibles. Copayments still exist and are often tiered to be more for specialist visits than for primary care visits.

There are four different models for HMOs, with the variation being primarily around the kinds of contract arrangements with physicians. The classic HMO model is called a *staff* model and involves employing its own staff of physicians, each of whom is salaried, mostly on capitation, just as in the original HMO Act of 1973. This model is the most restrictive, on both consumers and physicians. The *group* model occurs when an HMO company makes a contract with a group of physicians or a hospital. The physicians remain independent contractors, but the contract is between the HMO and the group, not the individual physician. The *network* model also uses a contract with a group of physicians, but typically makes contracts with

**Table 14.1 Types of Managed Care Plans**

| Type of Plan | % of Group Employees Selecting | How Physicians Are Paid | Consumer Cost Sharing Methods[a] | Network of Physicians | Use of Gatekeeper |
|---|---|---|---|---|---|
| HMO | 14% | Salary based primarily on capitation | Copayment | Closed: plan covers all services offered within network | Yes |
| PPO | 57% | Reimbursed by PPO, based on offered discounted rates | Coinsurance; (some) copayments; (some) deductibles | Tiered network with higher coverage (80%) for some physicians than others (70%) | Not commonly |
| POS | 9% | Reimbursement by plan, based either on discounted rates or FFS | Coinsurance; (some) copayment; (some) deductible | Tiered network with higher percentage coverage for some physicians | Yes |

*Source:* Data from Kovner, A.R. and Knickman, J.R., *Health Care Delivery in the United States*, 10th edition, New York: Springer, 2011; Shi, L. and Singh, D.A., *Delivering Health Care in America: A Systems Approach*, 6th edition, Jones and Bartlett, Burlington, MA, 2014; Teitelbaum, J.B. and Wilensky, S.E., *Essentials of Health Policy and Law*, 2nd edition, Jones and Bartlett, Burlington, MA, 2013.

[a] Besides premiums.

specific specialty groups, especially primary care physician groups. In this case, physicians are paid a capitated amount for each patient, but expected to manage the costs of any care referred out of the group. For both group and network models, a consumer may choose any physician in one of the approved groups. Even more freedom of choice exists in a type of HMO called an *independent practice association* model (IPA). In this arrangement, the IPA is an intermediary between the HMO and the group of physicians. The HMO has the financial responsibility, whereas the IPA has the responsibility for contracting with physicians. Among all forms of the HMO model, the IPA is the most popular, mainly because it is less restrictive in terms of selecting a physician. Not surprisingly, these plans also tend to have higher premiums (Teitelbaum and Wilensky, 2013; Shi and Singh, 2014).

## PPOs

The preferred provider model evolved in response to concerns from both consumers and physicians about the restrictions of the classic HMO model. These managed care plans establish a network of what are called preferred providers. These are physicians who have agreed to discounted rates ranging from 25% to 35% of their normal charges. If a patient chooses one of these providers, these discounted rates are passed on to them. However, they may choose to use physicians outside of this network, with the higher coinsurance rates passed on to the consumer. In this way, consumers maintain a high degree of choice of providers. These plans do not commonly use a strong gatekeeper function, which is another feature consumers like. All three methods of consumer cost sharing are used by these plans, including deductibles and coinsurance as well as copayments. As can be seen in Table 14.1, these plans are the most popular of all managed care plans offered by employers (Teitelbaum and Wilensky, 2013; Shi and Singh, 2014).

## Point of Service

Point of service (POS) plans combine features from HMOs and PPOs. POS plans require gatekeepers and have tight utilization controls, following the HMO model. However, they allow choice of provider at the time of service— that is, at the time at which a medical treatment is provided. As PPOs have become more popular, POS plans have declined, as shown in Table 14.1 (Teitelbaum and Wilensky, 2013; Shi and Singh, 2014).

As can be seen in Table 14.1, almost 80% of the health plans offered by employers to employees fall into one of these three managed care models. Although classic indemnity plans are seldom offered by employers, the most rapidly growing option is an example of the indemnity FFS model. This option consists of high deductible health plans, which are paired with health savings accounts, as described in Chapter 13. Almost 20% of the health insurance plans chosen by employees fall into this category, an increase from only 4% in 2006. These plans are cheaper in terms of premiums because they involve very high deductibles, and have fewer regulations placed on them in terms of what has to be covered (Shi and Singh, 2014). As will be described in Chapter 17, the ACA will gradually require these plans to be more comprehensive in coverage.

## Summary

Managed care is at the heart of financing medical care services, although FFS has not disappeared from the health care system. Most hospitals still link payment to a specific type of service, and in some HMOs, physician salaries are based on revenues brought into the group practice. These revenues are usually calculated based on some type of FFS technique. The result is a "mushing" of the models. The models are presented in this chapter as separate concepts primarily to help in understanding some of the financing policies being suggested today.

Despite the ubiquity of managed care in health insurance plans, it is safe to say this is a system that nobody loves. Neither consumers nor physicians appreciate the types of restrictions placed on them. Managed care has not reduced the cost of the medical care system as much as policymakers had hoped. The model has the potential for cost savings because of administrative savings attributed to the providers and insurers being part of the same organization. But because there are many different types of managed care plans available, hospitals and physicians must interact with a variety of plans, each of which have different payment guidelines. Many subsidiary for-profit industries have been established that act as separate, independent contractors, such as the increasing use of external, independent laboratories for diagnostic tests (Shi and Singh, 2014).

All European countries use some aspect of managed care, and it seems to work better for them than for the United States, as will be described in Chapter 22. Part of the reason for this is that the U.S. health care system maintains a very complex and fragmented method of paying physicians and hospitals for the services delivered to patients, requiring providers in the United States to be able to interact with multiple financing systems, each with different expectations. The next chapter addresses this issue, which is how money actually gets to physicians and hospitals.

## Acknowledgments

This chapter was contributed to by the following people: Alexandra Amaral-Medeiros, Diana Griggs, and Jennifer Salop. Their careful reading and constructive comments improved this chapter significantly.

*Chapter 15*

# The Payment Function: Money Moving through the System

The previous chapter considered health insurance from the perspective of the consumer. This chapter addresses how payment eventually reaches providers. For most nonhealth goods and services, there is a straightforward system for purchasing, consistent with the principles of the market justice model. The consumer makes a purchasing decision, comparison shops, and then buys the desired good or service. Actual payment may be postponed by using a credit card, but the purchase is easy and fairly transparent. The item is priced clearly. The producer of the good or service knows how much it cost to produce one item, and can calculate how much to charge to recover their costs and make a profit. Expensive items may require additional financing over time, which adds additional costs to the consumer for interest payments. Although not all costs are known to the consumer, there is a level of transparency to this purchasing process.

One of the primary reasons for health insurance is that many health care goods and services are very costly. Spreading risk and pooling money over a large group, as described in Chapter 13, increases access to expensive medical services. But the introduction of health insurance produces several significant complications in the purchasing process. Some are conceptual, as noted in Chapter 11. The insurance company becomes the broker between the consumer and the provider, so the consumer does not have free choice of medical services. The issue of using too much care (moral hazard) or of people getting care without paying for it (free riders) increases the cost to those who do pay. This creates negative feelings among those who are healthy, sometimes resulting in a decision to forgo health insurance, which increases the cost for everyone else.

This situation is not unique to the United States. Every country has created a health insurance system of some sort. Many countries have a multiple payer system, including some with for-profit companies, but as will be shown in Chapter 22, these are all under the same general regulatory system, so cost control functions are centralized, although many other decisions are decentralized. In the U.S. health care system, each of the third-party payers has different rules and guidelines for payments and reimbursements, and each also has different regulations to comply with at both state and federal levels. Additionally, in many cases, the health insurance payer does not pay for the full cost. This results in providers needing a system to bill and receive money from patients, and then coordinate it with payments received from the various insurance programs. Many families have more than one health insurance payer, so providers must coordinate payments from two different insurance payers for one person. This process is called coordination of benefits, and each insurance payer has guidelines for this.

Further complicating this process is that there is no transparency in terms of cost or price of each medical service or good. As will be discussed in Chapter 16, even the term medical cost is not clear, and it has different meanings for different stakeholders. The terms price or cost are not generally used in the payment function. Instead, the term reimbursement is used, which means what an insurance plan or third-party payer will pay for a specific service or good.

The first task within the payment function is determining the amount of money to be reimbursed for a specific service. This is usually called *rate setting*, and each payer has different methods of doing this. Negotiations between the insurance payer and the medical provider are around the appropriate charge or fee, as in fee-for-service (FFS), which was discussed in Chapter 14. From a technical perspective, the charge is set by the provider and the rate is set by the insurance payer. Each provider has a fee schedule, which is a list of the *desired* charges for individual services offered to a patient. Each payer decides how much of each desired charge or fee it will reimburse, with each one having different rules. Some insurance companies modify this FFS payment method to one based on usual and customary charges in order to reduce their *disbursements*, or actual payments to providers.

The general payment process starts when providers submit a claim to the insurance payer; the insurance payer disburses payment based on the rates acceptable to them, and the provider then bills the patient the remainder, an act called *balance billing*.

Although this general description is applicable to all third-party payers, the details of the payment process are quite different for the three major payers we have in the United States: Medicare, Medicaid, and private health insurance plans. This chapter will begin with a description of the payment function of Medicare. Medicare uses the most centralized payment function in the U.S. health system, so many cost-control experiments are started in this program, some of which are then implemented in the private insurance payment function.

## The Payment Function in Medicare

Figure 15.1 represents how physicians and hospitals receive payment for patients who are part of the Medicare system. As described in Chapter 14,

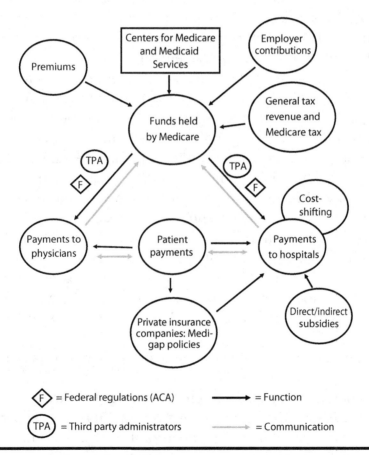

**Figure 15.1    Payment function: Medicare.**

all insurance begins with a central pool of money. In the case of Medicare, the contributions to this pool are from three different sources, each of which is described in Chapter 18. They will simply be noted here as the following: patient premiums for one part of Medicare (Part B); employer contributions through Social Security; and contributions from general tax revenues, including the Medicare tax contributions, a separate category for the Social Security tax. This fund is administered through an administrative office that is a branch of the Department of Health and Human Resources (DHHS) called the Centers for Medicare and Medicaid Services (CMS). As this is a federal program, all eligibility and benefits are the same.

## Payments to Physicians

There are several methods used by Medicare to determine how physicians are paid for services delivered to patients. Some payments are still made using an FFS method, with Medicare determining the fee. As noted in Chapter 12, this method of reimbursement is thought to increase costs by providing a financial incentive for excess services to patients. In an effort to control this, Medicare experimented with a slightly different way of setting the fees, beginning in 1992. This method is called the *Resource-Based Relative Value Scale* (RSBRVS) and is based not on specific fees for specific services, but rather on what are called relative value units (RVU) for each service. This is an effort to capture time spent with the patients, as well as intensity of services. This system also allows for administrative costs of practices, such as overhead expenses and malpractice expenses, as well as geographic variations (Hsiao et al., 1988; Shi and Singh, 2014). Using an RSBRVS to determine fees is less arbitrary than the FFS method and has been adopted by some private insurance companies. However, it is still a variation on FFS, with corrections for intensity of service, but no financial incentives for less care (Jessee, 2011).

Another innovation in determining how much money to pay physicians is *bundled services*. This is a modification of a global budgeting approach that provides incentives to physicians to provide all needed care to a patient for a set amount (Hussey et al., 2012; Shi and Singh, 2014). This experiment is also being encouraged by the ACA as part of the private insurance payment function, and will be described later in this chapter.

## Payments to Hospitals

Payments are made to hospitals for inpatient care through a unique method of prospective reimbursement, which was developed in 1983, in response to increasing hospital costs for Medicare patients. Prospective reimbursement provides incentives to hospitals to reduce costs by reducing duplication of services and examining the medical necessity of each service. Under this payment mechanism, a hospital predicts the cost of caring for Medicare patients for the upcoming year, based on the care delivered the year before. The hospital is allocated this amount of money in a yearly budget and must provide all necessary care in the upcoming year within the allocated amount. Any excess amount can be kept by the hospital, but additional expenditures must be absorbed by the hospital.

This payment method requires a new way to determine how much to reimburse for each patient. The system, Diagnosis-Related Groups (DRGs), creates groups of diagnoses that require similar hospital-based resources and reimburses the whole group at the same rate. More than 300 different diagnostic groups were created for this purpose (Starr, 2011). Although reimbursement is primarily based on groups of diagnoses that are similar in terms of resource use, there are also other modifications to setting the reimbursement rate for each group. This includes designation of whether the hospital is located in an urban or a rural area, and whether the hospital participates in the medical education of residents. An additional modification is whether the hospital takes care of a large number of uninsured patients (Shi and Singh, 2014). These modifications are some of the examples of direct/indirect subsidies shown in Figure 15.1.

The communication between providers and Medicare is fairly simple, especially when compared to the communication process involved in private insurance companies, as will be explained later. In the case of Medicare, providers know what type of reimbursement to expect, so there is no ongoing negotiation process. For payment of hospital services, this amount of money is based on a DRG system and paid prospectively. For ambulatory care, the fee or charge is paid based on one of the approaches described above.

Patients do have uncovered expenses in Medicare, for both ambulatory care and for hospital care. Medicare pays for 80% of all covered expenses. Consumers frequently buy a specific private health insurance policy to cover this remainder. This type of health insurance is called a medigap policy and will be described in Chapter 18. As shown in Figure 15.1, this means that hospitals may receive payments from consumers as well as individual private insurance companies.

## Payment Function: Medicaid

The payment process for providers through Medicaid (Figure 15.2) is similar except that more state level regulations are relevant, because Medicaid is both a federal and state level program. As with Medicare, Medicaid is administered by the CMS. However, it also has a state Medicaid Administrative Office, which sets policy guidelines and rates for services for a specific state, within the overall federal guidelines. Unlike Medicare, the funds that are pooled to pay for medical expenses for recipients are completely tax generated, either at the state or federal level.

Given the nature of the population receiving care under this program, it is very difficult to have individual cost sharing. Some states have experimented with low coinsurance amounts, usually less than 10% of the cost

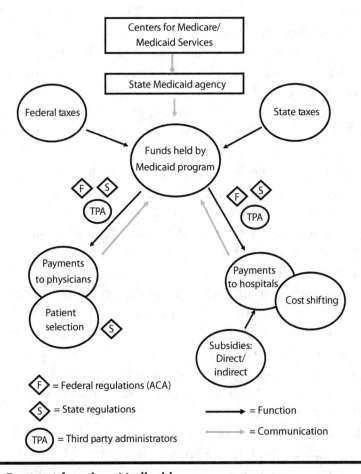

**Figure 15.2  Payment function: Medicaid.**

of services to the state (Teitelbaum and Wilensky, 2013). Medicaid is well known for the poor level of reimbursement for patients, both for ambulatory care and for hospital care. Physicians are not allowed to bill patients, so some physicians limit the number of Medicaid patients in their practice. Some studies show that less than one-third of physicians accept new Medicaid patients, while still accepting new patients from other payer sources (Boukus et al., 2009).

Physicians are paid under Medicaid by a variety of arrangements, depending on the state. Although there is some FFS, increasingly, Medicaid patients are enrolled in a managed care program that pays a set fee to physicians for the services they provide. In 2009, about 70% of all Medicaid recipients were enrolled in some sort of managed care plan (CMS, 2009).

Medicaid uses a set fee arrangement when paying for hospital services, which is lower than all other payers (Teitelbaum and Wilensky, 2013). At the time of Medicare's implementation of prospective payment based on DRGs, it was anticipated that private insurance companies and Medicaid would also switch to this method. This did not happen, although some state Medicaid programs did switch to a form of prospective reimbursement, based on a set per diem rate for each patient, irrespective of intensity of care.

## Payment Function: Private Insurance

As shown in Figure 15.3, the major source of money for private health insurance companies are premiums paid by consumers. The method for determining the premiums was explained in Chapter 13. The state also sets regulations on how much insurance companies can charge for premiums, and once the Affordable Care Act (ACA) is fully implemented, the federal government will also be involved in this type of regulation. The money held by the insurance company is used to pay claims to providers on behalf of patients, with the hope that there will be money in excess of the claims. In the case of for-profit health insurance companies, these excess revenues are profits. In the case of nonprofit health insurance plans, these excess revenues are invested back into the company. One of the specific requirements of the ACA is that private health insurance companies must demonstrate that they pay at least 85% of their revenues in benefits. This is an effort to control both profits and administrative costs, each of which detracts from paying benefits to patients.

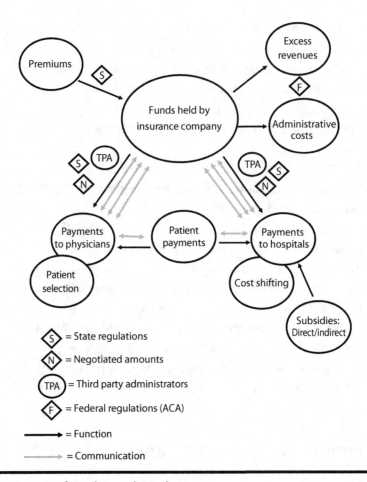

**Figure 15.3 Payment function: private insurance.**

## Payments to Physicians

As described at the beginning of this chapter, in most cases physicians present to insurance companies a statement of desired charges for each individual service they perform. These are often based on FFS, or sometimes an RBRVS method, as described earlier. Other payment arrangements are used by health maintenance organizations (HMOs) and other managed care organizations, as described in Chapter 14. The main alternative method is capitation, which pays physicians a flat rate for each patient, irrespective of what type of services are provided. Many HMOs pay physicians by salary, but the method of determining the salary may be based on an FFS method or on an intensity or resource value of the service.

Innovations in paying physicians include bundled services, described earlier for Medicare. This provides financial incentives for physicians to deliver all needed care to a patient for a set amount. Bundled payments for a group of services offered to one patient is the basis for *accountable care organizations*, an innovation encouraged by the ACA for use in private health insurance plans. In this model, a group of physicians and hospital(s) are responsible and accountable for all the health care needed by a specific group of patients. This is paid for by premiums, and physicians are paid by capitation. The goal is to emphasize preventive and primary care so expensive services will be needed less (DeVore and Champion, 2011; Shi and Singh, 2014). This global payment model should sound familiar, because it is the original classic HMO model.

This discussion highlights the difficulty of determining the appropriate amount of money paid to a physician for providing medical care to a patient. There is a balance between the desire to pay physicians fairly for their skill and knowledge base while creating a system that does not provide what are called perverse incentives, which are economic reasons for providing either too much or too little care. It is probably impossible to have a perfect payment system, which means that innovations will continue.

An additional problem that Figure 15.3 demonstrates is the complexity of the process of getting money to a physician. The solid line in Figure 15.3 represents the payment of funds to a physician, with the amount determined by one of the methods described earlier. However, this payment usually happens only after many rounds of communication between the insurance payer and the physician. The lighter lines represent this, although it is an oversimplification of the actual process. The nature and frequency of this communication depends partly on which insurance payer is disbursing funds. It is not unusual for a physician to have several rounds of communication between their office and the insurance payer before payment is received, including when claims are denied by the insurance payer. In all cases, the physician is trying to get more money from the insurance payer while the payer is trying to pay less.

Individual and group physician practices can select patients based on insurance coverage. Physician practices also have the right to refuse to provide service to a patient without any insurance. In most states, physicians also have the right to limit the proportion of Medicaid patients they accept in their practice, as shown in Figure 15.2.

Importantly, Figure 15.3 represents a communication pattern between a physician and one health insurance payer. As a matter of fact, many physicians must manage all three different categories of payers: private insurance companies, Medicare, and Medicaid. Each of these reimburses differently.

As an added complication, one physician practice may have to manage and respond to as many as 15 different private insurance companies, each with slightly different guidelines. As noted in Chapter 14, some physicians respond to this complexity by choosing to practice in more structured managed care organizations, which handles this financial aspect for them.

## Payments to Hospitals

Figure 15.3 also shows the process by which hospitals are paid. The method of determining the appropriate amount to disburse to a hospital for provided services is even more complex than physician payments, because many different services are provided to hospitalized patients. In general, there are two major methods by which insurance payers distribute money to hospitals. One is particular to Medicare, and used only by Medicare, which is the prospective method of reimbursement described earlier. The second method of reimbursement for hospital services used by all payers except Medicare is called *cost-plus retrospective reimbursement*. First of all, cost-plus means that some parts of the overhead expenses are allowed to be represented in the desired charges presented to the insurance company by the hospital. Overhead expenses include such things as the cost of cleaning and maintaining rooms, general infrastructure including lights, and the cost of operating rooms and diagnostic imaging machines. Although not every patient needs all these services, some insurance companies allow the hospital to charge a small percentage for each patient. Other insurance companies use a *per diem* (per day) rate for each patient, which may or may not include some overhead charges, as negotiated between the hospital and the insurance company.

The term *retrospective* means the hospital is paid after the services are delivered. The common procedure is to bill the insurance company after the patient has been discharged. Total reimbursement for a patient involves how long a patient has stayed (length of stay), the amount and type of services provided, and any acceptable overhead charges. Once the insurance company pays the amount it has negotiated, the hospital then sends a paper statement to the patient called an *explanation of benefits* (EOB), in which the amount paid by the insurance company is shown and compared to the amount the hospital charged. After this, the hospital will bill the patient for any remaining charges.

There is another step involved in this payment process. Once the service has been delivered, and the negotiations around acceptable charges have occurred, and all the claims made by the provider have been verified, the insurance payer then disburses funds. Some insurance companies do this internally using their own claims department. However, many insurance companies, as well as Medicare and Medicaid, also use what are called *third party administrators* (TPA in Figures 15.1 through 15.3) to process and also pay these claims (Shi and Singh, 2014). This adds another administrative cost to an already complicated system.

Once the provider—physician or hospital—is paid by the insurance payer, there are usually charges left over, for which the patient is responsible. Some managed care plans do not permit this practice of balance billing, because they have negotiated the payment as part of being in the network of the managed care plan. However, many of the less restrictive managed care plans, such as preferred provider organizations, do allow such charges—which are included in the share of patient costs known as coinsurance rates. All of the private health insurance plans sold as individual policies (consumer-driven market) are based on the traditional health insurance model described in Chapter 14 and involve such bills to patients. In Figure 15.3, this is shown as revenue to the provider. Not represented in this chart are the multiple times that paper bills are sent to consumers, as well as the not uncommon need to give this debt over to a collection agency.

## Consequences of the Payment Function in the U.S. Health Care System

Figures 15.1 through 15.3 represent the basic payment function in the U.S. health care system. Because of the complexity of this aspect of health care financing, much of the detail has been sacrificed in order to provide a general understanding of the payment system. The basic foundation for the payment function for Medicare, Medicaid, and private health insurance plans has several similarities. There is a pool of money contributed to in several ways. This pool is used to pay providers for care for the people covered by a particular program or insurance plan. Each program or company has its own set of guidelines and/or regulations that govern the amount of money given to a particular provider, either a physician or a hospital.

Not shown in these charts is the process by which people select into each of these three types of health insurance plans. Medicare enrollment is based on age or determination of a disability; private insurance is based on membership in an employment group or on individual consumer decisions. Medicaid involves yearly eligibility determinations, based on income and several other categories, which will be described in Chapter 19. There is an administrative cost for each of these decisions, for each communication with a patient, and for each dispersal of funds. This is understated in these charts, but is present everywhere in the background. Some of the administrative tasks are completed by the organization itself, but in many cases, all these responsibilities are contracted to independent, separate companies, including the TPAs, which actually disburse funds to providers. These intermediary organizations are used by all three types of health programs. Total administrative costs are very difficult to capture, because they are part of this general background. When specific efforts are made to explicitly calculate all these costs, the most well respected estimate is 31%, as noted in Chapter 13 (Woolhandler et al., 2003).

Also not fully represented in each chart is the background regulatory infrastructure that influences every step of this payment process. State and federal regulations are noted in each of these three figures, but these are only a few examples. Supporting all three flows of money into the central pots of money used to pay for medical care services is a regulatory network and also a network of publicly funded direct and indirect subsidies. Some of the indirect subsidies are in the form of not paying taxes, as in the case of nonprofit health care organizations. Medicare provides indirect and direct subsidies to hospitals in many ways, the most obvious of which is supporting the training of medical students during their residencies. Cities, towns, and states provide both direct and some indirect subsidies to help hospitals defray expenses related to providing medical care for uninsured people.

Also in the background of all three figures are a network of various policies that support the medical practice climate of both physicians and hospitals. As just one example of this, any third-party money, regardless of whether it is public or private, can go only to specific, legally recognized and state-licensed health care providers. Although this is viewed by some as being too restrictive, it does protect both consumers and providers, as noted in Chapter 7.

A more practical consequence of the multiple and independent payment functions occurs within the hospital accounting office, which has to be able to handle prospective reimbursements from Medicare based on DRGs; retrospective or prospective reimbursement from Medicaid based on a daily rate; and retrospective reimbursement from several different private health insurance companies, each of which use different guidelines.

Although the emphasis throughout this chapter has been on those third-party payers who pay frugally, especially Medicaid, there are some that are more generous in payment, especially with respect to overhead charges. Hospitals cope with this by routinely doing a process called *cost shifting*, a function that can be seen in all three figures. For example, maximum allow-able charges from private insurance companies may be applied to charges for other patients whose charges are disallowed by their payers, especially Medicaid. This process is not only perfectly legal, it is also viewed as the only way that hospitals can continue to take care of either uninsured or underinsured patients. Cost shifting is extensively studied to determine what factors impact it, as well as to determine the consequences on both hospitals as well as the overall costs of health care services (Robinson, 2011).

A payment function is not unique to the United States. Every country has to design a system to pay both individual and institutional providers. Figure 15.4 represents a generalized model used by other countries. Although details differ between countries, as will be seen in Chapter 22, the basic functions are the same. Although this is represented as a single payer sys-tem, this representation is also true for multipayer systems, because these systems have standardization of the payment function between all payers,

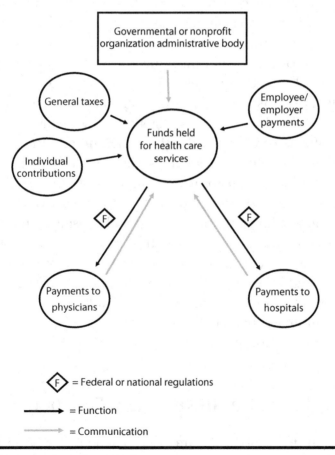

**Figure 15.4  Payment function: single payer.**

including private, for-profit insurance companies. Even in countries with a private insurance market, the same rules and guidelines apply to each payer, whereas in the United States the guidelines are quite different for each payer.

The independent multiple payer system used by the United States creates not only administrative inefficiency, as can be seen by comparing all four figures, but also inequities between hospitals. The financial health of a hospital is largely determined by its *payer mix*, which is the type of health insurance payers reimbursing a hospital for the care delivered. Hospitals develop an index called average costs, and they use this to compare with the daily rate paid by each category of payer. Medicare's reimbursements are about 90% of this index of average costs (AHA, 2009). Most private insurance companies reimburse at a rate above the hospital's average costs. Medicaid reimburses at only 60% or 70% of the hospital's index (Kovner and Knickman, 2011). A public hospital may have as much as 75% of their hospitalized patients being reimbursed under Medicaid or as uncompensated care, with as little as 5% of their patients being under some form of private insurance. Wealthier hospitals typically have about 40% of their patients covered by Medicaid or as uncompensated care, with at least one-third receiving care under some type of private health insurance (Kovner and Knickman, 2011). Even with additional public subsidies to help cover the expense of uncovered care, public hospitals are in a far more precarious financial position. Although Medicare is either at or only slightly below the average cost index, the volume of patients cared for under this program, and the predictability of reimbursement is beneficial to hospitals in terms of financial stability.

The ability of the hospital to provide a high quality of care is at least partly dependent on this payer mix, as well as the ability of the hospital to negotiate better rates with insurance payers. Both hospitals and third-party payers use their economic power to negotiate rates that are most beneficial to them. Medicare and Medicaid do not negotiate rates, but large third-party payers and large, highly regarded hospitals do routinely participate in such negotiations (Kovner and Knickman, 2011). As will be shown in Chapter 22, other countries eliminate this inequity by paying all hospitals the same amount for both public and private paying patients.

## Another Way to Look at the Payment Function

The four figures in this chapter illustrate the payment function in a general, fairly conceptual manner. Figure 15.5 captures the more practical impact

**1. Patient obtains health insurance coverage**
Private insurance: must select from among several plans, balancing coverage against cost-sharing responsibilities; must revisit selection yearly. Medicaid: apply yearly for eligibility and wait for notification. Medicare: apply once; if choosing a Medi-gap policy, must choose from one of 15 plans and select yearly; if doing Part D, must select yearly from among 15–20 plans.

**2. Providers negotiate with insurers**
Provider negotiates contracts with each insurer; must complete a separate credentialing form for each insurer.

**3. Patient schedules appointment**
Patient contacts provider office to make appointment; must determine if provider accepts patient insurance. Prior to appointment, office staff verify insurance for individual and also for level of coverage.

**4. Patient visit: treatment and/or diagnosis**
Provider must use appropriate diagnostic categories for each insurer; each claim must be submitted separately to each insurer. If treatment beyond office visit is needed, prior authorization may be needed. Patient, office staff and/ or provider may also need to check coverage of insurance plan.

**5. Billing and claims submission**
Provider and office staff must submit each claim separately. In the case of multiple insurers, must coordinate coverage between more than one insurer. No standard codes; no uniform way of submitting claim.

**6. Claims status inquiries, remittance, payment posting**
This process takes 3–6 months for most insurers. Office staff frequently contact insurer to verify receipt of claim by insurer and whether it has been posted in their system.

**7. Denials, reconciling over- and under-payments**
Denial of claim sends charge back to provider and to patient; insurers use a variety of denial codes which office staff must interpret. Uneven electronic capability across all insurers creates many errors. Patients contact provider office as well as insurer. In addition to denials, both over- and under-payments are common. Each of these must be returned to insurer for correction.

**8. Appeals**
Each insurer has an appeal process, which may be the responsibility of either the billing provider or the patient. Most appeals are manual, not electronic. Successful appeals involve resubmission of the claim, with the process starting all over.

**9. Reporting; possible billing of patient**
Payments often need to be reported to various organizations, such as coordinating insurers, other health plans, or hospitals. Provider practice may also have to then bill remaining amounts to individual patient.

**10. Patient payment**
Provider must have a system to receive payment from patients, including informal installment plans. Must also develop a reminder/collection system; and have a contract with a collection agency for delinquent/unpaid bills.

**Figure 15.5  Stages in the financial access/payment process. (Adapted from: Wikler, E., Basch, P., and Cutler, D., *Paper Cuts: Reducing Health Care Administrative Costs*, Center for American Progress, Washington, D.C., 2012.)**

of this process on a typical physician practice. Included in this figure is a detail very important to both physicians and patients. It is not uncommon for a claim to be denied or to be paid incorrectly. All of these instances result in another communication loop between the provider, the patient, and the payer. It also delays payment to the provider. In practices that are more structured and part of a managed care plan, many of these functions are carried out by staff, sometimes without much involvement from physicians. However, nationwide, every physician, regardless of practice setting, is estimated to spend at least 3 weeks every year interacting with insurers. The United States spends from 30% to 70% more on administrative costs than other countries, including those with multipayer systems that include both private and public financing (Wikler et al., 2012). This financing system is a source of frustration to physicians and patients alike.

## Summary

This chapter presents an overview of the payment function for each of the three major categories of third-party payers in the U.S. health care system: Medicare, Medicaid, and private health insurance companies. The existence of independently operated and regulated multiple payers in the U.S. health care system increases the need for administrative services and also decreases the transparency of costs of medical care. The pattern of communication involved in this payment process is strikingly more complicated in the U.S. health care system, especially in the private health insurance market. There have been many efforts at cost control, some of which were described in the context of this payment function. The next chapter focuses on the issue of cost and describes additional efforts to control costs.

## Acknowledgments

I appreciate Dr. Tom Duston reading and commenting on an early draft of this chapter. Four students read and commented on this: Ryan Barry, Jillissia James, Reema Chapatwala, and Renee Williams-Sinclair. Their comments helped in the revision of this chapter. Special thanks go to Dr. Bob Sherry, who found the source for Figure 15.5. Sincere appreciation goes to Jessi Duston, who went through several drafts of Figures 15.1 through 15.4, and to Julie Minnish, who made the final version of Figure 15.5.

*Chapter 16*

# Why Does Medical Care Cost So Much and What Can We Do about It?

"Health care costs too much." This is the single most common statement made about the U.S. health care system. The purpose of this chapter is to investigate this statement, beginning with an examination of what cost actually means, followed by a description of how much money is spent in the U.S. health care system and for what. Several factors contributing to the overall cost of health care will be described. Three different cost control approaches will be described, along with a few examples to illustrate how each approach is implemented. The chapter concludes with an analysis of whether the beginning statement is actually true.

## What Is Cost in the Health Care System?

In the previous chapter, the term cost was avoided as much as possible. This is primarily because reporting the cost of each service implies an accuracy and a transparency that cannot be achieved in the health care field. As demonstrated in Chapter 15, hospitals and physicians are paid based on what an individual health insurance payer will reimburse for a specific service, not on the cost of that service.

The very definition of cost is actually dependent on who is using the word. For policy makers and economists, cost is an aggregate term representing the total amount of money spent in the health care system. To a consumer, cost is synonymous with price, something they want to be lower. To a provider, cost is an expression of expenses of producing health care services.

Of the many stakeholders shown in Figure 12.1, several have special concerns about the cost of care. *Physicians* primarily relate cost to their own practice expenses. As noted in Chapter 11, physicians largely control the nature and amount of medical services that patients receive, but their perspective is on one individual patient at a time, not the system. Likewise, *the patient* is also relatively unconcerned about costs in a general way, except when it comes to a discussion of tax support for health care, or perhaps mandatory insurance coverage. Most of the time, the patient wants the maximum amount of high-quality care at the lowest price.

*Third-party payers* offer a set of services to a group of patients within a price structure supportive of the financial health of their organization. Their focus is on groups: not only patients, but also negotiating with groups of providers to provide services at the lowest cost possible. *Hospitals* are also focused on managing costs for a group: those who receive services in their hospital.

*Employers* have a strong vested interest in controlling the cost of medical care, specifically their employees. Employers mainly focus on finding the lowest premiums for the highest quality health plan they can offer. In their view, this is primarily related to employee retention and ensuring increased production of their company. For them, the cost of health insurance is a business cost (Kovner and Knickman, 2011).

Still another group with a deep interest in how much money is spent in medical care services are various companies that act as *suppliers*. These companies produce and deliver medical supplies, equipment, devices, and pharmaceuticals to providers and to patients (Kovner and Knickman, 2011). This group of stakeholders is very involved in a competitive for-profit market, so their primary interest is in decreasing costs so their profits can be higher.

Those who are invested in the larger system are *policy analysts* and/or *policymakers*, some of whom are part of government. Their major involvement is to design and evaluate cost control methods that can be used throughout the entire health care system, often by using one of several economic incentives. From their perspective, cost is a frustrating variable because of its uncertain connection to health outcomes and inability to be controlled. The *general taxpaying public* has an interest in the cost of medical care, but mostly in relation to their contribution to the public funds that support medical care services for the several targeted groups discussed in this book. This concern typically disappears when they are confronted with their own individual health needs.

## How Much Do We Spend and on What?

How much money is spent and on what is a subject of enormous research. The results of the research partly depend on which of the stakeholders described above is directing the investigation, which means the political perspective cannot be separated from the issue of how much money is spent on health care. Unfortunately, there are no standardized definitions used for identifying amounts of money within large and complex budgets, each of which uses different estimates. Also, there is always a year or two lag in having access to the data. This means comparisons must be made carefully, with comparable definitions and time periods. Because of this difficulty, it is not possible to simply state how much money is spent on health care in the United States. There are several commonly used estimates, which will be described here.

One indicator is *national health expenditures*, an estimate that comprises the total amount spent nationally in one calendar year on everything related to health, including direct medical care services, public health services, health supplies, health-related research, administrative costs, and investments in structure (Shi and Singh, 2014). In 2010, this amount was $2.6 trillion. Because this total amount is almost incomprehensible, a more useful estimate expresses this as a per capita figure, which is $8402 for each person in the United States. Even more helpful is to express this as a percentage of the whole production of the U.S. economy. This is 17.9% of the GDP (gross domestic product), and is probably the most frequently used indicator. This estimate measures total production and is also a measure of consumption (Shi and Singh, 2014). Whether this is a lot or a little is a matter of values, which will be addressed at the end of this chapter.

Another important consideration is how money is spent within the health care system. Figure 6.2 shows these categories in the way they are most commonly represented. As noted in Chapter 6, public health professionals feel this resource allocation understates the importance of public health activities in contributing to overall health and cost control. Also, as was noted in Chapter 14, this only represents public expenditures, and results in an especially large underestimate of system-wide administrative costs. A different way to examine this is the indicator related to *personal health expenditures*. This is the total amount spent on patient care. In 2010, about 84% of the total national health expenditures were spent on costs related to providing care to individual patients (Shi and Singh, 2014).

Another analytical issue concerns the source of the money spent in the health field, which is shown in Table 16.1. As can be seen from this, a little over one-half of the money spent in the health field comes from private money from individuals, including insurance premiums. This represents a decrease in the proportion of private money over time. In 1960, more than 75% of all medical expenses were paid for with private sources of money. The introduction of Medicare and Medicaid, in particular, caused an increase in public sources of money for health care. Most analysts agree that the Affordable Care Act (ACA) will continue this shift from private to public money funding the U.S. health care system (Kovner and Knickman, 2011; Teitelbaum and Wilensky, 2013; Shi and Singh, 2014). Whether this is a good or bad thing also depends on perspective, especially of the two allocation systems: market justice and social justice.

A continuing policy discussion is the rate of growth of national health expenditures. Whether that growth is reasonable and expected or "skyrocketing and out of control" is dependent on the perspective of the stakeholder. There have been periods when medical inflation exceeded 10% yearly, especially right after the implementation of Medicare and Medicaid (Shi and Singh, 2014). This was expected, since there is a well-known relationship between utilization and expenditures. Both Medicare and Medicaid created increased access for people, some of whom had postponed medical care. The annual percentage growth in national health expenditures has decreased

**Table 16.1  Sources of Money for the U.S. Health Care System**

| Source of Money | Percentage |
|---|---|
| Private health insurance | 35% |
| Federal dollars | 34% |
| State dollars | 12% |
| Out of pocket private payments | 12% |
| Other private funds | 7% |

*Source:* Data from Kovner, A.R. and Knickman, J.R., *Health Care Delivery in the United States*, 10th edition, Springer, New York, 2011.

steadily since 1990 to about 6% and then further decreased to slightly less than 4% in 2008, where it has remained (Shi and Singh, 2014).

How can we decide if this current annual increase of 3.8% is too high? There are three different methods used to put this number in context. The first is to compare the medical inflation rate to general inflation in the economy. With the exception of a brief period between 1978 and 1981, medical inflation has exceeded general inflation in the U.S. economy (Shi and Singh, 2014). A second way to set a context for increasing costs of health care is to compare this increase to the overall increase of the GDP. With only a very few exceptions, growth in health spending has exceeded growth in the whole U.S. economy. This means that an increasing share of the whole GDP is dedicated to the health care sector (Shi and Singh, 2014). Overlooked in many of these discussions is that cost increases do not occur evenly over the whole health care system. Growth in spending in the private sector far exceeds growth in the public sector (Altman, 2015). Whether shifting more costs from the private sector to the public is one way to control increasing costs is dependent on political perspective.

There does seem to be a general consensus among most stakeholders that health care costs are too high and need to be controlled, but there is much less agreement on how to accomplish this. Cost control strategies depend on the view of the reason for high costs and stakeholders have differing views of the main contributors of high costs, as discussed at the beginning of this chapter. The next section presents a method of identifying several important contributors to the cost of health care. Figure 16.1 shows several different

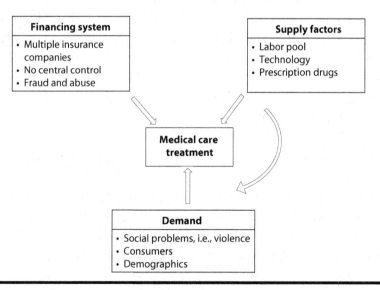

**Figure 16.1   Factors impacting cost of medical care treatment.**

categories, each of which is a contributor to health care spending. Each of these will be briefly discussed here, beginning with a category that is largely ignored by most stakeholders.

## Demand: Role of "Us" in High Health Care Costs

Consumers play a significant role in the high cost of health care in the United States, although this is seldom identified as a cost factor. This discussion will focus on several different considerations relating to the role of the consumer in the high cost of medical care. The first is general: consumers demand more and more services from the health care providers. As Roemer (1961) noted so long ago, utilization equals cost, so each time a consumer consults a health care provider, some cost is generated. Appropriate utilization is the challenge in the health field, not only for expensive services, but also primary care services. About one-half of all adults have at least one chronic disease, and 25% have two or more. Nearly 80% of all health care spending in 2006 was for this 50% of the population with a chronic disease (CDC, 2014c).

Some of the increase in chronic illness is related to the aging demographic profile of the U.S. population. Although it is not true that all elderly people are sick, it is true that on average utilization of the health care system increases with age, especially in terms of managing chronic diseases. In fact, health care costs nationwide are 2.6 times larger for those over the age of 65 than for those younger than 65 (Shi and Singh, 2014). Life expectancy has steadily increased in the United States, resulting in an ever-increasing percentage of people over the age of 65, with the biggest increase being in the over 85 group. In 2000, about 13% of the U.S. population was over the age of 65, which is projected to increase to about 20% by 2030. One result of the aging population is increased costs, especially in the Medicare program (Shi and Singh, 2014).

Of course, not all of the increase in the cost of caring for chronic illness is related to age. Four of the 10 leading causes of death are closely related to unhealthy personal health behaviors. Two specific health behaviors are well known for significantly contributing to the cost of health care. The first, which was discussed in Chapter 2, is use of tobacco. Direct medical costs of smoking-related illnesses account for about $75 billion every year. However, smoking illnesses have a larger impact, because the indirect costs of smoking-related illnesses amount to $167 billion every year (CDC, 2005).

The second costly health behavior is obesity. Nearly one-third of adults and almost 20% of children are obese (Ogden et al., 2014). In 2008, total expenditures in the health care system related to obesity amounted to more than $147 billion (Finkelstein et al., 2009). In both of these examples, public health professionals argue that increased spending on research to more completely understand the nature of these health behaviors would lead to more effective programs, which would then reduce costs to the whole health care system.

There is another part of consumer behavior that is seldom noticed. This concerns how consumers utilize the health care system. Part of this is demanding a higher level of medical care than is necessary, a form of moral hazard. The most costly part of this behavior is seeking care for nonurgent problems in the emergency room (ER) to obtain care more quickly or conveniently. Another consumer behavior factor seldom reflected in discussions about cost are patients missing scheduled visits to a health care provider. Missed visits are a significant cost to physician practices, because they mean idle time for a provider, as well as increased office staff time to reschedule and remind the patient. In one large group practice, nearly 40% of patients missed or canceled visits over the course of 1 year (Kovner and Knickman, 2011).

## More Demand from Us: Social Problems

The health care system exists within the larger context of U.S. society. The cost of larger social problems frequently becomes the responsibility of the health care system. Of the many examples of this, one that is drawing increasing attention is that of violence, especially gun violence. There are several types of cost, beginning with the ER, but they also include many others, including other hospital-based medical care costs, such as intensive care. Continued recovery involves a range of services including every level of care described in Chapter 6. Mental health costs for both the victim as well as family members are also a significant part of the cost of violence. In addition to these direct costs absorbed by the medical care system, there is also a large cost to the U.S. economy in terms of lost productivity and lost wages. A recent estimate of the total of these costs ranges from $50 to $174 billion every year (Corso et al., 2012; Miller, 2014). Because of the significant impact of gun violence on the U.S. health care system, the American Public Health Association now considers gun violence a public health issue (Weinberger et al., 2015).

# Supply Factors: Influence Felt throughout the Health Care System

Economists use the word supply to connote raw products, capital, and the technological processes used to make a product. The word supply is being used here in its broadest use to include various factors that influence cost. However, this is not a one-directional relationship, as Figure 16.1 demonstrates. Of the many factors included in this large category, only three will be discussed here: labor or the health care workforce, technology, and prescription drugs.

## *The Health Care Workforce*

The labor pool includes a whole variety of clinical and nonclinical professionals, as described in Chapter 7. This workforce is highly educated, professionally certified, and, in many cases, licensed by the state. This translates into higher salaries, with physician incomes usually given the most attention. Criticism of physician salaries in general oversimplifies a very complex issue, as noted in Chapters 7, 9, and 12.

Salaries of all health care professionals have increased, especially over the past 20 years. One particular group for which this is true is nurses, whose incomes historically have been quite low. One reason for increased nurse salaries is the increased unionization of nurses, especially in hospital settings. A second factor is shortages in the nurse labor pool, which is partly a result of consistently low wages (Spetz and Given, 2003). However, a third and very important reason is the increased awareness of the link between low wages and nursing turnover, which is a major cost to health care institutions. Nursing turnover in hospitals ranges from 5% to more than 15% yearly (Waldman et al., 2004). The cost of recruiting, hiring and training a new nurse ranges from $36,000 to $64,000 per nurse (Jones, 2004, 2005).

Labor costs are a significant part of hospital costs, as observed in Chapter 8. Labor costs are generally over half of the total operating expense of hospitals (Herman, 2013b). Some of these labor costs are attributable to new professionals who are required for the increasing technology in the hospital setting.

## *Technology*

This is usually the first factor mentioned in a discussion of the increasing cost of medical care. After all, technology is very expensive and medical care has become more intensive, so the association is natural. However, the relationship between technology and costs in the medical care field is more nuanced than it appears. The first problem is one of definition: what is medical technology? One increasingly important category of medical technology includes innovations in supportive and indirect care services such as electronic medical records, telemedicine, and general health information systems. Another very large category of medical technology includes diagnostic and imaging procedures such as computerized axial tomography (CAT) scanners and magnetic resonance imaging (MRI). There are also a range of medical technologies related to managing diseases such as kidney dialysis, pacemakers, cardiac catheterization procedures, and intensive care units. Although there are some differences with respect to each technological innovation, there are some general observations that are helpful in trying to determine the impact of technology on health care costs.

The first is that in the health field, new technologies do not necessarily replace old ones. One example of this is the continued use of the x-ray as the first imaging study, even if an MRI or CAT scan also seems appropriate. In cases where only an x-ray is necessary, this results in cost savings. However, in those cases where a more technological image is needed for diagnosis, the result is additional costs. Second, for each technological innovation, there is very commonly a new health professional required. Most of these new professionals are educated and certified. This produces increased costs because of increased labor specialization.

New clinical technology often leads to increased utilization, which does not always lead to decreased costs. The development of laparoscopic and arthroscopic surgical techniques has made a whole range of surgeries less risky, with each procedure being less expensive. However, because the intervention is safer, it is used more frequently, so overall costs have not decreased.

The United States is characterized as having an early-start–fast-growth method of adopting technological innovations in the medical field (TECH Research Network, 2001). This means that the United States adopts technological innovations quickly, and the use of the innovation spreads rapidly. The use of advanced imaging procedures as part of outpatient visits tripled between 1996 and 2001 for the Medicare population alone (NCHS, 2010). The United States has more advanced imaging machines available than any other country, with about twice as many MRIs and CAT scanners than any of the European countries (OECD, 2011b). American hospitals also perform more surgical procedures than do European hospitals, including knee replacements, cardiac catheterizations, and bypass heart surgeries (OECD, 2011b). American patients expect to receive highly technological innovations as part of their medical care (Kim et al., 2001), and this is a very important contributor to their view of a high-quality medical intervention (Schur and Berk, 2008).

This increased use of technological interventions has not produced improved health status, as will be discussed in Chapter 22. It is not accurate to describe European and Scandinavian countries as having less technology available. However, consistent with other features of their health systems, each country has devised a centralized method of allocating these expensive resources with a focus on the most medically needy patients. There is very little regionalization of technological resources in the United States; rather, each hospital needs all the latest technological equipment in order to successfully compete for patients.

## Prescription Drugs

As can be seen in Figure 6.2, almost 10% of the health care dollar is spent on prescription drugs. The pharmaceutical industry is a component of the health care system with a complicated private and public sector involvement, involving both research and development as well as in manufacturing and selling pharmaceuticals. The private sector involvement centers on for-profit drug companies, which estimate that it takes 8–9 years and more than $200 million to develop and obtain approval for a new drug (Toole, 2012). The role of the public sector is also significant in the drug research and development phase, because much of this research occurs either at public universities or under the financial support of grants from tax-supported governmental organizations such as the National Institutes of Health, under some of the allocative health policies described in Chapter 12.

It is difficult to balance the profit needs of private industry with safety and access needs of the public for pharmaceuticals. A good example of this is revealed in the development of what are called *orphan drugs*. These are drugs used to treat a rare disease, one that affects less than 200,000 people. These include well-known diseases such as cystic fibrosis, multiple sclerosis, and cancers such as multiple myeloma. The relatively small number of people who need these drugs limits the profit for the pharmaceutical companies. Several federal policies provide economic incentives to pharmaceutical companies to develop and market drugs for rare diseases, including the

Orphan Drug legislation of 1983 and the Rare Diseases Act of 2002 (Shi and Singh, 2014). Both of these provide an array of incentives including relaxation of several of the Food and Drug regulatory rules for the approval process, and extension of patent protections. These incentives have worked, because production of orphan drugs has increased by more than 38% in the past 2 years (Reardon, 2014). Price is not regulated in this market justice allocation model, so these drugs are expensive and frequently not covered by insurance policies. One of the newer drugs that targets one of the genetic deficits that causes cystic fibrosis can cost patients more than $300,000 yearly (Reardon, 2014).

This balancing of private and public interests is also demonstrated in making and distributing new vaccines, where the price is controlled by the federal government buying large quantities from pharmaceutical companies. Although the quantity is large for vaccines, the price is low and vaccines are not used frequently, so pharmaceutical companies view vaccines as not being profitable enough. Several policies have been used over time to provide economic incentives to pharmaceutical companies to produce more vaccines, with varied success (Frist, 2002; Toole, 2012).

Prescription drug costs are managed by health insurance plans by creating a list (formulary) of drugs and identifying the proportion of their price the insurance will cover. Most health insurance policies use a tiered formulary, with the consumer paying an increasing share of higher priced drugs. Another example of managing drug prices occurs in Medicaid programs, where recipients are required to use only generic drugs. Prescription drugs are distributed differently in many other countries, where they are more subject to price controls, and thus more freely available and cheaper to consumers than in the United States.

## Costs as a Result of the Financing System

The economic disincentives of a financing system that pays providers on a fee-for-service reimbursement method has been discussed previously. Also discussed previously is the increased administrative costs in the use of multiple, but independent, insurance payers. This section will briefly discuss one additional contribution to costs from the financing system: fraud and abuse.

Fraud occurs when a provider knowingly misrepresents a diagnostic code to increase reimbursement. As noted in Chapter 15, many insurance payers use what are called third-party administrators to actually disburse funds. These fiscal intermediaries do not routinely analyze whether the diagnostic codes that are given by a provider represent the services actually delivered. Independent studies estimate that fraudulent billings to insurance payers represent somewhere between 3% and 10% of total health care spending (Morris, 2009). This behavior is easier to detect for public payers than for private ones. The Health Care Fraud and Abuse Control program has been funded to identify use of fraudulent diagnostic codes in Medicare and Medicaid. In 2010 alone, the federal government recovered over $2 billion from Medicare and Medicaid programs (Shi and Singh, 2014).

Abuse refers to physicians referring patients to services for which they themselves also receive reimbursement. This is most frequently referrals to physician-owned diagnostic imaging or treatment facilities. This is very difficult to document, but is both unethical and illegal.

Both of these activities are a result of the lack of central control of the financing system, especially with respect to for-profit companies, which have less transparency than nonprofit health care organizations. Very few physicians participate in this behavior, but detection is often delayed for years, resulting in a loss of considerable amounts of money.

## Costs Arising from the Medical Treatment Process

An important focus of the public health field is on lack of access to medical treatment, and as will be shown in Chapter 17, most of health care reform efforts are attempts to increase access for certain groups of people. However, a significant contributor to high costs in the U.S. health care system is actually the phenomenon of overtreatment. Overtreatment is related to two distinct problems. The first is *lack of coordination* of services, so a patient gets the same diagnostic tests or medical services from multiple providers. In 2008, about one-third of all patients experienced duplication of services, at a cost of about $200 billion (Berwick and Hackbarth, 2013). The emphasis of the primary care provider as a gatekeeper and coordinator of services is an effort to curb this.

The second aspect of overtreatment is *unnecessary* care. This is somewhat subjective, because determination of need for services involves both consumer demand and provider judgment. Research to better identify this phenomenon investigates how economic and other incentives cause physicians to provide more care than may be clinically justified. One way to analyze this is using *small area variation*, implying that the variation in physician clinical decisions are influenced by factors other than clinical symptoms. John Wennberg demonstrated this first by identifying that the most important factor determining rate of tonsillectomies was not symptomology, but the presence of surgeons (Wennberg and Gittlesohn, 1973). This has been repeatedly demonstrated not only with respect to variation in clinical patterns, but also in cost differences (Baucus and Fowler, 2002; Fisher et al., 2003). The goal of any health care system is to deliver only needed services to patients, but determining appropriate treatment is very challenging. Recent research indicates that overtreatment has become a persistent and systemic part of the U.S. health care system (Nassery et al., 2015).

An important contributor to overtreatment is *defensive medicine*. This occurs when physicians fear a malpractice suit and thus provide diagnostic and/or treatment services that may not actually be warranted by the clinical condition of the patient. The malpractice system is a significant contributor to costs in the medical care field, especially as part of a physician's practice expenses. Rates for malpractice insurance vary by both geographic location of practice and specialty. In general, malpractice premiums are highest for those physician specialties that are more likely to have a claim filed against them, which include surgical specialties such as neurosurgery, orthopedic surgery, plastic surgery, and thoracic–cardiovascular surgery. Another specialty with generally high malpractice premiums is obstetrics–gynecology. Premiums range from $12,000 per year for nonsurgical specialties to almost $50,000 per year for the higher risk surgical specialties (Jena et al., 2011). Whether the nature of the malpractice system in the United States is appropriate is outside the scope of this chapter; the interest here is to identify it as a factor contributing to the cost of care in the U.S. health care system.

## Cost Control: Approaches and Targets

Controlling costs in the U.S. health care system is a formal goal of both political parties, and has been a persistent platform in state and national elections for the past 20 years. There is no agreement on whether these measures have been effective, mostly because this is so closely tied to political ideology, as was demonstrated in Chapter 12, especially in Figure 12.2.

The lack of success at cost control in the United States is in stark contrast to other countries that are able to successfully control costs in their health systems, as demonstrated by the much lower percentage of GDP spent by these countries, while still achieving successful health outcomes (see Chapter 22). What is the difference between the United States and other countries? The answer primarily lies in the lack of a centralized financing model in the United States. Other countries have multiple payers, but no other country allows the payers as much independence as the United States. This is directly related to the belief in the market justice allocation model, where for-profit organizations are less regulated than nonprofit ones. The for-profit organizational structure is far more dominant in the United States than in other countries; but other countries have the tools to implement cost-containment mechanisms across the whole health care system, including the for-profit sector. There are many regulations on private insurance payers, but they are at the state level. This independence of multiple insurance payers is economically inefficient, and leads to high administrative costs, as has been shown. However, another consequence of this multiple insurance payer system is the inability to control costs.

Table 16.2 summarizes the three general approaches to cost containment efforts in the United States. The first and by far the most common is regulatory, and is generally based on the ideas in the social justice model. The second approach is to encourage competition, which is based on the ideas of the market justice allocation model. The third approach is to decrease utilization of health care services by consumers. These will be briefly described here.

**Table 16.2   Categories of Cost Control Efforts**

| Regulatory |
| --- |
| • Decrease payments to hospitals |
| • Decrease payments to physicians |
| **Encourage Competition** |
| • Health exchanges under the ACA |
| • Increase cost sharing with consumers |
| **Public Health Approaches** |
| • Change behavior at the individual level |
| • Change behavior at the community level |

## Regulatory Methods of Cost Control

These methods are primarily used for medical care services paid for with public funds, because it is far easier to exert cost control measures on public dollars than private ones. There are many examples of this, including the development of the prospective payment system used in paying for hospital care of Medicare patients described in Chapter 15. Despite the evidence of the success of this approach in controlling hospital costs, private insurance companies declined to follow this reimbursement method and states did not require them to do so. As the vast majority of health care dollars are spent on expenditures on personal health, it is no surprise that most of the cost control efforts are directed at either physicians or hospitals. The regulatory cost control efforts are most common in Medicare, because of the central (i.e., federal) control in that payer. One example will be given for hospitals and one for physicians.

Because hospitals are very expensive, they have been a common target of cost containment regulations, dating back to the late 1970s and early 1980s. Several policies have tried to control the rate of growth in hospital spending, but the Carter administration was the only one to include private spending as well as public (Starr, 2011). Although this attempt failed, it led to the prospective method of reimbursement for hospitals based on Diagnosis-Related Groups, which was successful in controlling increases in Medicare spending. This effort also led to hospitals increasing outpatient care, because the reimbursement rates had not been modified in that setting. These losses in revenues also increased hospital activity in cost shifting uncompensated care to private insurance companies, as described in Chapter 15.

The story of cuts in Medicare payments to physicians is more complicated. Medicare uses a list of some 7000 defined services provided by physicians. Charges for these services are set by a group called the Medicare Payment Advisory Commission, an independent Congressional agency. Advice from this group is given to the Centers for Medicare and Medicaid Services (CMS), which updates the list annually. The total per capita spending for physician services under Medicare is not allowed to exceed the yearly increase in the GDP (Merlis, 2013). Because physicians have an increased volume of patients from Medicare, they are generally willing to agree to a lower reimbursement rate. In 1997, this became formalized into what was known as a *sustainable growth rate* (SGR), an estimate used to adjust charges, depending on volume (Ginsberg, 2012). Between 1997 and 2002, this seemed to work, but in 2002, this formula required a 5% price cut to physicians. Physicians complained about this, and when it happened again in 2003, Congress responded by overriding the increase and restoring the original fees for physicians. This process has repeated itself every year since (Merlis, 2013). This creates an ambiguous situation for physicians who have to wait for Congressional action to know how much they will be paid for taking care of Medicare patients. In 2015, the Obama administration signed legislation repealing the SGR, thus creating more financial stability for physicians caring for Medicare patients (KFF, 2015a).

These two examples demonstrate the regulatory cost containment process. It focuses on the one payer that can be centrally controlled—Medicare. Each cost-containment action must be authorized by Congressional legislation, a daunting task at best. Finally, providers respond to price cuts, sometimes in ways that are not anticipated, as noted in the response of hospitals to decreased revenues.

## Encouraging Competition

The second general approach to cost control is encouraging competition. This approach is most often utilized for private insurance payers, and the health exchanges set up under the ACA, described in Chapter 17, are examples of this. Another example is the continual experimentation with consumer cost sharing among private insurance payers. Many of these experiments demonstrate that if consumers pay more for health care services through increased premiums, copayments, and coinsurance, they decrease utilization of services for less serious problems, although not for more serious issues (Wong et al., 2001). Although this may decrease costs for the short term in one sector of the health care system, it will not cause an overall decrease in total costs. Also, if the managed care model and the economic principle of elasticity are to be believed, the cost savings will be in the short run, not in the long run.

## Public Health Approaches

Impacting people's health behavior is largely the interest and focus of the public health field. As described in Chapter 2, the field of public health is committed to emphasizing and encouraging individual healthy behaviors that will also result in less expensive interventions. Research into the reasons for health behavior is complicated, but has focused on understanding motivations and barriers for health behaviors. Much of this research is based on the Health Belief Model, described in Chapter 2 (Glanz et al., 2008). Another theory that has guided the development of interventions aimed at encouraging individuals to adopt healthy behavior is the *stages-of-change model*, which identifies the change process as involving several distinct and important steps (Prochaska and DiClemente, 1983). This creates an individualized plan for each individual who increases their chance of being successful in making changes in health behavior such as stopping smoking (Emmons and Rollnick, 2001).

However successful behavior change strategies are at the individual level, the field of public health has a very strong emphasis on health behavior change at the community level, in recognition of the importance of social determinants of health. A theoretical framework that has been very useful in designing more community-based health interventions is the *social learning theory*, which explicitly builds on social determinants of health. Interventions designed using this theory emphasize the interactions between the person and their social environment that either helps or hinders behavior change (Glanz et al., 2008).

The public health field focuses on improving the health status of individuals, but these efforts also impact cost of medical care services. It is ironic that the United States spends more on the administrative costs of public insurance payers than on actual funding of public health services, activities that could significantly reduce costs (Mays and Smith, 2011).

There is no shortage of cost control efforts, with the regulatory approach by far the most common. As noted earlier, health providers adapt their behavior in response to regulations. This adaptive behavior then causes more piecemeal cost control policies to be developed. The overall consequence is a continual stream of new, increasingly more specific cost-control regulations and a health care system that seems more oriented to cost control than to clinical services.

This does not mean that nothing has worked. However, it does mean that it is nearly impossible to decide what has worked, because no cost control mechanism impacts the whole system. The overall rate of growth of health care costs has decreased over the past 15 years, although the rate of growth in the public sector is lower than in the private sector. The percentage of GDP that is spent on health care services has steadily increased, however—indicating the importance of being able to develop centralized cost control mechanisms that influence the whole health care system.

## What Is the Real Problem?

Although this whole section of this book has been devoted to an exploration of health economics and health care financing, allocation of health care services is not primarily an economic issue. It is a philosophical issue based on political values. The philosophical question can be posed as follows: Who should *not* receive health care? One possible answer is that people with no money should not get health care services. If this is true, the health care system needs to be redesigned and health care professionals trained differently. Currently, people with no money receive the most expensive services—the inelastic ones—but not the cheaper, preventive services. We worry not only about the high cost of a system based on a social justice system but also about the abuses of a system based on a market justice approach. This chapter has demonstrated that the type of mixed private/public system that currently exists is costly and efforts to control costs have been largely unsuccessful. Four questions seem to direct thinking in terms of cost:

- Are we spending too much money on health care?
- Do we get our money's worth?
- Are we paying for the right services?
- Can we have a more efficient financing system?

About 18% of every dollar is spent on health care, but the United States is a very wealthy country, so who is to say that this is an amount that is too much? This first question is not helpful and should be discarded.

Most economists would argue that a more relevant question is whether we get enough value for the money spent. One way of answering this question is to assess quantifiable outcomes, which are captured in health status indicators, as described in Chapter 3. There are several possible indicators, ranging from death rates to life expectancy rates, and avoidable hospitalizations to treatment successes for a variety of diseases. For almost all of these outcome measures, the United States performs worse than other countries with economies similar to that of the United States. Furthermore, we spend more money in our health care system.

This leads to questioning whether the differences in health status outcomes are a result of Americans getting either an inappropriate combination of services or ineffective services. These are two different questions; both are controversial and both are investigated. One of the methods of analyzing this is to assess end-of-life medical services. The CMS periodically evaluates this category of expenditure, because Medicare is likely to be the payer of services delivered in the last year of a person's life. One study concluded that although only about 6% of beneficiaries died during that last year, nearly 30% of all Medicare and Medicaid expenditures were on this small group of patients (Kovner and Knickman, 2011). If Medicare saved only 10% on this group, it would translate to a 3% savings over the total Medicare budget, which is more than $14 billion (Kovner and Knickman, 2011). Of course, the question is much larger than money saved, but clinical studies indicate that end-of-life services are frequently painful interventions that do not increase either the length or quality of a person's life. Another way to address the question of whether the appropriate services are delivered is to evaluate the effectiveness of specific medical interventions. This research is often supported by the Institute of Medicine, with very mixed results.

This brings us to the last question. In many ways, this is less challenging to answer. The six chapters in this part of the book provide evidence that the health care financing system used in the United States is less efficient than any other, and more expensive. As noted in Chapter 15, this financing system costs the U.S. health care system almost one-third of every dollar spent on health care. Reforming the financing system is challenging, but this is because it is primarily an ideological issue, not a technical issue. One way to look at this is to ask one more question: Is belief in market justice worth 31 cents of every dollar spent in the health care field?

This is a challenging question, but other countries that all spend less money than the United States have been able to address some equally challenging questions about which medical services to fund freely and which to restrict. Restricting services, or rationing, is something that Americans prefer to not think about. In the United States, rationing of health care services is mostly invisible, occurring as a result of lack of financial access. The very high administrative costs of the U.S. health care system are also largely invisible.

It is important to create a more efficient and effective health care system that fits within the political and cultural environment of the United States. There have been many efforts to do this, some of which have been large, such as Medicare and the ACA. Others have been smaller, including the establishment of the prospective payment system for Medicare. All can be captured under the term health care reform, which is the subject of the next chapter.

## Acknowledgments

Dr. Thomas Duston has influenced my thinking on this topic for years. He continued to help with this chapter by finding many helpful references that are important to the arguments being made here. Thanks also go to Dr. Bob Sherry, whose feedback improved this chapter and who found many very interesting examples. I also thank my colleague, Dr. Maria Bulzacchelli, who found references related to cost of gun violence. Four students read and commented on this chapter: Annie Beach, Derek Luthi, Daniella Stern, and Elyssa Williams. Their comments improved this chapter. Annie constructed the figure.

# HEALTH CARE REFORM IN THE UNITED STATES: TARGETED PROGRAMS AND CONSEQUENCES

Section IV of this book begins with a chapter (Health Care Reform: Past as Prologue to Present) describing some of the most important efforts at reforming the U.S. health care system since 1935. This brief historical framework is necessary so we can understand how the most recent reform effort—the Affordable Care Act—fits into the American historical fabric. There have been many reform efforts in the United States, but all are consistent with our cultural belief in decentralized, administratively independent, targeted programs. The historical narrative also illuminates the tension between several political and philosophical values that are a theme of this entire book. This chapter concludes with a description of the Obama administration's Patient Protection and Affordable Care Act of 2010, which, although more comprehensive than other health care reform efforts, maintains the targeted program concept.

The next three chapters in this section describe several targeted programs that are a significant part of the U.S. health care system. Chapter 18 (Taking Care of the Elderly: Medicare) describes the Medicare program and Chapter 19 (Taking Care of the Poor: Medicaid) describes the Medicaid program. Chapter 20 (Taking Care of Almost Everybody Else) describes examples of other targeted programs within the U.S. health care system. Two of these—the Indian Health Service and the Military Health System—are usually not included in general books about the health care system.

This section—and book—concludes with analyzing some consequences of the U.S. targeted program model of organizing medical care services. Chapter 21 (A Persistent Problem: Racial and Ethnic Disparities in Health Outcomes) describes research on health disparities, an important aspect of the public health field's effort to evaluate programmatic efforts to provide medical care services. This chapter emphasizes the dramatic and persistent racial disparities in health status, using many of the health status indicators described in Chapter 3.

The last chapter (Alternative Models for Health Care Systems: International Perspectives) is devoted to exploring how other countries with economies similar to the United States organize and finance their health care systems. There is more diversity than expected in the seven comparison countries, although all are organized around an alternative conceptual model: universal care rather than targeted programs. This chapter is instructive in providing a larger context for thinking about our own health care system.

# Chapter 17

# Health Care Reform: Past as Prologue to Present

This chapter begins with a brief description of the history of health care reform in the United States, so as to provide the framework for the most recent reform: the Patient Protection and Affordable Care Act (ACA) of 2010. Because of their importance in the whole U.S. health care system, more detail is provided on the history of two specific pieces of reform legislation: Medicare and Medicaid, whose programs are fully described in Chapters 18 and 19. The tension of the attempt to balance the closely held values of the market justice allocation model with the assurances of the social justice model is a theme of this chapter. This chapter concludes with a description and analysis of some of the more important parts of the ACA.

## The Foundation

Because Medicare and Medicaid are linked to the Social Security program, many view the beginning of health care reform as dating to Franklin D. Roosevelt's (FDR) presidency. This is partially correct, in that FDR understood that health insurance should be part of the overall economic security he envisioned as part of his New Deal program. However, his main emphasis was on providing economic protection to people who were not able to work. Even by this early date, the philosophy of market justice and private ownership of medical practice was very firmly established, as described in Chapter 13. FDR was not interested in engaging the young American Medical

Association (AMA) in a protracted battle over health insurance. He did retain his interest in a national health insurance program, calling for an "economic bill of rights" that included a right to health care and freedom from financial worries over illness (Starr, 2011).

Even though it did not include health insurance, his hallmark program of Social Security provided a basic foundation for the principle of an income redistribution plan to ensure that those who worked their whole lives would not be poverty-stricken when they retired. Although this was a very progressive idea, there were several conservative features that remain a limiting part of the program today. The first of these is the reliance on a regressive tax, with the highest income people paying a lower percentage than lower or middle income citizens. Also, the only people receiving contributions from employers were those with regular employment. This Act did clearly establish the link between employment and benefits, and also made contributions toward the elderly the joint responsibility of private business and government. The Social Security Act also gave states matching funds for maternal and child health programs, disabled children, and aid to dependent children under the age of 16 (Starr, 1982). These provisions created the window for what would later become Medicaid.

## Too Close for Comfort

While the governmental policies in the United States were reinforcing a health system based on market justice and private ownership, many European countries were establishing health care systems based on the concept of social security for all, which included access to health care, as described in Chapter 13. As will be shown in Chapter 22, some of these countries (e.g., France and Germany) based their systems on the idea that sicker people should pay less for their health care. A national system that had particular influence on progressives within the U.S. government was the British National Health Service.

Just prior to the British system being established and for several years after (between 1938 and 1950), there was serious legislation in the U.S. Congress to establish a similar nationalized health insurance program in the United States. By 1945, Truman was president and he had campaigned on a platform that included establishing a national health insurance system. The Wagner–Murray–Dingell bill failed by only one vote because of the intense lobbying pressure from the AMA, which strongly protested what they viewed as socialist medicine. By 1950, the Cold War and Eisenhower's presidency made any collective attempt suspicious, with the pejorative term communist used to oppose several social justice actions, including in the health field. The label socialized medicine was used as a code for government intrusion into the private practice of medicine. Republicans took over control of the White House in the next two elections, which prevented further progressive legislation regarding health care reform (Starr, 1982; Shi and Singh, 2014).

## Health Insurance Becomes an Employment Benefit

Chapter 13 describes the evolution of increased acceptance of health insurance as an employment benefit in the United States. Health insurance became more common, mainly because of economic benefits to companies and to hospitals (Stern, 2003). The final step in making employment-based health insurance the foundation of the U.S. health care system came through the legal system. Both Supreme Court cases described in Chapter 13 provided strong economic incentives for employees and employers (Starr, 1982; Stern, 2003; Shi and Singh, 2014). After this, employer-based health insurance grew rapidly, but did not cover everybody. Other health insurance programs were targeted to those who did not have employment-based health insurance.

## Health Care as Part of a Social Services Network

One of the most significant moments in health care reform took place in 1965 under President Johnson. As with all reform moments, this one was created on the shoulders of previous events, and was the product of the political and cultural environment of the time.

By the 1960s, the U.S. health care system was dominated by hospital-based care, resulting in a proliferation of expensive services. At least partly because of this, having health insurance was necessary to ensure access to these services. As noted, health insurance was now viewed as a basic part of fringe benefits of employment. John Kennedy's presidential platform focused on improving the business climate so the overall economic environment would "rise all boats" (Starr, 1982). As his presidency progressed, however, he became convinced this would not work, so he developed a more broadly based antipoverty program that included access to health care. Lyndon B. Johnson continued this agenda with his war on poverty. Access to health care became a central piece of the social services network implemented through the Office for Economic Opportunity (Starr, 1982). Johnson's first initiative at national, universal comprehensive care was defeated in 1965.

After this defeat, Johnson and an array of stakeholders created a program that Shi and Singh (2014) describe as a three-layered one. The first of these was the original Medicare, composed of a hospital-based health insurance program (Part A), funded by the Social Security Administration, for people who had retired from employment. The second layer was a separate tax-subsidized health insurance program for physician's fees that grew out of the AMA's Eldercare proposal to help elderly individuals afford physician fees. This became Part B of the Medicare program (Starr, 1982; Kovner and Knickman, 2011; Shi and Singh, 2014). Symbolically, President Truman was present at the signing of the Medicare legislation and became the first person officially entered into the program (Starr, 2011).

Passage of the third layer was more challenging. This program was targeted to a more controversial group of people: the poor, including those with less systematic work experience. The Kerr–Mills program provided federal money to states to provide care for their poor elderly citizens. As with all other welfare and human services programs, this was limited to low income people. An important part of the Kerr–Mills program was allowing states a fair degree of freedom under broad federal guidelines, including the ability to identify their own additional benefits (Barr, 2002). Rather than creating a whole new program for the poor, Johnson used this Kerr–Mills framework to create the Medicaid program.

One of the stakeholders involved in defining the benefits of the Medicaid program were public health professionals. Based on their experience with providing care for the poor, it was understood that a comprehensive program was necessary. As a result, benefits under Medicaid are more comprehensive, similar to those contained later in the managed care or health maintenance organization (HMO) model. Medicare, however, is an insurance program designed from the traditional hospital insurance model, as described in Chapters 13 and 14, where the most pressing need was to pay for the most expensive services.

This package of programs, eventually passed as part of the Johnson Great Society Program, established three important principles, which are still followed today. The first principle is that employment-based insurance is the best way to cover the majority of the U.S. population. Those who are not covered by their employers should be covered by targeted publicly funded programs, specifically developed for them. Second, primarily because of the strong belief in private ownership of medical practice, the role of the government is restricted to a payer of services, with no direct involvement in the delivery of medical services. Finally, this established the incremental approach to health care reform, based on strong involvement of relevant stakeholder groups.

As these public programs became firmly established as part of the U.S. health care system, the philosophical idea of the relation of access to health care and the social and economic fabric of a national economy became lost. The emphasis shifted to the cost of these programs. Increased costs were expected, because these three programs increased access and utilization to health care for both the poor and the elderly, groups that had fairly high health needs. However, the extent of the increase was surprising. National health expenditures jumped by 78% between 1965 and 1970 and again by 71% from 1970 to 1975 (Shi and Singh, 2014).

## HMOs: The Beginning of Managed Care

These increasing costs led President Nixon to declare a crisis in the medical sector, one so severe that he predicted a breakdown in the entire medical system if this crisis were not dealt with adequately (Starr, 1982). Although there was bipartisan agreement that health care cost too much, there were many opinions about why and what to do about it. Gradually, a consensus evolved that the predominately fee-for-service (FFS) payment method that permeated both inpatient and hospital reimbursement methods provided economic incentives for too much treatment. Nixon proposed several comprehensive health plans, focusing on health maintenance. He began with the idea of prepayment of premiums, with physicians paid based on capitation and everyone enrolled in a group health plan whose function was to provide unlimited primary care for health maintenance while rationing more expensive hospital care. He proposed two programs: a private plan for those who were employed and a public plan that would replace Medicare and Medicaid (Teitelbaum and Wilensky, 2013). This national plan was opposed by hospitals, insurance companies, physicians, and liberal politicians, all for different reasons. Once again, a national health insurance plan failed to pass, probably because it was too broad in its scope and could not gather enough support from various stakeholder groups.

Nixon did finally pass the HMO Act of 1973, which was far more limited in scope, and is described in Chapter 14. This legislation marked several significant changes in the view of medical practice. First, it was based on the idea that group practices were more economically efficient than solo practices. The second was the explicit recognition that paying physicians using the FFS method was at least partly responsible for increasing costs in medical care. The third idea was to use economic incentives to change the nature of clinical practice, primarily by encouraging reduced hospitalizations. A final change in perspective was the assumption that the best way to reduce costs was to integrate the financing and delivery of care. A group practice became both an insurance company and a health plan. All of these views were contrary to the prevailing political positions of the AMA.

This legislation has had significant and far-reaching impacts on the health care system because the principles of managed care have become the basic way in which health care is financed today, and is fully described in Chapter 14. By 1998, more than 80 million people were enrolled in some kind of managed care plans, with two-thirds of these being in a for-profit managed care plan (Barr, 2002). Over a 25-year period, the U.S. health care system moved from a system of primarily FFS small nonprofit health care organizations to larger, more organized and increasingly for-profit health care organizations.

## Clinton and the Free Market

President Bill Clinton pursued two very different strategies for health reform, neither of which was successful. The first, politically progressive effort was to establish a national single-payer system, very similar to that used by Great Britain. Hillary Clinton was the primary leader in this effort. After this failed, he switched to a more politically conservative idea, based on the ideas of the economist Alain Enthoven. Enthoven believed costs could be controlled in the health field by a process of managed competition. Specifically, large regional health plans called Health Insurance Purchasing Cooperatives (HIPCs) would compete with increasingly large HMO plans. Clinton adopted this conservative economic view, although he modified it somewhat by standardizing benefits between competing plans and having state governments running and managing the HIPCs (Barr, 2002; Starr, 2011). The resulting legislation had many similarities to the national plans of the Netherlands or Switzerland, as will be described in Chapter 22.

His Health Security Act was defeated for many of the same reasons that previous efforts at creating national plans were defeated. Several stakeholder groups opposed it and offered their own competing plans, and midterm elections produced a very conservative Congress, led by Newt Gingrich (Starr, 2011). The health insurance industry was now well equipped for lobbying and produced a series of TV ads that are infamous among health policy analysts. The middle class was the target audience for the "Harry and Louise" ads, which portrayed the government as the means by which they would lose their employer-based health insurance (Barr, 2002).

The one piece of health care reform legislation Clinton did pass has had a significant impact on every part of the health care system. The Health Insurance Portability and Accountability Act (HIPAA) is mostly known for requiring patients to sign a lot of forms relating to privacy of medical information. However, the first and most important part of this legislation was to place restrictions on how health insurance companies treated those who changed jobs. Previous to this legislation, it was common for health insurance companies to deny immediate insurance coverage to those who were new to their policies, even if they had been previously insured. Waiting periods for preexisting conditions were common, including pregnancy. This legislation also required companies to make the comprehensive coverage available through the employment-based group plan to individuals who lost their jobs, although the person did have to pay the whole premium. These two features allowed many people to obtain or keep health insurance coverage as they changed or lost jobs.

Another important feature of this legislation is a significant part of the ACA. HIPAA has a clause called "Administrative Simplification," which required all medical records to be computerized by October 2003. Computerized medical records are intended to make the recall and tracking of health-related matters easier, especially for the payment function, as discussed in Chapter 15. Although this goal was not met, the computerization of medical records is an important part of predicted cost savings under the ACA (Sultz and Young, 2014).

## The ACA Builds on the Past

The ACA impacts every sector of the U.S. health care system, but it has not dramatically altered the basic structure of the targeted program approach of the U.S. health care system. The target group for this piece of legislation is the uninsured, which comprises at least 15%—and maybe 20%—of the U.S. population. As described in Chapter 13, this group is largely composed of young people, many of whom are employed, but who work at companies that do not offer health insurance. The uninsured do have access to some medical care. They receive urgent medical care as a free rider, as described in Chapter 13. Costs for this uncompensated care are passed on to others, either through increased health insurance premiums, or increased taxes, as has been described previously.

The ACA is consistent with the cautious, incremental approach to reform efforts that has been used by the United States since the establishment of Medicare and Medicaid in 1965. It is creating what is hoped to be the last targeted program. The legislation includes adjustments in many different parts of the health care system, but the market-based structure of private health insurance is not changed. The insurance sector of the economy now has increased controls, especially in the consumer-driven market. Whether it has—or will—reduce the amount of money the United States spends on health care depends partly on one's political perspective.

This section will first describe briefly the philosophy and overall goals of this legislation, and will then describe the impacts of the bill on the various sectors of the U.S. health care system.

## Philosophy and Goals of the ACA

There are three overall goals of the ACA. The overarching goal is to increase the percentage of Americans who have insurance from the current 80–85% to 96% by 2016, while maintaining a competitive market system for selling health insurance, and without interrupting the current employment-based health insurance system or any of the other targeted programs. The other two goals are to decrease overall costs of the U.S. health care system and to improve quality of care and patient safety. Although all three of these goals are clearly interrelated, the focus in this section will be on the first one. Whether the ACA will decrease costs in the health system will be discussed in the last section of this chapter.

The ACA is based on the idea of providing universal coverage through minimally invasive reform, as opposed to substantially redesigning the U.S. health care system. This is, of course, consistent with past examples of health care reform, and is the least politically sensitive idea. The basic idea of the ACA is to build on two major programs that currently provide health insurance for people under the age of 65: Medicaid and employer-based health insurance. Some adjustments would be necessary to both programs, but these were viewed as much easier to implement than the other proposed changes (Lambrew et al., 2005).

Several important consequences arise from this basic premise. The first is that by choosing to anchor this new program in Medicaid instead of Medicare, the concept of basing reform on a strong federalism was rejected (Starr, 2011). Of course, the federal government still provides most of the money and the general guidelines, but the states maintain significant control. Most analysts believed there would be a Medicare expansion rather than a Medicaid expansion. Although the increased role of the states has complicated the nationwide implementation of the ACA, coverage under Medicaid is actually more comprehensive than Medicare.

A second consequence is the continuation of the dominance of the free market in the health insurance industry, but with increased centralized regulation, similar to plans of the Netherlands and Switzerland. Insurance companies face a more regulated environment, but they have also gained a substantial benefit—an increase in the pool of people buying insurance. This larger, healthier group increases their revenues and reduces their financial risk.

A third consequence is reinforcement of the idea of shared responsibility, meaning that although individuals have a right to health care, they do also have a responsibility to share the financial burden. This idea underscores the responsibility of everybody to purchase health insurance, thus eliminating the free rider problem. Shared responsibility for health care includes the individual, the government, and the business sector. The result is a multi-payer system with funds coming from the individual, employers, and public tax dollars, with overall federal- and state-level governmental guidelines for access, safety, and quality. Finally, the idea behind moral hazard remains important in the American view of shared responsibility. Financing of the ACA includes increased cost sharing and several economic incentives to encourage more rational use of health care services.

## Why Was It Able to Get Passed?

There have been numerous reforms of the health care system involving specific limited adjustments, but the more broadly based reforms are much less likely to get passed in the U.S. polarized political system. There is wide agreement that an essential component is a very strong and powerful political advocate. This was certainly true with Johnson in 1965 and is also true with Obama in 2010, because this health care legislation became his first priority.

However important leadership is, it is not sufficient, and most would agree that a significant problem in previous health care reform efforts has been the power of opposing stakeholders. There were two important differences in the stakeholders that contributed to the passing of the ACA. The first is that the general public was used as an important stakeholder, primarily through political messages linking health care issues to the economy (Starr, 2011). At the same time, the consumer-driven market described in Chapter 13 was rapidly expanding, with widely publicized anecdotes about poor coverage.

Some of the most important opposing stakeholders in previous efforts at broadly based health care reform have always included the AMA and the American Hospital Association. More recent reform efforts have been directed by stakeholders in the health insurance industry, such as the Health Insurance Association of America and America's Health Insurance Plans, representing for-profit companies; and the Group Health Association of America, representing nonprofit health insurance companies. The pharmaceutical industry has become an increasingly important lobbying group, especially through the Pharmaceutical Research and Manufacturers of America. Another large stakeholder representing the business world is the Chamber of Commerce (Starr, 2011).

How all of these stakeholders came to be on the same page is beyond the scope of this chapter, but this is the second reason for the passage of the ACA. The short version is that rather than proposing a piece of legislation that all would oppose, the stakeholders were all brought to the table and allowed to help define the legislation so that each group gained something to offset potential losses. Having stakeholders make deals in exchange for support of the legislation was a new, more pragmatic process in Washington (Starr, 2011; Teitelbaum and Wilensky, 2013).

Including stakeholders in creating the legislation has one of two consequences, depending on one's political perspective. One perspective is that all stakeholders participated in discussions and negotiations so that no individual group was unduly harmed. The alternative perspective is that all the relevant industries were quick to make deals to ensure their favorable position would continue under the ACA. This position is developed in Brill's recent book, which critiques this legislation as allowing groups to maximize their profits and political power at the expense of a larger social good (Brill, 2014).

Although there are continuing arguments, including court cases, the implementation of the ACA is occurring in phases, beginning in 2010 and continuing through 2017. The remainder of this section will analyze the impact of the ACA on several specific groups, beginning with the health insurance industry.

## The Heart and Soul of the ACA: State-Run Health Insurance Exchanges

A state health exchange is a competitive health insurance market that is essentially a web-based store in which each health insurance company provides consumers with easily understood comparative information so they may select a health insurance plan. Premiums are set by using several variables, including income. Subsidies are available to those whose incomes are between 133% and 400% of the federal poverty level, which translates to an individual income between $14,500 and $43,600 (Chapter 19 describes federal poverty levels). Below $14,500, the consumer is eligible for the expanded Medicaid program, which will be described shortly, and the consumer receives no financial assistance for incomes above $43,500. The subsidies are in the form of tax credits, and are calculated based on the fact that the annual cost of premiums must be no more than 3% or 4% of a person's income (Starr, 2011; Teitelbaum and Wilensky, 2013).

Other variables used to set premiums involve the modified community rating described in Chapter 13. Older people may be charged three times more than younger people, although this is also partly determined by income level, and also by choice of coverage, which will be discussed next. Smokers may be charged substantially more than nonsmokers for premiums. The cost of premiums can be reduced by participating in a wellness and/or exercise program (Starr, 2011).

States are encouraged to set up and run these exchanges themselves, although the state may choose to have the federal government actually organize and administer the state exchange. All state exchanges receive subsidies funded by the federal government in order to cover the costs of subsidies offered to consumers. Each private health insurance company has to offer 12 essential benefits, although the extent of coverage within each benefit may vary, depending on the level of coverage selected.

Table 17.1 shows the 10 categories of required essential benefits that each health insurance policy must now offer, regardless of whether it is sold on the ACA exchanges or offered to employer groups. One noticeable essential benefit is mental health coverage including substance abuse counseling. The intent of this is to finally implement the principle of parity of coverage for

**Table 17.1   Essential Health Benefits Required under the ACA**

| Categories of Required Benefits | |
|---|---|
| Outpatient services | Emergency services |
| Hospitalizations | Maternity/newborn care |
| Prescription drugs | Laboratory services |
| Prevention/wellness, including chronic disease management | |
| Mental health services, including substance abuse | |
| Pediatric services, including dental and vision services | |
| Rehabilitative services, including devices | |

mental illness with physical illnesses, as discussed in Chapter 10. Deductibles, copayments, and coinsurance rates on each of these categories of benefits vary, depending on the type of coverage that is selected, as is shown in Table 17.2. The four levels of coverage represent levels of cost sharing with consumers. The lowest level of individual financial responsibility is found in the Platinum level, because the consumer only pays about 10% of health care costs. This coverage has higher premiums and is meant for those who expect more intensive health care costs during the year. The level of coverage with the highest amount of personal financial responsibility is the Bronze level, which is defined as the minimum acceptable coverage. In this level of coverage, the consumer will pay about 40% of the costs of health care.

Of the essential benefits shown in Table 17.1, there is one category that must be offered with no cost sharing: the prevention and wellness category. The reason for this specification comes from theory of the original HMOs, based on an understanding of elasticity, as described in Chapters 11 and 14.

**Table 17.2   Levels of Coverage Available through the ACA**

| Level of Coverage | Description |
|---|---|
| Bronze | Lower premiums; higher out-of-pocket costs<br>About 60% of health care costs are covered |
| Silver | Premiums higher than bronze<br>About 70% of health care costs are covered |
| Gold | Premiums higher than silver<br>About 80% of health care costs covered |
| Platinum | Highest premiums<br>About 90% of health care costs are covered |

It has been repeatedly demonstrated that financial barriers greatly reduce people's willingness to participate in preventive health activities. Despite this, most health insurance policies have maintained some level of financial responsibility for preventive services, including managed care plans.

The specific prevention services covered were not specified until after the legislation was passed, which is typical. When the U.S. Preventive Service Task Force announced the actual services to be covered at no cost to consumers in 2011 (shown in Table 17.3), there was immediate controversy over the inclusion of all FDA approved contraceptive services. Prominent among the opponents was the Catholic Church, which did not feel that it should have to offer this benefit to its employees. Also against this were many conservative Protestant evangelical groups, who specifically opposed those contraceptives that disrupt a fertilized egg, including IUDs and the morning-after pill. Women's groups have long argued about the unfairness of health policies that do not cover this important aspect of women's reproductive health. The end result was exemptions and/or accommodations for religious employers as well as nonprofit religious organizations. These accommodations involved the use of third-party administrators (TPAs; described in Chapter 15) to pay for contraceptive services for employees who wanted this benefit. In this way, these religious organizations would not have to "contract, arrange, pay, or refer" for any contraceptive coverage to which they objected (DHHS, 2011).

**Table 17.3 Prevention and Wellness: Services Covered with No Cost-Sharing**

| *For All Adults* | *For All Women* |
| --- | --- |
| Blood pressure screening | Contraceptive services and counseling |
| Alcohol abuse screening | Domestic/interpersonal violence screening |
| Cholesterol screening | Cervical cancer/HPV screening |
| Colorectal cancer: over age 50 | Mammography: over age 40 |
| Depression screening | Osteoporosis: over age 60 |
| Diabetes, type 2: people with high BP | Screening/counseling for sexually transmitted illness |
| Tobacco use screening/counseling | Breast feeding support/counseling |
| Immunizations | Pregnant women: anemia; gestational diabetes; Hepatitis B; Rh incompatibility; syphilis screening. |
| Obesity screening/counseling | |

Another discussion over women's reproductive services centered on the role of the state exchanges and coverage of abortion. The Hyde amendment has prohibited the use of federal funds for paying for abortions since 1976, as discussed in Chapter 5. However, most private insurance plans do cover abortion services. The presence of private insurance companies on federally subsidized exchanges presented a challenge. Supporters of women's reproductive rights argued that private insurance companies on the exchanges could segregate the federal subsidies from the private payments, and use only the private sources of premiums to pay for abortions. This was codified in the Stupak amendment, which prohibits any private insurance company from providing abortion coverage if they received any federal subsidies at all (Starr, 2011).

Table 17.4 shows the four basic categories of types of plans that are available on the state exchanges. The most restrictive are the types of plans

**Table 17.4   Types of Health Plans Available on State Exchanges**

| Type of Plans | Description |
|---|---|
| Strong network plans | Includes health maintenance organization (HMO) and exclusive provider organization (EPO) plans. These plans include a network for all services, including outpatient and inpatient. Very difficult to get referral for an out-of-network provider. High out-of-pocket costs when seeking care outside of the network. |
| Weak network plans | Preferred Provider Organization (PPO) plans, involve a network of all services. Referrals to out-of-service providers are required, but easier to get. Higher out-of-pocket costs for care outside the network.<br>Point of Service (POS) plans do not require a referral to go out of network. Patients may choose any health care provider they wish, with differing levels of out-of-pocket costs. |
| High Deductible Health Plans (HDHP) | Plans designed to have lower premiums, but with higher deductibles—usually about $2500 before the health plan pays for services. These plans are designed for those who have set up a Health Savings Plan. |
| Catastrophic plans | Plans designed for those who want only "bare bones" coverage. Limited to those younger than 30, or to others who cannot find a plan for less than 8% of their income. Annual deductible for an individual is over $6000, although the required preventive services must be offered without charge. Income subsidies are not available for these plans. |

that fall under one of the two HMO options. These plans are based on strongly defined networks of physicians, much like the original HMO plans as described in Chapter 14. There are other plans involving networks of physicians, but with fewer limitations, shown in Table 17.4 as weak network plans. There are two other types of plans that do not use networks. The High Deductible Health Plans, described in Chapter 12, are based on the conservative philosophy of making individuals more financially responsible in an effort to reduce moral hazard. As noted in Chapter 13, these plans have become more popular. These plans must include coverage at least at the Bronze level to be included on the state exchanges.

The inclusion of catastrophic plans on the state exchanges is controversial, for two reasons. First, these plans do not offer benefits that are equal to the Bronze level, which is the minimum required level. Second, these plans do not typically cover primary and preventive care services. In order to be included on the state exchanges, a catastrophic plan must provide all the benefits defined under prevention and wellness without any cost sharing. For all other benefits, these plans require a deductible of more than $6000 per year. Once this deductible is met, the catastrophic plan must pay 100% of all other costs. People who choose catastrophic plans may not have any of the premiums subsidized, mostly because the premiums of these plans are very low, since the deductibles are so high. Also, the only people who can enroll in these plans are those under the age of 30. These plans are only included as part of the transition period (Yagoda and Duritz, 2014).

Embedded in this new marketplace are several new restrictions on health insurance companies, which are applicable not only to policies offered on the state-run health exchanges, but to all policies, including those sold through employers. Most of these restrictions were specifically aimed at the consumer-driven market, such as refusing coverage because of a preexisting health condition, increasing premiums as an individual uses the policy, or rescinding the policy when claims were made (Teitelbaum and Wilensky, 2013). Other restrictions include elimination of the annual cap on benefits, known as the catastrophic cap described in Chapter 13. Another important restriction requires large health plans to demonstrate they pay out 85% of their revenues in benefits, and smaller plans must pay out 80% (Teitelbaum and Wilensky, 2013). When this ACA requirement took effect in 2013, some health plans had to reimburse employers and in some cases, consumers.

As noted previously, health insurance companies found these restrictions acceptable in light of the requirement for all people to purchase a required minimum amount of insurance, expressed as the Bronze level of coverage.

Although all health plans must cover the essential benefits noted in Table 17.1, there is room for insurance companies to limit their financial responsibility. For example, some health plans have redefined and narrowed their networks, so a larger percentage of care is done outside of the network, requiring more payments from consumers. Insurance plans retained the right to make these changes without prior notice, so consumers may experience unexpected changes in cost sharing.

## The Individual Mandate: Fair or Not Fair?

The impact of the ACA on individuals depends on the type of insurance a person has. Those who are currently on Medicare and Medicaid are only very minimally impacted by this legislation. Several benefits are provided to those who currently have health insurance through their employer. The first is to be able to include their children through age 26 on their existing policy, which will be explained shortly. The second is the elimination of caps on annual benefits (catastrophic caps) that most health insurance policies utilized. The third is to reduce out-of-pocket costs for preventive examinations, a common cost sharing technique used by most health plans. Finally, as noted above, all health insurance plans are now required to pay out 85% of their revenues to beneficiaries. A criticism of the ACA is that premiums of group health plans would increase, but the truth of that has not been determined.

By far the biggest impact of the ACA is on those who do not have health insurance. As was shown in Chapter 13, this is a diverse group. Some people in this group do not have insurance for economic reasons. However, not all individuals in this group have marginal incomes. In 2007, for example, there were at least 9 million people making more than $75,000 per year who chose to be uninsured (Teitelbaum and Wilensky, 2013).

This is not a new problem, and others have proposed resolving this by making insurance mandatory. In 1993, Clinton included individual mandates as part of his managed competition plan (Starr, 2011). In 1994, the Heritage Foundation accurately pointed out that the public was already paying for health care services for the uninsured—through taxes as well as higher premiums for private insurance. Although an individual mandate was unwelcome from a conservative political perspective, it was supported as a way to require people to be responsible (Moffitt, 1994). Governor Romney also cited the importance of personal responsibility when supporting individual mandates for the Massachusetts state plan in 2006 (Starr, 2011).

So it is not unprecedented for President Obama to include individual mandates as part of the ACA. He followed the example of Governor Romney by including penalties for failing to have health insurance. The first penalties were phased in beginning in January 2014. The penalty begins at 1% of income (or $95) and rises to a maximum of 2.5% of taxable income, or $695 by 2016 (Teitelbaum and Wilensky, 2013).

There has been substantial controversy around this requirement, mostly from conservatives, even though the idea of personal responsibility is very clearly a conservative ideal. The first lawsuit against the ACA was filed by the state of Florida on the very day the ACA was signed. This suit was joined by 25 states and the National Federation of Independent Businesses (Sultz and Young, 2014). The suit argued that under the Commerce Clause, people have the right to economic *inactivity* and therefore cannot be forced by Congress to purchase a good, including health insurance (Starr, 2011). In June 2012, the Supreme Court ruled that the individual mandate could stand as a tax, not as a matter of commerce (Jost, 2012).

Exemptions to the individual mandate exist for people of specific financial hardships or those opposed to the idea of insurance, including members of religious groups, the Amish, and members of a recognized Native American tribe (Shi and Singh, 2014).

## What Do Employers Have to Do?

Small employers have historically been opposed to efforts requiring them to offer health insurance to their employees. Health insurance is often more expensive for smaller employers because they involve risk sharing over a smaller group. Administrative costs for smaller health plans are also higher (Gabel et al., 2011). This has always been a delicate balance between the interests of businesses and the interest of larger society that winds up subsidizing the cost of health care for this uninsured group.

The ACA does require all employers to provide health insurance, except for those employing less than 50 people. For this group of small employers, the ACA uses two different incentives to make insuring their employees more affordable. The first is tax credits to help pay for the cost of insurance for their employees. The second is a special health exchange for small employers. This allows these employers to pool their groups to get lower premiums and purchase health policies from larger health plans (Teitelbaum and Wilensky, 2013; Yagoda and Duritz, 2014).

Businesses with more than 50 employees are not only required to offer health insurance, but the insurance has to be affordable and also has to offer a minimum level of coverage. Affordable is defined as premiums costing less than 9.5% of the person's individual annual income. The minimum level of coverage is defined as providing coverage for at least 60% of the cost of health care services, which is the standard for the Bronze level of coverage on the state exchanges. If businesses fail to meet this level of insurance or do not offer health insurance at all, they must pay a penalty, which is scaled to rise as the nationwide annual cost of premiums increases. The amount of the penalty is also tied to whether any of the employees of the business purchase insurance on one of the state health exchanges and have incomes low enough to get the highest subsidy for their premium. Using these two criteria, penalties on businesses will vary between $2000 and $3000 per employee (Teitelbaum and Wilensky, 2013).

This arrangement is consistent with the concept that financing health insurance should be shared between the individual, the general public, and businesses. It was feared that some businesses would allow employees to purchase health insurance through tax-subsidized exchanges, thus moving this business expense to the general public. The size of the penalties is crafted so that this choice will not be economically attractive to employers.

The ACA did not close one of the biggest loopholes for employers. Employers are required to offer health insurance only to full-time equivalent employees. This is a standard used by the Internal Revenue Service for tax purposes, and is calculated on the basis of total number of hours worked by the total number of employees, not counting seasonal workers. By employing workers hired for less than 120 days/year and by manipulating the weekly hours worked by nonseasonal workers, employers are able to reduce the number of employees for whom they are required to offer health insurance (Teitelbaum and Wilensky, 2013).

## Medicaid Expansion

Requiring each person to have health insurance and requiring businesses to offer health insurance makes progress at providing financial access to part of the group targeted by the ACA: those with enough financial resources to purchase health insurance at subsidized rates. Many of the uninsured do not have enough resources to purchase health insurance, even with subsidies. They are also not poor enough to qualify for Medicaid. The ACA expansion of the Medicaid program is specifically targeted to this group.

This expansion is intrinsically linked to the details of the Medicaid program, especially how eligibility based on income is determined. An explanation of this expansion is described in Chapter 19, along with the Medicaid program itself.

## Special Groups Impacted under the ACA

It is always interesting to discover how a very large, complex piece of legislation singles out specific groups. There are many such examples under this legislation, a few of which will be noted here.

### Young Adults under the Age of 26

One of the first groups targeted under the ACA were young adults under the age of 26. As noted previously, private insurance companies were required to allow parents to continue to cover them under their family policies, even if their child had married. This is a mostly healthy group with fairly high rates of accidents and very low rates of insurance. As of 2009, about 30% of the age group 18–24 years were uninsured, with a similar percentage in the 29–34 years age group (U.S. Census, 2010a). Most health insurance plans would not allow a child to remain covered on the family insurance policy after the age of 21, significantly contributing to the numbers of young people uninsured. Mandatory enrollment of this age group started in 2010, with more than 700,000 young adults being covered right away. This benefit did come with an increase in premiums to families who included their children on their policies (Cantor et al., 2012).

### Medicare Recipients

The ACA does not have many direct impacts on Medicare beneficiaries. The major one is that the prevention and wellness services covered by Medicare must be provided without any cost to the consumer. These are more limited than the preventive services required of private insurance plans as will be explained in Chapter 18.

### Breast-Feeding Women

One of the lesser-known rules of the ACA amends the Fair Labor Standards Act of 1938 to require employers to provide a reasonable break time and an adequate, private space for breast-feeding mothers to express milk while at work (AMCHP, 2012). This regulation is in support of the overwhelmingly positive impact of breast-feeding on an infant's health. Studies have very consistently demonstrated that workplace issues prevent mothers from continuing to breast-feed once they return to work (AMCHP, 2012).

## The Lesbian, Gay, Bisexual, and Transgender Community

The first part of the ACA has a strong statement regarding patient rights. This notes that no one can be denied coverage, face financial penalties related to increased premiums, or be subjected to exclusions of coverage for any reason—including gender, gender identity, or sexual orientation. Previous to the ACA, insurance companies selling policies on the individual market, as described in Chapter 13, were able to do all of these. Also, same-sex couples were unable to provide health insurance for each other in group health sponsored family plans. In 2013, the Federal Defense of Marriage Act was overturned, meaning same sex couples could insure each other as long as they purchased health insurance through a state exchange, since these are all subsidized by the federal government (Yagoda and Duritz, 2014). This right was fully realized by the 2015 Supreme Court decision in *Obergefell v. Hodges*, which made same-sex marriage legal in all states.

## Legal Immigrants

Undocumented people are not eligible to receive health care coverage under the ACA. The Medicaid expansion discussed in Chapter 19 kept the provision that legal immigrants have to reside in the country for 5 years before being deemed eligible for Medicaid. However, legal immigrants may purchase health insurance on state exchanges even if they have not been a resident for 5 years. As noted in Chapter 5, undocumented immigrants can generally only receive emergency care from hospital-based emergency rooms. The exception to this is federally designated community clinics (described in Chapter 20). Under the ACA, these have received increased funding. Increasing care through community clinics is intended to reduce the burden of uncompensated care from hospitals, especially in areas of the country with high numbers of undocumented people (Starr, 2011).

## General Public

There are several population-based initiatives in the ACA. One that impacts nearly everyone is the requirement for all large chain restaurants to post calorie counts for their food (Corby-Edwards, 2012). The nutritional labeling must be easily visible and set in the context of other nutritional labeling. This was included in recognition of the contribution of obesity to many chronic health problems, which contribute to high costs in the health care system, as noted in Chapter 16.

## Who Pays: Financing of the ACA

It is commonly noted that there was only one new tax specifically developed to help finance the ACA. This was a 10% tax on all tanning salons, an industry with little political representation, and one that is widely understood to be dangerous in greatly increasing the risk of skin cancer. There were other taxes and fees, all of which were placed on various components of the health industry. Some of these include excise taxes on certain medical devices, fees on the manufacture and importation of branded drugs, and an excise tax on very high premium health insurance plans (Sultz and Young, 2014).

Other means of financing included changing reimbursement patterns to both physicians and hospitals under Medicare to move further away from the FFS model. These include increasing the use of Accountable Care Organizations, and bundled payments discussed in Chapter 15. All of these initiatives have a goal of switching from a volume-oriented system to an outcomes-based system.

All penalties and fees from both individuals and employers also contribute to financing the ACA. This is expected to be about $70 million in fees over a period of 10 years (Teitelbaum and Wilensky, 2013).

Some current subsidies are expected to decrease as the ACA is implemented. An important one includes the federal subsidies to hospitals for caring for uninsured patients, called the disproportionate share hospital payments. These are expected to be gradually eliminated, because there will be fewer uninsured people. Other subsidies to Medicare Advantage plans, for example, will decrease (Teitelbaum and Wilensky, 2013).

Although several of these have been the subject of political discussions, all of these taxes, fees, and reimbursement changes were part of the discussion among stakeholders as the ACA was being designed. All stakeholders agreed to these.

The Congressional Budget Office (CBO) has performed several calculations predicting the financial impact of the ACA on the U.S. economy. Its original prediction was to estimate the total cost of implementation at about $940 billion, with a savings of the federal deficit of about $124 billion (Teitelbaum and Wilensky, 2013). As changes are made to the legislation, the CBO does new calculations, all of which continually indicate that the long-term impact of the ACA will be to decrease the federal deficit. However, this remains a matter of political perspective.

## Where Are We at Today?

The ACA is the most significant reform of the U.S. health care system since the establishment of Medicare and Medicaid. At its simplest, this legislation is another program that provides financial access to an identified target group, making it consistent with previous reform efforts in the United States. It also relies heavily on private health insurance companies, although these are regulated in what can be considered a model first described by Enthoven as managed competition. It does not restructure the health care system: it adds coverage for about 15% of the U.S. population by adding a series of regulations on the private insurance industry and by expanding a publicly funded program, Medicaid. And yet, this program seems to have drawn far more criticism than other reforms.

One reason for this is ironic. The general public was viewed as being originally supportive of changes in the health care system, because health care and the economy were the two biggest issues during the 2007–2008 presidential campaign. Many health analysts from both political parties agree that the economy and health care costs are linked, and Obama made that argument very powerfully during his campaign and during the year in which the ACA was being formulated. However, by the time the ACA was passed, it seems the public had turned against it. By 2010, public polling showed that almost two-thirds were opposed in some way to the ACA (Shi and Singh, 2014).

The main reason for this switch has to do with political messaging and the increased polarization of the U.S. political system. No Republicans voted for the ACA. A strongly conservative view is easily and frequently represented to the general public, often through alarmist rhetoric such as Sarah Palin's "death panels" and use of the term "government takeover" of health care (Starr, 2011). This is reminiscent of the alarmist language used in the 1950s related to government involvement in health care being labeled as communist.

The irony is that almost half of the U.S. population obtains health care coverage through some type of publicly funded program. Every American is protected by the many safety regulations exercised in the health care field, beginning with the many restrictions on health care professionals described in Chapter 7. Taking the government out of the health care industry is simply not an option. Another source of irony is that the most vocal opponents of this legislation are politicians, not the many professional associations and lobbying groups. These stakeholders helped create a legislation that was fair to all, or at least did not hurt any of them too much. Despite the continuing efforts by some Republicans to overturn this legislation, it has now become so entrenched in the fabric of the health care system that eliminating it would be not only difficult, but harmful.

One important and unanticipated impact of the ACA legislation is to demonstrate the nature of the interconnectedness of the financing of the health care system. For example, hospitals agreed to a reduction of federal subsidies for uncompensated care because the ACA would reduce this problem by increasing the number of insured individuals. Although 15% seems small, the cost of caring for uninsured people is a huge and expensive issue, especially for hospitals. As discussed earlier, some of the costs for the uninsured are covered by tax dollars, through indirect subsidies. As Starr (2011) points out, another invisible transfer is when hospitals shift the cost of uncompensated care to private health insurance companies, who then increase the price of premiums, as was described in Chapter 15. As the general public is not aware of exactly how health care is financed, it is easy to be drawn into overly simplistic explanations.

Health providers respond to reform efforts by protecting their revenues, as noted in Chapter 15. Health insurance companies have responded to the increased regulatory environment by restricting the lowest cost networks, thus increasing cost sharing to consumers. It is this corporate response that led to the criticism against the Obama administration when some people did have to switch insurance policies to maintain coverage, despite the administration's promise.

The idea behind the cost savings of the ACA is long term, which is a new perspective in health care reform. Over time, costs to the whole system and to the economy will be less from health care. Some of this cost savings comes from innovations in methods of reimbursement. As most of health care financing is not transparent, it is not surprising that some of the changes in reimbursement seem new and unfair to some people.

Unfortunately, the initial implementation of the ACA was very problematic. Just explaining the legislation itself was very difficult. Equally important was the very practical problem of people being able to sign up for a health care plan during the first enrollment period in 2014. The http://HealthCare.gov website repeatedly crashed because of a combination of factors, including poor website design, complex rules, and high demand. Because of this, fewer people enrolled than anticipated. Additionally, whether the people purchasing insurance on the exchanges were actually uninsured also became a point of contention. A RAND study claimed that out of the almost 4 million enrollees in the first enrollment period, less than half were previously uninsured. Everybody else was seeking cheaper health insurance than offered by their employer, something the Obama administration did not want to happen (Avick, 2014).

As enrollment periods have been added, and more accurate counts have been developed, it is clear that, in fact, people have been enrolling, and most of them have been uninsured. Table 17.5 shows enrollment data as of April 2015, as determined by DHHS. About 26 million people are now covered through some part of the ACA. The impact of this has been very significant in terms of reducing the number of uninsured in the United States. The percentage of uninsured has dropped from about 15% before the ACA to about 13.9% in 2014 and to 11.9% by April 2015 (Obamacare, 2015). Preliminary data from the 2015 National Health Interview Study show the percentage of uninsured dropping to 9.2%. This report also demonstrates that the ACA has had the most impact upon people whose incomes are just above the poverty level. Those states choosing to expand their Medicaid

**Table 17.5  Enrollments under the Affordable Care Act (ACA) as of April 1, 2015**

| Component of the ACA | Number of People Enrolled |
|---|---|
| Federal marketplace | 8 million |
| State health exchanges | 2.5 million |
| Medicaid expansion | 10 million |
| Young adults added to parents' policy | 5.7 million |
| Total | 26.2 million |

*Source:* Data from DHHS, Obamacare enrollment figures, 2015. Available from: http://www.obamacarefacts.org.

programs have experienced a larger drop in percentage of uninsured adults: from about 18% in the first quarter of 2013 to 10% by April 2015 (Cohen and Martinez, 2015). This difference in percentage of uninsured can be seen in further state comparisons. For example, in 2013, there were 14 states in which there were 20% or more uninsured. By April 2015, only Texas has that large an uninsured population. As of 2013, only Massachusetts had a level of uninsured below 5% due to its mandatory health insurance law. By April 2015, seven states have 5% or less uninsured (Pear, 2015).

Perhaps the most negative unwanted consequence of the ACA is the many lawsuits that have been filed challenging it—by states, religious organizations, and business groups. Four major suits are especially important, one of which was filed by a business arguing against the coverage of certain kinds of contraception in the required preventive services. In this suit by Hobby Lobby, religious organizations and religious-oriented private businesses won the right to accommodations around providing their enrollees contraceptive services, as described earlier in this chapter.

Of the three suits filed by states, the ACA was strongly supported by two. The less favorable Supreme Court ruling was that states did not have to accept the Medicaid expansion, as will be explained in Chapter 19. This did not threaten or even slow the implementation of the ACA, since the federal subsidies make it financially attractive to all but the most ideologically conservative states. A suit that was more threatening to the integrity of the ACA challenged the right of the government to require everybody to purchase health insurance. The Supreme Court supported this authority, although it described it as falling under the taxation responsibility, which the Obama administration did not agree with. However, the positive decision left the individual mandate intact, a feature of the legislation necessary for its success.

The final important suit strikes at the very foundation of the ACA: the public subsidies of the state exchanges. The ACA allows for states to either run their own exchanges or to have the federal government administer the exchanges for the states. The decision by the state is at least partly a political one, since Democratic states have mostly decided to organize and run their own exchanges. Many Republican states have declined this, but have chosen to have the federal government organize and administer their exchange for them. Some states have arranged for joint responsibility, especially if they have had trouble getting their own state-level enrollment websites operational. All of these subsidies come from the federal government, irrespective of whether the state or federal government is responsible for organizing and operating the exchanges.

The *King v. Burwell* suit argued that only residents of states in which the exchanges are organized and run by the states themselves should be able to receive federal subsidies. Their reasoning was that only states can pass on federal subsidies, and only states actually wholly running their own exchanges can legally pass on the federal subsidies. A decision against the Obama administration would not eliminate the ACA, but it would greatly damage the ability of the private insurance industry to participate, since over 85% of people purchasing health policies on the exchanges are eligible for some sort of subsidy. If this suit had been successful, at least 6 million people in 37 states would lose tax credits necessary for them to purchase health insurance (Sanger-Katz, 2014). The negative impact on the health insurance industry would certainly result in higher premiums for policies sold on the state exchanges. It was also feared that there would be a reversal of several agreements, especially policies sold on the individual market rejecting people for preexisting conditions, and increasing premiums as people made claims. These two limitations were agreed to by the health insurance industry because of the promise that federal subsidies would make it possible for the individual mandate to work, resulting in an increase in the number of healthy people purchasing health insurance. In June 2015, the Supreme Court ruled that the subsidies designed to help people purchase health insurance should be available to all who qualify, regardless of whether the health insurance exchange is administered by the state or the federal government. This decision was widely viewed as essential to the continued implementation of the ACA.

As a result of these Supreme Court decisions, the ACA has now achieved both legal and political stability, but this does not necessarily mean that this broad health care reform legislation will remain unchanged or unchallenged. Unlike other countries where the health care system is solidly established as part of the political and social culture, the ACA will continue to be challenged politically. For example, in the very week the Supreme Court upheld the federal subsidies to the health insurance exchanges, there were several bills filed in the Republican-controlled Congress challenging and/or limiting the ACA. Most of these focused on limiting necessary funds to administer and implement the ACA. Some argue that the 2016 election will be crucial in determining the longevity of this health care reform. It is very true that political ideology is an important determinant of success of the ACA. However, this is not the only determining factor. Importantly, none of the health care institutions and few of the health care businesses supported any of the legal challenges to the ACA. From their perspective, the provisions of the ACA have already been so integrated into the American health care system that it would be very damaging to the health care industry to make substantial changes to this legislation.

Health care reform is never easy and predicting the future in health care is a dubious activity. It is safe to acknowledge that the political opposition to the ACA has been dramatic, longer-lasting, and far more polarizing than any other health care reform efforts in the United States. This includes the creation of the two programs in which nearly 40% of people today obtain their health care: Medicare and Medicaid. The next two chapters describe these important targeted programs.

## Acknowledgments

The following people made significant contributions by writing background papers that contributed to the content of this chapter: Rachel Brown, Samantha Calabrese, Zach Clements, Nolis Espinal, Susannah Gleason, Avery Henniger, Laura Norton, Sarah Schlosstein, Samuel Taylor, and Kylie Wojcicki. Four students carefully read and made comments on this chapter. Each of these people had a special interest in health policy and their feedback improved this chapter. They include Emily Assarian, Christopher Lukasik, Daphna Raz, and Daniella Stern. I also appreciate the time and enthusiasm of Dr. Tom Duston, who found several important current references.

# Chapter 18

## Taking Care of the Elderly: Medicare

This chapter describes the Medicare program, beginning with the identification of the target group, and the overall description of the original program. Medicare now has four distinct parts, two of which have been added to the original. Each of these is described, including the coverage, how it is funded, and cost-sharing responsibilities of consumers. This chapter analyzes how effective this program is as an example of a targeted program, including how costly it is.

This is a public insurance program, with a significant amount of funding from the federal government, but there is also a substantial amount of cost sharing required of each individual enrolled in Medicare. Additionally, there are several private market initiatives that have developed in response to gaps in coverage. Because of this, Medicare makes an excellent case study for the continuing struggle to balance the concepts of allocations using market justice or social justice approaches.

## The Target Group: Changes over Time

The initial target group identified in 1965 by President Johnson consisted of those over the age of 65 who were losing their employment-based health insurance as a consequence of retiring. As noted in Chapter 17, this is a group that was viewed very favorably, so helping them preserve their economic stability was a politically acceptable idea, although not universally supported. Medicare is limited to those who have contributed enough to the Social Security program to be eligible for benefits. This required contribution aspect makes Medicare closer to a social insurance program than to an entitlement program, such as Medicaid. Those who are not eligible for Social Security benefits may buy into Medicare, as will be described shortly. A little more than 90% of those older than 65 years are enrolled in the Medicare program (KFF, 2013b).

In 1972, the U.S. Congress expanded the program to provide medical care to two other groups: people of any age with permanent disabilities who receive Social Security disability payments and those diagnosed with end-stage renal disease. Kidney dialysis had just been developed and was a life-saving treatment. It was very expensive, so Congress required Medicare to cover the procedure (Barr, 2002). This was the first specific health problem that was added to Medicare coverage legislatively, but it would not be the last. In 2001, Congress expanded the program to also cover younger people with Lou Gehrig's disease (amyotrophic lateral sclerosis) (Medicare.gov, 2001). Other services have been added legislatively such as mammography (1990) and an annual wellness examination (2005) (KFF, 2010d).

The demographic group served by Medicare is generally divided into three subgroups. The young elders are the 65–74 years age group, the mid-elders are the 75–84 years age group, and old or elderly elders are older than 85. In 2011, more than 13% of the whole U.S. population were older than 65, and when all the Baby Boomers have reached age 65 in 2030, this group will comprise 20% of the whole population, with 12% being in the over 85 age group (Shi and Singh, 2014). The over 85 age group is growing at the fastest rate of any age group, and this is expected to continue.

About 48 million people receive health care services that are paid for by Medicare, with about 85% of those being over the age of 65 (KFF, 2010e). As with most insurance programs, the vast majority of the money spent under Medicare goes to a small proportion of people enrolled: almost 75% of these funds are spent in the last year of a person's life (Kovner and Knickman, 2011). A total of about 15% of the federal budget is spent on services received under Medicare (KFF, 2012a; OMB, 2014). Only the Department of Defense receives a larger share of the national budget.

Although the major target group (people over the age of 65) is a very diverse group of people, they do share some social and health challenges. About 75% of people over the age of 65 have at least two different chronic conditions. This is much higher than that found in the general population, of which about 21% have one chronic condition, and only 7% have three or more (Machlin et al., 2008). Nearly half of Medicare enrollees have some kind of self-reported activity limitation, with about one-third having some sort of cognitive impairment (Shi and Singh, 2014).

The Medicare is frequently referred to as a single payer system, but it is actually quite complicated, mostly as a result of the political process described in Chapter 17. There are two governmental agencies that are responsible for the organization and supervision of the entire Medicare program. The first agency is the Social Security Administration, which is responsible for determining eligibility and for processing the premium payments from individuals. The second is the Centers for Medicare and Medicaid Services (CMS), which is part of the Department of Health and Human Services, which administers the Medicare program. As shown in Chapter 15, there are also private contractors that disburse funds to hospitals and physicians.

Medicare is composed of four separate programs. The original two components, enacted in 1965, are *Part A* and *Part B*. *Part C*, called Medicare Advantage, was first implemented in 1985, with continual adjustments, including currently. *Part D*, the Prescription Drug plan, was implemented in 2006. Although each of these is administered by the government through the CMS, each part is financed differently and the payment function operates differently. Also, not every person is enrolled in each of the four parts.

# Medicare: A Four-Part Program

This section will describe each of the four parts of Medicare. This description will include identifying what is covered, how the part is funded, and what the cost-sharing responsibilities are for each individual. Also included will be a brief reminder of the payment function for each (this has been presented in more detail in Chapter 15).

## *Part A: Hospital Insurance*

The only services covered under Part A are inpatient hospital stays, including a semiprivate room, food, diagnostic tests, nursing services, and the cost of any drugs and medical supplies provided as part of a hospital stay. Physician services while in the hospital are not included under Part A, but nursing and other services are. Medicare limits hospital coverage to 60 days of full coverage, and 30 more days with a daily copay requirement

(Medicare.gov, 2013). This coverage takes effect after a deductible of about $1000 is paid by the patient. Part A also covers expenses related to inpatient psychiatric care, with a lifetime limit of 190 days, under the same deductible and copayment rules as for hospital stays.

In 1982, hospice services were added to Part A by a piece of specific legislation that amended the Social Security Act. Hospice services (described in Chapter 6) are for those whose life expectancy is about 6 months. Participation requires the patient to agree to palliative care for comfort instead of aggressive curative treatments (Medicare.gov, 2000; Barr, 2002).

Medicare does not cover stays in long-term care facilities, unless there is a specific medical need for a skilled nursing home, as described in Chapter 10. The maximum limit in a skilled nursing home is 100 days, with Medicare fully covering only the first 20 days. The patient pays a copayment of about $150 per day for the remaining 80 days (Medicare.gov, 2013).

## Funding

Part A is almost totally funded by payroll taxes, which involves employers and workers each paying half. People with incomes of up to $200,000 pay 2.9%, increasing to a maximum of 3.8% as incomes rise (Social Security Administration, n.d.). These payroll taxes go into part of the Medicare Trust Fund known as the Hospital Insurance (HI) Fund. The money withdrawn from the HI Fund to pay for enrollees is based on the earnings of currently employed people. In order for this system to work most effectively, enough people need to be currently working. In 1998, there were about 3.9 workers to support one beneficiary. In 2030, when the baby boomers will be mostly retired and in the Medicare system, it is estimated that there will be about 2.3 workers for one beneficiary and in 2050, it is estimated there will be only two workers per beneficiary (Barr, 2002). This policy dilemma occupies a considerable amount of time, as will be noted at the end of the chapter.

## Cost Sharing Responsibilities

There is no premium for those who qualify for Social Security, or are a spouse of someone who has contributed to the Social Security system. Eligibility for Social Security (and Medicare) is obtained after about 10 years of working full-time and paying the required Social Security taxes. If a person is not eligible for Medicare, they may still buy into the program by paying premiums, which range from $248 to $451 per month, depending on how many quarters of Social Security eligibility a person has Social Security Administration (SSA).

There are both deductibles and some copayments for specific services. As of 2014, there is a $1000 deductible for a hospital stay of less than 60 days, with a copay of $304 per day for each day beyond that (Shi and Singh, 2014).

## Payment Function

Hospitals are paid through a prospective reimbursement system using Diagnosis-Related Groups. Money is disbursed from the HI Fund to a fiscal intermediary (third-party administrator [TPA]), as described in Chapter 15. Hospitals then bill patients directly for the remainder. In 2012, about one-third of all Medicare payments were drawn from the HI Fund to pay hospitals (Shi and Singh, 2014).

# Part B: Medical Insurance

This part of Medicare is based on the concept of a traditional insurance plan described in Chapter 14. Part B pays for a range of services needed to treat those seeking care for a diagnosable illness. Table 18.1 shows these services, which include payments to physicians for a whole variety of medical services related to care for an acute or chronic illness. Physician services for either inpatient or outpatient care are billed through Part B. Other services that can be linked to a specific diagnosis include physical therapy, mental health services, and a variety of laboratory and diagnostic tests. The diagnostic code is important because all payment is linked to a code by using a fee for service method of determining charges.

There is a very complex set of regulations used to define and manage these benefits, and there have been several changes over time. For example, outpatient surgical procedures are covered under Part B. Furthermore, prescription drugs were not originally included, but today drugs that require a physician for their administration are covered. This includes many chemotherapy drugs.

Some services have been added to Part B by specific legislation, such as annual mammograms, described earlier. Specific immunizations such as flu, pneumonia, and most recently, shingles have also been added. The Affordable Care Act (ACA) requires Medicare to cover a yearly wellness

**Table 18.1    Summary of Services Covered under Medicare, Part B**

| Acute Care Services (Outpatient and Inpatient) | Chronic Disease Management (Outpatient Setting) | Preventive Services (Outpatient Setting) |
|---|---|---|
| Physician services for acute medical care | Physician visits related to managing specific illnesses such as hypertension and diabetes | Annual wellness examination |
| Emergency department services | Laboratory and other diagnostic services | General preventive screenings, such as mammography, pap examinations; colonoscopy examinations |
| Outpatient surgery | Medically necessary medical equipment related to diagnosed chronic illness | Specific disease screenings such as diabetes, obesity, depression, or alcohol misuse |
| Diagnostic and laboratory tests related to acute medical illnesses | Cardiac rehabilitation programs | Specified vaccinations, such as flu and pneumonia |
| Mental health services (outpatient) | Chemotherapy | |
| Physical and occupational therapy services (outpatient) | | |

examination, which involves fewer covered laboratory services than a traditional physical examination.

Part B also covers some Durable Medical Equipment, especially those that assist in mobility including canes, walkers, mobility scooters, and wheelchairs. Prosthetic devices such as limbs are also included.

## Funding

The original plan was to have about half of the costs of this part of Medicare paid for by participants' premiums, with the other half coming out of general tax revenues. However, as the price of premiums continued to rise, the proportion of the costs coming out of general tax revenues increased. Currently, nearly 75% of the expenses of Part B are paid for out of general tax revenues, with the rest coming from premiums paid by those who choose to enroll. Enrollment is limited to those who have Part A, and premiums are scaled to income. The base premium as of 2013 is $104/month. People whose incomes exceed $85,000 for a single person ($170,000 for a married couple) have higher premiums, ranging from $139/month per person to $335/month per person for those whose income is above $214,000 ($428,000 for a couple) (Medicare.gov, 2013). In most cases, these premiums are deducted from Social Security payments: those who are not receiving Social Security payments are billed quarterly. Once a person is on Medicare, all coverage is individual, even for married couples. This means that a married couple, both of whom are on Medicare, are billed separately for their premiums.

## Cost Sharing

In addition to the premiums noted above, there is a low deductible for Part B—only $147 in 2013. Unlike Part A, however, there is also a coinsurance rate for Part B. The program pays for 80% of the cost of the services, and patients are responsible for paying for the remainder of the cost of the services. About 85% of people enrolled in Part B purchase a private health insurance policy specifically designed to cover these remaining costs (AHIP, 2013). These types of policies are called complementary plans, Medicare Supplemental Insurance Plans, or—more simply—*Medigap* plans. They are very specific to Medicare: it is illegal for an insurance company to sell a policy to someone who is not covered by both Parts A and B of Medicare. This is a highly regulated market, with 10 different plans available, although not all are available in all states.

These plans cover the deductibles and copayments for Part A, and the various coinsurance and copayment rates for Part B. Medigap plans will not cover any service not covered by Medicare. The premiums vary depending on the type of coverage, but are typically between $150 and $340 per month (AHIP, 2013).

## Payment Function

As with Part A, the role of the government is to collect and hold two sources of money coming into this program: the money from the general tax revenues and the money coming in from premiums. There is a separate part of the Medicare Trust Fund for the purpose of holding the monies for Part B. This is called the Supplemental Medical Insurance (SMI) Trust Fund. Physicians are paid based on the Resource-Based Relative Value Scale (RBRVS) with the funds being disbursed by private contractors or fiscal intermediaries (TPAs), as described in Chapter 15. Patients pay any remaining amounts directly to providers, as shown in Figure 15.1.

## Part C: Comprehensive Coverage: Public/Private Interaction

During the 1980s and 1990s, an increasing number of consumers enrolled in health maintenance organization (HMO)-type managed care plans. The premiums for these plans were mostly lower, and they covered a variety of preventive services, as well as prescription drugs. New Medicare enrollees increasingly came from these HMO-type plans, and insurance companies saw a potential volume of patients with a stable payer. In response to this, the CMS experimented with paying a capitation fee to both for-profit and nonprofit HMOs to enroll Medicare patients into their managed care plans. By 1987, there were almost 200 individual HMOs that had signed risk-based contracts with the Medicare Administration; however, by 1991, this fell to only 31 (Barr, 2002). Medicare enrollees were more costly than HMOs originally anticipated, mostly because of the cost of prescription drugs, but also because of the need of a few for very extensive medical services. As the HMO market expanded, managed care plans began to care for Medicare enrollees more efficiently, and by 1997 almost 15% of all Medicare beneficiaries were enrolled in HMO plans.

The Balanced Budget Act of 1997 was a complex set of changes, several of which directly impacted the Medicare program. One was the federal government significantly decreased the capitation rate paid to HMOs from the previous 95% of predicted costs to only 70%. Also, under Republican leadership in Congress, Medicare was moved to a more market-based approach (Barr, 2002). This was primarily accomplished by the establishment of what was known as the Medicare Plus Choice, which was Part C.

This new component of Medicare gave enrollees a range of choices of how to receive their Medicare benefits. They could keep the traditional Parts A and B, or they could establish a Health Savings Account, which was also created in the same legislation. A third choice involved combining the premium for Part B with the premium paid to a private Medigap policy to enroll in a managed care plan. Their individual contributions were paid to the Medicare Trust Fund and then disbursed to a participating HMO, from whom the beneficiary would receive all needed medical care services, including prescription drugs. The federal subsidy payment was added to the funds dispersed to the HMOs to participate. By 2003, this part of Medicare became known as Medicare Advantage plans. Although HMOs were required to provide services comparable to Medicare coverage, there was substantial variation, including in prescription drug coverage (Merlis, 2008). This required the consumer to carefully consider all the choices. A piece of legislation called the Medicare Modernization Act remedied this, requiring all HMOs to provide prescription drug coverage through Part D of Medicare, which will be described in the following discussion.

An important part of the 2003 legislation was increasing the federal subsidies by about 12%. This encouraged more HMOs to enroll Medicare recipients, so by 2013 almost 28% of Medicare beneficiaries are enrolled in some type of Medicare Advantage plan through an HMO (Gold et al., 2013).

These plans are controversial because their administrative costs remain higher than traditional fee for service or RBRVS Medicare reimbursement of individual physicians. Also, there does not seem to be much better quality (Jacobson et al., 2009). Subsidizing private insurance companies with public money is always controversial. The ACA plans to slowly decrease the government subsidies to HMO Advantage Plans, thus increasing the cost to the enrollees. It remains uncertain what the impact of reducing these federal subsidies will be on the number of participating HMOs (Shi and Singh, 2014).

## Part D: Another Experiment in Public/Private Interaction

Part D of Medicare began in January 2006, with the specific purpose of providing coverage for prescription drugs. People may enroll directly in Part D, as long as they are also enrolled in Parts A and B. Medicare Advantage Plans also use Part D to provide prescription drug coverage. As of 2012, about 60% of Medicare enrollees directly enroll in a prescription drug plan through Part D (KFF, 2012b).

The major fear associated with a prescription drug program has always been cost. Because of this, politicians favored a mixture of public and private funds, along with significant free market activity. Public funds for this program come from general tax revenues that are part of the SMI Trust Fund, which also provides funding for Part B. Private funds come from individuals, as will be described next. The free market activity arises from the insurance sector: all prescription drug coverage is offered through private health insurance companies, which are free to structure their individual policies in the way that best suits their market.

There is no standardized benefit in terms of which drugs must be covered, but there is a required minimum benefit structure. The benefit structure begins with a basic deductible of $310 per year. Each insurance company must pay for 25% of annual drug costs up to $2970. The consumer is responsible for all costs between $2970 and $4750. This gap in coverage is known as the donut hole. A person is said to be *in the donut hole* when he/she has spent $2970 in the benefit year, but not yet spent the upper annual limit of $4750. Once the top limit of personal responsibility is reached, the consumer is then eligible for catastrophic coverage, meaning the individual is responsible only for a copay of $2.65 for each generic drug and $6.60 for each brand name drug prescription (KFF, 2012b).

There has been a fair amount of controversy about Part D right from the beginning, and with time and evaluation, more criticism has developed. Four major concerns will be noted here. First, despite the standard benefit structure, insurance companies use a variety of ways to meet these requirements. Some use a tiered drug formulary instead of deductibles; some offer coverage during the donut hole gap, whereas others do not. Insurance plans vary widely on which drugs they cover, and insurance companies retained the right to change the coverage during the year, which is unusual (KFF, 2012b). The average monthly premium is about $40 (Hoadley et al., 2013).

A second source of criticism relates to how complicated the program is, not only in terms of the benefit structure itself, but also in the amount of consumer choice. By 2010, there were more than 1500 stand-alone plans. Each state has between 40 and 50 different plans approved, and each consumer is often confronted with more than 30 different plans (Hoadley et al., 2009). Medicare runs an online plan finder, as do most pharmacies, to help consumers choose the right plan for their needs. Increasing consumer choice is a strong part of the market justice model, but the positive impact of consumer choice on price is highly dependent on adequate information, as described in Chapter 11. Supporters of Part D point to the many online sources of information. Critics note the limitations of such online sources for this demographic group. Other critics note the complex financing structure is difficult for all ages to understand.

A third point of analysis is whether this targeted program meets the needs of its designated recipients. The individuals who receive the most benefit from Part D are those with very large annual drug costs. About

26% of all enrollees reach the donut hole threshold, but only 4% of all those who enroll in Part D obtain catastrophic coverage (SMI Trust Fund Report, 2009). On average, about 15% of the elderly either modify or stop prescription drugs because of the cost. This percentage dropped to about 11% after the passage of Part D (Madden et al., 2008). Out-of-pocket expenditures for drugs also dropped slightly (Liu et al., 2011). There also seems to be an increase in the use of brand name drugs over generic ones (Zhang et al., 2008).

A fourth concern is that of cost, especially in terms of public source of funds. As of 2007, the average per capita cost for each beneficiary was about $1000, which translates to an annual expenditure of about $49 billion (SMI Trust Fund Report, 2009).

Which of these concerns is important is a matter of political and philosophical perspective. Those who support more market justice allocations in the health field view this program as one that appropriately balances the needs of the drug industry with the needs of individuals for assistance with the cost of their prescription drugs. Those who support more social justice models of allocation feel the balance in this legislation is too far on the side of the free market. A specific point of contention is that the legislation forbade CMS from negotiating lower prices with pharmaceutical companies in exchange for volume buying. The Veterans Affairs system has this negotiating right, which has resulted in drug prices that are between about 40% and 60% lower for its beneficiaries. Estimates of what this has cost the taxpayers vary, but a well-accepted amount is about $50 billion a year (Austin et al., 2012). This is being at least partially corrected under the ACA, which requires a manufacturer discount on drugs while the beneficiary is in the coverage gap (the donut hole) (Shi and Singh, 2014).

## So, How Good Is Medicare?

At the time the Medicare legislation was passed in 1965, only 56% of people over the age of 65 had hospital insurance (Barr, 2002). Today, about 93% of the people over age 65 are covered by Part A of Medicare. About 45% of medical care expenses of this group are covered by Parts A and B of Medicare (Shi and Singh, 2014). Whether this is good or poor coverage is a subjective judgment and dependent on political perspective. Many in the public health field find this level of coverage to be less than ideal. Those who believe that people are more responsible if they contribute their own resources to pay for health care view 45% coverage as a liberal contribution of society to the medical needs of individuals.

There are several services that are not covered, including most preventive care, especially primary care visits that do not include a specific diagnosis. Several services frequently utilized by this demographic group are not covered, including dental care and eye care, except for eye surgeries, including cataracts. Hearing aids are also not covered, and home care services are only covered if they are medically necessary and provided by a skilled health professional (Shi and Singh, 2014). Perhaps the most important health services not covered is nursing home care. There are limits on the length of time that can be spent in a skilled nursing home, and Medicare will not pay for what is considered custodial care. This level of service is a completely free market activity, as described in Chapter 10. Medicaid does cover these services, which causes unanticipated consequences in that program, as will be shown in the next chapter.

Balancing the services not covered is that the most expensive medical services are covered by Medicare, although not without cost sharing.

The most severe criticism of Medicare is how much it costs, which is considerable. The total cost of Medicare in 2010 was about $523 billion, which is almost 15% of the entire federal budget. This is predicted to increase to about $923 billion by 2020 (KFF, 2010e). This money provides medical services to about 48 million people as of 2010, with a projected increase to about 79 million by 2020 (KFF, 2010e). The administrative costs of Medicare are lower than any other insurance, public or private, as shown in Table 13.1, but the overall cost predictions cause concern.

## Challenges Facing Medicare: Suggested Policy Changes

As was described in Chapter 16, there have been several cost control mechanisms developed within the Medicare program. Many of these have been successful and have had a significant impact on the medical field. For example, the RBRVS used to pay physicians has somewhat reduced the income differential between primary care specialists and more narrowly defined specialists (Goodson, 2007). Despite this and other cost control successes, per capita medical expenses reimbursed by Medicare are increasing faster than the per capita gross domestic product (MedPac, 2013). There are many worries about the future, especially the impact of the Baby Boomers on the Medicare program and the expected decrease in proportion of working people to retired people to financially support the Medicare program.

These concerns have led some people to question whether the public/private balance of funds should be adjusted in order to create a more sustainable future source of funding for Medicare. Currently, about 43% of all Medicare spending comes from general tax revenues, which supports Parts B and D. Another 39% comes from the Medicare tax, which goes into the HI Trust Fund to pay for Part A. About 13% is generated from individuals paying premiums on either Part B or D. The remainder is mostly revenue from interest on the Trust Funds (KFF, 2013b; MedPac, 2013). A range of policy options have been suggested, along with projections of how much money would be saved over a 10-year period for each one. The most common policy options are shown in Table 18.2 and will be discussed here. All but one option involves increasing costs to beneficiaries in some way.

One of the most common proposals is to *increase the age of eligibility* for Medicare, similar to the proposal for increasing the age for eligibility for Social Security. Most justify this idea by noting that life expectancy after age 65 has increased 5 years since 1965 (KFF, 2013b). Increasing the eligibility age by 2 years, to age 67, produces a projected savings of $113 billion, as shown in Table 18.2.

There are several proposals that suggest *increasing the cost sharing to* beneficiaries. One specific policy suggestion is to increase the Part B deductible from $147 per year to $222, a $75 yearly increase. There are a range of other suggestions, including increasing coinsurance rates on all laboratory

**Table 18.2  Some Proposed Policy Changes to Medicare and Projected Savings over a 10-Year Period[a]**

| Proposed Policy Change | Projected Savings over a 10-Year Period |
| --- | --- |
| Increase age of eligibility | $113 billion |
| Increase cost sharing to beneficiaries | $21 billion–$40 billion, depending on specific options |
| Increase cost sharing of Medigap policies | $53 billion |
| Higher premiums on Parts B and D for all beneficiaries | $241 billion |
| A 1% general tax increase | $651 billion |

[a] Proposals are from the Kaiser Family Foundation, 2013. Available from: http://www.kff.org.

services or on home health services. There are also suggestions about increasing or establishing copayments on several services.

One specific suggestion is to increase the *cost sharing of Medigap* policies. More than 80% of Medicare beneficiaries have some type of Medigap policy, either through buying one individually, obtaining one by enrolling in a Medicare Advantage Plan (through Part C), or being given one as a retirement benefit. Conservative economists argue that Medigap policies encourage overuse (moral hazard) of health care services, by eliminating cost sharing. The projected savings of $53 billion over 10 years shown in Table 18.2 is based on one specific option, which is to have a 50% coverage limit on the first $5000 of coverage (KFF, 2013b).

A more substantial amount could be saved by *increasing the premiums* on both Parts B and D. Currently, beneficiary premiums pay for 25% of the program costs of both Parts B and D. For Part B, this means a range of premiums from $104 per month to $335 per month, depending on income. Part D premiums range from about $30 per month to $50 per month (KFF, 2013b). A large majority of beneficiaries are in these two programs: nearly 90% of Medicare beneficiaries have enrolled in Part B and about 60% are in Part D (KFF, 2013b). The substantial cost savings shown in Table 18.2 is generated by increasing these two premiums so that 35% of the costs of the programs are covered by premiums.

The policy option with the largest predicted impact is the one that does not pass costs on to only beneficiaries. A *1% increase in general taxes* placed in the Medicare Trust funds would create solvency for Part A for several decades (KFF, 2013b).

These are only a few of the many policy options, most of which come from the more liberal side of the political spectrum. One of the more conservative suggestions is to change the balance of private–public money by privatizing medical care with individually purchased vouchers and increased use of Health Savings Accounts. As might be expected, there are many different stakeholders attached to each of the policy options.

## Summary

Medicare is a prime example of what this book labels a targeted program. It is designed to provide financial access to one specific group of people: those who have worked a substantial part of their lives, and who are losing their employment-related health insurance as a result of retiring from their job. This is an example of a social insurance program, not an entitlement program, because individuals contribute to this program, and pay for part of it with private money.

It is an entirely fair question to evaluate this program in terms of whether it provides the coverage needed by this specific group. This question can be answered by examining both financing and coverage. Is the fact that this program covers half of all medical expenses good enough coverage? Out-of-pocket medical expenses for the group covered by Medicare have been steadily rising as a share of household income (KFF, 2013b). This is a philo-sophical question, related to whether there is a social agreement to provide for the health needs of the aging population of Americans.

Medicare mainly covers the most expensive, inelastic medical services, including excellent coverage for care delivered at the end of a person's life. Medicare spends almost 75% of its funds on medical care in the last year of a person's life (Kovner and Knickman, 2011). However, the most expensive level of service that about 25% of the over 85 age population will need is not covered: nursing home and other long-term care expenses.

Another way to evaluate the accessibility of this program is how easily understood it is by the target group for which it is designed. The original design of Medicare, Parts A and B, are straightforward, although there are significant differences in deductibles, copayments, and coinsurance between these two components of Medicare. Adding coverage for Part B involves consumers making decisions about an array of private insurance companies seeking Medigap policies. However, this is a closely regulated market, with a total of 10 plans available. Coordination of benefits between Medicare and these private Medigap policies is done by cooperation between both the public and private payers and works smoothly and well, with little consumer involvement needed.

Both Part C (Medicare Advantage) and Part D (prescription drugs) require more effort on the part of the beneficiary. Part D especially requires close attention by consumers as they choose between many different kinds of insurance plans for prescription drugs. This remains a less well regulated market, with the result being substantial differences between each policy.

The Medicare program significantly impacts the U.S. health care system as a whole. For example, Medicare funds the majority of all residency train-ing programs in U.S. hospitals, including subsidies to hospitals who train residents. Historically, Medicare increased the racial integration of the U.S. health care system. One of the little-known provisions Johnson included in the original legislation made payments to health care providers—both hospitals and physicians—dependent on being able to demonstrate their medical practices or hospitals were not racially segregated (Starr, 1982).

In the final analysis, one's view of Medicare is highly dependent on one's political and philosophical values. There is no doubt that the elderly are better off with this program than without it. The question is whether this is the best or most appropriate program for this group. There is a wide range of perspectives here, with more conservative policy analysts noting that Medicare is a socialist program within the U.S. health care system, one that is financially insolvent and a drag on the U.S. economy. This group supports increased privatization of the Medicare program, including eliminating public subsidies in favor of health savings accounts with tax advantages. Those on the more liberal end of the political spectrum view this as a model of a larger single payer system—one that should be instituted nationwide. This group supports at least the continued level of public funds supporting this program, with many supporting an increase.

Despite this difference in perspective, there is no doubt that, although Medicare may be further altered, it is a permanent and important part of the U.S. health care system, one that has maintained very strong political support. The other significant targeted program—Medicaid—does not have as strong a political advocacy, as will be seen in the next chapter.

## Acknowledgments

Much credit goes to Dr. Thomas Duston, who read and made comments on this chapter. He also provided research and economic analysis for the financial sustainability of the Medicare program, as well as most other economic issues contained in this chapter.

*Chapter 19*

# Taking Care of the Poor: Medicaid

This chapter provides a description of the Medicaid program, beginning with the definition of the target group: the poor. This chapter begins with how poverty is defined in terms of several human services programs, including Medicaid. Eligibility for coverage under Medicaid is still income-dependent, but there are now other factors that determine who receives services, which is the next topic of this chapter. Financing of Medicaid is very different from that of Medicare, leading to more state-level variations in services, as well as controversies over some of these services. The Medicaid program is centrally involved in the implementation of the Affordable Care Act (ACA), which will be described here. This chapter concludes with an analysis of this program, as well as some of the challenges in dealing with the social problem of poverty and income inequality.

The political process of creating Medicaid was described in Chapter 17. Like Medicare, the Medicaid program was legislatively created with an amendment to the Social Security legislation, so it is sometimes known as Title 19. Despite the legislative anchor of the Social Security program, Medicaid was closely linked to the Kerr–Mills welfare program, which gives federal money to states, while allowing states to administer these funds, as long as broad federal guidelines are followed (Barr, 2002). As will be shown, this is still the framework.

The program was—and still is—voluntary, although every state does participate in the basic Medicaid program. States receive federal money based on the per capita income of the residents of their state. New York, for example, receives about 50% of the overall cost of the Medicaid program in that state, whereas Mississippi and West Virginia receive about 75%. Overall, federal tax dollars pay about 60% of the cost of Medicaid with state taxes paying for the rest (Barr, 2002).

The Medicaid program is responsible for covering more people than any other single payer, including Medicare or any single private insurance company. More than 62 million people receive services through Medicaid, including more than one-third of all children in the United States. Medicaid pays for 40% of all births in the United States every year. More than 60% of all people in nursing homes are paid for by Medicaid. Altogether, the Medicaid program pays for about one-sixth of all national spending on personal health care (KFF, 2013c).

Medicaid, like Medicare, is a targeted program. Although Medicaid is no longer available to all who are poor, the description of the targeted group begins there.

# Who Is Poor: Definitions of Eligibility

Welfare programs in the United States are based on what is called a means test, which is to say that the programs are limited to those whose incomes are below a certain amount. Deciding on this amount turns out to be a very complicated subject, once one moves past the fairly general idea of not having enough money to provide some sort of minimally acceptable lifestyle. This section will describe the formal, official method used to decide if people are eligible for some sort of health and/or human services assistance, including the ACA subsidies. The end of this chapter will consider some alternatives proposed to this official method.

There are two different methods of assessing poverty in the United States. One is used by the U.S. Census Bureau and is based on poverty thresholds (Schwartz, 2005). This guideline is used to monitor how many people are poor in various demographic groups such as age, ethnicity, and gender. The Department of Health and Human Services (DHHS) uses a slightly different method to create formal poverty guidelines, used to determine whether a person or a family qualifies for assistance (Poverty Guidelines, 2013). These DHHS guidelines will be used here, because they determine eligibility for a range of health and human services, one of which is Medicaid.

These poverty guidelines are based on absolute amounts of money, and come from the work of an economist who advised the Johnson administration, which created the first poverty guidelines based on the average amount of money spent on food. The poverty guidelines were calculated by multiplying the average amount of money spent on what was viewed as a basic weekly food basket by 3. This yearly income figure, modified by family size, created the eligibility criteria. Today, families spend only about 10% of their after-tax income on food, and the types of foods included in the basic or economy food basket are very different (Schwartz, 2005). Despite these significant changes in the 50-year interval, there has been only one small change in determining eligibility for welfare programs, which involved adjusting increases by the Consumer Price Index instead of on the cost of food in the economy basket (Fisher, 2003).

These official, federal-level poverty guidelines are published by the DHHS for each family size. The basic income level for one person in 2014 is $11,400. If a single person makes more than this amount, they do not meet the basic federal level income eligibility requirement for any of the health and human services programs. Each additional person adds about $4000, so a family of 4, for example, must make less than $23,500 in order to qualify for a means-tested program. States may go either above or below these levels, but all programs refer to the federal poverty guidelines. Several health and human services programs set the eligibility criteria at 133% of the poverty line. This means that a single person making $15,000 will qualify under the income guidelines and a family of four making about $31,000 will qualify. The maximum is 250% of the federal poverty guideline, which means that, in some states, a family of four with a yearly income of $58,000 would qualify for some assistance.

## How Many People Are Poor and Who Are They?

The number of people who are poor as well as their demographic breakdown is of great interest to researchers and policy analysts. Using this official, federal estimate, the poverty level in the nation is about 15%, which means that about 46 million people in the U.S. population are formally classified as being poor. Of this general population estimate, about 10% of white people are classified as being poor, whereas about 26% of all Hispanics or Latinos and a similar percentage of Black people are classified as being poor (Poverty Guidelines, 2013). This is in contrast to the demographic profile of the nation, with 64% white, 16% Hispanic or Latino and 13% African American (Shi and Singh, 2014). Even though the risk of experiencing poverty is higher for minority families than for white families, well over two-thirds of the people defined as poor are white.

More than 75% of all poor households are headed by women (Dail, 2012). This has led to the term feminization of poverty, with subsequent research on the impact of poverty on women.

Interestingly, the age group with the smallest proportion experiencing poverty are those over the age of 65, where only 9% are classified as being poor. This is a result of the positive impact of the Social Security program on the financial stability of the elderly population. On the other hand, nearly one-quarter of all people under the age of 18 are classified as poor (U.S. Census Bureau, 2013). For this reason, there are several programs further targeted to children, which will be described in the next chapter.

One persistent misperception about this group is that only a small number of people are officially poor, and this group has a long-term status of being so. The average time that people spend in poverty is usually relatively short. A typical pattern is for someone to experience poverty for a year or two; go above the poverty line; then to have another episode of poverty at some later time, due to either losing a job or having an illness that makes it impossible to work. Nearly 40% of Americans between the ages of 25 and 60 will experience poverty at some point in their lives. If all assistance programs are considered together, including unemployment as well as welfare and/or food stamps, nearly 80% of Americans will experience poverty at some point in their lives (Rank, 2005). As will be seen at the end of this chapter, the official guidelines underestimate the proportion of poor in the United States.

Poverty is not only found in urban areas, as only about 10% of those in poverty live in urban areas. Poverty is spread in all geographic areas of the United States, with the exception of suburban areas (Rank, 2005).

One pernicious myth is that welfare programs offer an incentive for people to stay poor. This is not true: because of various welfare reform measures over the past 40 years, public assistance programs of all types have become more limited in terms of eligibility and more scanty in their benefits. The most common group now eligible for assistance programs are those meeting the eligibility guidelines for extreme poverty, a group that is about 3% of the U.S. population (Poverty Guidelines, 2013). The United States expends the least amount of money to provide assistance to poor families of any developed nation (Rank, 2005).

The Medicaid program began as a program for all people who met income eligibility guidelines for other welfare programs. In 1980, 70% of those who were eligible for welfare were also eligible for Medicaid (Barr, 2002). However, by 1999, only about 30% of those eligible for welfare also received Medicaid. Some of this shift is attributed to the nature of the financing and administration of Medicaid.

## Financing and Administration of Medicaid: Federal and State

The Medicaid program is financed through both federal and state income taxes, and therefore is subject to both federal and state regulations. This financing method has profound effects on the benefits of this program. Although the federal government gives states about 60% of the costs of the Medicaid program, states find the program a financial burden. In many states, the Medicaid program accounts for 16% of a state's budget (Kovner and Knickman, 2011).

The same federal organization that administers Medicare also administers Medicaid—the Centers for Medicare and Medicaid Services (CMS). This organization identifies the basic minimum services that must be covered in order for a state to receive federal money. The CMS also identifies a mandatory population that must be covered, which will be described in the next section. Finally, the CMS sets the method of reimbursement for providers for covered services, whereas states set the actual rates paid to a provider. Each state has a Medicaid agency that has monitoring and policy responsibility. This state agency submits the state plan for providing benefits to the covered population, which is the contract between the state and the federal government (Teitelbaum and Wilensky, 2013). States frequently file requests to vary either the amount of coverage or the population being covered, or sometimes the method of payment to providers. These are called waivers, and are the most common way to alter or introduce innovations in the state Medicaid programs. The ACA is using this process to expand Medicaid, as will be described later.

Medicaid is actually a collection of 50 different programs, due to each state having so much local control. The one common theme of all states is cost control. Although there are many experiments, there are three general themes of cost control that are relevant to all states, and will be described here.

The *first* is that states try to pay providers as little as possible for providing health services to patients covered by Medicaid. States are required to set payment rates for providers that are "sufficient" to ensure that Medicaid patients have "equal access" to medical services (Teitelbaum and Wilensky, 2013).

Within this very broad mandate, states have wide latitude in paying providers and they use it. Medicaid rates of reimbursement are much lower for both hospitals and physicians than are reimbursement rates for either Medicare or private health insurance. As noted in Chapter 15, the consequence of this is that physicians try to limit the number of Medicaid-covered patients in their practices and states, in turn, try to restrict this action with legislative action.

The *second* way in which states try to save money is by changing the eligibility levels so fewer people qualify for health care services. As will be described in the next section, there are several other requirements besides income for eligibility for Medicaid, but low income remains an essential criteria. States have gradually lowered the income needed to receive health services from Medicaid, so the program now primarily provides services only to the very poor, as noted previously. The first federal rule controlling the state's eligibility criteria required that all pregnant women at 100% of the poverty level had to receive health services under Medicaid. Previously, many states were only covering pregnant women whose incomes were 50% of the federal poverty level (Kovner and Knickman, 2011).

The *third* method some states have used to save money is to attempt to collect small amounts of money from the beneficiaries, including copayments, coinsurance payments, deductibles, and even premiums. Before 2008, states were prohibited from trying to collect any money from this population, but a part of a larger Deficit Reduction Bill gave states the freedom to try to collect funds (Pear, 2008; Teitelbaum and Wilensky, 2013). Obviously, this population has only a very limited ability to participate in any cost sharing, especially as the income eligibility guidelines have made Medicaid increasingly a program that provides access to health care services only for the very poor.

## Who Is Covered under Medicaid?

Under current federal guidelines, an individual must meet five general criteria in order to be eligible for Medicaid (Teitelbaum and Wilensky, 2013). These include the following:

■ Must fit into one of the federally identified categories
■ Income must fit into specified limits
■ Must have limited other resources, such as car and household goods
■ Must be a resident of the state in which they are seeking coverage
■ Must be a legal resident of the United States for 5 years

Importantly, the person must meet all five of these criteria, not just one or two. There are more than 50 different categories of both mandatory and optional groups of people that a state may choose to cover, including variations in specified income levels (Teitelbaum and Wilensky, 2013). Medicaid programs have gradually evolved into ones focusing on three distinct categories of people: children, pregnant women, and the poor, frail elderly. Nearly one-half of all Medicaid beneficiaries nationwide are children, with another 25% being adults, nearly all of whom are pregnant women, who live with children (KFF, 2010f).

As shown in Table 19.1, children and adults living with children are a mandatory group for which states must provide health services. The basic federal requirement is now 133% of the federal poverty guidelines, and states cannot go under this for any of the mandatory groups. States may choose to also cover children and adults living with children at incomes higher than this, up to a limit of 250% of the federal poverty limit, as shown in Table 19.1. One group almost never covered by any state Medicaid program consists of adults living without children, regardless of income. This is the group specifically targeted under the ACA expansion of the Medicaid

**Table 19.1 Target Population for the Medicaid Program**

| Mandatory | Optional | Not Covered |
|---|---|---|
| Children younger than 6 years below federal poverty level | Medically needy | Undocumented immigrants |
| Children 6–18 years living in families below federal poverty level | Children of documented immigrants living in the United States less than 5 years | Documented immigrants who have not lived in the United States for 5 years |
| Pregnant women below federal poverty level | Families, between 133% and 250% of federal poverty line | Childless adults older than 21 |
| Seniors and people with disabilities on Supplemental Social Security Income | Children in families between 133% and 250% of poverty line | |
| | Pregnant women between 133% and 250% of federal poverty line | |

program, which will be discussed later in this chapter. As of 2012, 67 million people received health care under the Medicaid program, with 32 million of these being children under the age of 18. Also receiving care were 19 million adults, mostly pregnant women and those living with children, 6 million seniors, and 11 million with disabilities (CBPP, 2013).

The Medicaid program is viewed as the public program most likely to cover immigrants. As many legal immigrants are low income, this is true—but rules also require that they must have lived in the United States for at least 5 years, as explained in Chapter 5. States may choose to cover children of documented immigrant adults who have lived in the United States less than this 5-year period. Undocumented immigrants have the right to emergency care in a hospital setting, but are not supposed to receive any other type of care, as noted in Chapter 5. Immigration laws result in awkward situations in the health field. For example, if an undocumented woman has a baby in a U.S. hospital, the baby is a legal citizen, and is eligible for care under Medicaid if the family income is low enough. However, no matter how low the income, the mother is not eligible for nonemergency care (Barr, 2002).

Depending on the political and cultural climate of the state, some modifications of these restrictions are possible. Some states agree that publicly funded health services should go first to those who have paid taxes to support them. Others argue that many undocumented immigrants actually do pay taxes and should therefore be able to receive health services under Medicaid, as long as they meet all other criteria. Low-income immigrants are unlikely to receive preventive care, but are very likely to receive needed urgent care in an emergency room, thus increasing the overall costs to the state. As a result of this debate, 27 states have decided to authorize the use of state-only funds to provide some preventive health services to this group (Families, USA, 2011). There are other targeted programs specifically designed to cover children, including those who are in the United States illegally; these will be described in the next chapter.

One group identified in Table 19.1 as being optional has very wide acceptance among states. This is the medically needy group that includes individuals who have very high medical expenses. Thirty-two states have chosen to cover this group, within modified income and asset guidelines (KFF, 2010g). If they were healthy, people in this group typically have incomes that are too high to be eligible for Medicaid. When existing medical expenses are subtracted from their income, they become eligible for Medicaid. This coverage is generally temporary, and is calculated periodically, depending on the individual state (Teitelbaum and Wilensky, 2013). This process is known as the spend down method of qualifying for Medicaid.

One group that is even more likely to "spend down" in order to be covered by Medicaid are known as *dual eligibles* because they are eligible for Medicare, because of their age or disability, and have incomes low enough to be eligible for Medicaid. Unlike the medically needy, states are required to include this group in their Medicaid programs, and this group is unlikely to have a change in either health status or wealth. This group is most likely to need Medicaid for nursing home coverage, because Medicare does not cover this expense. Although only 15% of Medicaid recipients are in this group, nearly 40% of expenditures from Medicaid are spent on their health needs (KFF, 2010g).

## What Does the Medicaid Program Cover?

Medicaid has a scope of coverage that is more comprehensive than all but the most expensive private health insurance policy. This design is based on extensive research on the relationship of income and health status. Poor people tend to be less healthy because they do not have enough resources for either a healthy lifestyle, including good nutrition, or for preventive health care services. People sometimes become poor because of illness, resulting in the loss of their job, as well as their health insurance. This is a group that cannot contribute much, if any, to the cost of health care services. This is also a group that private health insurance companies are not willing to cover, because the medical needs are high and there is no way for a private health insurance company to limit their financial exposure (Rosenbaum, 2002). All of these realities lead to a publicly financed health program designed around the concept of heavy reliance on preventive and primary care services, such as used later in the original health maintenance organizations, as described in Chapter 14.

Medicaid uses a different standard of care for services. Most private health insurance plans and Medicare use the standard of medical necessity. This means all medical services necessary to *restore functioning* to what it was before the medical problem (Teitelbaum and Wilensky, 2013). This curative standard is one of the reasons for scant coverage of preventive care services under the Medicare program. The Medicaid program was initially designed to provide care for children and people with disabilities, including developmentally challenged adults. This group requires a different scope of services, as well as a different standard of care.

Table 19.2 shows an important set of services: the Early and Periodic Screening, Diagnosis, and Treatment (EPSDT) package (Teitelbaum and Wilensky, 2013). This type of coverage begins with using a range of health care services to prevent the onset of a health problem. These services are provided periodically, and when services are needed, they are provided to a treatment standard to "correct or ameliorate" the health problem (Teitelbaum and Wilensky, 2013). This results in a very comprehensive set of services that must be offered to all beneficiaries of the Medicaid program. This is very costly, and one reason why states attempt to limit the number of people eligible for services, as noted previously.

Just as with the defined population described in Table 19.1, the federal government identifies a set of mandatory services, a set of optional services, and several specific services that states may not use federal dollars to provide. These three categories are shown in Table 19.2. Within these mandatory services, states have considerable ability to determine exact coverage. Under this requirement, each nursing home resident covered by Medicaid receives periodic medical assessment by a physician, but the definition of

**Table 19.2  Benefits under the Medicaid Program**

| Mandatory | Optional | Prohibited |
|---|---|---|
| EPSDT services for eligible children younger than 21 years | Prescription drugs | Surgical abortions |
| Inpatient and outpatient hospital-based services | Dental and vision care services | Drug-induced abortions |
| Ambulatory care services for both acute and chronic care | Hearing aids | Substance abuse treatment unless linked to a diagnosed mental illness |
| Nurse midwife services | Rehabilitation services | |
| Disability support services | Prosthetic devices | |
| Laboratory and diagnostic services | Inpatient psychiatric services | |
| Nursing home care for eligible adults over age 21 | Home care services | |
| Family planning services and supplies | Hospice services | |

*Note:* EPSDT, Early and Periodic Screening, Diagnosis, and Treatment.

periodic is set by the state. The only mandatory coverage for the broad umbrella of services offered under the EPSDT coverage is for children under age 18 and persons with documented disabilities. The optional services identified in Table 19.2 may be offered to certain categories of people, to specified income levels, or for specific types of medical problems. These are all set forth in the state's Medicaid plan, which must be approved by CMS.

One specific required service raises an important discussion, which is Medicaid's coverage of nursing homes. As has been previously described, Medicaid covers not only skilled nursing homes, but also those that are also classified as custodial. This makes sense because one of the target groups are the disabled, including both physical and developmental disabilities. As noted in Chapter 10, the cost of nursing home stays has become extremely high—nearly $90,000 a year. Although the elderly are not the only group needing this level of care, they are a primary group. Because Medicare does not cover the cost of a custodial nursing home, and Medicaid does, individuals and families attempt to spend down their resources in order to meet the income qualification. This practice has been abused by some families who attempt to keep personal assets to pass on to the next generation while having public funds pay for the nursing home stay of their family member. This practice was so prevalent that the 2005 Deficit Reduction Act included specific language to require such transfers to be made 5 years before any nursing home placement (Teitelbaum and Wilensky, 2013).

Today, nearly 70% of the total money spent under Medicaid goes to nursing homes and other long-term care services (KFF, 2013c). This was not the intention of the original design of this program, and it is not part of the intended impact today either. However, with no other options for this expensive part of the health care delivery system, it is difficult to see how this use of Medicaid money might be reduced without a significant alteration in the Medicaid program. One such alteration will be discussed later when the Oregon waiver program is discussed.

Table 19.2 shows some services that are specifically prohibited. Two relate to abortion and one relates to care of substance abuse. The less controversial is the prohibition of treatment of substance abuse not related to an existing mental illness. Drug addiction or drug abuse is not permitted as the primary reason for defining a disability, a diagnosis that then makes a person eligible for Social Security Supplemental Income (SSSI). This is important because a person who qualifies for SSSI is automatically eligible for both Medicaid and Medicare. This dual eligible group must be fully covered, as shown in Table 19.1. A disability may include having a diagnosable mental illness, which is complicated by substance abuse, but which must exist independently of the substance abuse. A similar situation exists with respect to treatment. Substance abuse treatment is covered, but only in relation to the treatment of a mental illness, which is an optional coverage by Medicaid programs (Teitelbaum and Wilensky, 2013).

One of the most significant controversies surrounding the Medicaid program is its funding of women's reproductive services, which includes family planning services, as well as supplies, as shown in Table 19.2. Family planning services and supplies were a very important required benefit in the original legislation, although abortion was not legal at the time this legislation was passed. People who worked in the various health and human services programs of the time were very insistent on assisting poor women in having fewer children, primarily as a cost savings strategy for welfare programs. The actual specification of what constituted family planning services and supplies was left vague. Federal guidelines stipulate only that states must provide services that "aid those who voluntarily choose not to risk an initial pregnancy" (Ranji et al., 2009). There is an economic incentive to encourage states to cover family planning. Although the federal government pays for about 60% of a states' Medicaid program, it pays for 90% of all family planning services and supplies, irrespective of the wealth of the state (Ranji et al., 2009).

State Medicaid programs cover a range of contraceptive supplies, including prescription contraception, as well as over-the-counter ones. In a 2009 study of state Medicaid programs, 32 of 44 programs covered all three forms of prescription contraception: hormonal (birth control pills), diaphragms, and intrauterine devices. Only 17 covered all forms of over-the-counter contraception, which include condoms, the sponge, and spermicides. Thirty-seven Medicaid programs also covered sterilization procedures for both men and women. Other services such as screening for cancers (e.g., breast and cervical) or for sexually transmitted diseases may be covered, but some states include these under medical services rather than under family planning services. Twenty-four states have received waivers so they can cover family planning services for women who are above the income eligibility guidelines. They successfully argued that it is less expensive to cover contraception supplies for women than to pay for the care of the children born to low-income women (Ranji et al., 2009).

The most controversial women's reproductive health service is abortion. As noted in Chapter 5, the Hyde Amendment prohibits the use of any federal funds to pay for abortions except in the cases of rape, incest, or if the life of the woman is in danger as a result of the pregnancy continuing (Guttmacher, 2014). Currently, 32 states follow these federal guidelines. States may choose to use state funds to provide Medicaid coverage of abortions, but only 17 states currently allow this, with 13 of them doing so because court cases have ordered this (Guttmacher, 2014). State legislatures have passed many pieces of legislation restricting abortions in many ways, including limiting the number of abortion clinics allowed in the state; restricting the number and type of providers that can perform abortions; requiring counseling and/or imaging services before an abortion; and requiring parental notification for younger women. Although these actions do limit access to abortion for all women, it is Medicaid-covered women who have far less access to abortions than women with private insurance.

## State Modifications of Financing and Coverage

States may alter the population, as well as both the nature and scope of coverage by the waiver process, especially one known as Section 115 waivers (Teitelbaum and Wilensky, 2013). Section 115 of the Social Security Act permits states to design demonstration projects under their Medicaid programs. These programs may involve changing the nature of the population covered or the benefits themselves. These are submitted to the CMS, where they are reviewed before being approved. The proposed alteration must help promote the overall expressed objectives of the state's Medicaid program. It must also be budget neutral, meaning the project cannot cost the federal government more than the current Medicaid program does (Teitelbaum and Wilensky, 2013). If approved, the state has to report periodically to the CMS on various benchmarks related to the demonstration project. Each of these demonstration projects is viewed as providing important research on how best to provide for the needs of the target group for whom Medicaid was designed.

There are many different waiver projects submitted and approved each year. This section will describe only two examples of waivers. The first example, from Oregon, is one of the most extensive demonstration projects because it changed both the target population and coverage. The second example is how the ACA uses this state-level waiver process to expand Medicaid coverage as part of reducing the number of people without health insurance.

## Changing the Design of the Program: Oregon

The best-known example of a state making dramatic changes in its Medicaid program occurred in Oregon, whose first Section 115 waiver was approved in 1993 (Barr, 2002). Oregon's Medicaid program was providing complete health care for a smaller number of people every year. By the late 1980s, only those with incomes that were 60% of the federal poverty standard were receiving services. The state wanted to increase the number of poor children and pregnant women who received benefits, but did not want to commit more of the state budget to do so. A statewide commission was appointed to identify all medical procedures covered by Medicaid so it could assess which ones were most effective. The commission identified a total of 700 medical treatments and rated each in terms of preventing death and disability, reducing future costs, and improving public health. This involved community-based focus group discussions of citizens as well as a professional panel. At the end of the 3-year process, the Oregon legislature decided to limit Medicaid coverage to health and medical care services with demonstrated effectiveness. The consequence was to defund some medical interventions so other, more effective interventions could be offered to all people at 100% of the federal poverty guideline and to all children at 133% of the income guideline. Examples of services that were taken off coverage included organ transplants and chemotherapy for cancer where there was less than a 5% chance of survival for 3 years (Barr, 2002).

This changed the Oregon Medicaid program from one that covered 700 medical interventions for people whose incomes were 60% of the federal poverty guidelines to one in which the most effective 565 interventions were covered for everybody at the federal poverty line, with additional preventive and primary care services going to children and pregnant women who were at 133% of the federal poverty guidelines (Barr, 2002). The immediate result was to increase the number of people who were covered by Medicaid by more than 100,000 (Barr, 2002). Because of the intense community involvement, the people of Oregon supported this program, although there were people who were denied treatment as a result of this. This effort to ration care based on effectiveness was controversial, with several legal challenges, including a supportive Supreme Court decision.

The state of Oregon has continued to revise its Medicaid program. In 2004, Oregon was allowed to close its Medicaid program to all new enrollees in response to increasing costs. It reopened its program in 2008 to allow 3000 more people, with these individuals getting coverage by means of a lottery, because too many were eligible for the resources available. Oregon also increased enrollment of children to be consistent with both its state mandate and the federal guidelines on children as a specific target population (Skidmore, 2008; AHRQ, 2013).

## Expanding Medicaid under the ACA

The gradual evolution of the Medicaid program resulted in nondisabled adults not living with children mostly unable to receive Medicaid benefits, even with incomes low enough to meet eligibility standards. The Obama administration decided to cover this group by expanding the state Medicaid programs instead of by increasing the subsidies on the private health insurance exchanges that were described in Chapter 17.

This expansion is accomplished with an expedited Section 115 waiver process. Under the ACA expansion, every person with an income that is 138% of the federal poverty level is eligible for coverage under expanded Medicaid. This calculation is made without consideration of other assets, reducing the spend down phenomenon (Rosenbaum and Westmoreland, 2012).

A particularly controversial part of this program involved the legislation requiring that each state expand its Medicaid program, because state participation in the Medicaid program is voluntary. Some of the disagreement arose from political opposition to the ACA legislation. Some states distrusted the financial incentives being offered by the federal government. The federal government pays for all of the costs of this expansion until 2016. After that, the federal government will cover the costs of the expansion at the 90% level until at least 2020, possibly far beyond that date. The federal government provided further incentives to the states by including in the ACA legislation that states that refused to participate in this expansion would lose the federal contribution to the rest of their Medicaid program.

Several states and the National Federation of Independent Businesses (NFIBs) sued the Obama administration on the grounds that this mandated participation and threatened financial punishment was unconstitutional. The Supreme Court agreed to hear the case *NFIB v. Siebelius* in 2012. They ruled that this incentive was too coercive on the part of the federal government, and the states were given the right to choose to not participate without any loss to their existing Medicaid program (Rosenbaum and Westmoreland, 2012; Sonfield, 2012). Table 19.3 shows the position of the states as of January 2015. A total of 29 states have implemented this expansion, and seven are still in discussions. If all states participated in the Medicaid expansion, 33 million people would become insured (Chesney and Duderstadt, 2013).

**Table 19.3   States' Positions on Medicaid Expansion, as of January 2015**

| States That Have Decided to Implement Medicaid Expansion | States That Are Not Moving Forward toward Expansion | States with Open Discussion Ongoing |
| --- | --- | --- |
| Arizona | Alabama | Alaska |
| Arkansas | Florida | Missouri |
| California | Georgia | Montana |
| Colorado | Idaho | Tennessee |
| Connecticut | Kansas | Utah |
| Delaware | Louisiana | Virginia |
| Hawaii | Maine | Wyoming |
| Illinois | Mississippi | |
| Indiana | Nebraska | |
| Iowa | North Carolina | |
| Kentucky | Oklahoma | |
| Maryland | South Carolina | |
| Massachusetts | South Dakota | |
| Michigan | Texas | |
| Minnesota | Wisconsin | |
| Nevada | | |
| New Hampshire | | |
| New Jersey | | |
| New Mexico | | |
| New York | | |
| North Dakota | | |
| Ohio | | |
| Oregon | | |
| Pennsylvania | | |
| Rhode Island | | |
| Vermont | | |
| Washington | | |
| Washington, D.C. | | |
| West Virginia | | |

*Source:* KFF, Status of state action on the Medicaid expansion decision, J. Henry Kaiser Family Foundation, 2015. Available from: http://www.kff.org.

## Does Medicaid Do What It Was Designed to Do?

There are three issues to consider when analyzing any target program. The first is the impact on the beneficiaries of the program, both in terms of utilization and health status. The second is to assess how the money is spent. Finally, it is also important to examine the original intention of the program. As will be shown in this section, none of these are easy issues to address.

## *Impact of Medicaid on the Target Population*

There is no doubt that Medicaid has increased access to medical care. This is very clearly seen in the first analysis of utilization figures performed 10 years after Medicaid was implemented. Between 1964 and 1975, there was a substantial increase in visits to doctors by the poor. There was also a proportional increase, so that poor people actually saw doctors about 20% more often than nonpoor patients. This was true for both ambulatory care visits and for surgical visits. Just before the implementation of Medicaid, low-income people had only half the rate of surgical procedures, but by 1975, the rate for poor people was 40% higher than for higher income patients. There was also a dramatic impact on utilization of medical services by African-Americans. Their utilization of medical services had always been far less than that of white people, but by 1975, this differential in utilization was much less (Starr, 1982). This increase in utilization was expected, because this was a group of people who were known to have limited access to health services; however, the extent of the increase was greater than expected.

This pattern of increased utilization is still evident today. A 2012 study showed that 80% of people with private insurance visited a doctor in the preceding year, as did 80% of those covered by Medicaid. Only 40% of those who were uninsured had done so (CBPP, 2013). This impact is especially seen on children: low income children insured through Medicaid have very high rates of utilization of preventive services, including well child examinations and immunizations (KFF, 2010f).

Analyzing the impact of this increased utilization on health status is challenging. Most analysts accept that increased utilization of preventive services and ambulatory care services is indicative of a generally healthier target group. Several studies have attempted to directly assess health outcomes, and most show a significant impact; for example, one study demonstrated a 5% reduction in childhood deaths among children on Medicaid and an 8% reduction of low birth weight on pregnant women covered by Medicaid (CBPP, 2013). Another study that assessed a pre-ACA expansion of the Medicaid program in three specific states demonstrated several positive outcomes. There was increased utilization, decreased reduction of delay in obtaining care, and a significant decrease in mortality among adults (Sommers et al., 2012). A study based on Oregon's revised program showed that Medicaid adults had less medical debt and better self-reported physical and mental health (KFF, 2013c).

## Where Does the Money Go?

Medicaid is no different than any other insurance program, with the majority of money spent on a relatively small number of recipients. More than one-half of the money spent under the Medicaid program goes to about 5% of the recipients (Teitelbaum and Wilensky, 2013). Additionally, nearly 70% of all the money spent under Medicaid goes to cover long-term care for the roughly 25% who are either elderly or disabled (Kovner and Knickman, 2011b). Even though about half of the enrollees are children, only 20% of expenditures are for this group, whereas 42% is spent on the disabled, who make up about 15% of Medicaid enrollees (KFF, 2013c).

## What Was the Original Intention of Medicaid?

The original intention of Medicaid is actually not clear. The Medicaid program is viewed as a highlight of the liberal political forces in Washington at the time, with one of the stated goals to "bring the poor into the mainstream of medicine" (Starr, 1982). It was linked very clearly to the Kerr–Mills legislation, whose purpose was to provide medical services to everyone who qualified for other state-funded welfare services (Teitelbaum and Wilensky, 2013). The program is frequently described as focusing on poor families with children (Barr, 2002; Kovner and Knickman, 2011). Public health advocates view the program as just one piece of the larger antipoverty programs of the Kennedy administration, and then the Johnson administration (Starr, 1982; Bailey and Sheldon, 2013). The elderly poor and the disabled were included in the original designation of specified target groups, but the public perception remains that this is a program targeted at young, poor families.

Almost three-fourths of Medicaid recipients are in fact children and low-income women, even though the least money is spent on them. Over time, Medicaid has become increasingly targeted at the very poor. This group clearly needs the assistance provided by the Medicaid program. However, the basic reason for the Oregon experiment described in this chapter was to explore another way of allocating Medicaid dollars, which might increase the proportion going to children and mothers.

## How to Assess Medicaid?

Caring for the poor is a social issue, not just a health care issue, and it is not an easily solved problem. Because the design of the U.S. health care system is based on health insurance through employment, the public has to bear a substantial part of the cost of caring for people who have fallen outside the employment sector of the United States. As will be shown in the last chapter of this book, in other countries the costs of unemployment are borne by taxpayers through a wider scope of social services, including subsidized housing and education, subsidized day care, and other social services. In the United States, most of the health-related costs of unemployment are the responsibility of the health care sector and for the very poor, this is the Medicaid system. Like the Medicare program, there is no doubt that the beneficiaries are better off with this program than without it. However, also like Medicare, the issue is whether this is the best—and most cost-effective—program that can be designed for this group. It is best to approach this from a good news/bad news perspective, because there is some of both in any assessment of the Medicaid program.

## The Good News

The first example of good news is that utilization rates for poor people have dramatically increased, not only for acute care, but also for preventive and primary care. As has been shown in this chapter, this was an immediate effect and it has remained. Of course, this has driven up the cost of this program, so for some people, this news is bad, not good. Medicaid is a program that was created to give access to a group of people who did not have access, and their use of it is costly. This is a group that, on average, is in poorer health than those who are covered by private health insurance (Teitelbaum and Wilensky, 2013). Medicaid pays for care for a group of very sick people at a much lower cost than if these people had private health insurance (CBPP, 2013). Part of this is attributable to the comprehensive nature of the coverage, but much of it is the low rate paid to providers. This is also a good news/bad news situation.

Medicaid is an important source of access to health care for the minority population in the United States, because low income is related to race and ethnicity, as will be discussed in Chapter 21. Although the majority of Medicaid enrollees are white, minorities are far more likely to have health insurance through Medicaid, whereas white people are more likely to have insurance through a private company (Teitelbaum and Wilensky, 2013).

The poor elderly and disabled have significant health needs and deserve care. However, the possibility of preventing future poor health by investing in preventive health services for a larger number of low-income people has driven many state-level experiments, including the first one in Oregon. It is this balance between two very different groups that causes the most tension. Under the Medicaid program, low-income children and low-income elderly and disabled are valued more than low-income adults. States have some flexibility to modify these priorities, but not to ignore them.

The comprehensive coverage of services is a remarkable aspect of Medicaid, especially when considering that it was designed in 1965. The people who designed this program had a very clear understanding of the relationship between poverty and poor health. They understood that poor health and disability are sometimes the factors that produce poverty. They also understood that in an employment-based insurance system, this group would never be covered. The result was a program that had far more generous benefits than any of the private health insurance plans of the time. One of the most remarkable benefits included in the original legislation were family planning services, primarily to save money on welfare programs. Today, this benefit is one of the most controversial benefits of the Medicaid program.

The Medicaid program has low administrative costs, although not quite as low as Medicare, because each recipient has to demonstrate their income eligibility once a year. As shown in Table 13.1, Medicaid has about a 7% overhead rate, whereas Medicare has about a 3% overhead rate.

For people who have conservative political values, the fact that Medicaid is structured with a shared federal–state governance and funding is very positive. For those with a more liberal political value, this goes under the bad news category. From a social justice perspective, the Medicaid program is complicated by this issue of state-level control.

## The Bad News

One item of bad news that has wide agreement is the overly large proportion of resources spent on nursing home services. It was certainly not the original intention of this program to have nearly 70% of the total money spent under Medicaid dedicated to nursing home services, and it is not part of the intended impact today either. However, with no other options for this expensive part of the health care delivery system, it is difficult to argue that the immediate needs of the poor elderly should be set aside for the future of poor adults. Nearly all poor children are now covered, although it has taken specific programs that are outside of Medicaid to do so, as will be described in the next chapter. In the states that accepted the ACA Medicaid expansion, most of the low-income adults who were previously uninsured will now have access to health care.

Another item of bad news with wide agreement is the very low rate paid to physicians who provide medical services to Medicaid recipients. This is so low that in some states and some specialties such as obstetrics, physicians refuse to accept Medicaid patients (Zuckerman et al., 2009). This is clearly an unsustainable policy position, with states trying to save costs by restricting payments to doctors or by restricting the number of people who can receive medical coverage.

## Another Way to Think about This

Many policy analysts who believe in a social justice approach to allocating health care goods argue that a significant issue for Medicaid and other means-tested programs is the increasing income inequality in the United States. The income of the poorest families has decreased and the income of the richest has increased, with a resultant increase in income inequality that makes the United States one of the most economically unequal in the world (Desilver, 2013). This has occurred for many reasons, but certainly an important one is the tax structure that has increased the tax burden on lower and middle income families, who currently experience the highest tax burden they have ever seen (ITEP, 2015). Other countries also have poor people, but they provide health and human services programs more economically. There are many reasons for this, not the least of which is a more efficient health care system, without so many separate targeted programs, each of which must be managed separately by individualized guidelines. However, there is also a factor related to the income inequality and the actual definition of poverty.

There are many programs targeted at poor people in the United States, and all of them—including Medicaid—depend on the definition of poverty used by DHHS, as described in the first section of this chapter. By this definition about 15% of the U.S. population is defined as poor, and is eligible for some type of health and human services assistance. In 2011, the U.S. Census Bureau introduced a slightly different measure: the supplemental poverty measure. This includes not only income, but also tax credits and necessary expenses such as child care costs, transportation and housing costs, as well as food costs. When this definition of poverty is used, the estimate of the total number of Americans living in poverty increases slightly, bringing the estimate to about 50 million people. More importantly, it was estimated that almost half of all Americans were below 200% of this new estimate (Berlinger, 2012).

Few families even at 200% of this more generous supplemental poverty measure can actually support themselves without needing some kind of assistance. Another, more realistic method used to define who is poor is based on a political movement called the Living Wage movement (LWFS, 2009). Similar to those who support the use of the Supplemental Poverty guidelines, this group calculates the amount of money necessary to meet the minimum basic needs, including food, housing, transportation, medical care, and child care costs—without any help from an assistance program. They translated this into an hourly wage, resulting in a range of $11.00 to $18.00 per hour, depending on the state (Gertner, 2006). Under this method, nearly 30% of the U.S. population is defined as being poor (Clary, 2009). If this method were implemented in determining eligibility for assistance programs, it would significantly increase the costs to taxpayers.

However, the Living Wage movement has provided the political impetus to begin a state-by-state effort to increase the federal minimum wage, which is currently $7.25/hour. If the minimum wage were higher, there would be fewer people needing publicly funded assistance programs. Most businesses oppose this, saying that higher wages would adversely impact their businesses. Despite the negative response from businesses, 29 states have increased their minimum wages above the federal minimum of $7.25, including eight states with a minimum of $9.00 or higher (NCSL, 2015).

A new, admittedly liberal, economic analysis provides an alternative, more comprehensive way to think about this issue. More than half of workers in low-wage industries receive assistance from a tax-funded program, such as Medicaid, housing assistance, fuel assistance, or food stamps. The total cost of this is about $7 billion dollars every year, which acts as a public subsidy to these for-profit companies, because taxpayers provide money for these income-tested assistance programs. This subsidy is not visible, but if $7 billion were subtracted from the publicly funded programs, the impact on taxes would be felt throughout the economy (Allegretto et al., 2013). Interestingly enough, many of the companies that pay very low wages in the United States are required to pay higher wages in other countries. In Denmark, for example, fast food companies must pay employees $20.00/hour in order to be able to operate a franchise, under agreement with Denmark's largest union (Alderman and Greenhouse, 2014). Employees also receive additional benefits, including paid vacation weeks, a pension plan, and paid paternity and maternity leave. Some of these wages go to taxes that fund the network of social services that exists in Denmark, including child care, education, and health care. Profits are slightly less, but obviously enough because fast food companies are firmly established in the European and Scandinavian markets.

This reinforces the thought at the beginning of this chapter: caring for the poor is not just a problem for the health care system—it is a broad social problem that involves cultural, political, and philosophical dimensions. All countries face similar issues regarding providing health care services for the poor. The solution in the United States is to create a targeted program funded and administered separately. In other countries, the responsibility for this group is society-wide, and their care is paid for by taxes. In the United States, the cost of care for this group is also tax-based, but because health insurance is based on employment, the discussion in the United States centers on whether the cost of providing health care should be shared more equally by businesses.

There is no right or wrong answer to this dilemma. Those who believe that health care should be allocated more by the social justice model tend to feel that health care should not be linked to employment. Those who feel that health care goods and services should be allocated by the market justice model tend to be more supportive of targeted programs such as Medicaid, although they are also frustrated by the expense of caring for this group. There are several other even more specific targeted programs in the U.S. health care system, aimed at the people who are still not covered sufficiently by Medicaid. These will be described in the next chapter.

# Acknowledgments

The following people made significant contributions to the development of this chapter, including gathering material and references, as well as writing and analysis: Irene Eberbach, Michael Goulart, and Chandler Kaplan. I am indebted to Jessi Duston, who read and commented on this chapter and provided several recent references.

## Chapter 20

# Taking Care of Almost Everybody Else

There are many other targeted programs in the U.S. health system, each of which is designed to provide access to medical care services for a specific population or group. This chapter will describe some of the more important of these. Some of these are populations already covered by a targeted program, such as poor children or the frail elderly. Not all targeted programs focus on either the poor or the elderly, but provide access to care for those who are uninsured because of very high health needs, or because of becoming injured on the job. These programs address the needs of those who fall between the cracks of the coverage provided by existing targeted programs. Two additional populations that have not been described are Native Americans and U.S. military personnel and veterans. These two groups have their own targeted health programs. This chapter provides a brief description of each of these programs, which are summarized in Table 20.1. Not included in this chapter are the several disease-specific programs, including those designed for people with cancer, diabetes, or AIDS, among others.

## Programs Focusing on Low-Income Children

The Medicaid program has gradually evolved into one that is focused on people who are very poor, as noted in Chapter 19. The result is an increasing number of families with children who cannot afford health insurance but who make too much money for Medicaid. There are several health and welfare programs

**Table 20.1  Other Targeted Programs**

| Target Group | Program |
|---|---|
| Low-income children | Children's Health Insurance Program (CHIP)<br>Joint state–federal program designed to cover children in medically indigent families<br>Women, Infants, and Children Program (WIC)<br>Nutrition program for low income pregnant women, infants and young children |
| Poor, frail, elderly | Program for All-Inclusive Care for the Elderly (PACE)<br>Innovative program to avoid nursing home care<br>Funded by waivers from Medicare and Medicaid |
| Uninsured, poor, vulnerable populations | Community Health Centers (CHCs)<br>Federally funded primary care health centers focusing on the very poor |
| Very medically needy | State-funded high-risk insurance pools<br>Designed to subsidize private insurance for the very sick |
| Employees injured on the job | Workers' Compensation Program<br>Provides coverage for job-related injuries and income replacement for lost work<br>Funded by employers |
| Members of American Indian and Alaska Native Tribes | Indian Health Services (IHSs)<br>Federally funded health service for registered members of American Indian and Alaska Native tribes |
| Military and Veterans | Military Health System (TRICARE)<br>Federal health care system for current military and families<br>Veterans Administration (VA)<br>Federal health care system for veterans |

specifically directed at poor children. In addition to our altruistic view of needing to provide adequate care to children, there is a strong economic advantage to providing children with cheaper services so they do not seek care in the emergency room. Only two of these programs will be discussed here.

## The Children's Health Insurance Program

The State Children's Health Insurance Program (SCHIP) is sometimes called the Children's Health Insurance Program (CHIP). This program was originally created in 1997 as part of a long, argumentative legislative process.

Most of the arguments arose from the source of funding, which was originally slated to come from increased taxes on cigarettes. It was finally passed as part of a larger piece of legislation that involved balancing the federal budget (Pear, 1997; Barr, 2002; Milligan, 2008).

CHIP is a joint state and federal program, but the money is conveyed to the states as a block grant. The amount of federal money is based on the number of eligible children in the state, with estimates being revised every 2 years (Teitelbaum and Wilensky, 2013). Eligibility is defined as children under age 19 living in families that are between about 200% and 300% of the federal poverty line, which is an income range between about $42,000 and $72,000 for a family of four.

As with most federal programs, CHIP has to be reauthorized periodically by Congress. In 2007, Congress voted to increase the number of children covered, but President George W. Bush vetoed this, because he felt low-income children should be covered by private health insurance plans (Stout, 2007). In 2009, under President Obama, the program was significantly expanded, with broad bipartisan support (Racine, 2014).

States have three choices in organizing this program. One choice is to administer this as a completely separate program, which 17 states do. Twenty-one states have created a hybrid program between children on Medicaid and those on CHIP. Twelve states have chosen to administer their CHIP as an expansion of their Medicaid program (Teitelbaum and Wilensky, 2013). The administration of this program matters, because under a block grant, the federal dollars are capped, whereas under the Medicaid state–local funding matching process, this is not true.

Federal guidelines identify required services, which include regular preventive and screening examinations, including both eye and dental examinations, mental health services, immunizations, laboratory and diagnostic imaging services, and any needed hospital care (Teitelbaum and Wilensky, 2013). As with Medicaid, the details of coverage are left to the states. These services are offered only to the children in an income-eligible family, and not to any of the adults.

The total number of children enrolled in the first 3 years was low, because of a complicated eligibility process and a lack of communication about the program to eligible families. By 2007, there were more than 8 million children in this program (Kovner and Knickman, 2011). It is estimated that nearly 8 million eligible children are still not yet covered (Hudson, 2005; Kenney et al., 2011). The CHIP program seems to have decreased some of the persistent racial/ethnic disparities in access, which will be the topic of the next chapter (Shone et al., 2005).

There are two important policy questions about this program, the first of which relates to cost. It does seem to be cheaper to treat low-income children under the CHIP programs, especially because of the increase in emergency room visits by this population when they are disenrolled for some reason (Rimsza et al., 2007).

The second issue relates to the reason President G.W. Bush opposed the reauthorization of CHIP in 2007. During the first 10 years of implementation, the total proportion of children covered nationwide under private health insurance plans decreased significantly, whereas the percentage of children enrolled in either Medicaid or CHIP increased (Harrington, 2011; Racine, 2014). Some view this as a positive impact, because the rate of uninsured children nationwide was cut from about 14% to 6%, during a time in which the uninsured rate among adults was increasing (Harrington, 2011). However, others (including President Bush) argued this was a result of state support crowding out private health insurance companies. Because children are relatively cheap to insure, private health insurance companies experienced a loss of revenue, which could contribute to a poor economic climate within the state (Kovner and Knickman, 2011). Some of the families who were on CHIP have now been able to purchase a subsidized health insurance policy on the health exchanges of the Affordable Care Act (ACA), which will cover the adults as well as the children (Chapter 17 describes the health exchanges.).

## The Women, Infants, and Children Program

The Special Supplemental Nutrition Program for Women, Infants, and Children (WIC) is included here even though it is not a medical services program, but rather is a targeted nutrition and nutrition education program. This program began in 1969 when a group of physicians noticed that the poor nutritional status of low-income children contributed to poor health outcomes. These doctors wrote prescriptions for food, using funds from federally funded community health centers (CHCs), which will be described later in this chapter (Rossi, 1998). Federal funds from the Agriculture Department are allocated to states for the WIC program, and all states participate in this.

Unlike other targeted programs, the eligibility guidelines for this program are narrowly defined and consistent across all states. Families with incomes at 185% of the federal poverty level (about $42,000 for a family of four) are eligible for services. Services are targeted at pregnant women, children under the age of 5 with a documented nutritional need, and breast-feeding women. In order for a low-income family to qualify, they have a nutritional risk assessment performed, using measures such as height and weight charts; growth assessments; hemoglobin levels; a diet assessment; and a general health history (USDA, 2012). This requires access to a primary care provider, which is most often a federally funded CHC, which will be discussed later.

Participants receive food vouchers, which can be used to purchase nutritional foods, including high protein foods, juices, fresh fruits and vegetables (with the exception of potatoes, which are not allowed), brown rice, whole wheat breads and pastas, and low fat milk. Also included are infant formula and cereals, soy-based beverages, tofu, and a variety of baby foods (Whaley et al., 2012).

In addition to the food buying assistance, WIC participants receive educational and counseling sessions to improve their dietary choices. Educational programs supportive of breast-feeding are also provided to pregnant women (USDA, 2012). Unfortunately, in most states, only 30 minutes is allowed for this, and in too many programs, this is a one-time encounter (Besharov and Germanis, 2000).

In 2011, WIC programs had about 9 million people enrolled, with 5 million of these being children between the ages of 1 and 5; 2 million were infants and the remaining were pregnant or breast-feeding women (USDA, 2012). The WIC program has had continually positive evaluations from the very beginning. Studies consistently demonstrate that for every $1.00 spent on the WIC program, there is a savings of Medicaid expenditures ranging from $1.77 to $3.13 (Hoynes et al., 2011). There are many other positive outcomes noted, including longer pregnancies, fewer premature births, fewer infant deaths, improved prenatal nutrition, increased immunization rates, and increased growth rates of infants (Devaney, 2007; Hoynes et al., 2011).

# Poor, Frail, Elderly: The Program of All-Inclusive Care for the Elderly

The Program of All-Inclusive Care for the Elderly (PACE) is one that provides services to a very narrowly defined target group. This program is specifically designed to provide and coordinate comprehensive medical and health care services for the frail elderly. This includes people over age 55 who are eligible for nursing home services under Medicaid guidelines. Most have multiple health problems, with an average of seven diagnoses. This program is designed to provide home-based services so they can avoid a nursing home.

This program began as a demonstration project in San Francisco that was developed by a nonprofit group called the On Lok (Cantonese for "peaceful, happy abode"). The program began with day services, then expanded to include hospital care, paid for by Medicare (Ansak and Zawadski, 1983). Several grants from foundations such as the Robert Wood Foundation provided additional resources to further expand this model. As part of this expansion, they received waivers from both Medicare and Medicaid for a completely different financing system. They receive a per capita payment for each participant to provide all needed services. In 2006, the Centers for Medicare and Medicaid Services funded 15 rural PACE programs. As of August 2010, there are 76 PACE programs in 30 states, with slightly less than 20,000 people being served. Most are small, serving a few hundred beneficiaries (Sultz and Young, 2014).

All services needed to remain in their homes are provided. This includes day health centers; home care services, including meals and housekeeping; and a variety of therapies, including physical and occupational. This program also pays for any necessary modifications to a person's home. Hospital services are also covered, but the emphasis is on outpatient and preventive services. PACE programs are arranged and financed around a PACE center, an organization that is financially responsible for the provision of all needed services. This creates an incentive to keep enrollees as healthy as possible in order to avoid costly hospitalizations. The PACE centers are arranged in a team concept, including medical, nursing, and a full range of social services, all of whom coordinate with each other to provide the best chance for these enrollees to stay at home and out of the hospital.

This program is very successful, not only in terms of participant satisfaction and health outcomes, but also in terms of cost. PACE participants have fewer and shorter hospitalizations, longer survival times, lower nursing home admission rates, and higher self-reports of health status and satisfaction with their quality of life. Costs for participants in PACE programs are 15–25% lower than for an analogous group of people receiving services through Medicare and Medicaid (Hirth et al., 2009; Wieland et al., 2013). Only 6% of participants are admitted to nursing homes, even though all are medically and socially eligible for a nursing home placement. Not surprisingly, more participants are able to die at home than in a comparable group (Sultz and Young, 2014).

Several factors restrict a wider implementation of this program, some of which are political, but others are practical. This requires a Medicaid waiver to pay providers differently, which requires state legislative approval.

Medicaid programs are politicized in many states, which has limited the expansion of PACE programs. Overhead costs of PACE programs increased after the implementation of Part D of Medicare. Even though there is a capitated payment arrangement, PACE programs have to internally manage the reporting guidelines of Medicaid, and the three different parts of Medicare—Parts A, B, and D. Because the PACE programs are responsible for the costs of all the care provided, these increased overhead costs have made service provision much more challenging. The ACA includes several provisions to attempt to make the management of PACE programs easier.

# A Public Health Approach: CHCs

Many of the targeted programs described in this book are designed to provide access to those who are too poor to purchase health insurance. Because of financial and political pressures at the state level, the income eligibility guidelines have gradually decreased, so many of these programs now serve only the very poor. When this happens, the program transitions to a *safety net* program, meaning that the program is one that serves a disproportionately large number of uninsured individuals, and poor consumers, including those who are in vulnerable groups. Some institutional providers are also considered safety net providers. This includes public hospitals and some academic teaching centers (described in Chapter 8), and family planning programs and some public health programs, described in Chapter 9.

CHCs are organizations specifically funded to serve as a safety net provider. The primary goal and *raison d'etre* for the existence of the CHC is to serve uninsured, poor, and vulnerable populations. This is in contrast to other components of the U.S. health care delivery system that deliver care to the uninsured as part of their overall mission of providing health services to a population, or perhaps as part of their obligation to maintain their tax-exempt status. Although many public health clinics are called community clinics, this section is dedicated to describing the federally designated CHC, an organization officially designated as the core of the safety net of the U.S. health care system.

CHCs provide the full range of primary care services, as described in Chapter 9, as well as other services to improve access, including transportation and a variety of outreach services, and home-based primary care. These services are provided by a culturally sensitive multidisciplinary team of health providers, including not only physicians and nurses, but also nutritionists, social workers, and community health workers. They do not provide any medically specialized services. For those services, as well as for hospital care, CHC patients are referred to the closest public hospital (Teitelbaum and Wilensky, 2013).

The CHC is not a new innovation—some version of this has been in existence since the 1960s, although the funding and overall responsibility has shifted over the years. They were first established as part of Johnson's Economic Opportunity Act of 1964, as Neighborhood Health Centers. These centers had a dual purpose: delivering primary health care services and serving as the centerpiece of President Johnson's antipoverty programs (Taylor, 2004; Frey, 2013). They were funded and administered under the Office of Economic Opportunity, and completely supported by federal funds.

In the 1970s, the term Community Health Center replaced Neighborhood Health Center, and responsibility and funding was moved to the Public Health Service Administration. This move signaled the evolution of their major purpose from being part of an antipoverty effort to an emphasis on providing health care services. During this period, their strongest advocate was Senator Ted Kennedy, who strongly supported keeping CHCs a completely federal effort to avoid the state variations in services that are so prominent in the Medicaid program (Frey, 2013).

CHCs are organized as nonprofit clinical care organizations that meet federal standards, including having a Community Advisory Board (HRSA, 2014). Each CHC is situated in an area that has been designated as Medically Underserved. Those that are in rural, agricultural areas often have a specific mission to provide health care services to migrant farm workers, which include undocumented workers, as noted in Chapter 5. Funding for these CHCs comes from federal funds from the Public Health Service Act, but also from Medicare and Medicaid (HRSA, 2014).

There are about 1250 federally designated CHCs, with 9000 different delivery sites. There are CHCs in all 50 states, with more in those states with poorer economic indicators, especially a high unemployment rate. In 2010, more than 21 million patients visited one of the CHCs (Whelan, 2010; HRSA, 2014). More than 90% of all patients at CHCs are below 200% of the federal poverty guidelines, with almost one-third below 100% of the federal poverty level. Of these, about 75% were on Medicaid and 60% were a racial or ethnic minority (Teitelbaum and Wilensky, 2013). In contrast, about 40% of the U.S. population is below 200% of the federal poverty level; about 15% receive health coverage under Medicaid, and about 30% of the overall population is classified as a minority (Sultz and Young, 2014).

The most recent study of the cost-effectiveness of this model conducted by the National Association of Community Health Centers found that communities with CHCs saved about $1200 per year per patient. This is primarily because the emphasis on primary and preventive care significantly reduces the use of emergency rooms and other hospital-based services (NACHC, 2013). The ACA includes about $11 billion for CHCs, with the majority of those funds going to establishing new clinics. It is estimated that CHCs will double the number of patients they see to more than 40 million by the end of 2015 (NACHC, 2013).

## Too Sick to Be Insured: The State Approach

One group that is often difficult to insure consists of those who have significant existing medical problems. Most private health insurance companies will not insure this group because it is too expensive. Many lose their jobs because of their health status, but they frequently have enough resources that they do not qualify for Medicaid programs. Some states passed regulations prohibiting private health insurance companies from refusing to sell policies to very sick people, and also restricted the cost of premiums (Cassidy, 2010). Other states established a state-funded pool for these sick people, called a *high-risk pool* (Frantz et al., 2004). This pool provides financial assistance to individuals with high medical needs to obtain health insurance. Individuals pay premiums to the state pool; their contributions are combined with state money, and a designated, contracted health insurance company is paid to provide coverage.

Thirty-five states have set up a state-funded high-risk pool that covers more than 200,000 people at a cost of about $2 billion annually (NASCHIP .org, 2014). These pools protect individuals from significant medical expenses, but are also a form of public subsidy for the health insurance companies providing care to a group of people known to be very expensive to insure.

The ACA created a specialized health insurance plan called the Pre-Existing Condition Insurance Plan, which is one of the options under the state health insurance exchange plans (Carey and Galewitz, 2014; Cauchi, 2014). This is an effort to shift this group of people into the federally subsidized private health insurance market. As noted in Chapter 17, under the ACA, no health insurance company can deny health insurance coverage, and there are limits on premiums. This is an effort to move this high need group back into the private health insurance market, where federal subsidies and a larger pool of people paying premiums will be able to share the cost of their health care.

# Workers' Compensation Programs

Workers' Compensation Programs are fully funded by employers and are meant to help employees recover from work-related injuries that occur as part of job responsibilities. It does not matter who was at fault for the accident. Not only do these programs pay for medical care, they very importantly also provide some replacement for lost wages, as well as training programs if the person is unable to return to the original position. There are also lump sums for disabilities that may occur as a result of the injury (USDL, 2012). In exchange for these benefits, the employee agrees to not sue the employer. In fact, one of the original intentions of this program was to remove occupational injuries from the legal system. The federal government requires states to have some sort of workman's compensation program, but implementation is left to the state. Over time, these programs have evolved from only dealing with on-the-job injuries to also including occupational exposure as well as overuse and repetitive syndromes (Shi and Singh, 2014).

This program has experienced a fair amount of conflict, which is dealt with by state-appointed administrative agencies rather than courts, although some disputed claims still end up in the legal system. Some accuse employees of claiming more serious injuries in order to get the two-thirds income compensation. On the other hand, there is substantial evidence that workers are hesitant to file a workman's compensation claim for fear of losing their job or experiencing some other sort of retaliation against them. When employers dispute the claim, the conflict must be settled, sometimes by a state court, with some cases reaching the Supreme Court. Both consumers and physicians report significant difficulties in the claims process (Wertz, 2000).

The number of people served by this program varies considerably by industry. Slightly more than 4% of employer spending in construction is attributed to workers compensation claims, whereas in the service industries, this represents only about 1% of employer expenditures (USDL, 2013). Nationwide in 2012, there were 3.7 claims for every 100 workers (Kudla, 2013).

# Indian Health Services

The responsibility of the federal level of the U.S. government to provide health care services to all registered members of federally recognized American Indian and Alaska Native (AIAN) tribes was established in 1787. This obligation is actually included in the U.S. Constitution and has been reinforced by many treaties, several Supreme Court decisions, and Presidential Executive Orders. This makes this population the original example for a targeted program. Despite this, the members of this target group lag behind all others in the United States for all economic and health measures (Kunitz, 1996; Jones, 2006).

The Indian Health Service (IHS) is an operating division within the U.S. Department of Health and Human Services, and is completely funded at the federal level. Unlike the other targeted programs described in this chapter, this program provides payment for and actual delivery of a range of health and medical services to the eligible population. There are 12 area offices, which are defined geographically. These regional area offices are responsible for the organization and management of the health and medical services that are delivered within their specific geographic regions. Nationwide, the IHS (or tribes designated by the IHS) operates a total of 48 hospitals, 268 health centers, 135 health stations, 11 school stations, 164 Alaska village clinics, 34 Urban Indian Health programs, and 11 Tribal Epidemiology Centers. The IHS employs a full range of health care providers, including medical and health-oriented professionals, with an annual budget of slightly more than $5 billion (IHS, 2013). There are slightly more than 4 million people in the United States who identify as a member of this target group, but the IHS provides health and medical services to only about half of these individuals.

Originally, all medical services were provided on reservations, and only to people who were officially designated as members of the tribe. This included about 560 federally recognized tribes in 35 different states. However, American Indians have been moving off reservations for many years, a trend that has steadily reduced the number of people receiving services. In 1970, less than 40% of American Indians lived in urban areas, but by 2000 more than 60% do (Zuckerman et al., 2004). As Native Americans move off reservations, the whole idea of maintaining an official designated status with their tribe has significantly decreased. Because this is an intrinsic part of defining the target population, this has significantly decreased the number of people eligible to receive free health care. Until fairly recently, the response of the federal government to this situation was to encourage urban American Indians to apply for Medicaid.

In the late 1990s, the IHS contracted with 34 different nonprofit organizations in urban areas to establish what are known as Urban Indian Health Organizations (UIHOs). The purpose of these health centers is to provide health and medical services to the members of the AIAN group that live in an urban area. Despite the large numbers of Native Americans living in urban areas, the proportion of the IHS budget dedicated to UIHOs is only about 1% (Zuckerman et al., 2004). In fact, members of the AIAN group have less than one-third of the per capita expenditures of all other targeted groups in the United States. The main argument justifying this very limited funding is that this target group is eligible for other public programs, including Medicare and Medicaid. However, when members of the AIAN target group initially apply to either of these programs, they are generally rejected because the assumption is that they are provided free care by the IHS and therefore are actually not eligible for other publicly funded services (Zuckerman et al., 2004).

The health status of this group is well below that of the general U.S. population, despite recent significant improvements, as shown in Table 20.2. These health disparities indicate the need for a serious revision of the IHS, with special attention to providing more health services to members of the AIAN group who live in cities, and increasing the integration of the needs of this target group into other programs designed for low-income

**Table 20.2   Selected Health Status Measures for AIAN Target Population**

| Health Indicator | Estimate of Difference |
|---|---|
| **Comparison of AIAN Target Group with U.S. Population: 2010 Data** | |
| Life expectancy | 4.6 years less |
| Deaths from alcohol | 519% higher |
| Diagnosed cases diabetes | 195% higher |
| Diagnosed cases TB | 500% higher |
| Deaths from unintentional injuries | 14% higher |
| Deaths from homicides | 92% higher |
| Deaths from suicides | 72% higher |
| **Change between 1972–1974 and 2002–2004** | |
| Maternal mortality | Decreased 39% |
| Infant mortality | Decreased 28% |
| Deaths from cervical cancer | Decreased 76% |
| Deaths from homicides | Decreased 57% |
| Deaths from unintentional injuries | Decreased 60% |

*Source:* Data from Shi, L. and Singh. D.A., *Delivering Health Care in America: A Systems Approach*, 6th edition, Jones and Bartlett, Burlington, MA, 2014; Indian Health Service, Indian Health Disparities: IHS Fact Sheet, 2010.

individuals, including Medicaid (Jones, 2006). The ACA includes an expansion of Medicaid targeted to urban Native Americans and more support for the establishment of UIHOs (Shi and Singh, 2014).

# Military and Veterans Health Services Systems

The military health care system in the United States is an independent and separate, federally funded comprehensive health care system that is designed to provide health and medical services to the target group of those associated with the military. This is actually not one integrated whole system, but rather a series of smaller systems all designed to meet the needs of specific and slightly different targeted groups within the military. This section will provide an overview of this health care system, which is divided into two separate independent sections: those who are currently involved in the military (so-called active personnel) and those who used to be but are not currently involved, veterans. Although these are independent systems, there is some overlap in eligibility. Both of these are additional examples of programs targeted to the needs of a specific defined population, with the Veterans Administration (VA) being the second oldest target program, after the IHS program, which was described earlier.

## *Military Health System*

The Military Health System (MHS) is designed to provide health and medical services to active duty military personnel and their families. This health care system dates to the Civil War, where medical care was the responsibility of commanding officers and soldiers with some type of medical training, and was only for battlefield injuries. World Wars I and II created a much greater need for medical care, and not just for battlefield injuries. The Department of War and the Department of the Navy merged into one cabinet-level organization—the Department of Defense (DoD). This merger caused conflict between two very distinct medical groups that had developed: the Army Medical Corps and the Navy Medical Corps. Additionally, the Air Force, which was considered part of the Army, was established as a separate branch at this time, with its own distinct Medical Service.

During this same period, there were changes in the expectations of the general American public with respect to health insurance, as summarized in Chapter 13. Active military personnel started requesting similar coverage, including for their families. An early DoD study indicated that almost half of all active duty personnel had dependents with no access to medical care, and 40% of active military personnel did not have easy access to a military site for health care services (Jones and Casey, 2001; Dorrance et al., 2013). This led to the development of Civilian Health and Medical Program of the Uniformed Services (CHAMPUS) (Dorrance et al., 2013). This program provided health care for military employees and their families by using civilian health care providers to increase access.

By 1997, the managed care model was widely viewed as a way in which health care costs could be managed, so CHAMPUS was changed to a national managed care system called TRICARE. This included 12 regions, with one contracting organization responsible for coordinating and administering care for active military personnel and their families in each region (TRICARE, 2013). TRICARE has undergone several reorganizations since 1997, mostly aimed at controlling costs.

The entire system is under the administration of the DoD and currently serves more than 10 million people, which include active duty personnel and their families as well as retired military personnel and their families, with an annual budget of more than $52 billion. The system includes 65 hospitals, 412 medical clinics, and 414 dental clinics spread all over the world. More than 200,000 people work in this system. Each branch organizes and administers its own health care system, resulting in three independent systems: one each for the Army, the Navy, and the Air Force (Dorrance et al., 2013; Shi and Singh, 2014). Within each of the three departments, there are several different types of managed health care plans in which people can enroll.

The definition of the target group in all of these programs is very important. This determines who pays for a service, such as with Medicare and Medicaid. In the MHS, this also frequently determines who provides services. Table 20.3 summarizes the extensive eligibility criteria for both the MHS and the Veterans Administration, which will be discussed next. As can be seen from this table, there are several categories of active duty military, including full-time active military personnel, but also active member of the National Guard as well as the Reserves. Dependents of full-time active military are covered, but spouses and children of those who serve with either the National Guard or the National Reserves are not. Retirees are also covered here, although they may also be covered under the VA. Retirees may also be covered by Medicare, and they often use whichever plan provides the best coverage for them, although this often causes problems for health care providers in terms of managing the paperwork.

**Table 20.3 Eligibility Criteria for Military Health System (TRICARE) and for Veterans Administration Services**

| Eligibility Criteria |
|---|
| **Military Health System** |
| • Sponsor (Active Duty Military Personnel) |
| • Dependent of sponsor, including spouse and children |
| • Active members of the National Guard |
| • Active members of the National Reserves |
| • Retirees |
| *Priority Categories* |
| **Veterans Administration** |
| • Active Military or Air Service |
| • Minimum length of service (usually 24 months) |
| • Honorable Discharge |
| • Peace- or war-time service |
| • Eight priority groups based on: service-connected disability levels; former Prisoners of War (POWs); holders of either Purple Heart or Medal of Honor; specific exposure to one of several toxins; income level in comparison to geographic location |

*Source:* Data from DoD, Evaluation of the TRICARE Program: Access, Cost and Quality, Department of Defense, 2013, available from: http://tricare.mil; DVA, 2010 Organizational briefing book, Department of Veterans Affairs, 2010, available at: http://www.osp.va.gov.

TRICARE is a managed care organization. Services are both financed and delivered under the administration of the 12 regional offices. Services are delivered either at military facilities or by contracting with local civilian health care providers. There are three levels of plans that military personnel may select: there are different plans for those in the reserves; those who are retired from the reserves; those that are retired from the active military and are also Medicare-eligible; and also for young adults (DoD, 2013; TRICARE, 2013). These are all separate plans, each of which involves varying types of premiums.

## VA

As with medical care services for active duty personnel, care for veterans also has roots in early battlefield conflicts. The early history is instructive in order to understand the evolving definition of this target group. Medical care was originally provided only to those active military disabled by battlefield injuries as part of the Revolutionary War, or later the Civil War. By the early 1800s, residence-based facilities were established for veterans under the responsibility of the federal government. These served a wide variety of mostly indigent soldiers, who had been disabled in the Civil War, or in one of several other conflicts such as the Indian Wars, the Spanish–American War, and the Mexican Border conflict. By 1854, the first federal hospital specifically for veterans was established in Philadelphia (DVA, 2005).

World Wars I and II created more injured and disabled veterans, and also a number of specialized programs, each of which was targeted to a particular group, including disability compensation or vocational rehabilitation for disabled servicemen. Specific documentation for each program was required, and services became more fragmented (DVA, 2005). The large increase of veterans needing care caused a rapid growth of hospitals, clinics, and custodial Soldiers' Homes. This resulted in increasing public scandals over whether the veterans were receiving adequate care. In response to this, the VA underwent a process of decentralization, increasing the responsibility of its state and regional field offices (Iglehart, 1996).

The conflicts in Korea and Vietnam produced still more veterans in need of medical and health care. As the United States moved away from a mandatory draft to a volunteer armed forces, the issue of providing adequate medical services became a sensitive political issue. Two different court cases alleging both poor quantity and quality of care for veterans were heard by the Supreme Court. The result of this was another significant reorganization at the federal level, which resulted in the 1988 creation of the cabinet-level Department of Veterans Affairs (Iglehart, 1996).

Beginning in the 1990s, another new group of veterans began to demand better services and to especially demand mental health services. The Gulf War veterans also brought attention to a new syndrome called the Gulf War syndrome, a debilitating illness that many felt was covered up by the U.S. government. This group, along with veterans from the continuing battles in Iraq and Afghanistan, has also drawn attention to the need for mental health services for posttraumatic stress disorder. Additionally, these most recent groups of veterans often return home with very disabling physical injuries that require intensive rehabilitative services.

The VA is a very significant part of the whole U.S. health care system. Included in this integrated system are 153 hospitals, 956 outpatient clinics, 134 nursing homes, and 232 counseling centers, organized in about 1400 different care sites around the nation. This system serves about 7 million people and has a federal allocation of about $41 billion every year (DVA, 2010). Additionally, the VA system has affiliations with academic medical centers and teaching hospitals. In fact, almost half of the entire physician workforce has received at least part of their medical education in a VA facility (Kovner and Knickman, 2011).

Services provided by the VA are primarily designed to provide care to veterans, not family members. Because the system is run on a fixed federal allocation, treatment resources must be carefully managed. The VA has created a priority system for rationing care. General eligibility is first determined by length of service, which must be 24 continuous months, or the entire period in which the veteran was called for service, unless this was interrupted by a service-related disability. Veterans complete an application and then receive an ID card. Once in the VA system, the priority system dictates the type of care (i.e., comprehensive or acute), whether mental health is included, and level of payment responsibility for the veteran. The priority categories are shown in Table 20.3.

The VA system has gradually evolved to focus on two specific groups of patients: veterans with a service-related disability, and those who are low income (Kovner and Knickman, 2011). The highest priority is given to veterans who have a service-connected disability that is classified as being 50% or more and who are unemployable because of this condition. The lowest priority includes veterans who are not disabled and who have incomes that are above the VA standards for the geographic area, and who agree to pay a copayment for the services (DVA, 2010). Although the VA does not require a disability to be service-related, the ranking of the priority groups results in most veterans with nonservice-related disabilities not being eligible for services, unless the veteran is low income. In fact, owing to the rapid increase in-low income veterans, in 2011 about half of those served by the VA were low-income veterans with no service-related disability (Shi and Singh, 2014).

Some veterans are retired and thus eligible for TRICARE, as discussed earlier. Others are older than 65 and are thus eligible for Medicare, and some very low income veterans are eligible for Medicaid. Obviously, all of these programs require applications and determination of whether the veteran is eligible for coverage. Even within the VA system itself, most veterans have to undergo a yearly assessment of their priority group. In 2010, about 10% (more than 2 million) of veterans and their families were uninsured, with nearly half of these being under 45. The planned Medicaid expansion, which is part of the ACA, is designed to include some of the low-income veterans (Haley and Kenney, 2013).

Once eligibility for care is determined, the VA offers comprehensive health care benefits, which include primary and preventive care as well as medical care and mental health services, including substance abuse treatment. A range of occupational and physical therapy services are also provided, based on determination of what the eligible veteran needs. Hospital care is also covered, as is hospice care. There are no premiums for coverage, but there are copayments for various services, which vary depending on the priority group. Coverage does include prescription drugs. The VA system has always negotiated with pharmaceutical companies for prescription drugs, so these are far less costly.

The VA system has been periodically criticized over both quality and quantity of care, with the most recent criticisms involving the long waiting times for medical care. Efforts at identifying quality and performance indicators began in the 1990s, with a specific emphasis on improving surgical outcomes, which were viewed as being of a lower standard than non-VA care. Three significant structural reforms began in 1995, the first of which was to create 22 geographic-based units responsible for organizing and managing the care of veterans in a particular geographic area. The second reform was to shift from hospital-based care to primary care, and to implement the widespread use of quality indicators, similar to those used in non-VA hospitals to meet professional accreditation standards. Finally, there was implementation of electronic medical records and other mechanisms to prevent medical errors, including bar coding of patient wrist bands and drugs (Kizer, 2003; Shi and Singh, 2014).

These reforms resulted in a significant increase in the quality of care as well as coordination of care in the VA system. Several studies showed that care from the VA was either better or equivalent to that provided to Medicare recipients or patients in private managed care organizations (Asch et al., 2004; Yano, 2007; Watkins and Pincus, 2011). Studies that track patient satisfaction have also shown significant improvement over time. In 1993, a survey showed that almost 75% of veterans would get care outside the VA if a national system were available to them (Iglehart, 1996). However, in 2008, a study using a standardized Customer Satisfaction Index showed that people who received medical care at a VA hospital were more satisfied than those who received care at a non-VA hospital. Satisfaction levels were also slightly higher for outpatient care settings (Watkins and Pincus, 2011).

These gains in quality have been lost in the 2014–2015 scandal over waiting times for care. The VA released an internal audit in June 2014, which revealed that more than 120,000 veterans had waited so long for care for which they were eligible that some had died (Griffin, 2014). As a result of this, the Obama administration ordered a Federal Bureau of Investigation inquiry and developed 19 executive actions aimed at improving care for veterans (Cohen, 2014; White House, 2014). Both the Secretary of Veterans Affairs and the Medical Director of the VA resigned (Cohen, 2014). There have been several congressional actions giving more resources to the VA and also allowing veterans to get health care at other civilian settings, with the VA paying (RTT, 2014).

This latest scandal probably reveals more about limitations of resources than it does the competence of the health professionals who provide care to veterans. Caring for this particular target group is expensive. Not only is the group continuing to grow, but their health needs are significant and very diverse. Some will require long-term mental health care in order to be able to return to being a functional member of society. Others with significant physical disabilities require continuing medical care support, as well as income assistance if they are not able to work.

# Does the Targeted Program Approach Work?

The United States has a very long history of creating separate programs to provide access to people with no health insurance. These programs begin with a design that is based on the identified needs of the target population. Although these targeted programs are frequently described as filling in the gaps created by employment-based health insurance, some of these programs, such as the IHS, the Veterans Health Administration, and the MHS, predate the establishment of the employment basis of health insurance in the United States. It is very important to recognize that the targeted program approach is a basic conceptual foundation of the U.S. health care system.

This chapter has described only some of the many targeted programs that are part of the U.S. health care system. Two programs included are targeted to members of specific groups. One includes those who belong to the AIAN minority group, who may obtain care through the IHS. The second include members of the military, who may obtain care through either the MHS or VA systems. Other programs have been selected that are targeted primarily to low-income people, including CHIP, WIC, CHCs, and PACE. Some programs identify a very specific group, such as PACE. Also included here are programs that are for those who are uninsurable under any private health insurance plan, so the cost of their coverage is borne by the taxpayers of the whole state. The Workers' Compensation Program is included because it is an example of a program that not only provides coverage for health problems related to work, but also provides income assistance as well as retraining for a new job. It is an example of a program clearly designed around the specific needs of people who suffer injuries on the job. Some of these programs are very innovative and all are effective, based on evidence from several studies. These represent one of the greatest strengths of targeted programs—which is meeting specific needs of a particular group, sometimes by creative and innovative approaches.

Each of these programs requires a separate eligibility process; most also require periodic reauthorization. The eligibility process is often very cumbersome for the targeted recipients of the program. The VA's use of eight different priority groups creates a very difficult and hard-to-understand priority system.

These are not the only administrative expenses. Even when there is a model that is innovative in both financing and delivery, such as PACE, the program must meet the reporting guidelines of Medicaid and three different parts of Medicare. This administrative burden decreases the ability of this program to be more widely implemented, even though it is cheaper to care for this group under this program and it is also what most people want when they are facing a nursing home placement.

Targeted programs are closely related to the social justice model of allocating health care resources. These programs are almost always designed to provide access to those who do not have access, often because of lack of money. Sometimes, lack of access is because the private insurance market will not agree to provide health insurance to those with very expensive health problems, so the cost of their care must be spread out over the whole state population.

Targeted programs are often innovative and provide more comprehensive services than those provided by the medical care system. Ensuring that pregnant women and children receive adequate nutrition or ensuring that injured workers will have some income assistance while they cannot work falls outside the framework of medically necessary services. As will be shown in Chapter 22, other countries include these kinds of supplemental safety net services in their larger human services system, not just in the health care system.

Most of these programs care for people whose health needs are very expensive, and several studies focusing on this issue seem to indicate that it may be cheaper to provide care through these targeted programs. However, one cannot escape the feeling that these savings are diminished by the need for continuing eligibility assessment.

A very important question is whether these programs provide good outcomes for the targeted group. This is a very difficult question to answer, and research on all of these programs is mixed. Some programs—such as WIC and PACE—seem to be overwhelmingly positive. Others, such as the IHS, do not seem to produce very good health outcomes. There are many significant social and economic problems in this group that obviously impact their health outcomes, and having such limited resources makes it more difficult to provide adequate services to this group.

One of the continuing concerns about targeted programs is whether these specifically designed programs provide the same quality and quantity of care as private health care programs. This concern has a strong relationship to race, because minority populations are more likely to have less access to private health care. One of the major areas of focus in the field of public health is the analysis of the issue of equity of programs, primarily by assessing health outcomes of various ethnic and minority groups. The next chapter focuses on this analysis.

Chapter 22 continues the question of whether these targeted programs are the most economically efficient way of providing health care services to certain groups of people. This analysis also uses health status indicators, especially in comparison with health outcomes in other countries, whose health care systems are organized on a different concept.

# Acknowledgments

The following people made significant contributions to the content of this section, including gathering material and references, as well as writing and analysis: Molly Barlow, Ariana Lymberopoulos, Hayley Mandeville, and Joshua Prevatt. Special thanks go to Chandler Kaplan, whose interest in Community Health Centers led me to include them in this book. Her background paper provided much of the material for that section of this chapter. Three students read this chapter and provided valuable feedback, as well as helpful references. These include Bianca Doone, Derek Luthi, and Rashinda Key.

*Chapter 21*

# A Persistent Problem: Racial and Ethnic Disparities in Health Outcomes

One of the important research questions arising from targeted programs is whether they provide access to the same quality of care as people with employment-based insurance receive. Assessing quality of medical care is a complex problem and is outside the scope of this book. The most common substitute measure for quality of care is impact on the person, or the health outcome. This is also very difficult to quantify, but because improving people's health is the overall goal of the U.S. health care system, much effort is devoted to this, both in medicine and in public health. Health outcomes are generally measured by focusing on what are known as health status indicators, as described in Chapter 3.

These health status indicators are often used to compare the health outcomes of people who receive care from one of the several targeted programs with the health outcomes of those who receive health care from an employer-based private health insurance plan. There are significant differences between these two populations, including age, race and ethnicity, prior health status, and often gender. In controlling for the several differences between these groups, some very clear distinctions in health status indicators have consistently emerged over the past 40 years. Every study consistently reveals a lower health status among all minority populations, especially African-American and Latino or Hispanic-American groups. This has created a whole area of research in the field of public health that is called health disparities.

This is a very large research area, with a huge amount of data. This chapter will focus on how the research has been conducted, rather than the wealth of data. How the question has been framed is an important part of the evolution of this area; and methodology often influences results. Some of the most important findings will be summarized here, but the emphasis is on the question being asked. There is no disagreement in either medicine or public health on the existence of health disparities in health outcomes. There is also general consensus that these disparities are very clearly related to race. There are more questions about why these systematic differences persist, as well as strategies to resolve this long-standing problem.

## What Are Health Disparities?

The term health disparity is used by governmental agencies, including the Centers for Disease Control and Prevention (CDC), the Department of Health and Human Services, and the Census Bureau, to indicate a systematic difference in health status between two or more groups of people. These fundamental differences are linked to some type of disadvantage, which may be economic, social, and/or environmental. The factors are related to income, gender, sexual orientation, and race or ethnicity rather than medical conditions alone. The CDC specifically notes that health disparities are "…differences in health outcomes between groups that reflect social inequalities" (DHHS, 2010). Since the 1990s, research on health disparities has become increasingly focused on race and ethnicity (Braveman, 2006; Barr, 2008).

Even within this more narrow focus, this remains a very complex research issue. Just defining the concept of race is not simple. Some argue that race is a social construct, invented mostly for the ease of explaining physical differences that are not actually based on biology (Barr, 2008). Although this is true, the term *race* is still used throughout the research literature and will be used here also. Race is not easy to measure or quantify, especially because the definition has evolved considerably. Most of the national data are obtained from the U.S. Census Bureau, and in the 2010 census, there were 15 different racial categories, including several that involved more than one racial identity. Respondents can select more than one category, which is a more accurate reflection of reality, but which makes creating categories for purposes of research more complicated. Based on the 2010 census, about

36% of the U.S. population identified as a minority. This included about 13% who identified as being Black or African-American, 16% Latino or Hispanic-American, and 5% Asian-American (U.S. Census, 2010b). A final issue is which terminology is the most appropriate to use for the various minority groups. This chapter will follow most of the research by using the term Black or African-American, and the term Latino or Hispanic for what the U.S. Census Bureau defines as "non-white Hispanics or Latinos."

The United States is an increasingly diverse country, especially because of immigration patterns, as discussed in Chapter 5. The health status of recent immigrants seems to be diminished the longer they are in the United States. Also, not all immigrant groups experience disparities in the same way. In some cases, their cultural health practices are protective (Lara et al., 2014). In many, but not all, locations in the United States, immigrant populations are viewed positively and they are themselves glad to be in the United States. This is not true for African-Americans, because their historical immigration was forced, and the long history of slavery in the United States has created a much different culture around this group than more recent, willing immigrants. As will be seen in the next section, this history contributes to increased health disparities.

The general public recognition of the link between race and health status is complicated somewhat by the uneven distribution of minorities across the United States, as shown in Table 21.1. Racial and ethnic diversity in a population does not have to lead to health disparities. This chapter analyzes why this relationship exists in the United States more than in other countries.

The pattern of health disparities in the Black population is striking across many different measures, a few of which are shown in Table 21.2. These differences have been very well researched, so this chapter will focus primarily

**Table 21.1  Geographic Racial/Ethnic Diversity in the United States**

| States with Highest Percentage of Minority Citizens (Reported as % Minority) | | States with Lowest Percentage of Minority Citizens (Reported as % White) | |
|---|---|---|---|
| Hawaii | 77% | Vermont | 96.4% |
| Washington, D.C. | 64% | Maine | 96.4% |
| California | 60% | New Hampshire | 95.5% |
| New Mexico | 60% | Idaho | 94.6% |
| Texas | 55% | West Virginia | 94.5% |

*Source:* Data from U.S. Department of Commerce, The Statistical Abstract: State Rankings, available from: http://www.census.gov, 2012.

**Table 21.2 Summary of Health Status Indicators: Differences between Whites and Blacks**

| Indicator | Difference |
|---|---|
| Overall mortality | 37% higher for Blacks than Whites |
| Infant mortality rate | Black infants are twice as likely to die within first year as White infants |
| Mortality rates from specific diseases: Stroke Heart disease Cancer Diabetes HIV | 46% higher for Blacks than Whites 31% higher for Blacks than Whites 22% higher for Blacks than Whites 108% higher for Blacks than Whites 8 times higher for Blacks than Whites |
| Deaths from homicides | 10 times higher for Blacks than Whites |
| Prevalence of obesity | 1.7 times higher for Blacks than Whites |
| Prevalence of hypertension | 66% higher for Blacks than Whites |
| Rate of being uninsured | 1.5 times higher for Blacks than Whites |
| Life expectancy at birth | 5 years less for Blacks than Whites |

*Source:* Data from Isaac, L.A., Defining health and health care disparities and examining disparities across the life span, edited by LaViest, T.A., Isaac, L.A., *Race, Ethnicity and Health: A Public Health Reader*, pp. 11–34, Jossey-Bass, San Francisco, 2013.

on the differences in health disparities between White and Black Americans. Even though there are known measurement problems, as described in Chapter 3, results for the past 40 years are very consistent across many different ways of collecting data.

# How Health Disparities Are Investigated

The earliest efforts to explain why health disparities exist concentrated first on biological and genetic differences, with a focus on cultural differences emerging next. It is easy to understand why the genetic basis would be investigated in the 1970s. Some of the first differences in quantitative indicators such as blood pressure seemed to indicate an inherent genetic variation. Also, the definition of race in this period was assumed to have a biological basis. It has taken quite a bit of time and careful research for investigators to move away from this limited conceptual model (Garte, 2002; Goodman, 2014). The first modification of this research model was to consider various cultural practices of the African-American population that might contribute to their generally poorer health status (Thorpe and Kelley-Moore, 2014). This research path did not help to illuminate the differences noted, primarily because the immigrant experience that used this cultural framework was not appropriate to the Black population, as noted. It soon became clear that focusing on individual determinants of health, including genetics and individual health behaviors, was not sufficient to explain the observed differences in health status. The research models gradually shifted to an increased focus on various social determinants of health. This chapter will briefly describe research using three different models, all of which use the framework of social determinants of health.

## Role of the Environment in Health Disparities

Studies focusing on the role of the environment have revealed strong, convincing, and consistent patterns over 20 years of investigating several different variables. This research is based on the fact that residential segregation continues to be very much present, especially in urban areas (Massey and Denton, 1993; Williams and Collins, 2001). Minority neighborhoods are more likely to be populated by largely low-income people. Urban minority neighborhoods are more likely to have deteriorating buildings and structures with code violations, even though these structures are occupied (Perera et al., 2002; Cohen et al., 2003).

Much of the research in this area focuses on what is known as the *built environment*. This includes access to food, safe areas for exercise and walking, and access to public transportation. The research results are very consistent: urban minority neighborhoods have less access to the more positive aspects of the built environment. For example, proximity to large supermarkets is related to lower rates of obesity and hypertension (Morland et al., 2002), whereas proximity to convenience stores is related to higher levels of obesity and hypertension in the neighborhoods surrounding the stores (Morland et al., 2006). Urban minority neighborhoods are far more likely to have convenience stores than supermarkets (Morland et al., 2006). Walkable environments are more available to predominantly urban Latino areas than for Black neighborhoods (Small and McDermott, 2006). There are also many fewer other opportunities for physical activity such as parks and gyms in predominantly Black urban areas (Gordon-Larsen et al., 2006). This combination of poor access to positive aspects of the built environment is thought to contribute to the higher prevalence of obesity and hypertension as well as to the higher prevalence of chronic diseases these conditions are related to.

One part of the built environment that seems to be more prevalent in low-income, predominantly African-American urban neighborhoods are liquor stores (LaViest and Wallace, 2014). Previous studies have indicated that location of liquor stores is associated with increased drinking. Alcohol is highly related to several indicators of social problems, including violence (Rabow and Watts, 1982; Gruenewald et al., 1992).

Poor, predominantly Black communities are also more likely to be exposed to increased environmental pollution, including air pollution, pesticides, lead, and other industrial pollutants (Corburn 2002; Perera et al., 2002; Woodruff et al., 2003).

All of these studies lead to a general conclusion that there is a much greater exposure to environmental risk factors in minority neighborhoods, all of which lead to higher mortality and morbidity rates (Cubbin et al., 2001; Deaton and Lubotsky, 2003). The research effort now is to create a conceptual model that quantifies the relationship of these variables to better understand the relative weight of each in terms of contributing to the observed poorer health status of those who live in low-income predominantly Black neighborhoods (Gee and Payne-Sturges, 2014).

These results generate a conclusion regarding how these environmental risk factors impact people. Nearly all of the investigators frame this in terms of chronic stress and the toll this takes on the health of the individuals living in these communities. The understanding of the impact of stress on health was described in Chapter 1, and this emphasis is the center of another research model used to investigate health disparities.

## A Broader Model: Biopsychosocial Considerations

Any response to an environmental stimulus is the result of interactions of many different variables, inducing genetic or constitutional factors, sociodemographic factors including socioeconomic status, as well as individual psychological and behavioral factors (Clark et al., 2014; Paradies, 2014). The question is, what is the environmental stimulus? An environmental stimulus is an independent variable, which means it is the major factor that causes the identified outcome. In this case, the search is for an environmental stimulus that causes the different health outcomes that have been documented between White and Black Americans. The answer has always been implicit in the literature, but in recent years this environmental stimulus has become more explicit.

The independent variable is racism. This variable is commonly quantified by study participants' self-reporting feelings of discrimination and how they responded to these behaviors (Paradies, 2014). A whole body of research has built up over the years that produces very consistent results. One particular conceptual model used to frame this research will be described here: the John Henryism (JH) hypothesis (Bennett et al., 2014).

The JH hypothesis takes its name from the legend of the Black railroad worker who competed with a steam-driven drill in a contest in the late 1800s. Although he won this contest, he died shortly after (Williams, 1983). Even the superhuman strength of John Henry could not protect his body from the stress of proving himself. The idea behind this theory is that the continuous stress from interacting with an unfair White society over time results in poor physical health on the part of African-Americans, especially in terms of increased prevalence of hypertension and cardiovascular disease. This rate of increased prevalence of hypertension and heart disease has been studied since the 1970s (James et al., 1983), but it was in 1983 that the first study formally used the idea of these two health indicators being the culmination of a lifetime of coping with stress of perceived racism (Harburg et al., 1973). After 10 years of consistently finding a link between perceived discrimination and hypertension in a wide variety of studies, an empirical scale was constructed to quantitatively measure how respondents cope with perceived discrimination (James, 1996). A review of more than 20 published articles using this scale produced a much improved understanding of the various coping mechanism used by Blacks as they respond to discrimination and also the negative health consequences over time (Bennett et al., 2014). Although many of the health impacts are related to cardiovascular disease, some studies have also used this framework to analyze the higher infant mortality rates (IMRs) for Black babies. Their conclusion is that chronic stress is a significant cause of low birth weight babies and preterm births. Under this framework, IMR is a result of chronic stress from years of a Black woman experiencing discrimination, even when the woman is of a higher socioeconomic class (Bell et al., 2006).

The first chapter of this text discussed the impact of chronic stress on health, using the examples of unemployment and of bullying. In both of these examples, research has identified the biochemical chain leading to the increased presence of cortisol in the bloodstream. The same is true of research in this area. The stress response is a biological process whose purpose is that of a short-term exposure. When the body is exposed to increased levels of circulating cortisol over time, a variety of negative consequences are the result. The negative responses include hypertension, cardiovascular disease, low birth weight babies, preterm births, and obesity. In all of these examples, the biochemical process has been identified, as well as the health indicator itself (Jackson et al., 2014).

The most recent advance in this particular area of research bridges the gap between research based on the biological and genetic dimension and that which is founded on social and behavioral factors. It is clear that there is a complex interaction between what might be called the constitution of a person and the responses of that person to perceived racial discrimination. Some of these responses are mediated by social and psychological factors. This has spurred the development of a relatively new field termed life course epidemiological models to explain why some of the responses seem to occur even without any specific example of overt racism (Thorpe and Kelley-Moore, 2014).

All of the research in this area has a common goal: to develop conceptual models for researching this area in order to explain why health disparities exist so that possible resolutions may be developed. Other research has a more narrow focus on the health care system, analyzing how African-Americans are treated once they are patients.

## *Focusing on Health System Issues*

For many in the public health field, the time has come to create solutions based on the information obtained from the conceptual models. The most common suggested solution is to increase access to health care services for low-income minority populations. As a result, a variety of targeted programs that improve financial access to medical care have been established. However, these programs have not decreased the racially based health disparities. An especially effective method to study the impact of access is to compare clinical procedures and health outcomes for Whites and African-Americans who have the same kind of financial access. Two early studies produced definitive results, which revealed that just increasing access is not sufficient. One study compared the role of race in treatment received in the Veterans Administration (VA) system and the other looked at the role of race in the type of treatment given for Medicare recipients. In both cases, because the issue of access had been taken away, there should be no difference between how Black and White patients were treated.

However, both studies showed the same kind of unequal access in these two very different populations. In the VA study, Blacks were 33% less likely to undergo a cardiac catheterization procedure and 42% less likely to have an angioplasty to open blocked cardiac vessels. They were also 54% less likely to receive a surgical procedure where the blocked arteries were bypassed (Peterson et al., 1994). These differences did not result in a higher death rate, but they did result in a much lower quality of life for the patients. The Medicare study demonstrated the same pattern of Black patients being offered less aggressive care for heart disease, even though all had the same insurance coverage (Kahn et al., 1994). Other clinical studies that focused on other diseases demonstrated the same sort of findings. Black patients with early stage lung cancer were less likely to have surgery than White patients, resulting in higher death rates (Bach et al., 1999). Black patients with kidney failure were less likely than White patients to be referred for kidney dialysis (Ayanian et al., 1999), and African-American patients treated for a broken bone in the emergency room received less pain medication than White patients (Todd et al., 2002). These results of these early studies were unexpected, and stimulated more research, which demonstrated the same results (Van Ryan and Burke, 2014).

Because of this, there is an increased focus on why these racial differences in treatment exist. Some investigations examine communication differences; some examine implicit biases on the part of providers, whereas others examine factors related to individual patients themselves (Van Ryan and Burke, 2014). The conclusion that arises from this research is that historical racial bias survives today in a less explicit, more insidious way—one in which none of the White health care providers means to treat Blacks differently, but do so anyway. This sort of systematic, mostly invisible prejudice is termed *institutional racism*, and has become an important independent variable for many studies, and also a way to develop possible resolutions.

## What Can Be Done about Health Disparities?

When reflecting on the body of research that has been only very briefly summarized in the previous section, it is perhaps not surprising that as a group, Blacks do not trust the U.S. health care system. Reasons for this distrust can be found not only in the many examples of current and continuing differential treatment, but also in history, the most important of which is the infamous Tuskegee Study. This study was under the auspices of the

U.S. government through the U.S. Public Health Service and involved the purposeful lack of treatment for confirmed syphilis in African-American male patients so the natural course of the illness, including death, could be determined (Gamble, 1997; Brandon et al., 2014). Combating history as well as current practice is daunting. However, several important initiatives have been developed, which will be summarized here.

Two watershed reports were published by the Institute of Medicine. The first one in 2001 was titled Crossing the Quality Chasm (IOM, 2001b), and the second, 2 years later, was titled Unequal Treatment (Smedley et al., 2003). These two reports suggested a broad initiative for all health care organizations emphasizing provider training in cultural competence in order to improve the ability of the health care professional to deliver more patient-centered care. Both of these reports were anchored in the idea that White providers do seem to treat African-American patients differently, leading minority patients to not trust their care. This combination of factors is likely to lead to a lower quality of care. Training in cultural competence was suggested as a way for providers to become more sensitive not only to cultural differences, but also to the provider's own stereotypes. This training focuses on communication skills, but also includes assessing the patient's view of biomedicine and the use of alternative healing methods (Betancourt and Green, 2014). This is a specific recognition of the importance of providers keeping the context of their patients in mind, as described in Chapter 4.

Many health professionals are well aware of the general findings from the extensive research summarized in this chapter, but these two reports specifically focused on the clinical environment. Because of this, they became the catalyst for developing resolutions. Of the many different programs developed around the country, two specific ones with a national perspective will be described here.

The first is a project funded by the Robert Wood Johnson (RWJ) Foundation to develop an overarching set of national initiatives to reduce racial health disparities. One of the first goals was to produce a conceptual framework that could be used to guide health care institutions in developing approaches to reducing health disparities. Although other conceptual models have been developed, this one is more comprehensive, including the structure of the health care organizations themselves, as well as social norms and racial and ethnic stereotypes held by health professionals. Also included in this conceptual model are organizational and governmental strategies for resolutions (Chin et al., 2014). This important model acts to integrate several lines of research, including individual and social determinants of health, as well as factors related to the health care system itself.

At roughly the same time, another group was developing a different, more practical national plan for reducing health disparities. The National Health Plan Collaborative (NHPC) is a group of large health insurance plans, all of which were interested in developing plan-specific strategies for reducing health disparities. This group was also funded by RWJ as well as by the federal government through the Agency for Health Care Research and Quality to develop the NHPC to Reduce Disparities and Improve Quality. Although some of these health plans are competitors, they all felt it was in their interest to reduce racially based health disparities. The original organizations included the following: Aetna, CIGNA, Harvard Pilgrim, Health Partners, Highmark, Kaiser Permamente, Molina, United Health Care, and WellPoint. A variety of health plans were involved, including health maintenance organizations, preferred provider organizations, and Medicaid and Medicare plans (Lurie et al., 2014).

These plans have designed a variety of strategies, but what they have in common is a data collection phase to document quality of care issues that may be linked to racial disparities. As just one example, Harvard Pilgrim Health Plan discovered that three specific communities contained almost two-thirds of its Latino enrollees with diabetes who had not yet received an eye examination. Investigation determined that there was very limited access to eye providers in close proximity to these communities. Resolving this became one of their strategies for improving the quality of care for diabetes in this minority group (Lurie et al., 2014).

## Where Are We Today?

The question today is not whether there are any differences in the health status indicators of minorities in comparison to Whites, but rather why these differences exist, and how they can best be resolved. One of the first suggestions for a resolution came from McCord and Freeman in their 1990 study, which demonstrated that a Black male in Harlem had a lower life expectancy than a male in Bangladesh. Their suggested national resolution was to identify pockets of excess deaths and give these areas extra resources, much as we do when geographic areas receive federal money for excess property damage from natural disasters (McCord and Freeman, 1990).

Two important observations are relevant to this chapter as well as to the continuing effort to develop strategies for resolving this very persistent problem in the U.S. health care system. Both are related to Section I of this book, which described the environment of the U.S. health care system. The first is recognition of the complexity of determining all the factors that impact health status. Although this book focuses on the medical care system, social determinants of health are at least as important in influencing health status. Although race is not the only social determinant, it is certainly a very important one, not the least of which is the link to income. The latest Survey of Consumer Finances conducted by the Federal Reserve shows continuing gaps between both income and wealth of White and Black households. Income of Black households has slowly increased since 1989, but income of White households remains two or three times higher than that of Black ones. However, the wealth gap is even larger, with White households having 13 times more wealth than African-American households. This wealth gap is a much more sensitive measure because it takes all assets into account (Fry and Kochhar, 2014).

This relationship between race and income can be seen in all of the programs that are targeted to low-income people. Although these programs serve a majority of White people, when the percentage served in these programs is compared to the overall proportion of Whites in the U.S. population, minorities are disproportionately represented. For example, as noted in Chapter 19, about 26% of the Black population in the United States meet the federal poverty guidelines, although Blacks account for only about 13% of the overall population. Only about 10% of all White people meet the federal poverty guidelines. The Kaiser Family Foundation recently reported that almost 35% of Black families live in poverty as compared to about 13% of White families (KFF, 2011).

A very important second observation relates to the history of racial discrimination in the United States. Most people know about this in terms of a larger society, but do not realize the discrimination that existed in this country toward people of color was also an integral part of the health care system. For example, until the Civil Rights movement of the 1960s, hospitals, medical schools, and most doctor's offices were segregated by race. Black physicians were trained in Black medical schools and were not permitted on the staff of any White hospitals. In those few health care practices and hospitals that treated both Blacks and Whites, completely separate waiting areas and treatment areas existed. Several pieces of legislation related to the Civil Rights movement were directed at the health care environment, but what really desegregated the U.S. health care system was the passage of Medicare and Medicaid in 1965, as noted in Chapter 17. For both of these programs, no federal dollars were given to any health care facility that maintained racially segregated medical treatment services (Barr, 2002). Although this may seem like old history to some, this framework is essential for understanding the importance—and power—of institutional racism.

The United States is not the only country that is confronted with health disparities, but it is the only country that has such strong and racially based health disparities. The classic studies on income- and class-related health disparities came from Great Britain, where Marmot observed what he called health gradients between people in the highest income groups and those in the lowest income groups (Marmot et al., 1991). This was surprising, given the highly centralized and nationalized structure of the British National Health Service. The racially based health disparities in the United States exist independent of income. Many of the programs designed to increase access are targeted to low-income people. It may be that labeling patients by which insurance coverage they have perpetuates the systematic institutionalized, perhaps unconscious, racially based stereotypes of health professionals. The last chapter of this book explores alternative ways of organizing a national health care system, which may result in fewer racially based health disparities.

## Acknowledgments

Dr. William A. Darity, the first dean and founder of the School of Public Health at the University of Massachusetts, provided the inspiration for the overall direction of this chapter. His work in the area of racial inequities in all parts of medicine and public health have made a very significant contribution to our understanding of this complex and difficult topic. The following people made important contributions to the content of this section through their excellent background papers, which included gathering material and references: Molly Barlow, Evan Hill, Maria Kardaras, Sheighlyn Knightly, Hayley Mandeville, Jasmine Offley, and Loreiny Peñaló. I also thank the following four students who read and commented on this chapter: Nicolas Dundas, Sydney Leone, Julie Minnish, and Jonathan Rosenblatt. Each of them provided very helpful suggestions that improved this chapter.

*Chapter 22*

---

# Alternative Models for Health Care Systems: International Perspectives

---

The U.S. health care system starts with a foundation of employment-based health insurance with targeted programs added for those who do not have health insurance through their jobs. This results in many specific and fairly independent insurance programs providing access to health care services, several of which have been described in Chapters 18–20. This model has its rationale in the philosophical values of market justice underlying the U.S. economy and which are present, although in a more limited fashion, in the health care system. It has always been argued that this targeted program approach allows for more flexibility and innovation and is more likely to meet the special needs of the various target groups. There does not seem to be much evidence to support this. Each program has separate eligibility requirements, such as employment status, age, disability status, or income. Because of this, the targeted program system is administratively more expensive. No other country organizes their health care system in the way in which the United States does, with South Africa being the closest. All other countries with economies similar to the United States spend much less money, have fewer administrative costs, and obtain better health outcomes.

The alternative conceptual model of providing access to health care services is *universal care*, and is founded not only on the philosophical principle of social justice, but also on a core belief in administrative efficiency.

The term universal means that there is only one program and it applies to all people, including workers as well as nonworkers. Although the term *single payer* is frequently used to characterize this universal model of providing access to health services for a whole population, this is not accurate. Neither is the more pejorative term *socialized medicine*. Nationalized access or centrally regulated are more appropriate terms for this model of access. The many health care systems organized under the universal care model involve both private and public financing, as in the United States. There are some multipayer systems, just as the United States. In some countries, employers are also part of the financing, just as in the United States. However, employment status and health insurance coverage are very carefully separated in these systems, unlike in the United States. Decisions and regulations in these countries are not more centralized: the U.S. health care system also has an important central federal regulatory structure. However, unlike in the United States, central regulations apply to all parts of the health care systems, both public and private. This is primarily because there is less for-profit activity and a different cultural and political view of the nature of health care services.

Examining the health care systems of other countries does not mean that these models can be easily adopted in the United States. This book started with the cultural and political context that surrounds views of health and illness and the structure of a nation's health care system, and it will end on the same note. It is instructive to analyze the structure, function, and financing of health systems of other countries, as these approaches may provide some insights into the types of health care reform possible within the political context of the United States.

## What Countries Should We Examine?

Selecting appropriate countries to analyze is extremely challenging. The first decision is to select countries that are at the same economic development level as the United States. There are many poorer countries that have a very strong primary care–centered health care system that produce some better health outcomes than in the United States, but these systems are not very instructive for the United States. It is important to be able to compare many variables, which means selecting well-studied countries. Several organizations analyze and compare various health systems around the world. One of these is the Commonwealth Fund, which not only studies the structure of health care systems, but also routinely surveys patients and policymakers in selected countries. This creates a very rich source of information including perceptions of patients about their health care systems. Other organizations such as the World Health Organization (WHO), the World Bank, and the Organization for Economic Co-operation and Development also routinely analyze national health care systems. Data from all these are used in this chapter.

Accurately characterizing complex health care systems is another challenge. In this chapter, health care systems will be grouped into three categories, based on some of the most important characteristics of the system. The first group comprises those that have what can be called a true *single-payer* system. In these countries—the United Kingdom, Canada, and Sweden—private insurance exists, but primarily to supplement the large, publicly funded health care system. Of these, the English system is the most centralized. It is governed by the National Health Service of England (NHS), which is part of the national government. The NHS both finances and delivers health care: many hospitals are owned by the government and most physicians are employees of the government. Both Canada and Sweden have more decentralized health care systems, while retaining a single-payer financing mechanism. For Canada, the federal government sets guidelines, but each province and territory administers the health plans, and exercises a fair amount of power over both benefits and costs. The Swedish health care system is based on a philosophical value of social solidarity and a principle of cost-effectiveness. This translates into a system in which all health care services are covered, with priority given to those with the greatest medical need (Anell et al., 2012). Although guided by central principles, the actual governance is decentralized to the 21 city councils, which are able to vary benefits and somewhat modify financing (Glenngard, 2013).

The second group is composed of those that are based on an important philosophical value of *social security* and solidarity. These countries include Germany and France, both of which share the idea that sicker people should pay less for health care. For these two countries, the health care system is part of the overall national fabric of caring for all citizens. Although the health care system is publicly funded, there are private insurance companies whose major function is to supplement the care provided by the tax-supported system. The German health system is composed of many health plans, called sickness funds. Most of these are nonprofit, although there are also some private, for-profit insurance plans. All are governed by the same regulations on both benefits and cost, however. Germans may choose which sickness fund to enroll in. France is also a multipayer system, which is funded by employers, employees, taxes on alcohol and tobacco, and other government tax-based funding.

The final category includes those countries that have what can be termed a *shared responsibility* system, which includes both public and private funding, where the private funding is sometimes a replacement for public financing. What differentiates this group of countries—including the United States, the Netherlands, and Switzerland—is that the private insurance market is more prominent. The Swiss health care system has always been based on the same two ideas as many other European countries: a belief in health care as a basic human right coupled with a belief in a cost-effective system. This system was significantly reformed in 1996 with the passage of what is called LaMal. This health insurance law limited the ability of private insurance companies to compete, and also limited their ability to make profits (Bidgood et al., 2013). In the Netherlands, each person is mandated to purchase health insurance coverage from a private insurer which is subsidized by tax funds to keep the cost of premiums low, much like the approach used by the Affordable Care Act (ACA).

Selecting variables to measure is yet another challenge. This chapter includes six data tables summarizing the major characteristics of each of these systems for variables most relevant to the themes of this book. This includes the following: an overall description of some important structural dimensions of each health care system; a summary of some relevant demographic variables; a description of financing and cost sharing required of consumers; some of the more important resources needed for a health care system; a few of the most well-documented access and satisfaction measures collected by the Commonwealth Fund; and finally, four of the most commonly used health status measures.

## Overall Description of Health Care System and Demographic Features

Table 22.1 reveals significant diversity in the overall structure of these health systems. For example, even among the three single-payer systems, only one (United Kingdom) is highly centralized, with Canada and Sweden both having significant local control. In Germany, France, the Netherlands, and Switzerland, there are multiple payers, including private insurance companies, as there are in the United States. The major difference between the United States and these four countries is the central government regulates

**Table 22.1   Overall Description of Health Care Systems**

| | | *Group # 1: Single Payer Systems* | |
|---|---|---|---|
| *Descriptor* | *United Kingdom* | *Canada* | *Sweden* |
| General description | National Health Service with governance by groups of health care providers. | Group of publicly funded health plans, provided and administered by each province/territory. | Based on philosophy of public ownership; with decentralized governance at the level of 21 city councils. |
| Comprehensive coverage | Mostly, with dental and vision care limited to medically necessary. | Yes; includes all basic health care; drugs; vision and dental; as well as hospital-based care. | No set defined benefits, but broadly comprehensive, including prescription drugs, long-term care, mental, health and dental health for children. |
| Choice of provider | Can choose GP; less choice for specialist and hospital. | Can choose provider and hospital. | Can choose provider and site of primary care. |
| Medical education | Mostly publicly funded. | Public subsidies available. | Publicly funded. |

*(Continued)*

**Table 22.1 (Continued)  Overall Description of Health Care Systems**

| | Group #2: Social Security Systems | |
| --- | --- | --- |
| | *Germany* | *France* |
| General description | Sickness fund enrollment or private insurance. | Health insurance funds are public and private, and all nonprofit. Each person must have health insurance, which is usually through the employer. |
| Comprehensive coverage | Yes. | Yes. |
| Choice of provider | Can choose sickness fund; this influences both provider and hospital. | Can choose provider and hospital. |
| Medical education | Mostly publicly funded. | Publicly funded. |

*(Continued)*

**Table 22.1 (Continued)   Overall Description of Health Care Systems**

| | Group # 3: Shared Responsibility Systems | | |
| --- | --- | --- | --- |
| | *Netherlands* | *Switzerland* | *United States* |
| General description | Three components funded independently: sickness funds (66%); private substitute insurance (29%); civil servants (5%). | Significant reform in 1996 controlled competition/profits among health insurance companies. Each individual must be insured. | Based on philosophy of creating insurance programs targeted to specific needs of each group, each with own administration. Foundation of linking employment and health insurance. |
| Comprehensive coverage | Mostly long-term care and selected preventive care benefits; also high-risk prenatal care. | Dental care not covered. | Varies by health plan. |
| Choice of provider | Can choose health plan and provider. | Can choose health plan and provider. | Can choose health plan; this influences choice of provider and hospital. |
| Medical education | Publicly funded | Partly publicly funded with some private payment. | Largely private payment with some federal/state subsidies. |

*Source:* Data from CIA World Factbook, available from: http://www.cia.giv; Commonwealth Fund, Comprehensive Coverage, available from: http://www.commonwealthfund.org; Eurostat, available from: http://ec.eiropa.eu/eurostat; Ridic, G., Gleason, S., Ridic, O., Comparisons of health care systems in the U.S., Germany, and Canada, *Materia Socio-Medica*, 24, 112–120, 2012; Index Mundi, Country Demographic Profiles, available from: http://www.indexmundi.com, 2014; OECD, Organization for Economic Co-operation and Development, available from: http://www.OECD.org, 2012; World Bank, available from: http://data.worldbank.org.

private insurance in the same way as publicly funded insurance programs, so both costs and benefits are the same for all citizens.

Regardless of structure and level of centralization, coverage is mostly comprehensive, meaning that all medical needs are covered, ranging from primary care to hospital services. This comprehensive coverage, however, is somewhat limited by cost sharing, as will be discussed later. Also, just as in the United States, coverage of dental, vision, and mental health services is challenging.

One of the common myths is that consumers in the United States have more choice of providers than citizens in other countries. As Table 22.1 shows, this is not true. There is a similar amount of choice in each country, with choice of insurance payer often dictating both a physician and a hospital. One of the most striking differences in Table 22.1 is financing of medical education. Only in the United States is this primarily privately funded. In all other countries there are substantial public subsidies. For example, medical schools in England are public, and are highly subsidized so costs of medical school are very low. In Germany, medical education is integrated into undergraduate education, and is very low cost. Medical schools are free in the Netherlands, with entrance of qualified applicants determined by a lottery. The medical education system in France is longer than in the United States, but is essentially free. In Canada, medical education is very similar to the United States, but there are many more financial assistance programs available to help defray the expense of medical school. This means that new medical school graduates in these comparison countries can start their careers without having to pay a large debt. This results in very different practice patterns and different specialty choices.

There are some striking demographic differences in this group of eight countries, summarized in Table 22.2. The United States is by far the largest in population, with Sweden and Switzerland being much smaller. The United States also is the most diverse in terms of racial and ethnic diversity, although the other seven countries also demonstrate considerable diversity. The percentage of uninsured is much less in each of these countries than in the United States, reflecting that health insurance is mandatory. It is interesting that the percentage of uninsured in the United States has dramatically decreased as a result of the implementation of the ACA, but is still well above the other countries. Table 22.2 shows the percentage of uninsured as a range, because it is being reduced as more people enroll in one of the ACA programs. Also, in all countries, the emphasis on providing access is focused on citizens, just as it is in the United States.

**Table 22.2 Selected Demographic Indicators**

| Group # 1: Single Payer Systems | | | |
|---|---|---|---|
| *Descriptor* | *United Kingdom* | *Canada* | *Sweden* |
| Population | 64 million | 35.9 million | 9.7 million |
| % over age 65 | 17% | 15% | 19% |
| % Minority population | 13% | 17% | 14% |
| % Uninsured | 0, except for noncitizens | 0, except for noncitizens | 0, except for noncitizens |
| Unemployment rate | 5.7% | 6.5% | 7.8% |
| Group # 2: Social Security Systems | | | |
| | *Germany* | *France* | |
| Population | 80 million | 64.9 million | |
| % over age 65 | 21% | 17% | |
| % Minority population | 9% | 15% | |
| % Uninsured | 0, except for noncitizens | 0, except for noncitizens | |
| Unemployment rate | 4.8% | 10.6% | |
| Group # 3: Shared Responsibility Systems | | | |
| | *Netherlands* | *Switzerland* | *United States* |
| Population | 16.8 million | 8 million | 318 million |
| % over age 65 | 16% | 18% | 14% |
| % Minority population | 19% | 17.5% | 36% |
| % Uninsured | 3% | 1.5% | Between 9% and 13% |
| Unemployment rate | 7.1% | 3.5% | 5.5% |

*Source:* Data from CIA World Factbook, available from: http://www.cia.giv; OECD, Organization for Economic Co-operation and Development, available from: http://www.oecd.org, 2012; U.S. Census Bureau, available from: http://www.census.gov; World Bank, available from: http://data.worldbank.org.

One particular pressure on health care systems is the proportion of the population over the age of 65, because this group tends to utilize more extensive and expensive services. All of these countries (including the U.S.) have at least 14% of their population in this age range, with Germany having 21%. The unemployment rate ranges from a low of 3.5% in Switzerland to a high of about 7% in Sweden and the Netherlands. Since employment status is not related to health insurance, this does not have a specific impact on the health care system, although it does impact the overall economic situation in the country.

## Financing and Cost Sharing

Table 22.3 provides more details about financing issues, including ways in which providers are paid and the amount of costs borne by individual consumers in each country.

Method of physician payment varies between these eight countries, with the majority being paid using some sort of a fee-for-service (FFS) method. In England and the Netherlands, physicians are paid differently, based on specialty. In Canada and Sweden, they are paid differently based on whether their payment is from public or private funds. Regardless of the method of payment, there are government controls on amount, with the most strict being in the United Kingdom, where some physicians are public employees, and in France, where all physicians are paid on an FFS basis by a negotiated national schedule. As has been shown in this book, the most variation occurs in the United States, where physician payment varies by insurance payer. Physician income is an important variable, and this will be discussed later.

There is more similarity in how hospital services are reimbursed. In all three structural types, it is typical for hospital costs to be global in nature, meaning that the central payment source provides an annual budget, based on a process very similar to the Diagnosis-Related Group method used for Medicare in the United States. Global budgeting allows a nation to explicitly identify spending priorities in health care and also includes a mechanism to monitor and control expenditures.

All of these countries have some private health insurance, but as shown in Table 22.3, this varies from a low of 5% in Sweden to a high of 90% in France. The role of private insurance varies considerably. For example, in France, the role of private insurance is to supplement the public plan, and

**Table 22.3  Financing and Cost Sharing**

| Descriptor | Group # 1: Single Payer Systems | | | |
| --- | --- | --- | --- | --- |
| | *United Kingdom* | *Canada* | *Sweden* | |
| Payment to physicians | Primary care: capitation Specialists: salary | Private: FFS Public: salaried | Mostly public: salaried. Some private: FFS | |
| Payment to hospitals | Global budgets from NHS | Nonprofits: FFS or per diem | Global budgets from city councils | |
| Deductible for core benefits | No | No | No | |
| Limit to individual costs | Yes | No | Yes (about $300/year) | |
| Type of cost sharing | None on primary care; hospital stays Yes to long-term care, dental/ eye care | Only for noncovered items such as prescription drugs | Limited; prescription drugs on a sliding scale | |
| Role of private insurance | Supplementary | Supplementary: cannot duplicate covered services; can provide extra coverage | Supplementary: provides faster access, use of private providers | |
| % with private insurance | 10% | 67% | 5% | |

*(Continued)*

**Table 22.3 (Continued)    Financing and Cost Sharing**

| | Group # 2: Social Security Systems | |
| --- | --- | --- |
| | Germany | France |
| Payment to physicians | Paid by sickness funds: mostly capitation | FFS by national schedule |
| Payment to hospitals | Paid from sickness funds: FFS by negotiated schedule | Nonprofit: global, DRG budget For-profit: itemized FFS |
| Deductible for core benefits | No | No |
| Limit to individual costs | Yes, limited to no more than 2% of income. Limits also for those with chronic diseases | No |
| Type of cost sharing | Copays for prescription drugs also limited | 30% on all physician visits, including primary care; 35% drug costs; 40% laboratory tests. No cost sharing for thosse with chronic illnesses |
| Role of private insurance | Supplemental. May opt out of national coverage. All insurance plans must be nonprofit | To help with out-of-pocket expenses; may also expand coverage |
| % with private insurance | 20% supplemental 10% opt out | 90% |

(Continued)

**Table 22.3 (Continued)   Financing and Cost Sharing**

| | Group # 3: Shared Responsibility Systems | | | |
|---|---|---|---|---|
| | *Netherlands* | *Switzerland* | *United States* |
| Payment to physicians | GPs: capitation<br>Specialists: FFS | FFS by insurance payers | Varies by insurance payer: FFS and salaried; a few capitation |
| Payment to hospitals | Global, DRG budget | Global, paid by negotiation with insurance payers | Varied, depending on insurance payer |
| Deductible for core benefits | Yes | Yes | Yes |
| Limit to individual costs | No | Yes (about $700/year) | None, before ACA<br>Now, percentage of income |
| Type of cost sharing | None for primary care; 20% for all other services, including hospital services | Deductibles and coinsurance for some services | Depends on insurance program |
| Role of private insurance | Supplementary; can be substituted for governmental plan | Supplemental to expand coverage; cover out-of-pocket costs; or to replace governmental core benefits. Insurance plans can only make profits on supplemental plans | Provides access to specific groups |
| % with private insurance | 80% | 70% | 66% |

*Source:* Data from American Medical Student Association, available from: http://www.amsa.org, 2010; Kaiser Family Foundation, available from: http://www.kff.org; Kovner, A.R., Knickman, J.R., *Health Care Delivery in the United States,* 10th edition, Springer, New York, 2011; Schoen, C., Osborn, R., Squires, D. et al., How health insurance design affects access to care and costs, by income, in eleven countries, *Health Affairs,* 29, 2323–2334, 2010.

*Note:* ACA, Affordable Care Act; DRG, Diagnosis-Related Groups; FFS, fee-for-service; GP, general practitioners; NHS, National Health Service.

is widely used by the population to defray out-of-pocket expenses. Health insurance is generally supplemental to the public plan in all of these countries, although in Germany, the Netherlands, and Switzerland, private insurance may be used to replace the public plan. In all cases, there is no cost or benefit difference between private and public plans. Private health insurance is largely nonprofit in these countries.

Individual consumers must pay for some of the services in each of these countries, although in four countries, there are explicit limits on the amount that is required of a consumer. Once the ACA is completely implemented, the United States will be added to this list. The role of private insurance is mostly to reduce payments by individuals. Also, in most of these countries, it is uncommon for individuals to pay anything for preventive care services. This is also a measure put in place in the United States through the ACA.

## Resources

The percentage of GDP (gross domestic product) of the health care system varies from a low of around 9% in the United Kingdom and Sweden, to a high of almost 18% in the United States. This is also reflected in the per capita expenditures represented in Table 22.4 (Schoen et al., 2010). Two important resources for any health care system are physicians and hospital beds. This table shows that the United States is near the bottom in both of these resources. Canada, the United States, the United Kingdom, and the Netherlands have a similar physician/population supply, whereas France, Sweden, and Germany have a larger supply of physicians. Switzerland has the most physicians, with 4.1/1000 people. Both France and Germany have significantly more hospital beds for their populations than all other countries. The supply of hospital beds/population in the United States is among those with lower capacity, similar to that of Sweden and England. This is a little unexpected, since hospital-based care is more expensive than outpatient care.

One of the key resource indicators is how much public money is spent on the health care system. This is difficult to compare because each of these nations have such a different tax structure. For example, in the United States, most of the tax burden is through individual taxes, but in many European countries, a good deal of the tax burden is from value-added taxes on consumption goods. One indicator commonly used to compare different tax

**Table 22.4  Selected Resources for Each Health Care System**

| Group # 1: Single Payer Systems | | | |
|---|---|---|---|
| Indicator | United Kingdom | Canada | Sweden |
| % GDP for health care | 9.4% | 11.2% | 9.6% |
| Per capita expenditures/ health care | $3129 | $4079 | $3470 |
| # Physicians/population | 2.8/1000 | 2.07/1000 | 3.8/1000 |
| # Hospital beds/population | 2.9/1000 | 3.2/1000 | 2.7/1000 |
| Average tax burden | 39% | 32% | 45% |
| Group # 2: Social Security Systems | | | |
| | Germany | France | |
| % GDP for health care | 11.3% | 11.7% | |
| Per capita expenditures/ health care | $3737 | $3696 | |
| # Physicians/population | 3.8/1000 | 3.38/1000 | |
| # Hospital beds/population | 8.2/1000 | 6.6/1000 | |
| Average tax burden | 40% | 44% | |
| Group # 3: Shared Responsibility Systems | | | |
| | Netherlands | Switzerland | United States |
| % GDP for health care | 12.4% | 11.6% | 17.9% |
| Per capita expenditures/ health care | $4063 | $4627 | $7538 |
| # Physicians/population | 2.9/1000 | 4.1/1000 | 2.2/1000 |
| # Hospital beds/population | 4.7/1000 | 5.0/1000 | 2.8/1000 |
| Average tax burden | 40% | 30% | 27% |

*Source:* Data from CIA World Factbook, available from: http://cia.gov, 2014; Heritage Foundation, Macro-economic data, available from: http://www.heritage.org, 2015; OECD, available from: http://www.oecd.org, 2014; Schoen, C., Osborn, R., Squires, D. et al., How health insurance design affects access to care and costs, by income, in eleven countries, *Health Affairs*, 29, 2323–2334, 2010; World Bank, available from: http://worldbank.org, 2015; World Health Organization, available from http://www.who.org, 2014.

structures is the average tax burden, which calculates a country's total tax revenue as a percentage of its GDP (Heritage Foundation, 2015). As can be seen from Table 22.4, the average tax burden of these countries is lowest in the United States (27%) and Switzerland (30%) and highest in France and Sweden (about 45% for both). About one-third of costs for the U.S. health care system is borne by individuals, which is much higher than in any other country. Also, all seven of these comparison countries provide many health and human services under this tax burden besides health care. This includes the cost of medical school, as discussed in Table 22.1.

## Indicators of Utilization and Financial Access

Having sufficient capacity in both physicians and hospitals is an important descriptor, but another is whether the population has access to these health care services. Table 22.5 summarizes the results of one of the continuing surveys performed by the Commonwealth Fund. Access to primary care is an especially important indicator, because a strong and available primary care infrastructure is significantly related to better health indicators (Starfield, 2004). As can be seen, the country with the most rapid access to primary care is Switzerland. In fact, 93% of the respondents in Switzerland indicated they were able to have same- or next-day access (Schoen et al., 2010). Interestingly enough, access to primary care does not seem to be closely related to the structure of the system. England and Switzerland have the fastest access to primary care, despite their very different structures. Only Canada and Sweden have longer waits for primary care than the United States.

Access to specialists and access to elective surgery are two other indicators often used to compare health care systems. The United States performs better on both of these measures. Waiting times for elective surgeries are somewhat higher in those countries with a single payer system. These countries organize their health care systems on the principle of giving the highest priority to services based on medical need, so wait times for elective surgery are longer.

Not surprisingly, the United States performs worst on both measures of financial access shown in Table 22.5. In fact, on every affordability and financial access measure asked, both by the Commonwealth Fund and other organizations, U.S. adults are consistently more negative. In some countries, there are explicit limits on out-of-pocket spending. For example, Germany

**Table 22.5  Indicators of Utilization and Financial Access**

| Group # 1: Single Payer Systems | | | |
|---|---|---|---|
| Indicator | United Kingdom | Canada | Sweden |
| Wait 6 or more days to get primary care | 8% | 33% | 25% |
| Wait 2 months or more to see specialist | 19% | 41% | 31% |
| Wait 4 months or more to have elective surgery | 21% | 25% | 22% |
| Owe more than $1000 in medical bills | 1% | 12% | 2% |
| Problems paying medical bills in past year | 2% | 6% | 5% |
| Group # 2: Social Security Systems | | | |
| | Germany | France | |
| Wait 6 or more days to get primary care | 16% | 17% | |
| Wait 2 months or more to see specialist | 7% | 28% | |
| Wait 4 months or more to have elective surgery | 0 | 7% | |
| Owe more than $1000 in medical bills | 8% | 4% | |
| Problems paying medical bills in past year | 3% | 9% | |
| Group # 3: Shared Responsibility Systems | | | |
| | Netherlands | Switzerland | United States |
| Wait 6 or more days to get primary care | 5% | 2% | 19% |
| Wait 2 months or more to see specialist | 16% | 5% | 9% |
| Wait 4 months or more to have elective surgery | 5% | 7% | 7% |
| Owe more than $1000 in medical bills | 9% | 25% | 35% |
| Problems paying medical bills in past year | 4% | 6% | 20% |

*Source:* Data from Schoen, C., Osborn, R., Squires, D. et al., How health insurance design affects access to care and costs, by income, in eleven countries, *Health Affairs*, 29, 2323–2334, 2010.

has income-related limits and France limits out-of-pocket spending for those who have a serious health problem (Schoen et al., 2010). The United States is the only country where one-fifth of adults report serious problems with medical bills. The exposure of U.S. adults to these costs is mostly a result of gaps in insurance coverage, as opposed to having no health insurance. A similar percentage of insured people under the age of 65 (38%) and uninsured (35%) both paid more than $1000 in medical bills last year. In contrast, only 4% of French citizens owed more than $1000 in medical costs (Schoen et al., 2010).

## Selected Health Status Indicators

Chapter 3 described several health indicators, and three of these are summarized in Table 22.6: infant mortality rate (IMR), and two different life expectancy rates. All of these countries have low IMRs and high life expectancy rates, which is not surprising, given their economies. Sweden's IMR is one of the lowest in the world. The U.S. IMR is much higher than any of these seven countries. As noted in Chapter 3, the IMR is an indicator of broad access to primary care. The life expectancy rate includes the impact of more technological interventions, especially life expectancy after age 65. The United States is at the bottom for these two indicators, although the differences are not as great as in the IMR.

Table 22.6 shows one additional health indicator. The WHO, in association with the United Nations, ranks 191 national health systems using a variety of indicators, including access, health status, and satisfaction (WHO, 2013). In this comprehensive study, France is ranked as having the best health care system in the world, and the United Kingdom ranks ninth. Germany, the Netherlands, Switzerland, and Sweden all rank between 14th and 23rd. Canada is 30th and the United States is 37th.

## What Can We Learn from These Health Systems?

There is no ideal national health care system, and none of the systems presented in this chapter are perfect. All have significant and continuing challenges in order to provide health care services to a whole population within some sort of reasonable cost parameters and consistent with their own cultural and political framework. How successful these health care systems are

**Table 22.6    Selected Health and System Indicators**

| Group # 1: Single Payer Systems | | | |
|---|---|---|---|
| Indicator | United Kingdom | Canada | Sweden |
| Infant mortality rate | 4.4 | 4.7 | 2.0 |
| Life expectancy at birth | 80.4 | 81 | 81.7 |
| Life expectancy at age 65 | 19 | 20.2 | 24 |
| Overall health system performance | 9th | 30th | 23rd |
| Group # 2: Social Security Systems | | | |
| | Germany | France | |
| Infant mortality rate | 3.4 | 3.3 | |
| Life expectancy at birth | 80.4 | 81.6 | |
| Life expectancy at age 65 | 19 | 21 | |
| Overall health system performance | 14th | #1 | |
| Group # 3: Shared Responsibility Systems | | | |
| | Netherlands | Switzerland | United States |
| Infant mortality rate | 3.0 | 3.7 | 6.2 |
| Life expectancy at birth | 81.1 | 82 | 79 |
| Life expectancy at age 65 | 19 | 21 | 19 |
| Overall health system performance | 17th | 20th | 37th |

*Source:* Data from CIA World Factbook, available from: http://www.cia.gov; OECD, available from: http://www.oecd.org; World Bank, available from: http:///www.world bank.org; World Health Organization, available from: http://www.who.org.

is generally measured by the use of health status indicators, some of which were introduced in Chapter 3, and four of which are summarized in Table 22.6. Although limited, these quantitative estimates do allow for interesting and valuable comparisons. There are also several other criteria that can be used to assess the success of a national health care system. These criteria are from the perspective of the public health field and therefore focus on providing health care services to an entire population, using the principles of the social justice perspective. These six criteria are briefly described in the following discussion.

## Comprehensive Services and Universal Coverage

Comprehensive services means that all health services—including preventive and health promotion services—are available to the whole population, as well as medical services needed once someone becomes ill. The definition of medically necessary is challenging and does vary between countries. Some countries include decision making about limits of care at a centralized level, such as the United Kingdom, whereas others (such as Canada and Sweden) allow this process to occur at lower governmental levels. Some countries use capacity of the system as well as judgments related to medical urgency to manage timing and amount of care available. These methods of rationing seem different from those used in the United States, but capacity and medical urgency especially for scarce high-technology interventions is also commonly used in the United States to manage timing of medical services.

Universal coverage means that everyone is eligible for care under the same financing system, with no additional eligibility determination. These countries all view this as a very important part of having a cost-efficient system. This arrangement is a specific rejection of the targeted program approach utilized by the United States.

## Zero Cost at Point of Delivery

For most countries, collection of money at the time of receiving medical care services is not worth the cost in administrative resources. In the United States, the belief in moral hazard has created a very different practice, where personal financial responsibility is viewed as leading to more responsible health behavior. In some countries, economic challenges have led to the introduction of fees to help in cost sharing, although the cost of collecting these fees has inhibited most countries from adopting this method of cost sharing.

## Ability to Control Supply of Health Professionals, Including Specialty and Geographic Distribution

This is a very important criterion, as this means that there is some control over the specialty mix and also some control over where physicians practice. This is accomplished in most of these comparison countries by taxpayer subsidization of medical school costs, and specific control of residency slots, especially with respect to primary care physicians. Medical school costs in the United States are somewhat subsidized, not only by state and federal funds, but also by Medicare, which funds residency slots in teaching hospitals. However, the level of subsidy is not enough to be able to control the composition of the physician workforce. Most of the cost of medical school is the responsibility of those wanting to become a physician.

## Simple Financing and Simple, Effective Cost Containment Measures

This criterion is key to the ability to implement and sustain a cost-efficient health care system. For most countries, this involves a central administrative system to control both costs and benefits: in some cases, this is a part of the government, whereas in other cases, it is an independent nonprofit organization. Implied in this criterion is designating an appropriate balance of public and private sector control and activity. In most of the countries included in this chapter, there is a private market. In all cases, however, the private market is regulated not only for what may be charged for premiums, but also in specifying required benefits. From the perspective of the United States, this is a system with little or no competition, but in reality, competitive forces are still very active within most of these health care systems, primarily aimed at producing administrative efficiency. For example, the Netherlands has a private health insurance exchange, with private insurance companies offering plans that compete with the public one. Switzerland has many private health insurance companies, offering plans that can substitute for the governmental plan, as well as supplementing the basic plan. Individual cost sharing, however, is limited and premiums are regulated by the government. The same is true in Germany, which has a great many different sickness plans, which are analogous to health insurance plans. All offer the same benefits, and costs of premiums are also the same.

It is not true that there is more regulation in these more centralized systems. As we have seen repeatedly throughout this book, there is extensive regulation, both federal and state, in the U.S. health care system. However, the nature of the regulation is different than in the United States, especially with respect to private companies. In many of these countries, such as Germany and Switzerland, for-profit private health insurance companies are limited, but in all countries where for-profit insurance companies exist, they are regulated in the same way as the public insurance program.

## Separation of Employment and Health Insurance

One important observation is that every country with a universal model of health insurance very intentionally separates employment status from health insurance, even though in many cases health insurance is partly paid for by employers. These countries explicitly recognize the very high social and economic cost of taking care of people who are both unemployed and uninsured.

## Satisfying to Health Care Professionals/Patients

No health care system is perfect, and each country continues to make modifications and reforms to its system, within the philosophical parameters of the design of the system. It is important that both health professionals and patients support a system. If the patients are unhappy, public confidence in the system deteriorates, and some may choose to seek care in other places. Physicians may respond to a deeply dissatisfying health care system by practicing in another country. This is an economic loss to the country that provided the training, as well as demoralizing to the health care system itself.

Physician salaries are an important part of this, and countries vary in how they determine these salaries. U.S. physicians do make somewhat less than physicians in other countries, although this comparison is difficult to make, as discussed in Chapter 17. National data on income of U.S. physicians are usually based on estimates of gross incomes, not net incomes. This is very important because physicians in other countries have many fewer practice costs, including malpractice costs. Moreover, medical schools are highly subsidized in most of these comparison countries, so physicians do not have the large amount of debt that U.S. physicians have.

# Summary and Final Thoughts

This book ends where it began: culture and political ideology is critical to the design of any national health care system. France and Germany have a very different cultural philosophy, where they view the health system as part of their national social support network. They feel sick people suffer enough and should not have to pay more for medical care. The U.S. culture is more oriented to individualism: it is an essential American value that we take care of ourselves. These two different views of the role of government have profound consequences for the design of a health care system.

In many European countries, there is a high value on efficiency, and in health care, a desire to spend more on providing services than managing them. This sometimes leads to behavior that is confusing to an American perspective. For example, identifying those who overuse the system—moral hazard—is a major concern in the United States, but is viewed by European countries as costing too much to monitor. It is easier and cheaper to just accept some overutilization, especially at the primary care level. This leads to a system where primary care services—elastic care—are freely allowed and encouraged, but the more expensive, inelastic care is rationed based on medical need. The result is primarily a delay in elective procedures, and not urgent and emergent procedures. And, as Table 22.5 shows, these delays are not larger than in the United States. Overall health status indicators are not impacted by these resource decisions, as can be seen in Table 22.6. Utilization regulations in the United States are also acts of rationing resources. Since care is primarily rationed by insurance coverage, the result includes delays in both elastic and inelastic services, as described in Chapter 11.

Many differences between the United States and these seven countries remain, but three specific parts of the Affordable Care Act move the US health care system in a direction more comparable to the health care systems of these countries. The first is the mandate for all citizens to have health insurance, spreading the cost of care over a larger group. The second is extending regulations on the private health insurance market on both cost of premiums and required coverage. This makes centralized cost control more possible. The third is limiting the out-of-pocket costs for American consumers, something that every other comparison country does. These changes move the US health care system closer to the shared responsibility systems of Europe, especially of the Netherlands and Switzerland.

The gold standard of health care is outcomes, and it is certainly much too soon to determine this. Whether our health *and* economic outcomes will become more comparable to those of the countries discussed in this chapter depends on whether the ACA will be weakened by legislative amendments and changes. The ACA has started the United States down a path closer to a social justice model for the US health care system. Whether this direction continues depends largely on the hearts and minds of both politicians and the American public.

## Acknowledgments

Two distinct groups of students made significant contributions to the content of this chapter. The first group included Tia DiNatale, Sarah Kelly, Ariana Lymberopoulos, Alexandra McGowan, and Pratiksha Yalakkishettar. Because of their work, I was able to design this chapter around the six tables included here. The second group of students—Jillisia James, Christopher Lukasik, Daphna Raz, and Renee Williams-Sinclair—completed the tables, found references and other source materials, and contributed significantly to the analysis and final version of this chapter. I would not have been able to complete this chapter without their assistance. I also thank two colleagues in the School of Public Health and Health Sciences. Dr. Rosa Rodriguez-Monguio made several suggestions about the appropriate comparison countries and the variables to include in the analysis. My appreciation goes to Dr. Krishna Poudel, who helped me think about the role of the primary care infrastructure in these countries.

# References

AAASC (2012). Ambulatory Surgery Centers: A Positive Trend in Health Care. American Association of Ambulatory Surgery Centers. Available from: http://www.aaasc.org.

AACPM (2013). American Association of Colleges of Podiatric Medicine. Available from: http://www.aacpm.org.

AAMC (2013). Physician Data Resources—Masterfile. Association of Medical Colleges. Available from: http://www.ama.assn.org.

AAN (2009). Directors of Health Plans. Alliance for Advancing Non-Profit Health Care. Available from: http://www.insweb.com.

AANP (2007). American Association of Nurse Practitioners. Available from: http://www.aanp.org.

AAPA (2011). Physician Assistant Census. American Academy of Physician Assistants. Available from: http://www.aapa.org.

AARP (2013). Long Term Care Insurance: 2014 Update. American Association of Retired Persons. Available from: http://www.comparelongtermcare.org.

AARP (2014). Profile of Nursing Home Utilization. American Association of Retired Persons. Available from: http://www.assets.aarp.org.

ABMS (2013). American Board of Medical Specialties. Available from: http://www.abms.org.

Abrams, R. (2014). In ambitious bid, Wal-Mart seeks foothold in primary care services. *New York Times*, August 8, 2014, pp. B6–B8.

Adashi, E.Y., Geiger, H.J., and Fine, M.D. (2010). Health care reform and primary care—The growing importance of the community health center. *New England Journal of Medicine* 362(22): 2047–2050.

AHA (2009). Underpayment by Medicare and Medicaid: Fact Sheet. American Hospital Association. Available from: http://www.aha.org.

AHA (2014). Fast Facts on US Hospitals. American Hospital Association. Available from: http://www.aha.org.

AHIP (2013). Trends in Medigap Coverage and Enrollment, 2012. America's Health Insurance Plans. Available from: http://www.ahip.org.

AHRQ (2013). State Medicaid Program Adopts Multiple Policies to Significantly Increase Screening Rates and Enhance Access to Services for Young Children at Risk of Developmental Disabilities. Agency for Healthcare Research and Quality. Available from: http://www.innovations.ahrq.gov.

Alderman, L. and Greenhouse, S. (2014). Serving up fires, for a living wage. *New York Times*, October 28, 2014.

Allegretto, S., Doussard, M., Graham-Squire, D., Jacobs, K., Thompson, D., and Thompson, J. (2013). The Public Cost of Low-Wage Jobs in the Fast Food Industry. Institute of Research on Labor and Employment, University of California and Center for Labor Research and Education, University of Illinois. Available from: http://laborcenter.berkeley.edu.

Allotey, P. and Redipath, D. (2003). Infant mortality rate as an indicator of population health. *Journal of Epidemiology and Community Health* 57(5): 344–346.

Altman, D. (2015). Public vs Private Health Insurance on Controlling Spending. Kaiser Family Foundation. Available from: http://wsj.com.washwire.

AMA (2004). Physician Characteristics and Distribution in the US. American Medical Association, Division of Survey and Data Resources. Available from: http://www.ama.org.

AMCHP (2012). Health Reform: What Is in it to Promote Breastfeeding? Association of Maternal and Child Health Programs. Available from: http://www.amchp.org.

AMHCA (2013). Facts about Clinical Mental Health Counselors. Available from: http://www.amhca.org.

American Student Medical Association (2010). Comparison of International Health Plans. American Medical Student Association. Available from: http://www.amsa.org.

Anell, A., Glenngard, A.H., and Merkur, S.S. (2012). Sweden health system review. *Health Systems in Transition* 14(5): 1–159.

Angermyer, M., Matschinger, H., and Corrigan, P. (2004). Familiarity with mental illness and social distance data from a representative population survey. *Schizophrenia Research* 69(2–3): 175–182.

Ansak, M. and Zawadski, R. (1983). On Lok CCODA: A consolidated model. *Home Health Care Services Q* 4: 147–170.

Antonuccio, D.O., Danton, W.G., and McClanahan, T.M. (2003). Psychology in the prescription era: Building a firewall between marketing and science. *American Psychologist* 58(12): 1028.

AOA (2012). American Optometric Association. Available from: http://www.aoa.org.

APA (2013). Mental Health Insurance under the Federal Parity Law. American Psychological Association. Available from: http://www.apa.org.

APA (2014). What Is a Psychiatrist? American Psychiatric Association. Available from: http://www.psychiatry.org.

APHA (2014). ACA Advocacy and Policy. American Public Health Association. Available from: http://www.apha.org.

Appleby, J. (2013). FAQ: Obamacare and coverage for immigrants. *KSN: Kaiser Health News*. Available from: http://www.kaiserhealthnews.org.

Arias, E., Anderson, E.N., Kung, H.C., Murphy, S.L., and Kochanek, K.D. (2003). Deaths: Final data for 2001. *National Vital Status Reports* 52: 1–115.

Arrow, K.J. (1963). Uncertainty and the welfare economics of medical care. *American Economic Review* 53: 45–52.

Asch, S.M., McGlynn, E.A., Hogan, M.M. et al. (2004). Comparison of quality of care for patients in the Veterans health administration and patients in a national sample. *Annals of Internal Medicine* 14(1): 349–359.

ASHSP. American Society of Health-System Pharmacists (2008). ASHP statement on racial and ethnic disparities in health care. *American Journal of Health-System Pharmacy* 65: 728–733.

ASLF (2012). Assisted Living 2012. Assisted Living Federation of America. Available from: http://www.alfa.org.

Austin, F., Pizer, S.D., and Feldman, R. (2012). Should Medicare adopt the veteran's health administration formulary? *Health Economics* 21(5): 485–495.

Avick, R. (2014). RAND comes clean: Obamacare's exchanges enroll only 1.4 million. *Forbes Business.* Available from: http://www.forbes.com.

Ayanian, J.Z., Clearly, P.D., Weissman, J.S., and Epstein, A.M. (1999). The effect of patients, preferences on racial differences in access to renal transplantation. *New England Journal of Medicine* 341(11): 1661–1669.

Bach, P.B., Cramer, L.D., Warren, J.L., and Begg, C.B. (1999). Racial differences in the treatment of early-stage lung cancer. *New England Journal of Medicine* 341(11): 1198–1205.

Bailey, K. (2012). Dying for Coverage: The Deadly Consequences of Being Uninsured. Families USA. Available from: http://familiesusa.org.

Bailey, M.J. and Sheldon, D. (2013). *Legacies of the War on Poverty.* New York: Russell Sage.

Baker, B. and Rytina, N. (2013). Estimates of Unauthorized Immigrant Population Residing in the US in January 2011. Dept of Homeland Security. Available from: http://www.dhs.gov.

Balint, M. (1957). *The Doctor, His Patient and the Illness.* New York: International Universities Press.

Bardia, A., Nicoly, N.L., Zimmerman, B.M., and Gryzlak, B. (2007). Use of herbs among adults based on evidence-based indications: Findings from the national health interview survey. *Western Journal of Medicine* 82(5): 561–566.

Barnes, P.M., Powell-Griner, E., McFann, K., and Nahin, R.L. (2004). Complementary and alternative medicine use among adults: United States, 2002. *Advance Data* 2004(343): 1–19.

Barr, D.A. (2002). *Introduction to US Health Policy: The Organization, Financing and Delivery of Health Care in America.* San Francisco: Benjamin Cummings.

Barr, D.A. (2008). *Health Disparities in the United States: Social Class, Race, Ethnicity, and Health.* Baltimore, MD: Johns Hopkins University Press.

Barton, P. (2007). *Understanding the US Health Services System,* 3rd edition. Chicago: Health Administration Press.

Batalova, J. (2009). Temporary Admissions of Nonimmigrants to the US. Migration Policy Institute. Available from: http://www.migrationpolicy.org.

Baucus, M. and Fowler, E.J. (2002). Geographic variation in Medicare spending and the real focus of Medicare reform. *Health Affairs* July–December, suppl web exclusives: W115–W117.

Beaglehole, R., Bonita, R., Horton, R., Adams, O., and McKee, M. (2004). Public health in the new era: Improving health through collective action. *Lancet* 363: 2084–2086.

Beauchamp, T.L. and Childress, J.F. (2001). *Principles of Biomedical Ethics*, 5th edition. New York: Oxford University Press.

Becker, M.H. (1974). The health belief model and personal health behavior. *Health Education Monograph* 2: 324–508.

Bell, J.F., Zimmerman, F.J., Almgren, G.R., Mayer, J.D., and Huebner, C.E. (2006). Birth outcomes among African-American women: A multi-level analysis of the role of race residential segregation. *Social Science & Medicine* 63: 3030–3045.

Bennett, C.G., Merritt, M.M., Sollers, J.J., Edwards, C.L., Whitfield, K.E., Brandon, D.T., and Tucker, R.D. (2014). Stress, coping and health outcome among African Americans. In *Race, Ethnicity and Health: A Public Health Reader*, pp. 139–158. Edited by T.A. LaViest and L. Isaac. San Francisco: Jossey-Bass.

Berlinger, J. (2012). A new poverty calculation yield some surprising results. *Business Insider*, November 12, 2012. Available from: http://www .businessinsider.com.

Berman, B., Langevin, H., Witt, C., and Dubner, R. (2010). Acupuncture for low back pain. *New England Journal of Medicine* 363(5): 454–461.

Berwick, D.M. and Hackbarth, A.D. (2013). Eliminating waste in US health care. *Journal of the American Medical Association* 307(14): 1513–1516.

Besharov, D.J. and Germanis, P. (2000). Evaluating WIC. *Evaluation Review* 24(2): 123–190. Available from: http://erx.sagepub.com.

Betancourt, J.R. and Green, A.R. (2014). Linking cultural competence training to improved health outcomes. In *Race, Ethnicity and Health: A Public Health Reader*, pp. 689–694. Edited by T.A. LaViest and L. Isaac. San Francisco: Jossey-Bass.

Bidgood, E., Clarke, E., Daley, C., and Gubb, J. (2013). Healthcare systems: Switzerland. *Civitas*, pp. 1–15.

BLS (2012). *Occupational Outlook Handbook: 2012–2013 Edition*. United States Dept of Labor, Bureau of Labor Statistics, Washington, DC. Available from: http://www.bls.gov.

BLS (2013). Occupational Employment Statistics: Occupational Employment and Wages. Bureau of Labor Statistics. Available from: http://www.bls.gov.

Blum, M.H. (1974). *Planning for Health: Developmental Application of Social Change Theory*. New York: Human Sciences Press.

Bodenheimer, T., Chen, E., and Bennet, D.H. (2009). Confronting the growing burden of chronic disease: Can the US health care workforce do the job? *Health Affairs* 28: 64–74.

Boukus, E.R., Cassil, A., and O'Malley, A.S. (2009). A Snapshot of US Physicians: Key Findings from the 2008 Health Tracking Study Physician Survey. Center for Studying Health System Change. Available from: http://hschange.com.

Brandon, D.T., Isaac, L.A., and LaViest, T.A. (2014). The legacy of Tuskegee and trust in medical care: Is Tuskegee responsible for race differences in mistrust of medical care? In *Race, Ethnicity and Health: A Public Health Reader*, pp. 557–568. Edited by T.A. LaViest and L. Isaac. San Francisco: Jossey-Bass.

Braveman, P. (2006). Health disparities and health equity: Concepts and measurement. *Annual Review of Public Health* 27: 167–194.

Brewer, C.S. and Kovner, C.T. (2001). Is there another nursing shortage? *Nursing Outlook* 49(1): 20–26.

Brill, S. (2014). *America's Bitter Pill: Money, Politics, Backroom Deals, and the Fight to Fix our Broken Healthcare System*. New York: Random House.

Campbell, J.B., Busse, J.W., and Injeyan, H.S. (2000). Chiropractic and vaccination: A historical perspective. *Pediatrics* 105(4): 43–50.

Cantor, J.C., Monheit, A.C., DeLia, D., and Lloyd, K. (2012). Early impact of the Affordable Care Act on health insurance coverages of young adults. *Health Services Research* 47(5): 1773–1790.

Carey, M. and Galewitz, P. (2014). HHS extends coverage for patients in federal high-risk pools. *Kaiser Health News*. Available from: http://www.kaiserhealthnews.org.

Carter, B.D., Abnet, C.C., Freskanich, D. et al. (2015). Smoking and mortality: Beyond established causes. *New England Journal of Medicine* 372: 631–640.

Case, A. and Paxton, C. (2005). Sex differences in morbidity and mortality. *Demography* 42: 189–214.

Cassidy, A. (2010). Health policy brief: Pre-existing condition insurance plan. *Health Affairs*. Available from: http://www.healthaffairs.org.

Cauchi, R. (2014). Coverage of Uninsurable Pre-Existing Conditions: State and Federal High-Risk Pools. Available from: http://www.ncsl.org.

Cauchi, R., Landess, S., and Thangasamy, A. (2014). A National Conference of State Legislators. State Laws Mandating or Regulating Mental Health Benefits. Available from: http://www.ncsl.org.

Cawley, J.F. and Hooker, R.S. (2013). Physician assistants in American medicine: The half-century mark. *American Journal of Managed Care* 19(10): e333–e341.

CBO (2006). Nonprofit Hospitals and the Provision of Community Benefits. Congressional Budget Office. Available from: http://www.cbo.gov.

CBO (2007). The Impact of Unauthorized Immigrants on the Budgets of State and Local Governments. Congressional Budget Office. Available from: http://www.cbo.gov.

CBO (2011). Overview of Congressional Budget Office. Available from: http://www.cbo.gov.

CBO (2013). Health Related Options for Reducing the Deficit: 2014–2023. Congressional Budget Office. Available from: http://www.cbo.org.

CBPP (2013). Policy Basics: Introduction to Medicaid. Center on Budget and Policy Priorities. Policy Brief. Available from: http://www.cbpp.org.

CCE (2008). Council on Chiropractic Education. Available from: http://ccc-usa.org.

CDC (2000). Report on US Health Statistics. Centers for Disease Control and Prevention. Available from: http://www.preventdisease.com.

CDC (2004). The Health Consequences of Smoking: A Report of the Surgeon General. Centers for Disease Control and Prevention. Available from: http://www.ncbi.nlm.nih.gov.

CDC (2005). Annual smoking-attributable mortality, years of potential life lost, and productivity losses—United States, 1997–2001. *Centers for Disease Control and Prevention Morbidity and Mortality Weekly Report* 54(25): 625–628.

CDC (2010). Overview of US Health Care System. Centers for Disease Control/National Center of Health Statistics. Available from: http://www.cdc.gov.

CDC (2011). CDC Health Disparities and Inequalities Report—United States, 2011. Centers for Disease Control and Prevention. Available from: http://www.cdc.gov/mmwr.

CDC (2012a). Diagnoses of HIV Infection in the United States and Dependent Areas. HIV Surveillance Report, Vol. 23. Available from: http://www.cdc.gov.

CDC (2012b). Reproductive Health: Infant Mortality. Atlanta, Georgia: Centers for Disease Control and Prevention. Available from: http://www.cdc.gov.

CDC (2013). Collaborative Practice Agreements and Pharmacists' Patient Care Services: A Resource for Pharmacists. Centers for Disease Control and Prevention. Available from: http://www.cdc.gov.

CDC (2014a). Outbreak of *Salmonella heidelberg* Infections Linked to Tyson Brand Mechanically Separated Chicken at Correctional Facility (Final Update). National Center for Emerging and Zoonotic Infectious Diseases (NCEZID) Division of Foodborne, Waterborne, and Environmental Diseases (DFWED), January, 14, Atlanta, GA.

CDC (2014b). Injury Prevention and Control: Data and Statistics. Centers for Disease Control and Prevention. Available from: http://www.cdc.gov.

CDC (2014c). Chronic Disease Prevention and Health Promotion. Centers for Disease Control and Prevention. Available from: http://www.cdc.gov.

CDC/NCHS (2009). Healthy People 2010. National Center for Health Statistics. Available from: http://www.cdc.gov.

Champion, V.L. and Skinner, C.S. (2008). The health belief model. In *Health Behavior and Health Education*, 4th edition. Edited by K. Glanz, B. Rimer, and K. Viswanth. San Francisco: Jossey-Bass.

CHCF (2014). Health Spending by Distribution, by Sponsor. California Health Care Foundation. Available from: http://www.chcf.org.

Cherkin, D. (1989). AMA policy on chiropractic. *American Journal of Public Health* 79(11): 1569–1570.

Chesney, M.L. and Duderstadt, K.G. (2013). Affordable Care Act: Medicaid expansion key to increasing access to care. *Journal of Pediatric Health Care* 27(4): 312–315.

Chick, D.A., Friedman, H.P., Young, V.B., and Soloman, D. (2010). Relationship between COMPLX and USMLE scores among osteopathic medical students who take both exams. *Teaching and Learning in Medicine* 22(1): 3–7.

Chin, M.H., Walters, A.E., Cook, S.C., and Huang, E.S. (2014). Interventions to reduce racial and ethnic disparities in health care. In *Race, Ethnicity and Health: A Public Health Reader*, pp. 741–785. Edited by T.A. LaViest and L. Isaac. San Francisco: Jossey-Bass.

CIA World Factbook (2013). Country Comparisons: Infant Mortality Rates. Available from: https://www.cia.gov.

Clark, R., Anderson, N.B., Clark, V.R., and Williams, D.R. (2014). Racism as stressor for African Americans: A biopsychosocial model. In *Race, Ethnicity and Health: A Public Health Reader*, pp. 79–103. Edited by T.A. LaViest and L. Isaac. San Francisco: Jossey-Bass.

Clary, B. (2009). Adam Smith and living wages: Arguments in support of a mandated living wage. *American Journal of Economics and Sociology* 68(5): 1063–1084.

CMA (2012). Center for Medicare Advocacy. Is There a Difference in Care? 2012. Available from: http://www.medicareadvocacy.org.

CMMS (2009). Centers for Medicare and Medicaid Services. Medicaid Managed Care Enrollment as of June 30, 2009. Available from: http://www.cms.gov/Medicaid.

CMMS (2011). Centers for Medicare and Medicaid Services. Available from: http://www.cms.gov/.

Cohen, T. (2014). Audit: More than 120,000 veterans waiting or never got care. *CNN News*. Available from: http://www.cnn.com.

Cohen, D.A., Mason, K., Bedimo, A., Scribner, R., Basolo, V., and Farley, T.A. (2003). Neighborhood physical conditions and health. *American Journal of Public Health* 93: 467–471.

Cohen, R.A. and Martinez, M.E. (2015). Health Insurance Coverage: Early Release of Estimates from the National Health Interview Survey. Centers for Disease Control/National Center for Health Statistics. Hyattsville, MD. Available from: http://www.cdc.gov.

Collins, R., Wong, E., Cerully, J., Schultz, D., and Eberhart, N. (2012). Interventions to Reduce Mental Health Stigma and Discrimination. Rand Corporation. Available from: http://www.rand.org.

Colwill, J., Cultice, J., and Kruse, R. (2008). Will generalist physician supply meet demands of an increasing and aging population? *Health Affairs* 3: 232–241.

Cooper, R.A. and McKee, H.J. (2003). Chiropractic in the US: Trends and issues. *Milbank Quarterly* 81(1): 107–138.

Copeland, W.E., Wolke, D., Lereya, S.T., Shanahan, L., Worthman, C., and Costello, E.J. (2014). Childhood bullying involvement predicts low-grade systemic inflammation into adulthood. *Proceedings of the National Academy of Sciences of the United States of America* 111(21): 7570–7575.

Corburn, J. (2002). Combining community-based research and local knowledge to confront asthma and subsistence-fishing hazards in Greenpoint/Williamsburg, Brooklyn, NY. *Environmental Health Perspectives* 110(Suppl 2): 241–248.

Corby-Edwards, A.K. (2012). Nutrition Labeling of Restaurant Menus. Congressional Research Service. Available from: http://facs.org.

Corrigan, P. (2004). How stigma interferes with mental health care. *American Psychologist* 59(7): 614–625.

Corso, P., Finkelstein, E., Miller, T., Fiebelkorn, I., and Zaloshnja, E. (2012). Incidence and lifetime costs of injuries in the United States. *Injury Prevention* 12: 212–218.

Coulter, I.D., Adams, A.H., and Sandefur, R. (1997). Chiropractic training. Contained in chiropractic in the US: Training, practice and research. Edited by D.C. Cherkin and R.D. Mootz. Rockville, MD: Agency for Health Care Policy and Research.

Cox, M. and Irby, D.M. (2006). American medical education 100 years after the Flexner report. *New England Journal of Medicine* 355(3): 1339–1344.

Creswell, J. and Abelson, R. (2013). New laws and rising costs create a surge of supersizing hospitals. *New York Times*, August 13, 2013, p. B1. New York City.

Cubbin, C., Hadden, W.C., and Winkleby, M.A. (2001). Neighborhood context and cardiovascular risk factors: The contribution of material deprivation. *Ethnicity & Diseases* 11: 687–700.

Dail, P. (2012). *Women and Poverty in the 21st Century*. Jefferson, NC: McFarland Publishing Co.

Dannenberg, A.L., Bhatia, R., Cole, B.L., Heaton, S.K., Feldman, J.D., and Rutt, C.D. (2008). Use of health impact assessment in the US: 27 case studies, 1999–2007. *American Journal for Preventive Medicine* 34(3): 241–256.

Davis, K. (2004). Consumer-directed health care: Will it improve system performance? *Health Services Research* 39: 1219–1233.

Deaton, A. and Lubotsky, D. (2003). Mortality, inequity, and race in American cities and states. *Social Science & Medicine* 56: 1139–1153.

Dental Salaries (2013). Available from: http://www.salary1.com/dentist.

Desilver, D. (2013). Global Inequality: How the US Compares. Pew Research Center. Available from: http://pewresearch.org.

Devaney, B. (2007). WIC Turns 35: Program Effectiveness and Future Directions. National Invitational Conference of the Early Childhood Research Collaborative. Available from: http://www.earlychildhoodrc.org.

DeVore, S. and Champion, R.W. (2011). Driving population health through accountable care organizations. *Health Affairs* 30(1): 41–50.

DHHS (2003). US Department of Health and Human Services, Health Resources and Services Administration. Available from: http://www.hrsa.gov.

DHHS (2005a). Health, United States. Department of Health and Human Services. Available from: http://www.hhs.gov.

DHHS (2005b). Substance Abuse and Mental Health Services Administration. Transforming Mental Health Care in America: The Federal Action Agenda. Dept. of Health and Human Services. Available from: http://www.samhsa.gov.

DHHS (2010). Disparities. Available from: http://www.healthypeople.gov/2020.

DHHS (2011). Contraceptive Services and the ACA. Health and Human Services. Available from: http://www.hhs/healthcare.gov.

DHHS (2015). Obamacare Enrollment Numbers. Department of Health and Human Services. Available from: http://www.obamacare.org.

DoD (2013). Evaluation of the TRICARE Program: Access, Cost and Quality. Department of Defense. Available from: http://tricare.mil.

Dorrance, K.A., Ramchandani, S., Neil, N., and Fisher, H. (2013). Leveraging the military health system as a laboratory for health care reform. *Military Medicine* 178(2): 142–145.

Dumpe, M.L., Herman, J., and Young, S.W. (1998). Forecasting the nursing workforce in a dynamic health care market. *Nursing Economics* 16(4): 170–179, 188.

DVA (2005). VA History in Brief. Department of Veterans Affairs. Available from: http://www.va.gov.

DVA (2010). 2010 Organizational Briefing Book. Department of Veterans Affairs. Available from: http://www.osp.va.gov.

Edelstein, B. (2010). Training New Health Providers in the US: Training of Dental Providers. Available from: http://www.kkf.org.

Elfawal, M.A., Towler, M.J., Reich, N.G., Golenbock, D., Weathers, P.J., and Rich, S.M. (2012). Dried whole plant *Artemsisia annua* as an anti-malarial therapy. *PLoS One* 7:e52746.

Emanuel, E. (2014). *Reinventing American Health Care*. New York: Perseus Books.

Emmons, K.M. and Rollnick, S. (2001). Motivational interviewing in health care settings: Opportunities and limitations. *American Journal of Preventive Medicine* 20: 68–74.

Ernst, E. (2011). Acupuncture: Does it alleviate pain and are there serious risks? A review of reviews. *Pain* 152(4): 755–764.

Everett, C.M., Thorpe, C.T., Palta, M., Carayon, P., Gilchrist, V.J., and Smith, M.A. (2013). Division of primary care service between physicians, physician assistants, and nurse practitioners for older patients with diabetes. *Medical Care Research and Review* 70(5): 531–541.

Fairman, J.A., Rowe, J.W., Hassmiller, S., and Shalala, D.E. (2011). Broadening the scope of nursing practice. *New England Journal of Medicine* 364(3): 193–196.

Families, USA. (2011). Expanding Coverage for Recent Immigrants: CHIPRA Gives States New Options. Available from: http://www.policyarchive.org.

Feinberg, L., Reinhard, S.C., Houser, A., and Choula, R. (2011). Valuing the Invaluable: The Growing Contributions and Costs of Family 2011 Update. AARP Public Policy Institute. Available from: http://assets.aarp.org.

Feldstein, P.J. (2005). *Health Care Economics*, 6th edition. Clifton Park, NJ: Thompson-Delmar Learning.

Felt-Lisk, S., McHugh, M., and Howell, E. (2002). Monitoring local safety-net providers: Do they have adequate capacity? *Health Affairs* 21(5): 277–283.

Fielding, J.E., Teutsch, S., and Koh, H. (2012). Health reform and healthy people initiative. *American Journal of Public Health* 102(1): 30–33.

Finkelstein, E.A., Trogdon, J.G., Cohen, D., and Dietz, W. (2009). Annual medical spending attributable to obesity: Payer and service-specific estimates. *Health Affairs* 28(5): w822–w831.

Fisher, G.M. (2003). The Development of the Orshanky Poverty Thresholds. Available from: http://www.census.gov.

Fisher, E.S., Wennberg, D.E., Stukel, T.A., Gottlieb, D.J., Lucas, F.L., and Pinder, E.L. (2003). The implications of regional variations in Medicare spending: Part 1. The content, quality and accessibility of care. *Annals of Internal Medicine* 138(4): 273–287.

Flexner, A. (1910). Medical Education in the United States and Canada. Study funded by the Carnegie Foundation. Available from: http://www.carnegiefoundation.org.

Forbes (2007). America's Best-and-Worst Paying Jobs. Available from: http://www.forbes.com.

Frantz, A., Pizer, S., and Wrobel, M. (2004). High-risk pools for uninsurable individuals: Recent growth, future prospects. *Health Care Financing Review* 26(2): 1–4.

Frey, C. (2013). Community Health Centers: In the Beginning. Alliance for Rural Communities. Available from: http://www.cpca.org.

Frist, B. (2002). Public health and national security: The critical role of increased federal support. *Health Affairs* 21(6): 117–130.

Frum, D. (2000). *How We Got Here: The 70's*. New York City: Basic Books.

Frumkin, H., Hess, J., Luber, G., Malilay, J., and McGeehin, M. (2008). Climate change: The public health response. *American Journal of Public Health* 98(3): 435–445.

Fry, R. and Kochhar, R. (2014). The Racial Wealth Gap after the Great Recession. PEW Research Center. Available from: http://pewresearch.org.

Gabel, J., Whitmore, H., Pickreign, J., Satorius, J., and Stromberg, S. (2011). Small Employer Perspectives on the Affordable Care Act's Premiums, SHOP Exchanges, and Self-Insurance. Available from: http://www.healthafffairs.org.

Galanti, G. (2008). *Caring for Patients from Different Cultures*, 4th edition. Philadelphia, PA: University of Pennsylvania Press.

Galewitz, P. and Kaiser Health News. (2013). How Undocumented Immigrants Sometimes Receive Medicaid Treatment. Available from: http://www.pbs.org/newshour.

Gamble, V. (1997). Under the shadow of Tuskegee: African Americans and health care. *American Journal of Public Health* 87: 1773–1778.

Garte, S. (2002). The racial genetic paradox in biomedical research and public health. *Public Health Reports* 117: 421–425.

Gee, G.C. and Payne-Sturges, D.C. (2014). Environmental health disparities: A framework integrating psychosocial and environmental concepts. In *Race, Ethnicity and Health: A Public Health Reader*, pp. 493–522. Edited by T.A. LaViest and L. Isaac. San Francisco: Jossey-Bass.

Gelbier, S. (2005). 125 years of development in dentistry. *British Dental Journal* 199(7): 470–473. Available from: http://www.nature.com/bdf/journal.

Gertner, J. (2006). What is a living wage? *New York Times*, January 15, 2006. Available from: http://www.nytimes.com.

Ginsberg, P.B. (2012). Fee-for-service will remain a feature of major payment reforms, requiring more changes in Medicare physician payment. *Health Affairs* 31(9): 1977–1983.

Glabman, M. (2005). *Hospitalists: The Next Big Thing*. Chicago: AHA. Center for Healthcare Governance, Trustee Forum.

Glanz, K., Rimer, B.K., and Viswanath, K. (2008). Theory, research and practice in health behavior and health education. In *Health Behavior and Health Education: Theory, Research and Practice*, 4th edition, pp. 23–41. Edited by K. Glanz, B.K. Rimer, and K. Viswanth. San Francisco: Jossey-Bass.

Gleckman, H. (2009). *The Future of Long Term Care: What Is Its Place in the Health Reform Debate?* Washington, DC: Tax Policy Center, Urban Institute and Brookings Institute.

Glenngard, A. (2013). The Swedish Health Care System. The Commonwealth Fund. Available from: http://www.commonwealthfund.org.

Glied, S.A. and Frank, R.G. (2009). Better but not best: Recent trends in the well-being of the mentally ill. *Health Affairs* 28: 639–640.

Gold, M., Jacobson, G., Damico, A., and Neuman, T. (2013). *Medicare Advantage 2013 Spotlight: Enrollment Market Update*. Menlo Park, CA: Henry J. Kaiser Family Foundation.

Goodman, A.H. (2014). Why genes don't count (for racial differences in health). In *Race, Ethnicity and Health: A Public Health Reader*, pp. 49–56. Edited by T.A. LaViest and L. Isaac. San Francisco: Jossey-Bass.

Goodson, J.D. (2007). Unintended consequences of resource-based relative value scale reimbursement. *Journal of the American Medical Association* 298(19): 2308–2310.

Gordon, J.E., Purciel-Hill, M., Ghai, N.R., Kaufman, L., Graham, R., and VanWye, G. (2011). Measuring food deserts in New York City's low-income neighborhoods. *Healthy Place* 17(2): 696–700.

Gordon-Larsen, P., Nelson, M.C., Page, P., and Popkin, B.M. (2006). Inequality in the built environment underlies key health disparities in physical activity and obesity. *Pediatrics* 117: 417–424.

Greyson, S., Chen, C., and Mulan, F. (2011). A history of medical student debt: Observations and implications for the future of medical education. *Journal of the Association of Medical Colleges* 86: 840–845.

Griffin, R.J. (2014). Interim Report: Review of Patient Wait Times, Scheduling Practices, and Alleged Patient Deaths. VA Office of Inspector General, VA Health Administration; Dept of Veterans Affairs. Available from: http://www.va.gov.

Gruber, J. (2002). The economics of tobacco regulation. *Health Affairs* 21(2): 146–162.

Gruenewald, P.J., Ponicki, W.R., and Holder, H.D. (1992). The relationship of outlet densities to alcohol consumption: A time-series cross-sectional analysis. *Alcoholism: Clinical and Experimental Research* 17: 38–47.

Guttmacher (2014). State Policies in Brief: State Funding of Abortion under Medicaid. Guttmacher Institute. Available from: http://www.guttmacher.org.

Haley, J. and Kenney, G. (2013). Uninsured Veterans and Family Members: State and National Estimates of Expanded Medicaid Eligibility under the ACA. Robert Wood Johnson Foundation and the Urban Institute. Available from: http://www.urban.org.

Hancock, J. (2013). Who Knew? Patient Share of Health Spending Is Shrinking. Kaiser Family Foundation. Available from: http://kaiserhealthnews.org.

Hankin, B.L. (2006). Adolescent depression: Description, causes, and interventions. *Epilepsy & Behavior* 8(1): 102–114.

Hanley, B.E. (1998). Policy development and analysis. In *Policy and Politics in Nursing and Health Care*, 3rd edition. Edited by K.J. Leavitt, D.J. Mason, and M.W. Chaffee. Philadelphia, PA: WB Saunders.

Harburg, F., Erfurt, J.C., Hauenstein, L.S., Chape, C., Schull, W.J., and Schork, M.A. (1973). Socio-ecological stress, suppressed hostility, skin color, and black–white male blood pressure: Detroit. *Psychosomatic Medicine* 35(4): 276–296.

Harrington, M. (2011). Interim Report to Congress. Children's Health Insurance Program: An Evaluation (1997–2010), December 21. Available from: http://aspe.hhs.gov.

Harrington, C., Olney, B., Carrillo, H., and Kang, T. (2012). Nurse staffing and deficiencies in the largest for-profit nursing home chains and chains owned by private equity companies. *Health Services Research* 47: 106–128.

Harris, G. (2011). Talk doesn't pay, so psychiatry turns instead to drug therapy. *New York Times*, March 5, 2011. Available from: http://www.nytimes.com.

Helman, C.G. (2007). *Culture, Health and Illness*, 5th edition. London, England: Hodder Arnold.

Henry, L.R., Hooker, R.S., and Yates, K.L. (2011). The role of physician assistants in rural health care: A systematic review of the literature. *Journal of Rural Health* 27(2): 220–229.

Heritage Foundation (2015). Macro-Economic Data. Available from: http://www.heritage.org.

Herman, B. (2013a). What does the Tenet–Vanguard merger mean for healthcare? *Becker's Hospital Review*. Available from: http://www.beckershospitalreview.com.

Herman, B. (2013b). 10 Statistics on hospital labor costs as a percentage of operating revenue. *Becker Hospital Review*. Available from: http://www.beckershospitalreview.org.

Hesketh, T. and Zhu, W.X. (1997). Health in China: Traditional Chinese medicine: One country, two systems. *British Medical Journal* 315(7100): 115–117.

Himmelstein, D.U., Thorne, D., Warren, E., and Woolhandler, S. (2009). Medical bankruptcy in the United States, 2007: Results of a national survey. *The American Journal of Medicine* 122(8): 741–746.

Hing, E. and Burt, C.W. (2007). Office-Based Medical Practices: Methods and Estimates from the National Ambulatory Medical Care Survey: Advance Data, No. 383, March 12. Available from: http:/www.cdc.gov.

Hing, E. and Hsiao, C.J. (2014). State Variability in Supply of Office-Based Primary Care Providers 2012. NCHS Data Brief # 151. Atlanta, GA: CDC.

Hirth, V., Baskins, J., and Dever-Bumba, M. (2009). Program of all-inclusive care (PACE): Past, present, future. *Journal of the American Medical Directions Association* 10(3): 155–160.

Hoadley, J., Cubanski, J., Hargrave, E., Summer, L., and Neuman, T. (2009). Medicare Part D Spotlight: Part D Plan Availability in 2010 and Key Changes Since 2006. The Henry J. Kaiser Family Foundation. Available from: http://www.kff.org/medicare/upload/7986.pdf.

Hoadley, J., Cubanski, J., Hargrave, E., and Summer, L. (2013). Medicare Part D: A First Look at Plan Offerings in 2014. Available from: http://kff.org/medicare /issue-brief/medicare-part-d-a-first-look-at-plan-offerings-in-2014.

Hoge, C., Castro, C.A., Messer, S.C., McGurk, D., and Koffman, R.L. (2004). Combat duty in Iraq and Afghanistan, mental health problems, and barriers to care. *New England Journal of Medicine* 351(1): 13–22.

Holohan, J. (2011). The 2007–09 recession and health insurance coverage. *Health Affairs* 30(1): 145–153.

Hooker, R.S. and McCraig, L.F. (2001). Use of physician assistants and nurse practitioners in primary care, 1995–1996. *Health Affairs* 20(4): 231–238.

Hoynes, H., Page, M., and Stevens, A.H. (2011). Can targeted transfers improve birth outcomes? Evidence from the introduction of the WIC programs. *Journal of Public Economics* 95(7–8): 813–827.

HRSA (2014). Health Center and the Affordable Care Act. Bureau of Primary Health Care. Health Resources and Services Administration. Available from: http:// bphc.hrsa.gov.

Hsiao, W.C., Braun, P., Dunn, D., Becker, E.R., Chen, S.P., and Couch, N.P. (1988). A National Study of Resource-Based Relative Value Scales for Physician Services: Final Report to the Health Care Financing Administration. Publication 17-C-98795/1-03. Boston: Harvard School of Public Health.

Hudson, J.L. (2005). The impact of SCHIP on insurance coverage of children. *Inquiry* 42(3): 232–254.

Hussey, P.S., Mulcahy, A.W., Schnyer, C., and Schneider, E.C. (2012). *Bundled Payment: Effects on Health Care Spending and Quality*. Rockville, MD: Agency for Healthcare Research and Quality.

Iglehart, J.K. (1994). The American health care system: Managed care. In: *The Nation's Health*, 4th edition, pp. 231–237. Edited by P.R. Lee and C.L. Estes. Boston: Jones and Bartlett.

Iglehart, J.K. (1996). Reform of the Veterans Affairs health care system. *New England Journal of Medicine* 335(18): 1124–1132.

IHS (2013). Agency Overview, 2013. Indian Health Service. Available from: http:// www.ihs.gov.

Inglehart, J.K. (2006). The new era of medical imaging—Progress and pitfalls. *New England Journal of Medicine* 354(10): 2822–2828.

IOM. Institute of Medicine (1996). *Primary Care: America's Health in a New Era*. Washington, DC: National Academy Press.

IOM (2001a). *Coverage Matters: Insurance and Health Care*. Washington, DC: Institute of Medicine National Academy Press.

IOM (2001b). *Crossing the Quality Chasm: A New Health System for the 21st century*. Committee on Quality of Healthcare in America. Washington, DC: National Academy Press.

IOM (2003). *Hidden Costs, Value Lost: Uninsurance in America*. Washington, DC: Institute of Medicine. National Academy Press.

ITEP (2015). Who Pays? 5th edition. Institute on Taxation and Economic Policy. Available from: http://www.itep.org.

Jackson, C. (2002). Cutting into the market: Rise of ambulatory surgery centers. *American Medical News*. Available from: http://www.ama-assn.org.

Jackson, J.S., Knight, K.M., and Rafferty, J.A. (2014). Race and unhealthy behaviors: Chronic stress, the HPA axis, and physical and mental health disparities over the life course. In *Race, Ethnicity and Health: A Public Health Reader*, pp. 159–174. Edited by T.A. LaViest and L. Isaac. San Francisco: Jossey-Bass.

Jacobson, G., Damico, A., Neuman, T., and Huang, J. (2009). What's in the Stars? Quality Ratings of Medicare Advantage Plans. The Henry J. Kaiser Family Foundation. Available from: http://www.kff.org.

James, S.A. (1996). The John Henryism scale for active coping. In *Handbook of Tests and Measurements for Black Populations*, pp. 417–425. Edited by R.J. Jones. Hampton, VA: Cobb and Henry.

James, S.A., Harnett, S.A., and Kalsbeek, W.D. (1983). John Henryism and blood pressure among black men. *Journal of Behavioral Medicine* 6(3): 259–278.

Jena, A.B., Seabury, S., Lakdawalla, D., and Chandra, A. (2011). Malpractice risk according to physician specialty. *New England Journal of Medicine* 365: 629–636.

Jessee, W.F. (2011). Is there an ACO in your future? *MGMA Connexion* 11(1): 5–6.

Joffe, M. and Mindell, J. (2002). A framework for the evidence base to support health impact assessment. *Journal of Epidemiology and Community Health* 56(1): 132–138.

Jones, C.B. (2004). The cost of nursing turnover: Part 1. An economic perspective. *Journal of Nursing Administration* 20(5): 562–570.

Jones, C.B. (2005). The cost of nursing turnover: Part 2. Application of the nursing turnover cost calculation methodology. *Journal of Nursing Administration* 35(1): 41–49.

Jones, D.S. (2006). The persistence of American Indian health disparities. *American Journal of Public Health* 96(12): 2122–2134.

Jones, M.D. and Casey, D.E. (2001). Unification of the Military Health System: A Half-Century Unresolved Debate. Strategic Research Project. US Army War College. Available from: http://stinet.dtic.mil.

Jost, L. (2012). Supreme Court on Individual Mandate's Constitutionality. Available from: http://Healthaffairs.org.

Kahn, K.L., Pearson, M.L., Harrison, E.R. et al. (1994). Health care for black and poor hospitalized Medicare patients. *Journal of the American Medical Association* 271(8): 1169–1174.

Kaptchuk, T.J. (2002). The placebo effect in alternative medicine: Can the performance of a healing ritual have clinical significance? *Annals of Internal Medicine* 136(11): 817–825.

Katz, S. and Akpom, C.A. (1979). A measure of primary sociobiology functions. In *Sociomedical Health Indicators*, pp. 127–141. Edited by J. Elinson and A.E. Siegman. Farmingdale, NY: Baywood.

Keating, J.C. (2005). A brief history of the chiropractic profession. In *Principles and Practices of Chiropractic*, 3rd edition. Edited by S. Haldem, S. Dagenais, and D. Bugdell. New York: McGraw-Hill.

Kenney, G.M., Buettgens, M., Guyer, J., and Heberlein, M. (2011). Improving coverage for children under health reform will require maintaining current eligibility standards for Medicaid and CHIP. *Health Affairs* 30(12): 2371–2381.

Kessler, R.C., Chiu, W.T., Demler, O., and Walters, E.E. (2005). Prevalence, severity, and co-morbidity of twelve-month DSM-IV disorders in the National Comorbidity Survey Replication (NCS-R). *Archives of General Psychiatry* 2005: 62(6): 617–627.

KFF (2010a). Hospitals by Ownership Type. Kaiser Family Foundation. Available from: http://kff.org.

KFF (2010b). The Uninsured: A Primer—Key Facts about Americans without Health Insurance. Kaiser Family Foundation. Available from: http://www.kff.org.

KFF (2010c). Employer Health Benefits. 2010. Kaiser Family Foundation and Health Research and Educational Trust. Available from: http://ehbs.kff.org.

KFF (2010d). Medicare: A Timeline of Key Developments: 1965–2009. Kaiser Family Foundation. Available from: http://kff.org.

KFF (2010e). *Medicare Chart Book*, 4th edition. The Henry J. Kaiser Family Foundation. Available from: http://facts.kff.org, Menlo Park, CA.

KFF (2010f). The Medicaid Program at a Glance, 2010. J. Henry Kaiser Family Foundation. Available from: http://www.kff.org.

KFF (2010g). Medicaid Financial Eligibility: Primary Pathways for the Elderly and People with Disabilities, 2010. J. Henry Kaiser Family Foundation. Available from: http://www.kff.org.

KFF (2011). Poverty Rate by Race/Ethnicity. J. Henry Kaiser Family Foundation. Available from: http://kff.org/.

KFF (2012a). A Primer on Medicare Financing. The Henry J. Kaiser Family Foundation. Available from: http://www.kff.org/medicare/upload/7731-03 .pdf.

KFF (2012b). The Medicare Prescription Drug Benefit Fact Sheet. The Henry J. Kaiser Family Foundation. Available from: http://kff.org.

KFF (2013a). Employer health benefits: 2013 summary of findings. Available from: http://www.kff.org.

KFF (2013b). Policy Options to Sustain Medicare for the Future. The Henry J. Kaiser Family Foundation. Available from: http://kff.org.

KFF (2013c). Medicaid: A Primer. The Kaiser Commission on Medicaid and the Uninsured. Kaiser Family Foundation. Available from: http://www.kff.org.

KFF (2015a). Obama eliminates the Doc fix. *Health News*. Available from: http://www.khn.org.

KFF (2015b). Status of State Actions on the Medicaid Expansion Decision. Kaiser Family Foundation. Available from: http://www.kff.org.

Kim, M., Blendon, R.J., and Benson, J.M. (2001). How interested are Americans in new medical technologies? A multi-country comparison. *Health Affairs* 20(5): 194–201.

King, M.L. (2007). *Immigrants in the U.S. Health Care System: Five Myths that Misinform the American Public*. Washington, DC: Center for American Progress. Available from: http://www.cap.org.

Kizer, K.W. (2003). Effects of the transformation of the Veterans Affairs health care system on the quality of care. *New England Journal of Medicine* 348(22): 1716–1721.

Kochanek, K.D., Murphy, S.J., Xu, J., and Arias, E. (2014). Mortality in the United States, 2013. Centers for Disease Control/National Center for Health Statistics. Hyattville, MD. National Center for Health Statistics Data Brief No. 178.

Koh, H.K. (2014). Healthy People 2020: A report card on the health of the nation. *Journal of the American Medical Association* 311(24): 2475–2476.

Kouri, B.E., Parsons, R.G., and Alpert, H.R. (2002). Physician self-referral for diagnostic imaging: Review of the empiric literature. *American Journal Roentgenology* 179: 843–850.

Kovner, A.R. and Knickman, J.R. (2011). *Jonas and Kovner's Health Care Delivery in the United States*, 10th edition. New York: Springer.

Kowalczyk, L. (2014). Urgent care centers. *Boston Globe*, February 17, 2014. Available from: http://www.bostonglobe.com.

Kristol, I. (1978). A capitalist conception of justice. In *Ethics, Free Enterprise, and Public Policy*. Edited by R.T. De George and J.A. Pichler. New York: New York Academy of Medicine.

Kudla, J. (2013). Analysis of 2011, 2012 and 1st Half of 2013 Workers' Compensation Questionable Referrals and ISO Claims. Available from: http://www.nicb.org.

Kuehn, B.M. (2009). Alternative therapies. *Journal of the American Medical Association* 301(4): 370.

Kullgren, J.T. (2003). Restrictions on undocumented immigrant access to health services: The health implications of welfare reform. *American Journal of Public Health* 93(10): 1630–1633.

Kunitz, S.J. (1996). The history and politics of US health care policy for American Indians and Alaskan natives. *American Journal of Public Health* 86(3): 1464–1473.

Lam, T.P. (2001). Strengths and weakness of traditional Chinese medicine and Western medicine in the eyes of some Hong Kong Chinese. *Journal of Epidemiology and Community Health* 55(10): 762–765.

Lambrew, J.M., Podesta, J., and Shaw, T.L. (2005). Change in challenging times: A plan for extending and improving health coverage. *Health Affairs* 24 (March 23): w5-119–w5-132.

Langevin, H.M. and Yandow, J.A. (2002). Relationship of acupuncture points and meridians to connective tissue planes. *The Anatomical Record* 269(6): 257–265.

Lara, M., Gamboa, C., Kahramanian, I., Morales, L.S., and Bautista, D.E. (2014). Acculturation and Latino health in the United States: A review of the literature and its sociopolitical context. In *Race, Ethnicity and Health: A Public Health Reader*, pp. 215–252. Edited by T.A. LaViest and L. Isaac. San Francisco: Jossey-Bass.

LaViest, T.A. and Wallace, J.M. (2014). Health risk and inequitable distribution of liquor stores in African-American neighborhoods. In *Race, Ethnicity and Health: A Public Health Reader*, pp. 485–492. Edited by T.A. LaViest and L. Isaac. San Francisco: Jossey-Bass.

Lee, M.S. and Ernst, E. (2011). Acupuncture for pain: An overview of Cochrane reviews. *Chinese Journal of Integrative Medicine* 17(3): 187–189.

Levin, B.L., Hennessy, K.D., and Petrila, J. (2010). *Mental Health Services: A Public Health Perspective*. New York: Oxford University Press.

Link, D., Perry, D., and Cesarotti, E. (2014). Meeting new health care challenges with a proven innovation: Nurse managed health care clinics. *Nursing Administration Quarterly* 38(2): 128–132.

Litow, M.E. (2006). Medicare versus Private Health Insurance: The Cost of Administration. Milliman Group. Available from: http://www.cahi.org.

Liu, F.X., Alexander, G.C., Crawford, S.Y., Pickard, A.S., Hedeker, D., and Walton, S.M. (2011). The impact of Medicare part D on out-of-pocket costs for prescription drugs, medication utilization, health resource utilization, and preference-based utility. *Health Services Research* 46(4): 1104–1123.

Longest, B.B. (2010). *Health Policymaking in the US*, 5th edition. Ann Arbor, MI: Health Administration Press.

Lurie, N. (1999). Healthy People 2000: Setting the nation's public health agenda. *Academic Medicine* 74(8): 559–568.

Lurie, N., Freemont, A., Somers, S. et al. (2014). The national health plan collaborative to reduce disparities and improve quality. In *Race, Ethnicity and Health: A Public Health Reader*, pp. 741–760. Edited by T.A. LaViest and L. Isaac. San Francisco: Jossey-Bass.

LWFS (2009). Living Wage Fact Sheet. Available from: http://www.vibrantcalgary.com.

MacDorman, M. (2011). Race and ethnic disparities in fetal mortality, preterm birth, and infant mortality in the United States: An overview. *Seminars in Perinatology* 35(4): 200–208.

Machlin, S., Cohen, J.W., and Beauregard, K. (2008). Health Care Expenses for Adults with Chronic Conditions, 2005. Statistical Brief #203. Rockville, MD: Agency for Healthcare Research and Quality.

Madden, J., Graves, A.J., Zhang, F. et al. (2008). Cost-related medication nonadherence and spending on basic needs following implementation of Medicare Part D. *Journal of the American Medical Association* 299(16): 1822–1928.

Maio, F.D. (2010). From Engels and Virchow to Wilkinson: An Analysis of Research on Health Inequities. *Radical Statistics*, 101, BC, Canada. Available from: http://www.radstats.org.uk.

Manasse, H. and Speedie, M. (2007). Pharmacists, pharmaceuticals, and policy issues shaping the work force in pharmacy. *American Journal of Pharmaceutical Education* 71(5): 82. Available from: http://www.ncbi.nlm.nih.gov.

Marmot, M.G., Smith, G.D., Stansfeld, S. et al. (1991). Health inequalities among British civil servants: The Whitehall II study. *Lancet* 337: 1387–1393.

Marmot, M., Friel, S., Bell, R., Houweling, T., and Taylor, S. (2008). Closing the gap in a generation: Health equity through action on the social determinants of health. *Lancet* 372(9650): 1661–1669.

Martin, J.A., Hamilton, B.E., Osterman, M.J., Curtin, S.C., and Matthews, T.J. (2015). Births: Final data for 2013. *National Vital Statistics Report* 64(1): 10. CDC/NSHC, Atlanta, GA.

Massey, D. and Denton, N. (1993). *American Apartheid: Segregation and the Making of the Underclass*. Cambridge, MA: Harvard University Press.

May, L.A. (1993). The physiologic and psychological basis of health, disease, and care seeking. In *Introduction to Health Services*, 4th edition, pp. 31–45. Edited by S.J. Williams and P.R. Torrens. New York: Delmar Publishers.

Mays, G.P. and Smith, S.A. (2011). Evidence links increases in public health spending to declines in preventable deaths. *Health Affairs* 30(8): 1585–1593.

McAlearney, J.S. (2002). The financial performance of community health centers, 1996–1999. *Health Affairs* 21(2): 219–225.

McCluskey, P.D. (2014). A new source for the old house call. *Boston Globe*, April 17, 2014. Boston.

McCord, C. and Freeman, H.P. (1990). Excess mortality in Harlem. *New England Journal of Medicine* 322: 173–177.

Mechanic, D. (1994). Managed care: Rhetoric and realities. *Inquiry* 31(2): 124–128.

Medicare.gov (2000). Medicare Hospice Benefits. Available from: http://www.medicare.gov.

Medicare.gov (2001). Questions.medicare.gov. Available from: http://questions.medicare.gov.

Medicare.gov (2013). Medicare 2013 Costs at a Glance. Available from: http://www.medicare.gov.

MedPac (2013). *A Data Book: Health Care Spending and the Medicare Program*. Rockville, MD: CMS. Available from: http://medpac.gov.

Merlis, M. (2008). The Value of Extra Benefits Offered by Medicare Advantage Plans in 2006. The Henry J. Kaiser Family Foundation. Available from: http://www.kff.org.

Merlis, M. (2013). Medicare Payments to Physicians: Health Policy Brief. Available from: http://www.healthaffairs.org.

MetLife (2012). The 2012 MetLife Market Survey of Nursing Homes, Assisted Living, Adult Day Services, and Home Care Costs. MetLife Mature Market Institute. Available from: https://www.metlife.com.

Meza, R. and Pletcher, M. (2014). Half-Century of Smoking Prevention Extended 8 Million Lives: Study. US Department of Health and Human Services website. Available from: http://www.healthfinder.gov.

MHANY (2007). President Signs Critical Respite Bill for Family Caregivers. Mental Health Association in New York State, January 3, 2007. Available from: https://mhanys.org.

Miller, T.R. (2014). The Cost of Firearm Violence. Children's Safety Network. Available from: http://www.childrensafetynetwork.org.

Milligan, S. (2008). Clinton role in health program disputed. *Boston Globe*, March 14, 2008. Available from: http://www.boston.com.

Minkler, M. (1992). Community organizing among the elderly poor in the US. *International Journal of Health Services* 22(2): 303–316.

Mitka, M. (2010). The Flexner report at the century mark. *Journal of the American Medical Association* 303(15): 1465–1466.

Moffitt, R.E. (1994). Personal freedom, responsibility and mandates. *Health Affairs* 13: 101–104.

Monga, P., Keller, A., and Venters, H. (2014). Prevention and Punishment: Barriers to Accessing Health Services for Undocumented Immigrants in the United States, pp. 50–60. Available from: http://www.mdpi.com.

Monger, R. (2013). Nonimmigrant Admissions to the United States: 2012. Annual Flow Report, pp. 1–8. Available from: http://www.dhs.gov.

Moniz, C. and Gorin, S. (2007). *Health and Mental Health Care Policy: A Biopsychological Perspective*. Boston: Pearson Press.

Moody's Investor Service (2014). Moody's Outlook for US for-Profit Hospitals has been Changed to Positive. Available from: http://www.moodys.com.

Morland, K., Wing, S., and Diez Roux, A. (2002). The contextual effect of the local food environment on resident's diets: The Atherosclerosis Risk in Communities Study. *American Journal of Public Health* 92(11): 1761–1767.

Morland, K., Diez Roux, A., and Wing, S. (2006). Supermarkets, other food stores and obesity: The Atherosclerosis Risk in Communities study. *American Journal of Preventive Medicine* 30(4): 333–339.

Morris, L. (2009). Combatting fraud in health care: An essential component in any cost containment strategy. *Health Affairs* 28(5): 1351–1356.

Moseley, J.B., O'Malley, K., Petersen, N.J. et al. (2002). A controlled trial of arthroscopic surgery for osteoarthritis of the knee. *New England Journal of Medicine* 347(2): 81–88.

Mukherjee, P.K. and Wahile, A. (2005). Integrated approaches towards drug development from ayurveda and other Indian system of medicines. *Journal of Ethnopharmacology* 103: 25–35.

Munoz, C. (2014). The Affordable Care Act and Expanding Mental Health Coverage. DHHS. Available from: http://mentalhealth.gov/blog.

NACHC (2013). A Sketch of Community Health Centers—Chart Book 2013. National Association of Community Health Centers. Available from: http://www.nahc.com.

NAHCH (2010). Basic Statistics about Home Care: Updated 2010. National Association for Home Care and Hospice. Available from: http://nahc.org.

NAMA (2013). Schools and Programs. National Ayurvedic Medical Association. Available from: http://www.ayurvedanama.org.

NAMI (2014). Mental Illness. National Alliance on Mental Illness. Available from: http://www.nami.org.

Nandi, A., Loue, S., and Galea, S. (2009). Expanding the universe of universal coverage: The population health argument for increasing coverage for immigrants. *Journal of Immigrant & Minority Health* 11(6): 433. doi:10.1007/s10903-009-9267-2.

Nandi, A., Glymour, M.M., and Subramanian, S.V. (2014). Association among socio-economic status, health behaviors and all causes of mortality in the United States. *Epidemiology* 25(2): 170–177.

Nardin, R., Zallman, L., McCormick, D., Wolhandler, S., and Himmelstein, D. (2013). The Uninsured after Implementation of the Affordable Care Act: A Demographic and Geographic Analysis. Health Affairs blog. Available from: http://healthaffiars.org.

NASCHIP.org (2014). National Association of State Comprehensive Health Insurance Plans. Available from: http://naschip.org.

Nash, E., Gold, R.B., Rowen, A., Rathburn, G., and Vierboom, Y. (2014). Laws Affecting Reproductive Health and Rights: 2013 State Policy Review. Guttmacher Institute. Available from: http://www.guttmacher.org.

Nassery, N., Segal, J.B., Chang, E., and Bridges, F.P. (2015). Systematic overuse of healthcare services: A conceptual model. *Applied Health Economics and Health Policy* 13: 1–6.

NASW (2005). NASW Standards for Clinical Social Work in Social Work Practice. National Association of Social Workers. Available from: http://www.socialworkers.org.

Navarro, V. and Shi, L. (2001). The political context of social inequalities and health. *Social Science and Medicine* 52: 481–491.

NCCAM (2005). Ayurvedic Medicine: An Introduction. National Center for Complementary and Alternative Medicine. Available from: http://nccam.nih.gov.

NCCAM (2007). Chiropractic: An Introduction. National Center for Complementary and Alternative Medicine. Available from: http://nccam.nih.gov.

NCCAM (2011). Exploring the Science of Complementary and Alternative Medicine: Third Strategic Plan 2011–2015. NIH Publication No. 11-7643, D458. National Center for Complementary and Alternative Medicine. Bethesda, MD. Available from: http://nccam.nih.gov.

NCEA (2012). Fact Sheet: Elder Abuse of Residents of Long Term Care Facilities. National Center for Elder Abuse. Available from: http://www.centeronelderabuse.org.

NCHS (2001). Healthy People 2010 Final Review. National Center for Health Statistics. Available from: http://www.cdc.gov.

NCHS (2010). *Health, United States, 2009: With Special Feature on Medical Technology. National Center on Health Statistics.* Hyattsville, MD: US Dept of Health and Human Services.

NCHS (2012). Underlying Cause of Death 1999–2010. CDC Vital Statistics Cooperative Program. National Center for Health Statistics. Available from: http://wonder.cdc.gov.

NCSL (2015). State Minimum Wage Chart. National Conference of State Legislators. Available from: http://www.ncsl.org.

Needleman, J., Buerhaus, P., Pankratz, S., Leibson, C.L., Stevens, S.R., and Harris, M. (2011). Nurse staffing and inpatient hospital mortality. *New England Journal of Medicine* 364(11): 1037–1045.

Newman, J.F. (2001). CEO performance appraisal: Review and recommendation. *Journal of Healthcare Management* 46(1): 21–37.

Newman, J.F. and Anderson, R. (2005). Societal and individual determinants of medical care utilization in the United States. *The Milbank Quarterly* 83(4): 1–28.

NHPCO (2012). NHPCO Facts and Figures: Hospice Care in America, 2012. National Hospice and Palliative Care Organization. Available from: http://www.nhpco.org.

NILC (2014). Immigrants and the Affordable Care Act (ACA). National Immigration Law Center. Available from: http://www.nilc.org.

Niles, N. (2011). *Basics of the US Health Care System*. Boston: Jones and Bartlett.

NIMH (2013). The Numbers Count: Mental Health Disorders in America. National Institutes of Mental Health. Available from: http://www.nimh.nih.gov.

Norman, R. (2011). The social stigma of mental illness. In *Applied Research and Evaluation in Community Mental Health Services: An Update of Key Research Domains*, pp. 115–128. Edited by E.R. Vingillis and S.A. State. Montreal, Canada: McGill-Queen University Press.

NRA (2014). Crisis Management Primer. National Restaurant Association. Available from: http://www.schospitaltiy.org.

NRRC (2010). Adult Day Care: One Form of Respite for Older Adults. National Respite Network and Resource Center. Available from: http://archrespite.org.

O'Mullane, M. (2013). *Integrating Health Impact Assessment (HIA) with the Policy Process: Lessons and Experience from Around the World*. Oxford, UK: Oxford University Press.

ODPHP (2010). What Are the Leading Health Indicators? Office of Disease Prevention and Health Promotion. DHHS. Available from: http://www.healthy people.gov.

OECD (2011a). General Health Status. Healthy People. Available from: http://www .healthypeople.gov.

OECD (2011b). OECD Health Data: 2011. Paris: Organization for Economic Co-operation and Development. Available from: http://www.oecd.org.

OECD (2013). Organization for Economic Co-operation and Development. Economic, Environmental and Social Statistics: Infant Mortality. Available from: http://www.oecd.org.

Ofri, D. (2013). *What Doctors Feel*. Boston: Beacon Press.

Ogden, C.C., Carroll, M.D., Kit, B.K., and Flegel, K.M. (2014). Prevalence of child-hood and adult obesity in the US 2011–2012. *Journal of the American Medical Association* 311(8): 806–814.

Oleckno, W.A. (2002). *Essential Epidemiology: Principles and Applications*. Prospect Heights, IL: Waveland.

Oleckno, W. (2008). *Epidemiology: Concepts and Methods*. Long Grove, IL: Waveland Press.

OMB (2014). Budget of the US Government. Office of Management and Budget. Available from: http://www.omb.gov.

Optometrists Salaries (2013). Available from: http://www.salary1.com/optometritsts.

Ostibye, T., Yarnall, K., Pollak, K., Gradison, M., and Michener, K. (2005). Is there time for management of patients with chronic diseases in primary care? *Annals of Family Medicine* 3: 209–214.

Ostir, G.U., Carlson, J.E., Black, S.A., Rudkin, L., Goodwin, J.S., and Markides, K.S. (1999). Disability in older adults: Prevalence, causes and consequences. *Behavioral Medicine* 24(4): 147–156.

Owens, B. (2005). The plight of the non-profit. *Journal of Healthcare Management* 50(4): 237–250.

Pampel, F.C., Krueger, P.M., and Denney, J.T. (2010). Socioeconomic disparities in health behaviors. *Annual Review of Sociology* 36: 349–370. Available from: http://www.ncbi.nlm.gov.

Paradies, Y. (2014). A systematic review of empirical research on self-reported racism and health. In *Race, Ethnicity and Health: A Public Health Reader*, pp. 105–138. Edited by T.A. LaViest and L. Isaac. San Francisco: Jossey-Bass.

Passel, J. (2005). Estimates of the Size and Characteristics of Undocumented Population. Pew Hispanic Center. Available from: http://www.pewhispanic.org.

Passel, J. and Cohn, D. (2012). Unauthorized Immigrants: 11.1 Million in 2011. Pew Hispanic Research Trends Project. Available from: http://www.pewhispanic.org.

Pauly, N.W. (1968). The economics of moral hazard. *American Economic Review* 63: 120–125.

Pear, R. (1997). Hatch joins Kennedy to back a health program. *New York Times*, October 5, 2007. Available from: http://query.nytimes.com.

Pear, R. (2008). New Medicaid rules allow states to set premiums and higher co-payments. *New York Times*, November 27. Available from: http://www.nytimes.com.

Pear, R. (2015). Number of uninsured has declined by 15 million since 2013. *New York Times*, August 12, 2015. Available from: http://nytimes.com.

Penner, S. (2004). *Introduction to Health Care Economics and Financial Management: Fundamental Concepts with Practical Applications.* Philadelphia, PA: Lippincott, Williams and Wilkins.

Peregoy, J.A., Clarke, T.C., Jones, L.J., Stussman, B.J., and Nahin, R.L. (2014). Regional Variation in Use of Complementary Health Approaches by US Adults. National Center for Health Statistics. Bethesda, MD. NCHS Data Brief 146, April. Available from: http://www.cdc.gov.

Perera, F.P., Illman, S.M., Kinney, P.L. et al. (2002). The challenge of preventing environmentally related diseases in young children: Community-based research in New York City. *Environmental Health Perspectives* 110: 197–204.

Peterson, E.D., Wright, S.M., Daley, J., and Thibalt, G.E. (1994). Racial variation in cardiac procedure use and survival following acute myocardial infarction in the Department of Veterans Affairs. *Journal of the American Medical Association* 271(8): 1175–1180.

Pierret, C.R. (2006). The sandwich generation: Women caring for parents and children. *Monthly Labor Review*, September 2006, pp. 1–9. Available from: http://www.bls.gov.

Pinto-Foltz, M.D. and Logsdon, M.C. (2008). Stigma towards mental illness: A concept analysis using postpartum depression as an exemplar. *Issues in Mental Health Nursing* 29(1): 21–36.

Poverty Guidelines (2013). US Dept of Health and Human Services. Available from: http://aspe.hhs.gov.

Povolny, B. (2008). Acupuncture and traditional Chinese medicine: An overview. *Techniques in Regional Anesthesia and Pain Management* 12: 109–110.

PPA (2014). The Affordable Care Act. Planned Parenthood of America. Available from: http://www.plannedparenthood.org.

Prochaska, J.O. and DiClemente, C.C. (1983). Stages and processes of self-change of smoking: Toward an integrative model of change. *Journal of Consulting and Clinical Psychology* 51: 390–395.

Pushfor (2013). Certified Professional Midwives (CPMs) Legal Status by State. Available from: http://pushformidwives.org.

Rabow, J. and Watts, R.K. (1982). Alcohol availability, alcohol beverages sales and alcohol-related problems. *Journal of Studies on Alcohol* 43: 767–801.

Racine, A. (2014). Children's health insurance program (CHIP): Accomplishments, challenges, and policy recommendations. *Pediatrics* 133(3): e784–e793. Available from: http://pediatrics.aapublications.org.

Rakel, D. and Faass, N. (2006). *Complementary Medicine in Clinical Practice: Integrative Practice in American Healthcare*. Sudbury, MA: Jones and Bartlett.

Rampell, C. (2009). How much do doctors in other countries make? *The New York Times*. Available from: http://economix.blogs.nytimes.com.

Ranji, U., Salganicoff, A., Stewart, A.M., Cox, M., and Doamekpor, L. (2009). State Medicaid Coverage of Family Planning Services: Summary of State Findings, 2009. The J. Henry Kaiser Family Foundation. Available from: http://kff.org.

Rank, M.R. (2005). *One Nation, Underprivileged: Why American Poverty Affects Us All*. New York: Oxford University Press.

Reardon, S. (2014). Regulators adopt more orphan drugs. Science News and Comment. Available from: http://www.nature.com/news/regulators -adopt-more-orphan-drugs-1.14970.

Rhoman, A. and Wagner, E. (2003). Chronic illness management: What is the role of primary care? *Annals of Internal Medicine* 138: 256–261.

Rimsza, M.E., Butler, R.J., and Johnson, W.G. (2007). Impact of Medicaid disenrollment on health care use and cost. *Pediatrics* 119(50): 1026–1032.

Robert, S.A. and Booke, B.C. (2011). US opinions on health determinants and social policy as health policy. *American Journal of Public Health* 101(9): 1655–1663.

Robinson, J. (2011). Hospitals respond to Medicare payment shortfalls by both shifting costs and cutting them, based on market concentration. *Health Affairs* 30(7): 1265–1271.

Roemer, M.I. (1961). Bed supply and hospital utilization: A natural experiment. *Hospitals* 35(21): 36–42.

Rosenbaum, S. (2002). Health policy report: Medicaid. *New England Journal of Medicine* 346: 635–640.

Rosenbaum, S. and Westmoreland, T.M. (2012). The Supreme Court's surprising decision on the Medicaid expansion: How will the federal government and states proceed? *Health Affairs* 31(8): 1663–1672.

Rossi, P.H. (1998). *Feeding the Poor: Assessing Federal Food Aid*. Washington, DC: AEI Press.

RTT (2014). Senate Approves VA Reform, Highway Funding Bills before August Recess. Available from: http://www.rttnews.com.

Ruggie, M. (2004). *Marginal to Mainstream: Alternative Medicine in America*. New York: Cambridge University Press.

Russell, L. (2010). Mental Health Services in Primary Care: Tackling the Issues in the Context of Health Care Reform. Washington, DC. Center for American Progress. Available from: http://www.americanprogress.org.

Saltman, R.B. (2009). Cost Control in Europe: Inefficiency Is Unethical. The Hastings Center. Available from: http://www.thehastingscenter.org.

SAMHSA (2014). Mental Health Parity and Addiction Equity. Substance Abuse and Mental Health Service Administration. Available from: http://beta.samhsa.gov.

Sanger-Katz, M. (2015). What's at stake in health law case. *New York Times*, February 3, 2015. Available from: http://NYtimes.com/upshot.

Santerre, R.E. and Neun, S.P. (2004). *Health Economics: Theories, Insights, and Industry Studies*, 3rd edition. Mason, OH: Thomas South-Western.

Schlesinger, M., Cleary, P., and Blumenthal, D. (1989). The ownership of health facilities and clinical decision-making: The case of the ESRD industry. *Medical Care* 27(3): 244–258.

Schoen, C., Osborn, R., Squires, D., Doty, M.M., Pierson, R., and Applebaum, S. (2010). How health insurance design affects access to care and costs, by income, in eleven countries. *Health Affairs* 29(12): 2323–2334.

Schur, C.L. and Berk, M.L. (2008). Views on health care technology: Americans consider the risks and sources of information. *Health Affairs* 27(6): 1654–1664.

Schwartz, J.E. (2005). *Freedom Reclaimed: Rediscovering the American Vision*. Baltimore: Johns Hopkins University Press.

Selvam, A. (2012). Number of for-Profits Rising. Modern Health Care. Available from: http://www.modernhealthcare.com.

Shi, L. and Singh, D.A. (2014). *Delivering Health Care in America: A Systems Approach*, 6th edition. Burlington, MA: Jones and Bartlett.

Shi, L. and Starfield, B. (2000). Primary care, income inequality, and self-related health in the US: Mixed-level analysis. *International Journal of Health Services* 30: 541–556.

Shi, L. and Starfield, B. (2001). Primary care physician supply, income inequality, and racial mortality in US metropolitan areas. *American Journal of Public Health* 91: 1246–1250.

Shi, L., Collins, P.B., and Aaron, K.F. (2007). Health center financial performance: National trends and state variation, 1998–2004. *Journal of Public Health Management and Practice* 13(2): 133–150.

Shone, L.P., Dick, A.W., Klein, J.D., Zwanziger, J., and Szilagyi, P.G. (2005). Reduction in racial and ethnic disparities after enrollment in the state children's health insurance program. *Pediatrics* 115(6): 697–705.

Shore, H.H. (1994). History of long term care. In *Essentials of Long-Term Care Administration*. Edited by S.B. Goldsmith. Gaithersburg, MD: Aspen.

Sirey, J.A., Bruce, M.L., Alexopoulos, G.S., Perlick, D.A., Friedman, S.J., and Meyers, B.S. (2001). Stigma as a barrier to recovery; perceived stigma and patient-rated severity of illness as predictors of antidepressant drug adherence. *Psychiatric Services* 52(12): 1615–1620.

Skidmore, S. (2008). Oregon Holds Health Insurance Lobby. Associated Press. Available from: http://ap.google.com.

Small, M.L. and McDermott, M. (2006). The presence of organizational resources in poor urban neighborhoods: An analysis of average and contextual effects. *Social Forces* 84(3): 1697–1724.

Smedley, D.B., Smith, A.Y., and Nelson, A.R., eds. (2003). *Unequal Treatment: Confronting Racial and Ethnic Disparities in Health Care.* Washington, DC: National Academy Press.

SMI Trust Fund Report (2009). Operations of the Part D Account in the SMI Trust Fund during Calendar Years 2004–2018. Annual Report of the Boards of Trustees of the Federal Hospital Insurance and Federal Supplementary Medical Insurance Trust Funds. Available from: http://www.cms.hhs.gov.

Smith, J.N. (2014). *Epic Measures: One Doctor, Seven Billion Patients.* Philadelphia, PA: Harper Collins.

Social Security Administration (n.d.). Available from: http://www.ssa.gov.

Sokolec, J.E. (2009). Health care for the undocumented: Looking for a rationale. *Journal of Poverty* 13(3): 254–265. doi:10.1080/10875540903163943.

Sommers, B.D., Baicker, K., and Epstein, A.M. (2012). Mortality and access to care among adults after state Medicaid expansions. *New England Journal of Medicine* 367(11): 1025–1034.

Spetz, J. and Given, R. (2003). The future of the nurse shortage: Will wage increases close the gap? *Health Affairs* 22(6): 199–206.

Spotlight (2014). Spotlight on private equity investing in urgent care. *Law360.* Available from: http://www.law360.com.

Sprately, E., Johnson, A., Sochalski, J., Fritz, M., and Spencer, W. (2001). The Registered Nurse Population, March 2000: Findings from the National Sample Survey of Registered Nurses. DHHS. Available from: http://www.dhhs.gov.

Stamps, P.L. (1997). *Nurses and Work Satisfaction: An Index for Measurement.* Chicago: Health Administration Press.

Stamps, P.L. and Cruz, N.T.B. (1994). *Issues in Physician Satisfaction: New Perspectives.* Ann Arbor, MI: Health Administration Press.

Stanfield, P.S., Hui, Y., and Cross, N. (2012). *Introduction to the Health Professions,* 6th edition. Burlington, MA: Jones and Bartlett.

Starfield, B. (1994). Is primary care essential? *The Lancet* 344(8930): 1129–1133.

Starfield, B. (2004). Is US health really the best in the world? In *Health Policy: Crisis and Reform in the US Health Care Delivery System,* pp. 46–49. Edited by C. Harrington and C. Estes. Boston: Jones and Bartlett.

Starfield, B. and Shi, L. (2004). The medical home, access to care, and insurance: A review of evidence. *Pediatrics* 113: 1492–1498.

Starr, P. (1982). *The Social Transformation of American Medicine*. New York: Basic Books.

Starr, P. (2011). *Remedy and Reaction: The Peculiar American Struggle over Health Care Reform*. New Haven, CT: Yale University Press.

Stephens, J. and Artiga, S. (2013). Key Facts on Health Coverage for Low-Income Immigrants Today and Under the Affordable Care Act. Kaiser Family Foundation. Available from: http://kff.org.

Stern, A.L. (2003). Labor rekindles reform. *American Journal of Public Health* 93(1): 95–98.

Stevens, R. (1989). *In Sickness and in Wealth: American Hospitals in the Twentieth Century*. New York: Basic books.

Stout, D. (2007). Bush Vetoes children's health bill. *New York Times*, October 3, 2007. Available from: http://nytimes.com.

Strope, S., Daignault, S., Hollingsworth, J.M., Ye, Z., Wei, J.T., and Hollenbeck, B.K. (2009). Ownership of ambulatory surgery centers and practice patterns for urological surgery. *Medical Care* 47(4): 403–410.

Suddick, R.P. and Harris, N.O. (1990). Historical perspective of oral biology: A series. *Critical Reviews in Oral Biology and Medicine* 1(2): 135–151. Available from: http://www.ncbi.nlm.hih.gov.

Sullivan, L. (2004). Missing Persons: Minorities in the Health Profession. A Report of the Sullivan Commission on Diversity in the Workforce. Available from: http://www.sullivancommission.org.

Sultz, H.A. and Young, K.M. (2014). *Health Care USA: Understanding Its Organization and Delivery*, 8th edition. Burlington, MA: Jones and Bartlett.

Taylor, J. (2004). The Fundamentals of Community Health Centers. National Health Policy Forum. Available from: http://www.nhpf.org.

TECH Research Network (2001). Technology change around the world: Evidence from heart attack care. *Health Affairs* 20(3): 24–42.

Teitelbaum, J.B. and Wilensky, S.E. (2013). *Essentials of Health Policy and Law*, 2nd edition. Burlington, MA: Jones and Bartlett.

Thorne, S., Paterson, B., Russell, C., and Schultz, A. (2002). Complementary/ alternative medicine in chronic illness as informed self-care decision making. *International Journal of Nursing Studies* 39: 671–683.

Thornicroft, G. and Tansella, M. (2009). *Better Mental Health Care*. Cambridge, MA: Cambridge University Press.

Thorpe, R.J. and Kelley-Moore, J.A. (2014). Life course theories of race disparities: A comparison of the cumulative dis/advantage theory perspective and the weathering hypothesis. In *Race, Ethnicity and Health: A Public Health Reader*, pp. 355–374. Edited by T.A. LaViest and L. Isaac. San Francisco: Jossey-Bass.

Timmrock, T.C. (1994). *An Introduction to Epidemiology*. Burlington, MA: Jones and Bartlett.

Todd, K.H., Deaton, C., D'Adamo, A.P., and Goe, L. (2012). Ethnicity and analgesic practice. In *Race, Ethnicity and Health: A Public Health Reader*, pp. 507–515. Edited by T.A. LaViest and L. Isaac. San Francisco: Jossey-Bass.

Toole, A. (2012). The impact of public basic research on industrial innovation: Evidence from the pharmaceutical industry. *Research Policy* 41(1): 1–12.

Travis, J.W. and Ryan, R.S. (2004). *Wellness Workbook: How to Achieve Enduring Health and Vitality*, 3rd edition. Berkeley, CA: Ten Speed Press.

TRICARE (2013). Available from: http://themilitaryzone.com.

U.S. Census (2010a). Income, Poverty, and Insurance Coverage in the United States, 2009. Current Population Reports: US Census Bureau. Available from: http://www.census.gov.

U.S. Census (2010b). The 2010 US Census Questionnaire: Informational Copy. Available from: http://2010.census.gov/2010/census/pdf/2010_questionnaire_info_copy.pdf.

U.S. Census Bureau (2013). Income, Poverty and Health Insurance Coverage in the US 2010. Available from: http://www.census.gov.

United Health Foundation (2013a). Premature Deaths. America's Health Rankings. Available from: http://www.americashealthrankings.org.

United Health Foundation (2013b). America's Health Rankings. 2013 Annual Report. Available from: http://www.americahealthrankings.org.

USDA (2012). WIC—The Special Supplemental Nutrition Program for Women, Infants and Children. United States Department of Agriculture. Available from: http://www.fns.usda.gov.

USDA (2014). Federal Subsidies of Tobacco, 2012. United States Dept of Agriculture. Available from: http://www.fsa.usda.gov.

USDL (2012). Office of Workers Compensation Programs. United States Department of Labor. Available from: http://www.dol.gov.

USDL (2013). Economic News Release: Nonfatal Occupational Injuries and Illnesses Requiring Days Away from Work, 2012. United States Department of Labor. Available from: http://www.bls.gov.

Van Ryan, M. and Burke, J. (2014). The effect of patient race and socio-economic status on physicians' perceptions of patients. In *Race, Ethnicity and Health: A Public Health Reader*, pp. 607–636. Edited by T.A. LaViest and L. Isaac. San Francisco: Jossey-Bass.

VanLeeuwen, J.A., Waltner-Toews, D., Abernathy, T., and Smit, B. (1999). Evolving models of human health toward an ecosystem context. *Ecosystem Health* 5(3): 204–219.

Vaughn, E.J. and Elliott, C.M. (1987). *Fundamentals of Risk and Insurance*. New York: John Wiley and Sons.

Villanueva-Russell, Y. (2011). Caught in the cross hairs: Identity and cultural authority within chiropractic. *Social Science & Medicine* 72(11): 1826–1837.

Vogt, D. (2011). Mental health related beliefs as a barrier to service use for military personnel and veterans: A review. *Psychiatric Services* 62(2): 135–142.

Wahl, O.F. (1999). Mental health consumers' experience of stigma. *Schizophrenia Bulletin* 25: 467–478.

Waldman, J.D., Kelly, F., Sanjeev, A., and Smith, H.L. (2004). The shocking cost of turnover in health care. *Health Care Management Review* 29(1): 27–33.

Wanberg, C.R. (2012). The individual experience of unemployment. *Annual Review of Psychology* 63(1): 369–396.

Wang, G. and Watts, C. (2007). The role of genetics in the provision of essential public health services. *Epidemiology* 97(4): 620–625.

Wang, P.S., Lane, M., Olfson, M., Pincus, H.A., Wells, K.B., and Kessler, R.C. (2005). Twelve month use of mental health services in the US: Results from the national comorbidity survey replication. *Archives of General Psychiatry* 62(6): 629–640.

Watkins, K.E. and Pincus, H.A. (2011). Veterans Health Administration Mental Health Program Evaluation: Capstone Report. TR-956-VHA. Santa Monica, CA: Rand Corp.

Weil, A. (1995). *Spontaneous Healing*. New York: Random House.

Weinberger, S.E., Hoyt, D.B., Lawrence, H.C. et al. (2015). Firearm-related injury and death in the United States: A call to action from 8 health professional organizations and the American Bar Association. *Annals of Internal Medicine* 162(7): 324–325. Available from: http://annals.org.

Weiner, J.P. (2004). Prepaid group practice staffing and US physician supply: Lesson for workforce policy. *Health Affairs* 23(2): W43–W59.

Weissman, J. (2005). The trouble with uncompensated hospital care. *New England Journal of Medicine* 352(12): 1171.

Wennberg, J.E. and Gittlesohn, A. (1973). Small area variations in health care delivery. *Science* 183: 1102–1108.

Wertz, K. (2000). *Managing Worker's Compensation: A Guide to Injury Reduction*. Chicago: CRC Press.

Whaley, S.E., Ritchie, L.D., Spector, P., and Gomez, J. (2012). Revised WIC food package improves diets of WIC families. *Journal of Nutrition Education and Behavior* 44(3): 204–209.

Whelan, E. (2010). The Importance of Community Health Centers. Center for American Progress. Available from: http://www.americanprogress.org.

White, A. (2009). Western medical acupuncture: A definition. *Acupuncture in Medicine* 27(1): 33–35.

White House (2002). President's New Freedom Commission on Mental Health. Office of the Press Secretary. Available from: http://www.whitehouse.gov.

White House (2014). Statement by the President. Office of the Press Secretary. The White House. Available from: http://www.whitehouse.gov.

WHO (1948). *Preamble to the Constitution*. Geneva, Switzerland: World Health Organization. Available from: http://www.who.

WHO (1978). *Primary Health Care*. Geneva, Switzerland: WHO. Available from: http://www.who.org.

WHO (2008a). Commission on Social Determinants of Health: Final Report. Geneva, Switzerland: WHO Report. Available from: http://www.who.int/socialdeterminants.

WHO (2008b). Primary Care: Now More Than Ever. World Health Organization. Available from: http://www.who.int/whr/2008.

WHO (2013). Comparison of International Health Systems. World Health Organization. Available from: http://www.who.int.org.

WHO (2014). Artemisinin as Standard Malaria Treatment. World Health Organization. Available from: http://www.who.int.

Wieland, D., Kinosian, B., Stallard, E., and Boland, R. (2013). Does Medicaid pay more to a program of all-inclusive care for the elderly (PACE) than for fee-for-service long term care? *Journal of Gerontology* 68(1): 47–55.

Wikler, E., Basch, P., and Cutler, D. (2012). *Paper Cuts: Reducing Health Care Administrative Costs*. Washington, DC: Center for American Progress. Available from: http://www.americanprogress.org.

Wilkinson, R. and Marmot, M. (2003). *Social Determinants of Health: The Solid Fact*, 2nd edition. Copenhagen, Denmark: World Health Organization.

Williams, B. (1983). *John Henry: A Bio-Bibliography*. Westport, CT: Greenwood Press.

Williams, D.R. and Collins, C. (2001). Racial residential segregation: A fundamental cause of racial disparities in health. *Public Health Reports* 116(5): 404–416.

Wilson, F.A. and Neuhauser, D. (1985). *Health Services in the United States*, 2nd edition. Cambridge, MA: Ballinger.

Wong, M.D, Andersen, R., Sherbourne, C.D., Hays, R.D., and Shapiro, M.F. (2001). Effects of cost sharing on care seeking and health status: Results from the medical care outcome study. *American Journal of Public Health* 91(11): 1889–1894.

Woodruff, T.J., Parker, J.D., Kyle, A.D., and Schoendorf, K.C. (2003). Disparities in exposure to air pollutants during pregnancy. *Environmental Health Perspectives* 111: 942–946.

Woolf, S.H., Braveman, P.A., Christensen, K. et al. (2013). Understanding Cross-National Health Differences among High Income Countries. National Research Council; Institute of Medicine. Available from: http://www.nationalacademies.org.

Woolhandler, S., Campbell, T., and Himmelstein, D.U. (2003). Costs of health care administration in the United States and Canada. *New England Journal of Medicine* 349(8): 766–775.

World Bank (2011). The History of Life Expectancy. Available from: http://www.worldlifeexpectancy.com.

World Bank (2015). Hospital Beds per Population. The World Bank Indicators. Available from: http://www.data.worldbank/indicators.

Wright, W.L. (2012). Malpractice prevention: What NPs and PAs need to know. *Nurse Practitioner Perspective* 3(6): 23–26.

Xie, Z. and Dong, H. (2003). *Acupuncture: Review and Analysis of Reports on Controlled Clinical Trials*. Geneva, Switzerland: World Health Organization.

Yagoda, L. and Duritz, N. (2014). *Affordable Care Act for Dummies*. Hoboken, NJ: John Wiley.

Yano, S.H. (2007). The evolution of changes in primary care delivery underlying the Veterans Health Administration's quality transformation. *American Journal of Public Health* 97(12): 672–678.

Young, A., Chaudhry, H., Rhyne, J., and Dugan, M. (2011). Physician census. *Journal of Medical Regulation* 96(4): 10–20. Available from: http://www.nationalahec.org.

Zhang, J., Yin, W., Sun, S., and Alexander, G.C. (2008). Impact of the Medicare prescription drug benefit on the use of generic drugs. *Journal of General and Internal Medicine* 23: 1673–1678.

Zhang, X., Liu, Y., Guo, Z. et al. (2012). The Herbalome—An attempt to globalize Chinese herbal medicine. *Analytical and Bioanalytical Chemistry* 402(2): 573–581.

Zuckerman, S., Haley, J., Roubideaux, Y., and Lille-Blanton, M. (2004). Health Service access, use and insurance coverage among American Indians/Alaska Natives and Whites: What role does the Indian Health Service play? *American Journal of Public Health* 94(1): 53–59.

Zuckerman, S., Williams, A.F., and Stockley, K.E. (2009). Trends in Medicaid physician fees, 2003–2008. *Health Affairs* 28: w510–w519.

# Index

Page numbers followed by f and t indicate figures and tables, respectively.

Printed in the United States
by Baker & Taylor Publisher Services